Four Feet Small

Billy Bean

This book is in the memory of Mr and Mrs Head, without whom, this book would not have been possible. Rest In Pieces and good riddance.

Acknowledgment

I would like to say a huge thank you to all the people who contributed to the publishing of this book. I will not mention any names as I do not want to implicate anyone regarding any fallout due to the content.

Firstly, to the proofreaders, particularly those who had the unenviable task of reading the first draft. I knew I was never the best at grammar and spelling, but just how bad it was, still shocked me and was slightly embarrassing, to say the least. But I am a lot bitter now!

Seriously though, I would just like you to know that if I asked you to proofread the first draft, you were someone whom I trusted and respected as much as anyone I know.

If I asked you and you declined, I totally understand. Some of the language in this book is most definitely not to everyone's taste.

To those whom I didn't ask, please do not be offended. It was just that I knew you already had a lot on your plate, and I did not want to burden you with what would have been a considerable undertaking. I hope you understand and are in no way offended.

To my Graphic Designer, for her patience with me in designing the covers for the book.

To my publishers, for your advice, guidance, and support.

To you, for purchasing this book.

To those who have perhaps borrowed the book from a friend and therefore, avoided paying for it. Fuck off.

To the few and far between people who stood by our family in our darkest days. You know who you are, your conscience will tell you that. What you may not know is how much your kindness meant to us at that time. It is something I will never forget and will be eternally grateful for.

To the many bastards who ruined a decade of our lives. You made me realise that no matter what, no matter how good we think life is, no matter how good a person we think we are, we are so fragile, and our life can change completely in the blink of an eye by someone or something that we have no control over – an accident, illness or being a victim of crime, for example.

I want to thank you because what happened to our family was one of those events we had no control over, but it proved to our family that we are strong – stronger than we could ever have imagined. Strong enough to not only withstand the enormous stress and strain of the past ten years and counting, but to eventually have the strength to fight against the many members of the public and local police force who, for reasons I do not know, dedicated their lives to destroying ours.

Please read on at your leisure, I hope you enjoy it, and thank you again.

Table of Contents

Introduction

Justice is Everything

Hello and welcome. I was going to use the pseudonym of N. Emesis for this book because, without the full stop, it becomes Nemesis. The definition of the word Nemesis is, *'the inescapable agent of someone's or something's downfall'*, for this book, the *'inescapable agent'* is honesty, and the *'someone's'* is the many members of the public and local police force, whom I now refer to as Numpty Police. Numpty Police, or NP for short, controlled every aspect of our family's lives and took great pleasure in doing so, and most importantly, the *'something's'* is quite simply the word injustice. However, due to the input of my grandson, I will call myself Billy Bean and our family is therefore the Bean family.

The actions of these people cut our family so deeply and hurt so much more than we could ever have imagined. I have to right this wrong. I must do everything in my power to hold Numpty Police accountable for their actions and vindicate our family of the inequality, incrimination, discrimination, and blatant and deliberate misconduct heaped upon us by the powers that be. As the head of the family, I feel a great sense of personal responsibility to take on this role. To be honest with you, it is something I must do if I ever want to recover as much of the person that I was before we became the victims of crime.

If I am unable to right the wrong of their injustice, then it will remain a void in my life and the hurt will never stop. There will always be a hole in my heart and soul until justice is done. Justice is everything.

This book will detail the harassment, misconduct, and injustice. For some, it will be a difficult read at times, but for most, I hope it will be a bit of an eye-opener to the level some people, including police officers, will go to try to destroy an innocent family.

I bet some of you have switched off already, *'Oh my God, another whiner complaining about our wonderful heroic police force.'* I beg to differ.

1

However, some of you may have your ears pricked, you may have been the victim of the same or something very similar. We cannot be the only family to have been through this. In fact, I know we are not, you only have to turn on the Telly to hear stories like ours, the program Nightmare Neighbour Next Door is a prime example that we are not alone.

Our family is the victim of a particularly nasty and vile type of harassment which is described and recognised in British Law as Collective, Community, Organised, or Group Harassment. This type of harassment has several forms, rather than the more common harassment where one person targets another person. Group harassment can be when an individual targets a group, or a group targets an individual, or where one group targets another group, it could be a club, mosque or as in our case, a family. Whatever word you choose to describe it; we are the victims of it, and it is truly devastating.

It is impossible for our family to fully recover from something that has taken so much from us all. So many values and beliefs that determine the person you are or that you aim to be. It is also impossible for me to put into words the full extent of the impact the harassment and injustice has had on us all and in many ways, so on most occasions, I will not even try. I am sure you will make your own mind up regardless of what I say, and fair play to you. I will include some points regarding this impact where it is necessary to give some context. Some of you may get it, some may not.

I won't bore you with the legal stuff either, again only where necessary. But if you are interested, all the information you need regarding the offence of Harassment can be found on the Government Legislation and Crown Prosecutors Service websites. You may also find various documents online regarding police conduct including the College of Policing Code of Ethics that you may want to refer to. Although to be fair, I do not think you will need to refer to anything to decide whether Numpty Police acted with equality, impartiality and the slightest bit of honesty. There is no doubt in my mind that throughout our involvement with NP, they broke every rule in the book, and more.

All I think you need to know for now, in layman terms, is The Prevention of Harassment Act became law in 1997 and was amended in 2012 to include the section 4 offence of Harassment and Stalking Causing Fear of Violence. This was because of several high-profile celebrities being victims of

Stalking around that time. At that time, there was a loophole in the Harassment Act which allowed offenders to get away with the continued harassment of their target and even if they were prosecuted, they were only given ridiculously light sentences relative to the impact their *'Course of Conduct'* had on their victim, which on some tragic occasions resulted in the offender taking the life of their target. I will not mention any names as I would not want to upset anyone.

When the Act became law in 1997, there was no provision for the offence of Stalking contained in the Act, so it was amended in 2012 to include the offence of Stalking and also introduced the offence of *'Causing Fear of Violence'* for both the offences of Harassment and Stalking. The standard offence of Harassment and Stalking were considered to be a relatively minor 'Section 2 offence' and punishable with a short prison sentence, a fine, Community Service or a combination of the three. The section 2 offence was also subject to a six-month time frame for the case to be presented by the police to the Crown Prosecution Service (CPS).

From 2012, however, Harassment Causing Fear of Violence, was considered a more serious Section 4 offence, which carried a much higher punishment including a lengthy prison sentence. It was also not subject to the same time frame as a section 2 offence for the case to be presented to the CPS. To be accurate, and I am in no doubt about this, our family are the victims of the Section 4 offence of Group Harassment Causing Fear of Violence.

I am confident that if you read this book and believe just a fraction of what is contained in it, you will also be sure that our family were the victims of this offence. Not only that but NP deliberately failed to protect our family from that Harassment and were also complicit to and on many occasions actively joined in with the harassment of our family to a shockingly disgraceful level.

The vast majority of what is contained in this book, incidents, allegations and misconduct can be fully evidenced. In some cases where that evidence is not or no longer available, because NP have refused to disclose it to me or have destroyed it. I will give you my opinion. In those cases, and there will not be many, I will try to make it clear that it is only my opinion.

I have no fear of being called out or exposed in any way for writing this book. That is one benefit of living my life the way I have, it is what I call clean living. There are no skeletons in my closet, I do not have to waste a second of my time wondering if the police have found out about this or do they have evidence of that. I know 100% that if they try that, whatever they claim to have on me will be false. I would not put it past them to try because this book will piss a lot of people off, especially many police officers. To be fair, they have already tried to get me and my family on several occasions. As you will find out if you read on, I was prosecuted for an alleged offence made to NP by the harassers who were also our next-door neighbours, even though they, NP as well as myself, all knew the allegation to be false.

Thankfully, and because they had no choice, the CPS discontinued their prosecution against me when they realised NP had fucked up. But not before I had to attend court and stood in the dock to plead not guilty. And had two suspected heart attacks in the space of five days due to the stress it caused. A little more interested now?

It may seem a little of an overkill to write a book about our experience. I mean, it is only a bit of harassment, after all, it cannot have been that bad, I hear you say. And I do understand if you feel that way at this stage. Let's face it, nobody has died, and with so many terrible events happening in the world at this time, the conflicts in Ukraine and the Middle East for example, it might appear petty to some that I am going on about the harassment as though it is the worst thing in the world. Trust me, I do know it is not the worst thing in the world, but it is the worst thing that has ever happened to our family. This is our war, our fight for survival, our fight for equality and most importantly, our fight for justice.

If I had to choose one word to summarise why I am writing this book, it would be the word, *'Justice.'* Before the harassment, I, like most of you, would not have given the word Justice much thought, I had never needed to. I, neither any member of my family had ever been in trouble with the police. We had never been arrested, cautioned or convicted of any offences, we were and still are good people and a strong, law-abiding family. My wife does annoy the hell out of me, but I guess I am not alone there, and it is not an offence, although whether it should be or not is debatable!

It was not until I suffered injustice that I realised the importance of the word justice. It is a basic human right for everyone and anyone, even the most despicable people on the planet, rapists, murderers, terrorists, paedophiles and police officers (oops sorry, should not have said that, slipped out!), are entitled to justice. So, when that justice was denied to our family due to the discrimination, inequality and misconduct by NP, it was devastating and the impact on our family was ten times worse than the harassment itself. It felt as though we did not have any rights, no right to be protected by the police or the law of this fair land. It was like we were worthless and did not deserve to be treated with any sort of respect.

It is not just that NP failed to protect our family from the harassment, they encouraged, facilitated, were complicit to and sometimes actively joined in with the harassment, abusing their position, powers and responsibilities as police officers. When you are the victim of crime, the only place you can turn for help is to the police (legally anyway). You cannot say, *'Oh well, the police have failed us so we will call the Army instead.'* The police are the only public authority that can help anyone from being a victim of crime, so when they fail you, of course, it has a huge impact. So now, for me, the word Justice is the most important word in the English language because without the right to Justice, you have no rights at all, you are nothing.

So, my fight for justice is not about getting revenge on the harassers. At the end of the day, some of them lost far more than we did. They lost everything they had ever worked for their entire lives, including respect, dignity, innocence, and even their home. One of our former next -door neighbours even lost his mind and was reduced to needing round the-clock care, lying in a bed shitting himself, literally, shitting himself and waiting for some poor carer to change his nappy. Well, serves him right, our former next-door neighbours have no one else to blame but themselves for their predicament.

The Thin Blue Line

Many of the people who know what our family went through often say, *'How did you cope, how did you manage to even survive, let alone come out the other side relatively intact? It would have killed me, I would not have been able to do that, I would not have had the strength.'* To be honest, there were times when I thought the same and how we managed, I will never know. I can put it down to two things. Firstly, the fact we knew we were right, we knew we were innocent victims. No matter the intense level of intimidation, provocation and on occasions, temptation, we did not instigate any of the incidents and we did not retaliate to any of the extreme acts of harassment that we were subjected to for several years. We did not harass our next-door neighbours or their associates, ever. I am very proud of my family for having the strength and resolve to be able to do that, not that it helped us in any way at the time. Secondly, the human body and mind are unbelievably resilient, but also fragile at the same time. You only have to look at the wreckage of a car crash and you wonder how anyone could have survived that, but sometimes – not all – they do, sometimes they can even walk away relatively unscathed. I think most people have an inner strength that they do not think they have and which most of us never need to call on, thankfully.

Most of us will go through life without having to call on the depths of that inner strength, but for those who do, it is more often than not there. Most of us will never know what we can cope with or what we are capable of because we never need to go there. Unfortunately, our family has had to go there. But we found that strength, and we are better people because of it.

It is not that I want to see these officers and members of staff of NP who tried to break our family punished for their failings. I couldn't care less what happens to them, well, most of them. To be honest, I would like to see one or two of them hung, drawn and quartered in public (Bit harsh! Nah fuck 'um). It is about that word justice, it is about NP accepting they failed our family and acknowledging we are right to feel the way we do and the harassment was not down to what NP considered to be our family's imagination, or that we are unreasonable people, or most disgusting of all, our mental health issues.

If the powers that be within NP still want these officers to work for them after what they did to our family, the multiple acts of gross misconduct and criminality, then that is up to them. To be honest, if the powers that be within NP read this book, not only will they still want them to work for NP, they will probably promote and commend them.

'Oh well done Cuntstable, you fucked up an innocent family good and proper, have a promotion and enhanced pension, why don't ya?'

It is no secret that a significant percentage of people join the police force with the intention of abusing their position and powers. It is also no secret that a percentage of people join the police force because they have a mental health condition called Narcissistic Personality Disorder (NPD), and being a police officer allows them to fulfil their desire to abuse and control others. In my experience, if an officer does not have NPD when they join, most of them quickly develop it, or leave the force before they do.

There is also the theory of *'Good Cop, Bad Cop'*. I do not go along with that. In an organisation like the police force, people work closely together regularly, often in very challenging circumstances. In my opinion, it would be very difficult not to gain an understanding and insight as to what their fellow officers are doing. In other words, I do not think it would be possible for a *'Good Cop'* not to know who a *'Bad Cop'* was and what they were up to, but they choose to do nothing about it. Wayne Cousins and David Carrick are two prime examples. The colleagues of both these officers knew of their conduct but did nothing about it.

So, does that make the so-called *'Good Cop'* worse than the *'Bad Cop'*? To be clear, I do understand the very difficult, distressing and challenging nature of the work of police officers, attending accidents and suicides for example. It must be horrific, and I do not know if I could do that, it does take a special type of person.

Just like police officers, a Nurse, Doctor, Carer, Paramedic, Fire Fighter, they too have difficult, distressing and challenging jobs. So, the police are not unique in their role, but they are unique in their powers. It would appear, you need higher qualifications and are subjected to higher levels of background checks to become a carer than a police officer.

No wonder the police are fucked up!

A police officer is, in my opinion, the same as a surgeon or consultant for example. When a surgeon gets it right, it can be life-changing, lifesaving, in fact. But when they get it wrong, even accidentally, it can be life-changing, life-ending, in fact. A police officer is just the same, they have the power to save or destroy lives, almost without regulation or accountability.

Of course, we all make mistakes, even the best surgeons in the world cannot save everyone. But when a surgeon or a police officer gets it wrong, even accidentally, we have to accept it as part of life, it is something that will always happen (until Artificial Intelligence takes over the world). We can never completely eliminate human error; it is what makes us human.

But when a surgeon or police officer gets it wrong deliberately, it is absolutely devastating. There are no excuses, unlike making a mistake, a deliberate failure should not happen. That is one thing I really struggled with

7

over the period of the harassment, how is this happening, why is this happening, this should not be happening. I know there is the odd nurse or doctor that abuses their position to commit dreadful crimes, but it is a rare occurrence. Unlike the police force where every day seems to bring a new and disgraceful abuse of power. I watched the news only yesterday and an article came on about yet another Metropolitan Police Officer being jailed for life for sexually abusing over two hundred underage girls, often carrying out this abuse while on duty. The news reader also said that over one thousand Met Police Officers were either suspended or placed on restricted duties due to complaints being made against them. And since 2021, 18 Met Police Officers had been jailed for child sex offences and 13 more had been sacked but not jailed, also for child sex offences. That is in the Met alone! So even though the NHS for example, must have many more employees than the police, the police have by far the greater issues regarding abuse of power and position than any other organization. So, something is clearly wrong.

There have been many other battles against injustice in the past in a different league to mine, Hillsborough, Grenfell, The Post Office Scandal, Stephen Lawrence, for example. So, as the fight against the harassers was our family's war and fight for survival. My fight against the injustice and misconduct of NP, is our Hillsborough, our Grenfell, our Post Office Scandal, our Stephen Laurence. And I will not stop until justice is delivered. The one problem I have at this time is that I do not know exactly what that justice will look like. At the moment, I feel it will not be revenge or punishment of the offenders, but simple vindication could well be the answer. Vindicating that we were victims of criminality, NP failed our family, and we were right to fight against injustice.

Let me ask you one question before I move on, just to explain where I am coming from. If it was a Liverpool fan who opened the gate at Hillsborough which led to 97 police officers being crushed to death, would the relatives of those officers still be waiting for justice?

To Hate or not to Hate

I have always thought hate is a very powerful word. When our kids were growing up, they would use the word hate far too often, I hate you, I hate my teacher, I hate my best friend, you know the sort of thing. I can remember telling them the word hate is not nice and shouldn't be used so flippantly, hate to me is strike three, bridges burned. So, if you asked me if I hate

Numpty Police the answer would be, ABSOLUTELY, I hate them with a passion you could not imagine. To me. living with hate is like living with stress, you may think you are coping and in control of your feelings, but hate can eat away at you and one day you just might implode. In my opinion, hate and stress will get you in the end. I do not want to live the rest of my life with hate coursing through my veins, I want rid of it and the only way that can happen is through achieving justice.

I also never understood the impact that harassment could have on a person or a family. I feel it is one of those things that you must experience first-hand, to be able to fully understand the impact of the non-stop drip, drip, drip of the behaviour of the harassers. Our family never had time to recover from the last act of harassment before the next act would happen. There was no respite, no chance of a break.

When we were at home, it felt like we were in prison, and if we left the house, walked to the end of our drive, and turned left, we would have to walk past our next-door neighbour's house. If we turned right, we would have to walk past our next-door neighbour's relative's house who lived a few doors away. If we got to the junction at the end of the road, we would be opposite the house of our next-door neighbour's friend and builder who also joined in with the harassment, to the extent that in 2017 and 2018, he was convicted of harassment against me. There really was no escape. I can vividly remember driving home from work and when I got close to our village, I could see a big black cloud hanging over our house. It was like driving back to hell but having no choice because that is where we lived.

I will use bad language at times because that is me. One of my Achilles' heels is that I have always used bad language far too much. I will stop short of using the horrible word for female genitalia, instead, I will substitute it with CU Next Tuesday, I hope that suits you all. To be honest with you now, there is one occasion I have used that word, when you come across it, I hope you understand why.

I do know I run the risk that using bad language may make some of you think I am as bad as the rest and deserve what we got and may even put you off reading. All I can do is assure you that is not the case. In fact, there is no language bad enough to describe what happened to our family and the people who did it, but if you are offended by any bad language, I apologise.

Also, what I hope you will see, if you haven't already, is a sense of humour, which despite everything you will read, and everything that happened to our family, never left me. It indeed helped as much as anything in being able to survive the hell our lives had become. One thing that I have been strongly advised to do is to change the names of the people involved. I have been advised that this will help protect me from any fallout from the content of this book. I am not happy about that because everything I write is the absolute truth. If these people felt they were big and brave enough to harass our family, they should be big and brave enough to be exposed for what they are. If you can't do the time, don't do the crime. If I had my way, I would name them and expose them, all of them, whoever they are and whatever position they hold – a member of the public, police officer, judge, solicitor, insolvency practitioner or even the knight of the realm that got themselves involved. Honestly, a Sir actually got involved in the harassment, only in a small way, that I know of, but involved nevertheless.

But I have others to consider, first and foremost my family. We have had enough heartache and battles to last any family a lifetime. I would hope not to bring any more, but sometimes, some things just have to be done. My life experience leads me to believe if you do not deal with something, it will never be sorted and it will come back to bite your butt, probably when you least expect it and least need it. It is part of life's rich tapestry.

It is the easiest thing in the world to just close the door on something and pretend it is sorted and can be forgotten, but that tends not to happen. If you do that, it is a door that you cannot open again and when you keep closing the doors, it ends up you have nowhere to go. Your life is so restricted that you are unable to do anything. Sometimes you have to kick your way through the door no matter how much you may not want to. In my experience, the consequences of closing the door are far greater than kicking the door down. Short-term pain for long-term gain.

So, out of consideration for everyone, I will change the names of all concerned, but I will have a bit of fun with the name changes but only me and my family will be aware of that most of the time. So, if anyone reads this book and considers themselves to be one of the characters contained in it, you are probably correct. It is a true story, after all.

However, no liability will be taken for any perceived distress or defamation caused.

There may be Trouble Ahead.

I am fully aware that writing this book will probably get me in a whole load of trouble, but this story is too important not to be told, at least to me. To be too scared of the consequences for being honest, too scared of the repercussions and impact on my life for slating and exposing the pathetic law enforcement services and the broken criminal and civil justice systems in this country, is not an option. The British law and justice system are the envy of the world, supposedly. No wonder this world is fucked up!

I am confident that if any reader has experienced something similar to what we have, and I know there are plenty of people out there who have, they will be able to understand not just the content of this book, but also the impact. For those who haven't experienced anything similar, I understand it may be a lot more difficult to comprehend. I feel it is one of those things that you must experience to be able to fully understand. Like becoming a parent, losing a relative, or getting married. To the people involved, it is everything, a major life event, but to anyone else, it is an everyday occurrence and no big deal. What happened to our family is one of these events. To our family, it was everything, allconsuming. It dominated and controlled every aspect of our lives, emotionally, physically, mentally, and financially.

As stated earlier, the non-stop drip, drip, drip of harassment is like torture. You never know what is coming next or when it will happen. The only thing we were sure of was that it was coming, and it was never going to stop. While our next-door neighbours could harass, they would harass and when they could no longer harass, they incited others to continue where they left off. In isolation, some of these acts, or *'course of conduct'*, to give it the legal term, might seem quite trivial, with minor inconveniences that you could just brush off or even laugh about. But when they are put together, and never stop, it's a whole different ball game. I think this is why most people who haven't experienced harassment struggle to understand. And I get that, I really do. We have experienced it to a very great degree, and we still struggle to understand it. Why would someone, particularly your next-door neighbours, want to behave that way towards you? Why would an entire family, who we had not wronged in any way, develop such a hatred of our family that they were prepared to risk losing everything they had ever worked for? Why would our next-door neighbours want to live their lives that way, two of them were pensioners for God's sake. Why did they just not want to live out their later years in peace? Why would they just not let our family live our lives in peace? It's as insane as it is tragic.

In this case, it is not just our family that has been ruined, it is their family too. The big difference between them and us is that they had a choice whether to ruin their lives, and we did not. They are the only ones responsible and to blame for what has happened to them and us.

One of the very few pieces of good advice we ever received from a police officer was very early on in the involvement of NP in the harassment. We were visited by a PCSO, who advised us to record every incident as soon as possible and in as much detail as possible after the event, no matter how small or insignificant the incident might seem at the time. And to also keep a detailed log of when and where these incidents took place.

So, I did, and thanks to him, I can write this book. I am able to detail the incidents and provide all the irrefutable evidence to back up what I write. That is why I do not care about any repercussions. Whatever happens, I can provide the evidence to back up what I say. I have no fear of being exposed as a liar. Unlike many others mentioned in this book.

So, let's crack on, shall we?

Chapter One
Our Family

Motherly Love

I won't go into my life before I met my wife or even before the harassment started, other than to say my mum was the strongest person I have ever met. Unfortunately, she was seriously ill for most of her adult life. Despite everything she was going through, she never moaned, grumbled, or complained, but most importantly, she never stopped being a mum to me, my brother, and my sister. I have tried to live my life like she had lived hers, being the best person I can be. I feel my mum is why I have been able to stand up to the harassers and police. She has given me the strength to carry on, despite the odds, to never give up and to fight for my family and for right to prevail over wrong. My mum was amazing, I love you and I miss you. XX.

One other thing I need to mention before I start on the negative is the biggest positive that happened to our family during our decade of destruction. In early 2016, we became the very proud grandparents to a little boy. Not just any little boy, but the best human being I have ever met in my life. Well, equal with my mum, to be honest. He arrived right in the middle of the harassment which was at the most difficult time in our family's history. We were absolutely on our knees. I make no bones about it, that little boy saved my life, he was a gift. I am not religious, so I do not think he was a gift from God or heaven, but he was a gift, from where, I do not know, or care. He was here and he gave me the reason to live and the strength to fight. Bless you, Gitster.

If that wasn't a blessing enough, in 2021, our grandson was joined by his little sister.

Amazingly, she is as special as our grandson, as well as much as a stinky girl can be. Thankfully, we were in a better place when she was born, still not the ideal place, but better. They are two absolute diamonds, and we

13

all love them to the moon and back. Seriously though, I am sure most grand-parents feel the same way about their grandkids. But these two little rugrats are like nothing I have ever come across before. I could go on and on about the little characteristics that make them special. But I think you will get bored after a couple of days of reading. I thought our children were the best you could get, but our grandkids top even them. No offence, kids!

Our House

We moved into our current house in May of 1998. Our new house was a threebedroom detached house in a well-sought-after and respected village just outside of the main town. From my humble beginnings, I never thought I would ever own a threebedroom detached house in an area like that. To be honest, I do not think anyone who knew me as a teenager would have be-lieved it either. It was one of the proudest days of my life and I loved living there.

Just a week after we moved in, it was our daughter's birthday. We had the usual party and invited her friends as well as our new neighbours and their children who were of a similar age to our kids. At that time, I was work-ing for my brother's company, the secretary owned a horse. On the afternoon of the party, she came around on the horse and gave all the children a ride up and down the street. The kids loved it, and it was very kind of her to do this for our daughter. Thanks, Kazza.

As you would expect, the horse had a tip out in the road. I thought, *'Oh my God, what must the neighbours think?'*

We had only moved in a week ago and here we were parading a horse up and down the street. The neighbours must have wondered what had hit them. As it turned out, we needn't have worried. As soon as the horse had tipped out, one of the neighbours came rushing out with a shovel. I apolo-gised to him for the mess, but he said, *"Don't apologise, this will be brilliant for my Roses."*

It turned out that our next-door neighbours were very keen gardeners, and a big dollop of horse poo was just what they needed. Phew!

That is how things seemed to happen from the very beginning in our new home. Our family and life blossomed. Everyone got on with everyone, most of the time, there were the odd hiccup in the neighbourhood as there would be anywhere.

Recovery

As stated, to move on, I have to feel that the injustice we have been subjected to is corrected. I am fully aware that the likelihood of that happening is remote, but I must try my best. If we get to the end of the line and my best has not been good enough, then so be it. Some people may think it is the wrong thing to do, that the likely outcome will be too much for me to take and I will not cope with the stress it will cause. But I am not like that. For me, the option of doing nothing about the injustice and trying to correct the wrongs of the past (taking the easy option), is far more stressful than fighting for justice. In my eyes, I have nothing to lose. If I do nothing, I have to close the door and I will never be able to go back and open it again. The injustice will restrict my life and keep me prisoner forever. I will not allow that to happen without trying my best to prevent it. He who dares win my son, he who dares win.

I am fully aware that taking on NP is a massive undertaking, and I do not underestimate the task. But I know I am right to do so, and our family has done nothing to deserve what happened to us. I am no saint, I have made mistakes like everyone else, but I am fundamentally a good person, like most of us. I have never gone out of my way to hurt someone; I cannot see the point of that.

During and since the harassment started, I have been placed in many situations that before the harassment I would have been a nervous wreck, such as appearing in court as both a victim and alleged offender, being interviewed under caution by the police, threatened and assaulted. Those experiences have left me nerveless. Just a couple of weeks ago, my wife and I had a cheeky week in Spain, we were walking down a street holding hands (I know, disgraceful behaviour and I am not proud) and there was a great big bang, like an explosion. My wife squeezed my hand really tightly and jumped through the air in fright. We realised we were passing a BMX cycle track and a tyre on one of the bikes had exploded, it made one hell of a bang. When my wife calmed down, she said to me, *"You never even flinched."*

I didn't even realise I had not reacted until she said that. However, it may have its benefits occasionally, but I do not think it is a good thing on the whole. I would much rather be the way I was before the harassment.

Chapter Two
First Impressions

In the beginning

It was the summer of 2012. We knew our next-door neighbours had sold their house and would be moving but we did not know when. We were sad that they were moving as we had built a very good relationship with them over time. Just like our family and the family who lived next door on the other side and the family next to them, we thought all neighbours were like this. Big mistake!

We returned from our family holiday in August 2012 to find we had new next-door neighbours. I will call them the Head family. There was the mum and dad who were both retired, and two younger men, one who looked to be in his forties and another who looked a bit younger. I naturally assumed they were their two sons. As it turned out, I was wrong to assume this. The older man was indeed their son, I will call him Little Head, and the other younger man was the partner and to become the husband of Little Head. I will call him Sponger.

The next morning, I was in our back garden and so were our new neighbours. We were talking over the fence; the usual stuff new neighbours talk about. Introducing each other, where they had moved from, what football team we supported, what we did for a living, all that sort of thing. Mr. Head said he was a retired Fire Safety Officer for the Fire Service and Mrs. Head said she was a retired School Dinner Lady. One thing, well, two things actually that I found a little surprising given it was our first-ever meeting, was that they told me Mrs. Head was in remission from Stage 4 bowel cancer and their daughter had passed away when she was only 15 years old. I thought this was a little deep for our very first meeting.

However, the first warning sign of what was to come didn't take long. My wife's sister who was house-sitting while we were on holiday told us that on the day our old neighbours moved out, late in the afternoon, the lady from next door knocked on our door and asked my sister-in-law if they could put some of their possessions in our front garden and they would collect them as soon as possible. The sister-in-law said our neighbour was quite distressed when she called round. The sister-in-law put it down to the stress of the move and didn't think any more of it. True to their word, our now ex next-door neighbours collected their belongings soon after.

However, a week or so after we had returned from our holiday, our ex-next-door neighbours came to visit. We thought it was to thank us for letting them put their belongings in our garden and to tell us how they were settling into their new home only a few streets away. The lady suddenly got emotional and told us about their ordeal with the Heads on the day of the move. She started by saying, *"I am really sorry but I think we have dropped you in it."*

They then told us why they needed to put their belongings in our front garden. As often happens with house moves, the transfer of funds was delayed between our old neighbours and the people they were buying off, so they could not start moving their belongings into their new home until later in the day, this, in turn, delayed them from removing some of their possessions from their now old house. As it was only a few streets away, our old neighbours were using their cars and a transit van they had hired to move all their possessions, which would have taken several trips. While sitting in the van outside their new home, waiting for the funds to change hands, they received a phone call from the Heads telling them that they had to get the rest of their possessions out of the house straight away. They explained to the Heads that they couldn't unload their van and cars because the funds had not changed hands yet. The Heads told our old neighbours that they had thirty minutes to get the rest of their possessions out of the house, or they would dump them in the street. So, they came and asked the sister-in-law if they could put those possessions in our front garden until they could unload their van.

My wife was upset that our new neighbours had treated our ex-next-door neighbours this way. But me being me, said we should just wait a minute before we judge our new next-door neighbours. It could well have been a misunderstanding and the stress of moving. We should give our new neighbours a chance and judge for ourselves, after all, they seemed okay to me. As usual, my wife was right and in hindsight, I regretted even doubting my former neighbours' words, they were a lovely couple.

Apart from that, all seemed fine at first, there were no issues between us. In fact, because of my family's busy lives, with our children training and competing in their sports, we had little contact with them, just as with everyone else in the street. We exchanged the usual pleasantries when our paths crossed, and all seemed okay. But we were soon to find out what was in store for our family.

Let the Games Begin

The first incident was in December 2012, we had put our recycle bins out as usual. The following morning, my wife noticed that our blue bin was in the Heads front garden and my wife thought the Heads must have brought our bin in as well as theirs by mistake. So, my wife asked our son to nip next door and get our blue bin back. A few hours later, my wife noticed that the blue bin was back in the Heads garden and their house number had been painted on the bin! We did not think any more of it other than it had just been a mistake and ordered another bin from the Local Council.

The first major incident happened in February 2013. The Heads started to have a block paved driveway installed by a local builder, I will call him Trigger. Trigger was also a neighbour and lived in the house opposite the junction at the top of our street, just 50 metres or so from our house. Although we had been neighbours with Trigger for the past fifteen years, like with our other neighbours, we had not had much contact with him except exchange of pleasantries, which wasn't often.

A couple of days after Trigger had started working on our neighbour's driveway, I returned home from work to find that without our knowledge or permission, Trigger had removed our fence panels from the concrete posts between the two front gardens and moved two large plant pots from the Heads front garden and placed them in our front garden. Although a little peeved, I did not make a fuss. That evening, Trigger and I had a brief chat in the front garden, and he asked if he could step over the fence into our garden, if necessary. He had obviously already done so, but I agreed as I could see no harm in him doing so.

A couple of days later, I returned home from work as normal. Given the time of year, it was dark, Trigger and his crew were still working next door and I said hello when I got out of my van. I went in the house and my wife came up to me before I could even close the front door. I knew something was wrong by the look on her face, she looked very stressed and tearful. My wife then said to me, *"Your rose bush is gone, the builders have dug it up."*

I went outside to find that the builders, again, without our knowledge or permission, had done far more than step over the fence. They had excavated a metre-wide trench between the two front gardens, the entire width of the trench was on our side of the boundary. This trench ran from the front wall of our house to the pavement, about five metres in length. To be clear, this trench was excavated entirely in our front garden, not in the Heads garden, or even on the boundary between the two properties, but entirely in our front garden.

In excavating this trench, the builders had dug up all our plants in this area. One of these plants was a rose bush that my father gave me in memory of my mother's passing. I had kept this rose bush for 25 years, it had been with me wherever I had been, and when we moved houses, it came with us. There is no headstone, no memorial, no plaque, to commemorate my mother's life. This rose bush is what I had to remember her by, it was, of course, one of my most treasured possessions and was of extreme sentimental value. I asked Trigger where the rose bush was, and he replied, *"What rose bush?"*

I explained to him there was a rose bush where the trench had been excavated. He said, *"It will probably be in a landfill site by now as the digger driver put the soil straight onto the back of a truck which had gone."*

In desperation, I asked what landfill site the soil had been taken to but he said he didn't know. I explained to Trigger what the rose bush meant to me and to be fair, he was apologetic, at the end of the day, he knocked on our door to apologise again.

Later that evening, I knocked on the Heads door to tell them I wasn't happy that Trigger had excavated a metre-wide trench in our front garden and that he had dug up and destroyed my rose bush. Mr. and Mrs. Head came out of their house to look at the trench. Both Heads then started a tirade of abuse and aggression, shouting and swearing at me. Mr. Head shouted, *"I am not standing on my fucking drive talking to you about a fucking rose bush."*

This tirade took me by surprise, and I was naturally upset. The last thing I needed was confrontation, so I returned home. The Heads had mistaken our kindness for softness for the first time. Strike one.

If that wasn't bad enough. The following day, I returned home from work to find Trigger had again, without our knowledge or permission, erected a low-level retaining wall in the trench by placing 600mm square concrete slabs on end to form the retaining wall. To hold the slabs in place, the trench had been filled with concrete on either side of the slabs to serve as foundations. This meant the retaining wall had permanently taken a metre-wide strip of our front garden. To be clear, this area of our front garden was now completely unusable as it was now solid concrete. I asked Trigger what he was doing and informed him that he had erected the retaining wall on our side of the boundary, and he did not have our permission to do so. After what had happened the previous day, I could not believe he had done this. He said the retaining wall was not part of the original job and that Mr Head had asked him to erect the retaining wall after he had started the driveway.

The next day, I saw Mr and Mrs Head in their front garden, I said to them, *"The retaining wall was out of order as it had permanently taken up to a metre of our land."*

The next thing I knew, Mrs Head came flying towards me shouting, *"It's our land, it's our land, we have claimed it, we have claimed it, just fuck off."*

I explained to them that you cannot just claim land, but the tirade of abuse and aggression did not stop. There was no talking to them, they would not even listen. They kept shouting and swearing until I had no choice but to give up and return indoors. I could not believe they had behaved like this again.

I wish I had removed the retaining wall there and then. But as I was taken aback by what happened in the past few days – losing the rose bush had cut me very deep, so I did nothing. As had happened many times before in my life, I had allowed myself to be bullied, this time by our next-door neighbours and Trigger. They all must have known exactly what the job entailed before Trigger started the job. Trigger is a builder, and I am a carpenter, we both know how these things work. Trigger would have been fully aware when he priced up the job that he would need to erect the retaining wall to retain the block paving. We both know you need the landowner's permission before you carry out any work on their property.

A few days later, when the driveway was finished, my wife was in our front garden. As if the events of the previous week or so had never happened, Mrs Head called to my wife out of her bedroom window and asked if we wanted our windows cleaned because of the dust. My wife said to Mrs Head, *"No, we want your concrete out of our garden."* Mrs Head just laughed and closed the window.

At no time did Mr and Mrs Head or Trigger ask our permission, and permission was never given to erect the retaining wall in our front garden. And every subsequent request for the retaining wall to be removed from our garden was met with abuse, aggression and point-blank refusal. To this day, TWELVE years on, the retaining wall is still in place. The Heads and Trigger had mistaken our kindness for softness, for the second time in a matter of days. Strike two.

Just to be clear. Ours and the Heads houses are detached properties. The HM Land Registry Plans of the two properties clearly show the line of the boundary is in a dead straight line running the entire length from front to back of the two properties. The plans indicate the line of the boundary is approximately 350mm from the side wall of our house and is roughly denoted by the edge of a concrete path that runs between the two side walls of our houses.

There can be no dispute or mistake regarding the line of the boundary. This will become much more relevant to events detailed later in this book, but I just wanted to make it clear early doors to prevent any confusion.

Because of these events, we did not have any communication with the Heads for a couple of months. Then, one morning in early April 2013, my wife was sitting in our front room when an almighty noise started and everything in our front room started to shake like there was a mini earthquake. My wife went into our front garden to find it wasn't an earthquake at all but a man drilling into the side wall of our house. My wife asked the man what he was doing, and he replied, *"I am fitting a new gate post."*

My wife asked the man to stop and wait until I got home to discuss it with him as the Heads had not asked permission to fit the new post to the side wall of our house. The man said, *"Okay, I will have a word with Mr Head."*

A little while later, my wife left the house to do some errands. When she returned home, to my wife's amazement, not only had the gate post been fitted to the side wall of our house, but a new gate had been fitted to the new post. My wife asked the man why he had carried on working on our property when she had asked him to stop and wait until I got home. The man said, *"I had a word with Mr Head and he told me to carry on."*

To be clear, as I am sure most of you are aware, Mr Head does not have the right to instruct anyone to carry out work on our property without our knowledge and permission. And the builder must have known this. Just to make you fully aware, this builder was not Trigger.

I called at the Heads the following morning, which was a Saturday, to inform them of our disgust and annoyance following the events in February, that yet again, they carried out work on our property without our knowledge or permission. This resulted in another tirade of abuse and aggression from Mr and Mrs Head. Once again, Mrs Head was very abusive and Mr Head was very aggressive. There was no talking or reasoning with them again, they just kept on shouting and swearing until I had to give up trying to talk to them and go back home. I assume it was a familiar tactic of the Heads to try to intimidate people when they were challenged. They picked on the wrong family, I'm afraid. The Head family had mistaken our kindness for softness for the third time. Strike three.

When it comes to deciding enough is enough, I have always worked on a three-strike principle. The first time you cross me or my family, strike one, it's not ok, but everyone has an off day and may act out of character for one reason or another, live and let live. The second time you cross me or my family, strike two, and I will distance myself from whoever it is, friend, family, or knob, there is clearly a problem that can be avoided, so avoid it. If that does not work and it happens again, strike three, you are out, that's it, bridges burned, stay out of my way and I will stay out of yours. The Heads by this time had hit strike three. Strike one, the rose bush, strike two, the erecting of the retaining wall in our front garden, and strike three, the fitting of the gate post to the side wall of our house.

I wasn't going to go after them. They were both pensioners and I had the utmost respect for pensioners (well, most of them) as I worked in the Care Home environment, but it was strike three. Not that I had a choice, the Heads had made it very clear they were not interested in getting on. They just wanted to do whatever they wanted regardless of whether they had the right to do it or not.

Due to this latest incident and the fact there was no chance of rational dialogue with the Heads, we wrote a letter to them. It sounds daft I know, writing a letter to your nextdoor neighbours. But if we wanted to get matters sorted and make our position clear, we had no choice as we simply could not have any sort of rational conversation with them. The letter was simple and unthreatening, firm, and fair. We informed them that we were not happy about several issues including, and in particular, the two occasions: they had, without our knowledge or permission, carried out work on our property and that the boundary between the two properties was not the metre or so into our front garden as the Heads clearly wanted it to be. Also, we wanted the retaining wall, concrete and gate post removed from our land as soon as possible.

False Hopes

We thought the letter might have done the trick as there were no further issues for a few months after that. In fact, there was no contact between us at all, although the retaining wall and concrete remained in our front garden. Then in October 2013, there was another recycle bin incident. As usual, we put our recycle bins out in the evening. The following morning, we went to bring our bins in after they had been emptied, and our red bin was missing. I noticed that the Heads had two red bins in their front garden!

Realising that relations between ourselves and the Heads were very fractious, shall we say, I needed to be diplomatic about the situation and not jump to any conclusions? So firstly, that evening, I called at our next-door neighbours on the other side to ask if they had taken our red bin by mistake. They said they did not think so and looked to confirm they only had one red bin. Following this, I called the Heads, Mrs Head answered the door and I asked her the same question I had asked the other neighbour whether they had taken our red bin in by mistake, without even glancing at where their bins were, Mrs

Head replied, *"No, we have always had two."*

I replied, *"Okay, no problem, we will get another one from the council."*

I went on to say to Mrs Head that we were still unhappy about the retaining wall in our front garden and that we would still like it removed. The conversation between Mrs Head and me was polite and amicable, surprisingly. And as far as I was concerned, the matter had been dealt with when I left the Heads front door to return home.

A few minutes later, however, there was a constant knocking on our front door and a ringing of the doorbell. I answered the door to receive a tirade of abuse from the Heads son, Little Head. He told me that his dad was going berserk next door, that his mother nearly died of cancer, and that our non-stop harassment of them was making them ill.

It was clear that Little Head was unable to control himself, he was crying like a baby. I informed him that as he did not appear able to behave rationally, I was going to close the door, and I thought the matter was closed when I left his parents' house. I was more than willing to discuss the matter with him if he was able to do so in a civilised and rational manner. I then closed the door and he went away. However, a couple of minutes later, he was back hammering the door. It was clear how Little Head was hammering the door that he had not calmed down. So, I did not answer the door, fearing a repeat of a few minutes earlier. Or worse.

A day or two later, we received a letter from the Heads'. We couldn't really complain about that as we had already sent them a letter. However, I had posted our letter through their front door myself, and the Heads letter arrived via first-class post! The content of this letter was quite disturbing as it did not acknowledge that their encroachment into our front garden and the drilling into the sidewall of our house, were in any way inappropriate or wrong. In fact, it was the complete opposite. The letter sought an apology from us and threatened legal action against us regarding the retaining wall and our continued harassment. The letter also pointed out that we would have to disclose any neighbour dispute upon the sale of a property.

Considering what had happened since the Head family had moved in, the content of the letter was unbelievable. For the Heads to think that it was our family harassing them was absurd and delusional. All of this led us to believe this was not the first time the Heads had been involved in a dispute with their neighbours. I still believe that to this day. If they had not been involved in a previous neighbour dispute or harassment, they seemed to somehow have a great deal of knowledge about it.

We replied to this letter the following day stating our argument against the points raised in their letter and making it clear that the only party who was the victim of harassment was our family. There would be no apology from our family as we have nothing to apologise for.

There were a few minor incidents over the following months, but nothing really worth mentioning in this book. If I detailed every single incident, this book would put War and Peace in the shade.

Chapter Three
Turn for the Worse

First Assault

It was early June 2014, the day before our daughter's birthday. A family friend, well much more than a family friend, to be honest, the friend's mum and my wife had been best friends since they were very young. They got up to all sorts of mischief by all accounts, some good, some not so good. And although they didn't see each other as much when they got older, they remained firm friends. Very sadly, my wife's friend was diagnosed with Mesothelioma which is better known as Asbestosis and passed away in late 2009, she was just 43 years old. This was just a few months after my father passed away from lung cancer. Life's rich tapestry!

Our daughter's friend had popped around to bring her a birthday present. Thanks to the close bond between my wife and her friend, our daughters have been friends since before they could even walk. The friend was a single mum and had a son who was four years old at the time. She also suffered from Chronic Arthritis, particularly affecting her knees and shoulders. The arthritis hindered her from playing with her son like most parents, so my daughter would often take her son down to the park to play on the swings or to kick a ball about. Sometimes he would come around for tea to give his mum a break, he got quite partial to my beef stew and spag-boll (not at the same time though). We did a lot for her and her son. Although we enjoyed their company, my wife thought it was also her duty to look out for them after her friend passed away.

It was a lovely day in early summer, so my daughter and our friend's son went into the back garden to play. After a few minutes of play, the boy kicked a football and it hit the fence between ours and the Heads rear gardens. It was a 5-foot-high larch lap panel fence, so it wasn't difficult to see over the top. Mrs Head must have been in her garden at the time and almost immediately shouted, *"Stop kicking that fucking ball against our fucking fence."*

Our daughter replied, *"There is a child here."*

Mrs Head said, *"I don't give a fuck about that fucking little toe rag."*

The family friend was in the kitchen with my wife and heard Mrs Head shouting and swearing. She went into the back garden to tell Mrs Head not to swear at her son, Mrs Head replied, *"Shut the fuck up, you fucking ginger twat."*

Unfortunately, as well as having chronic arthritis in her early twenties, she was also ginger (I know, life is just a bitch sometimes, poor girl). Mrs Head was then joined by Mr Head, both launched the now familiar tirade of abuse towards our daughter and her friend. When my wife heard the tirade coming from next door, she also went into the garden. The Heads continued their abuse and taunted my wife, daughter, and friend, saying things like, *"Come round here, I will have you."* and *"Out the front now."*

Things calmed down and Mr Head said to my wife, *"If you want to come around and discuss it, feel free."*

At this point, my wife decided it would be best if they all went indoors. When they got indoors, the little boy was very upset, he asked, *"Why did that lady shout at me?"* and *"Have I been a naughty boy?"*

My wife was trying to calm him down and reassured him that he had not been naughty. After he had calmed down, my wife decided to pop next door to discuss the matter with Mr Head as he had offered.

As my wife walked onto the Heads driveway, Mr Head came around from the side of his house. When he saw my wife, he charged towards her. He got right in her face and started snarling like a rabid dog. He had one fist clenched and raised towards her face.

Mr Head was shouting at my wife, *"Get your husband round here, get your husband round here!"*

My wife said, *"My husband is not here."*

Mr Head replied, *"Yea I know, so why don't you fuck off back home, little girl?"*

28

It was at this point, my wife noticed that Mr Head was holding some sort of tool in his other hand, like a pair of pliers, scissors, or a screwdriver. My wife realised she was in danger, so she returned home, locked the doors, and windows and called Numpty Police. My wife was very distressed. To be clear, my wife is as hard as nails, so for her to be as distressed as she was, it must have been bad.

The whole event was witnessed by our daughter who was standing on our driveway. Due to the commotion and the fact that it happened on the Heads driveway, which is on the corner of a busy junction and in broad daylight, this assault by Mr Head on my wife was probably witnessed by many other people.

That night I had the first of what would become regular and very distressing nightmares. I have always been a light and active sleeper. For example, when I worked for British Rail, in the vicinity of the track, we used what was called a *'Look Out'*. It was this person's job to look out for trains coming along the line and warn the others so they could get out of the way. The *'Look Out'* would blow a horn and depending on which way the train was travelling shout, *'One on the up'* or *'One on the down'*, *'Stand clear.'*

It was always *'On the up'* if the train was travelling to London, and *'On the down'* if it was travelling away from London, no matter where in the country you were. Most of the time, we all managed to get out of the way, there were a few occasions that were a lot closer than I would have liked and we did lose the odd workmate, but it was the eighties!

Anyway, I would often sit bolt upright in bed and shout, *'One on the up'* at the top of my voice, at which point my wife would wake me up.

Also, I am a keen fisherman, oops, sorry, Sam Smith, I mean fisher them, I wouldn't want to upset anyone. On occasions, my wife would wake me up and I would be sitting up in bed as though I was sitting on the riverbank, rod in hand, fishing.

Anyway, I digress. This nightmare was truly harrowing. It started with me sitting in my front room and I heard my wife and daughter pull up on our drive in the car, they had been to visit my mother-in-law. No, that's not the nightmare, I didn't imagine they had brought the mother-in-law back with them for tea, it wasn't that horrific!

A few seconds later, I heard my daughter screaming and I looked out of our front window and Mr Head was attacking her with a chainsaw. He drew the chainsaw right down her face and body and she fell to the floor out of sight behind our hedge at the front of our garden. I started to run towards our front door and at the same time called the police on my mobile phone. As I opened the front door, I was speaking to an officer at Force Control. It was a female officer and I said to her, '*My next-door neighbour has attacked my daughter with a chainsaw, and he is just about to cut my wife's head off.*'

As I said that, Mr Head cut my wife's head off with the chainsaw and she too fell to the floor behind the hedge. At that point, I dropped my phone, it fell to the floor in slow motion and when the phone hit the floor, it smashed and I woke up. I was sweating and my heart was pounding. I had this nightmare regularly for years and it was the same every time.

Although it remained a nightmare, as the harassment progressed and the Heads became more deluded and dangerous, it could easily have become a reality. The Heads were intent on not just harassing our family but causing all of us serious physical harm, nothing was off limits and everything was justifiable to them and Numpty Police. Thankfully, I have not had this particular nightmare for several years now. Obviously, writing this book brings all these memories to the fore and it is not pleasant – not pleasant at all, but it is a necessary evil.

This was only one of the nightmares that would plague my life for years. All of which were equally horrific and distressing. It sends shivers down my spine just putting it down in words. It is one of those doors I had no choice but to close back then. I could not deal with it, and I will not be able to deal with it until justice has been done and our family vindicated. If that does not happen, then that door will have to remain closed for the rest of my life, which will restrict how far along the road to recovery I can travel. I must do all I can to exorcise the demons that live rent-free in my head.

Numpty Police

This assault on my wife signalled the involvement of our local police force, NP, in what was to become the worst decade in our family's history. We thought that getting to the stage with our next-door neighbours that NP needed to get involved would signal the end of the problems with the Heads. Little did we know, our problems had not even started. The involvement of

NP started a sequence of events that we could not believe were happening. But it was happening, and it was all too real and it went on year after year after year.

That evening we were visited by two police officers from NP. It did not get off to the best of starts. They played the role of good cop, and bad cop, a role that we would become very familiar with over the following years. The good cop was what we would expect from a police officer who attended our property after we had reported my wife being assaulted by our next-door neighbour – polite, patient and calm. The other was an arrogant, ignorant, impatient and rude arsehole and a clear misogynist. The bad cop was asking all the questions and taking notes in a hard-backed A4-size notebook. He was asking my wife and daughter what happened. After about ten minutes or so, he slammed the book shut and said to my wife and daughter, *"If you are not going to let me speak, I might as well leave."*

We were all shocked, including the good cop, he actually looked embarrassed at the actions of his colleague. Naturally, my wife and daughter started to cry, it was the last thing they needed after what happened earlier that day.

My wife apologised, even though she had nothing to apologise for. In fact, it was the officer who should have apologised, but that is not in their makeup. If they apologise for anything, they are accepting they did something wrong and they would never do that, would they?

It was very distressing to see my wife this way. The good cop kept looking at my daughter with a look on his face as if he was saying sorry. The bad cop continued with the same balshy attitude until they left our house to visit the Heads.

A few minutes later, the good cop returned to our house and said, *"It looks as though the Heads have gone to bed as all the lights were off and we didn't want to disturb them, so we will send an officer out to see them tomorrow"*

Trifik. So, if you want to know how to get away with speaking to the police when you have been reported for assaulting your next-door neighbour, just go to bed, or pretend to go to bed and the police will not disturb you. I mean, that wouldn't be fair would it, to disturb someone who was alleged to have assaulted the woman who lived next door. Not fair at all!

The bad cop was rude, arrogant and aggressive. He showed a total lack of compassion and understanding towards the assault on my wife by Mr Head. He made my wife feel as though it was all her fault. This was our first involvement with NP and it was the first but not the only time by far, that NP treated our family with an unacceptable level of disdain. It was also our first exposure to what would become the familiar tactic used by NP, to incriminate and intimidate the victim, in this case, my wife, so they do not have to deal with the matter.

You may ask why we did not object to the conduct of the officer. Before this day, we had not dealt with the police. We may be different to most people, but I do not think so. To us, the police are the authority, they are the ones you trust and respect, you do what they say and don't argue. We found the whole situation to be very intimidating, having a police officer in your front room shouting at you is not a pleasant experience, particularly, when you have been the victim of crime. It is only natural to do what they say because you're desperate for their help. I wish I knew then what I know now.

The following day, which was our daughter's birthday, we received a visit from a PCSO from NP. He informed us that he was not able to deal with the assault but would arrange for an officer to call to progress the allegation. He informed us that the reason for his visit was to ask if we would be prepared to try mediation with the Heads to attempt to resolve the issues between us. We, of course, agreed to take part in mediation so the PCSO visited the Heads to ask if they would take part. A little while later, the PCSO returned to our house and told us that the Heads had refused to take part in mediation.

Even at this stage, if the Heads genuinely believed they had issues with our family and we were harassing them as they claimed in their letter, why would they refuse to mediate?

This was the officer who advised us to keep a record of any incident, in as much detail as possible and as soon as possible after the event. So, that is what I did. So, thanks to this PCSO for this bit of advice. It is probably the only piece of good advice we ever received from an NP Officer. I am not sure some of his colleagues will be so thankful when this book is published.

A couple of days after that, we received a visit from PC Bruce Willis, that is not his real name by the way, but he was one of the very few officers who actually treated our family with respect and equality. Well, as much as he was allowed to before he was abruptly *'moved on'* to another department, surprise, surprise. Anyway, he said he had been tasked with taking statements from my wife and daughter regarding the assault by Mr Head and that he would be asking Mr Head to attend an interview. After the initial visit from the two officers on the day of the assault, we hoped the attitude of the bad cop may have been a blip, strike one if you like. And the attitude of this officer was more along the lines of what we could expect from an NP officer. Wrong!

Just a few days later, we noticed that the Heads had placed a gas bottle against the side wall of our house, it was the type of blue gas bottle that you would use for your BBQ. This was very concerning as there was an article on the news that day about a gas bottle that had exploded in the garden of someone's house causing extensive damage to their property. The article included an interview with a Fire Safety Officer from the Fire Service who explained the dangers of this type of bottle and how they should not be kept in the vicinity of your home.

As mentioned previously, Mr Head was a retired Fire Safety Officer from the Fire Service himself, so he would have been fully aware of the danger this gas bottle posed to us and our property. They had also placed some long decking timbers leaning up against our fence between the two properties. This wouldn't have bothered me if it wasn't for their previous conduct. After all, Mr Head had assaulted my wife, so I was not prepared to allow them to take further liberties, they had used all their strikes a while ago. The Heads had also fitted a CCTV camera to the soffit board in their rear garden which was pointing directly into our back garden.

Over the following few days, every time our paths crossed with any of the Head family, there was an incident, such as our son being called a *'Fucking little prick'*. Or if we were in our back garden, Mrs Head would shout obscenities over the fence and sing songs, the Queen classic, *'We are the Champions'* was a particular favourite of hers. Every time we went into our back garden almost without exception, within ten seconds, the Heads patio doors would open and out would come Mrs Head with her usual odd behaviour.

It was obvious that Mrs Head was watching their CCTV camera that pointed into our back garden and whenever she saw us in our back garden, she would come out to say, sing or do something. She was so fucked up, even at this stage.

Mrs Head would also regularly shout over the fence that she had recorded evidence of our family harassing them on their CCTV cameras. We knew this to be bollocks as we had not harassed them.

The penny had dropped by now and we knew we had a serious problem. It was clear that the Head family had developed a delusional fixation that our family was harassing them, when, in fact, it was the Head family harassing us. This would again become a familiar theme with the Heads as they would reverse the truth. We would contact the police to report an incident, NP would visit the Heads, and the Heads would tell the police it was our family who had harassed them. This again, led me to believe they had done this before. They knew exactly how to play the police and because they were pensioners, NP would always believe them. Because of their age and, dare I say it, Mr Head was a retired member of the Emergency Services, NP just refused to accept that it could possibly be the Head family at fault. Due to the level of aggression the Heads had previously displayed, this was very concerning for our family. They must have been thinking, we have committed one assault, so why not do it again? And guess what, they did.

A couple of weeks passed and we had not heard anything from NP regarding the assault on my wife. So, my wife contacted the Officer in Charge (OIC) of the case, PC Willis. He informed my wife that he had sustained a serious hand injury and had been placed on long-term sick leave so had not progressed the case. We had no reason to doubt him. But we did wonder why another officer had not picked up the case.

A few days later, my wife was away for a few days with her sister when she received a phone call from a female officer from NP. The officer informed my wife that she had taken on the workload of PC Willis and that she had filed the case regarding the assault by Mr Head with No Further Action. The officer gave no reason for the decision.

My wife was naturally taken aback by the call. She was not expecting the call and she certainly was not expecting to be told that the case had been filed with No Further Action. When my wife returned, she contacted NP to ask why the case had been filed with No Further Action. Those three words, NO FURTHER ACTION, are three words we would hear time after time after time from NP over the following few years regarding offences committed by the Heads and their associates. My wife later received a call from another PC, who told her that the case had been filed due to the lack of an independent witness!

To be clear. NP had not conducted any investigation, had made no house-to-house inquiries, and had made absolutely no attempt to find out if there was an independent witness. As mentioned, this assault took place at the junction of a busy road and the chances that this assault was witnessed by someone other than my daughter must have been very high. My wife was told by NP that although our daughter witnessed the entire assault and had provided NP with a statement, as our daughter is a relative to the alleged victim, she cannot be considered as an independent witness and her statement cannot be used as evidence. So, because of the lack of an independent witness, the case will remain closed! Well, it was the Heads, so a little bit of crime didn't matter.

I fully understand that it would have been beneficial to have an independent witness, despite the fact NP had done nothing to find out if there was one. But with the lack of an independent witness, surely, the next best thing would suffice. For instance, if someone broke into a house and assaulted your spouse, but because it happened inside your property, and the only witness was you, would the police close the case with no investigation and NO FURTHER ACTION? No, firstly, they would or should do everything in their power to find out if there was an independent witness, conduct house to-house inquiries, or gather any evidence such as CCTV footage. What's the word I am looking for, oh yeah, INVESTIGATE!

Also, if their investigation did not find any witnesses or evidence, then the eyewitness account of the other person or people in the house, whether related to the victim or not, would be considered tangible evidence and can be used in a court of law.

It was absolutely crystal clear that NP did not want to take any further action against Mr Head for not just assaulting a woman but assaulting the woman who lives next door. Could it have been because Mr Head was a pensioner? Could it have been because Mr Head was a retired member of the Emergency Services, and the registration plate of his car was N999 HEAD?

No, surely not, NP would not allow someone to get away with assaulting the woman who lived next door just because he was once one of them, would they?

However, before going on long-term sick leave, PC Willis did interview Mr Head regarding the assault on my wife. We were later informed by PC Willis that in his interview, Mr Head admitted putting his head in my wife's face, but he denied he was holding anything in his hands. This was a lie and would be proven to be so by Mr Head himself much further down the line. In any event, for Mr Head to admit to putting his head in my wife's face constitutes an assault.

There was also a witness to the assault who provided NP with a statement, admittedly it was our daughter. So, there was an admittance to the offence by Mr Head, an eyewitness to the offence, and a witness statement. But despite all this which I consider to be enough evidence to at least investigate, NP failed and refused to take any action whatsoever against Mr Head. In the not-too-distant future, the decision to take no further action against Mr Head for assaulting my wife would have serious consequences for our family, and myself, in particular. It also gave the Heads the green light to carry on with their harassment, and boy, did they carry on.

It would appear that we were not the only ones who had contacted NP. We received a visit from another PCSO from NP, to discuss the ongoing problems with the Heads. She told us that the Heads had reported our whole family to NP for harassment. We told her our side of the story and she made what the police refer to as a Scheduled Appointment with an Officer to see what could be done to help resolve the ongoing issues.

We mentioned to the PCSO our concerns regarding the gas bottle the Heads had placed against the side wall of our house and the angle of the Heads CCTV camera that was pointing into our rear garden.

The PCSO informed us it was okay for the CCTV camera to be pointing into another person's property as long as it was not pointing into a bathroom or bedroom window, but she would ask the Heads if they wouldn't mind changing the angle, so it wasn't pointing into our garden. She also said she would ask the Heads to remove the gas bottle from the side wall of our house. She then went to speak to the Heads.

The PCSO returned a while later and told us that the Heads had refused to move the gas bottle from the side wall of our house but because of the danger the gas bottle posed, she had moved the gas bottle herself. She also told us the Heads said the CCTV camera was a dummy camera so they would not be changing the angle. The PCSO then left and what a total waste of time her visit was.

So, if the police ask you to do something you don't want to do, just say NO and they will go away! Well, it's the Heads, so a little bit of crime didn't matter.

Within ten minutes of the PCSO leaving our house, the Heads replaced the gas bottle back against the sidewall of our house. They made sure we knew they were doing this as they dragged the gas bottle along the concrete path that ran between the two properties. Considering Mr Head was a retired Fire Safety Officer with the Fire Service, he would be fully aware of the dangers this gas bottle posed and the fear it would cause to our family. This is an example of how deranged, deluded, and dangerous the Heads had already become.

I know the chances of the gas bottle exploding are remote, but it was possible, it had happened only a few days before. If it exploded, it would have caused as much damage to their property as it would ours. But the Heads did not care about that. Their only concern was to cause our family as much fear, alarm and distress as possible.

As arranged with the PCSO, an officer from NP visited our house for the Scheduled Appointment as planned, I will call him PC Blankbrain. We spoke at length regarding the problems with the Heads and he seemed sympathetic and advised us we would be best to go for an Anti-Social Behaviour Order against the Heads as it would be easier to gain and enforce than a Harassment Order.

We again expressed our concerns regarding the gas bottle the Heads had placed against the side wall of our house again. We told Blankbrain that the PCSO had moved the bottle a few days ago but within ten minutes of her leaving, the Heads had replaced it. PC Blankbrain said he would pop next door and have a word with the Heads. That was good of him!

PC Blankbrain returned about 30 minutes later and his attitude had completely changed. First of all, he asked our daughter who had been present throughout his visit, to leave the room!

He then said the Heads had shown him social media comments posted by our daughter regarding the Heads' LED lighting on their driveway.

He then said the Heads had shown him footage of our son harassing them. He said the CCTV footage showed our son had turned the corner in his car, driven forward onto the Heads drive, reversed off, and parked over their drive. Also, our son and his mates, who were in the car with him, harassed the Heads.   PC Blankbrain said (Blankbrain is in italics),

"The car in the footage was a silver Renault Megane, does your son drive a silver Renault Megane?

"No, he drives a grey Citroen C4"

"Yeah, that's it, a grey Citroen C4." He was clearly lying.

I asked Blankbrain what the registration plate of the car in the footage was. He said he couldn't see the registration plate. I told him that he had just told me that the CCTV footage showed the car driving forwards onto the Heads drive, reversing off and parking over the Heads driveway, which would have been in clear view of the Heads CCTV camera, so how could you not see the registration plate?

Blankbrain replied, *"I could not see the registration plate but I know it was your son's car by the alloy wheels"*

Blankbrain had never seen our son or his car before, so he could not possibly know what the alloy wheels on our son's car looked like. In any case, our son's alloy wheels had *"Citroen"* written on them, so why would Blank-brain think our son's car was a Renault Megane? He was clearly lying again.

Blankbrain then said the time on the footage shows it happened at 6.10 pm on Thursday. We told Blankbrain that our son was in a different county coaching tennis at 6.10 pm on Thursday.

Blankbrain then said, *"The time on the footage may be wrong and it may be 8.10 pm on Thursday."*

We then told him that our son was playing football with many other players at 8.10 pm on Thursday.

Blankbrain then said, *"Well, I know it was your son because things were said."*

The Heads CCTV does not record audio. Blankbrain was lying again.

When Blankbrain had gone, we asked our daughter about the social media posts the Heads alleged she had placed on social media. She had no knowledge of these posts. So, we searched her social media history and found no record of these posts. On top of that, Blankbrian could not show us any evidence of these posts, even though he claimed he had just seen them when he visited the Heads. Blankbrain was clearly lying, again and again and again.

But what had changed his attitude from when he left our house to visit the Heads, to when he returned?

Several weeks later and after much persistence, we were eventually informed by another Officer of NP via text message, that our son was not identified in the CCTV footage. Thus, confirming the Heads had lied to PC Blankbrain and Blankbrain had lied to us.

Blankbrain also said that Mr Head had refused to move the gas bottle, stating he was a former Fire Safety Officer, and it did not present a danger. Blankbrain told us he was not prepared to move it himself.

Brilliant. So, the Heads again refused to move the gas bottle from the sidewall of our house when asked to do so by a police officer. And the police officer was not prepared to move it himself. So, between the Heads refusal and Blankbrain's incompetence, we were left with the danger this gas bottle posed, against the sidewall of our house for weeks. Well, it's the Head's so a little bit of crime didn't matter.

Blankbrain also advised us that the Heads were planning to do some privacy work to the front of their property. He would not expand on that, and I didn't give it much thought. I was too preoccupied by the lies the Heads had told Blankbrain and more to the point, the lies PC Blankbrain told me and my wife.

There is absolutely no doubt. PC Blankbrain knowingly and deliberately lied to us regarding our son harassing the Heads. We have proven 100% that our son did not do what was alleged. Also, Blankbrain clearly lied to us regarding the allegation that our daughter had posted comments on social media regarding the Heads LED lighting. That was why he asked her to leave the room, because he knew he was going to lie.

We cannot emphasise enough the impact this had on our family. At a time when our family was already going through hell, PC Blankbrain lied through his teeth to us in this way. There is no excuse, no misunderstanding, these were deliberate lies by an officer of NP in order to intimidate and incriminate our family. The actions of PC Blankbrain were disgraceful and unforgivable. C U Next Tuesday.

In mid-July 2014, Little Head posted two videos on YouTube that were recorded on their CCTV, alleging I was harassing them by removing timbers from the Heads Garden. I was doing nothing of the sort. I was moving the timbers the Heads had repeatedly placed on our property without our knowledge or permission. The timbers I moved were on our property and I placed them neatly on the Heads side of the retaining wall which was still on our property. I did not steal the timbers, and I did not trespass onto the Heads land to remove them as Little Head stated I did.

Little Head had no right to be recording me in my own front garden and he had no right to post videos of me on social media stating I was committing a criminal offence. Although these videos were posted in mid-July, I was not aware of their existence until mid-September.

A few days after this, we were visited by another two Officers from NP. I will call one of them PC Sloth and I will not mention the name of the other one as we never saw him again although he seemed to be the 'good cop' in the usual double act. PC Sloth informed us he had been assigned as our Dedicated Police Officer for the ongoing neighbour dispute. We were advised by PC Sloth that the Heads were planning to erect a large fence from front to back between the two properties. We informed PC Sloth about the previous issues we had with the Heads carrying out work on our property without our knowledge or permission. Due to these problems with the Heads regarding the position of the boundary between the two properties, we applied to the HM Land Registry for a copy of the Official Plans for our properties.

I provided PC Sloth with a copy of these Plans and asked PC Sloth if he could pass the Plans on to the Heads so they would know the line of the boundary before erecting the fence. All sorted, or so I thought. Silly me!

Second Assault

About a week later, it was the 24 July 2014, just four days after my 50th birthday. We received another visit from PC Sloth. He informed us he had passed the Plans on to the Heads and they had told him they knew the line of the boundary and area of land between the retaining wall Trigger had erected in February 2013 and the boundary belonged to us. He said that he had told the Heads not to erect the fence on our side of the boundary. PC Sloth also told us that the Heads told him that we had been singing songs over the fence and that we had relatives who lived around the corner who were also harassing them.

This is how delusional the Heads are, not to mention pathological liars. It was in fact, the Heads who were singing songs over the fence, although that can be disputed. But what cannot be disputed is the fact it was the Heads who had relatives living around the corner who were harassing us. We do not have any relatives living around the corner, in fact, we do not have any relatives living anywhere in the entire village. The Heads were again reversing the truth but to a totally ridiculous degree. How can you deal with that?

How is it possible to resolve the issues with a family that is so delusional and such pathological liars and who are not prepared to mediate a solution? Clearly, the harassment was never going to stop, while the Heads could harass, they would harass.

We told Sloth that the Heads had lied to him, and it was them who had relatives living around the corner who were harassing us. We also tried to inform Sloth of the impact the behaviour of the Heads was having on our family, particularly, our daughter who already suffered from Chronic Anxiety. Witnessing the assault on her mum had a real negative impact on her, and not surprisingly. But Sloth couldn't give a shit, he couldn't care about the Heads lying. I told Sloth the number of the house on the same road to us where the Heads relatives lived and their names. All he had to do was knock on their door and ask if they were related to the Heads or the Beans and it would prove the Heads were lying, but he could not be arsed. Sloth by name, Sloth by nature.

As mentioned, I have only included the major incidents in this book. On top of these, there were less serious incidents happening on an almost daily basis. That is what we found to be very difficult to handle, the drip, drip, drip, impact of harassment.

Unfortunately, the day went from bad to worse, much worse. At approximately 3.50 pm that day, while PC Sloth was still at our house, our daughter left our house to feed a friend's cat. Shortly after that, Sloth also left our house. The last thing I said to Sloth was, *"Two things, as soon as you are gone the Heads will do something to antagonise us and we are going on holiday tomorrow and when we return the Heads will have erected the high-level fence on our side of the boundary."*

Sloth nodded his head in agreement and left.

We were going to Vilamoura in Portugal for a special holiday to celebrate my 50th birthday. That may not seem too grand to some, but compared to our usual Sun Newspaper holidays, it was luxury. We had electricity, a shower, proper beds, and even the toilet had a lid. Woohoo!

I will have to forget the humour for a bit because what happened next was not funny in the slightest, in fact, it was horrible. That evening, I returned home from running a Community Youth Football Club. It was called *'Friday Fun Football'* and it was a place where kids of all abilities could come along for an hour on a Friday evening and have a good kick about in an organised, well, not so organised, manner.

I returned home at about 7.15 pm. The sister-in-law had come around to see the wife because as mentioned above, we were going on holiday the next day and it was my wife's birthday the day after that. My wife and I have our birthdays within six days of each other although I am two years older than her. It has always been like that since the day we met! Sorry, I said I would forget the humour. DOH!

Our son, his girlfriend, now wife and our daughter were also at home. Because I had been at the Football Club and the wife needed a Sat Nav to find the kitchen, they decided to have a Chinese Takeaway. As it was a lovely evening, I warmed my tea up in the Microwave and took it into the back garden to eat on the patio. I often did this as I am a bit of a sun worshipper and love to be outdoors. Whilst eating my tea, I was thinking about the visit earlier by PC Sloth. I was thinking about what I had said to him when he left our house and started to wonder what the Heads would have done to antagonise us. The Heads had regularly placed various items on our side of the boundary, often leaning up against the sidewall of our house, like the gas bottle for example. I finished my tea and went to have a look and sure enough, the Heads had placed a pack of 1.8 metre-long floorboards, like what you get from Wickes, against our fence return running from our conservatory wall to the fence that was on the boundary between the two properties. It was not the first time they had placed items there and it served no purpose other than to annoy, antagonise, and harass. I moved the wood from our fence return and went back to the patio to finish the drink I had with my tea.

The next thing I knew, I heard Mrs Head shouting, *"Ere Dick (that would make him Dick.*

Head by the way), that bastard has moved that fucking wood."

Mr Head came charging into the back garden and shouted at me over the fence,

"What the fucking hell do you think you are doing?"

I said, "I have moved the wood that you have yet again, placed on our property"

Both Mr and Mrs Head then launched the usual tirade of abuse. With both of them shouting and swearing at the same time, it was only the swear words that were coherent. I asked Mr and Mrs Head to calm down as this was not doing anyone any good. Mr Head was trying to climb over or tear down the fence between us. He was angry, very angry.

Mrs Head then said she had video evidence of our daughter harassing their son, Little Head. She said that when Little Head left their house earlier in the day, our daughter had tailgated him along the road.

This relates to when earlier that day, our daughter left our house to feed her friend's cat. By coincidence, as was bound to happen at some point when you live next door to each other, Little Head had left his house at the same time which resulted in our daughter being behind Little Head for about

100 metres along the road until they got to the junction. Little Head pulled out onto the main road while our daughter waited at the junction for the traffic to pass before pulling onto the main road herself. Our daughter was about four cars behind Little Head for a further few hundred metres before our daughter turned right at a junction.

I said to the Heads, "*Our daughter would not have done that, she is a good girl*"

At this point, Mr Head lost the plot completely. He again tried to climb over or tear down the fence. He repeatedly thrust his arms over the fence to try and either punch or grab hold of me. If it wasn't so scary, the sight of a sixty-something obese, vertically challenged man trying to climb the fence would have been hilarious.

I moved back, so he couldn't hit or grab me and then Mr Head disappeared behind the fence. The next thing I knew, the pack of floorboards that I had moved earlier was coming over the fence heading straight for my head. I managed to dodge to the side to avoid the wood hitting me in the face and moved further back from the fence. To be clear, if I had been a fraction slower in moving out of the way of this pack of wood, it would have hit me smack in the face and would have caused me serious injury if not worse.

I could then see that Mr Head had reappeared and was holding the pack of wood with both hands and was repeatedly thrusting it towards my face. When he realised he could not reach me, he made several gestures to throw the wood at me. He then threw the wood down on his side of the fence and tried to either climb or break through the fence again.

He was like a raging bull, his face seemed to be twice its normal size. He had a look of pure hate and evil in his eyes which were bulging out of his head and he was literally foaming at the mouth and spit was flying everywhere when he was shouting and swearing at me. I banged on our conservatory window and the wife and visitors came into the back garden. They said that when they came out, I was frozen to the spot with both the Heads ranting and raving at me. Mr Head was still trying to get through or over the fence. When Mrs Head noticed my wife and daughter in the garden, she shouted, "If

I see your daughter in the street, I will have her"

44

When our daughter heard this, she became upset. Not only had she witnessed her mum being assaulted by Mr Head, but she had now witnessed her dad also being assaulted by Mr Head and Mrs Head threatening to attack her. Mr and Mrs Head then went into their house, Mrs Head immediately came back out and said, *"If I see your daughter harassing my son again, I will have her."* Mrs Head then called us all *"Dickheads,"* and went indoors.

I am convinced that if Mr Head had managed to get over or through the fence, he would have caused me serious harm or even worse. There is no doubt in my mind about that. And what we were to discover later about this incident, proved I was right. It was very scary, even for a grown man. I have never seen anyone as angry as that before or since.

I have come close to death on several occasions in my life. As mentioned, I used to work for British Rail as a carpenter in their Civil Engineers Department in the 1980s. Some of the things we were expected to do and the conditions we were expected to work in were ridiculously dangerous. I once came within a few inches of losing my life twice in the same shift. But I can honestly say, I have never feared for my life more than on this day. When something happened with British Rail, you could not see it coming, so you couldn't be afraid. With this incident, I could see it coming, I could see a man just a few feet away from me who seriously wanted to kill me. I have never seen a look on someone's face like that before and I hope I never see it again. It is something I will never forget. But worst of all, I now knew what my wife had faced just a few weeks earlier. I am a six-foot-tall man, and I was genuinely scared for my life. For my five-foot-tall wife to face a snarling, raging bull of a man, my wife described him as being like a Pit Bull, it must have been terrifying. I do not know what else I can say about that.

We all came indoors and my wife called NP. They informed my wife that the incident had already been called in by the Heads via 999 and that officers were on their way via blue light and as the Heads had called the incident in, the officers would visit them first. What the hell the Heads said to NP when they called, I cannot imagine, *"Hello officer, I have just tried to kill my next-door neighbour, can you come and arrest him, please?"*

Well, I do not have to imagine. Later in this saga, I would receive a written copy of the 999-call made by Mr Head to NP regarding this incident. The content of the call confirmed that Mr Head was not finished with me, and he was intent on getting to me and hurting me again. I swear, if anyone other than Mr Head had made that 999 call to NP, they would have been arrested immediately when the officers arrived, but even though things went downhill from there, the officers did not arrest him, in fact, they did fuck all. Even though it was the second assault against his next-door neighbours in less than two months. Well, it's the Heads, so a little bit of crime didn't matter.

About 5 minutes later, two officers from NP arrived. As expected, they went to the Heads house first. About 10 minutes later, they came to our house. The Officers informed us that Mr and Mrs Head had alleged that our daughter was harassing their son by tailgating him along the road. The Heads had also told the officers that our daughter was harassing their son because he was gay.

We informed the officers of the circumstances regarding the allegation and that our daughter was not harassing Little Head because he was gay, or at all. We also explained that she had not tailgated Little Head along the road and that PC Sloth was actually at our house at the time our daughter left the house to go to her friend's and it was pure coincidence that Little Head left his house at the same time.

We told the Officers what really happened and that Mr Head had assaulted me. One of the officers said, *"It's a shame they only have a CCTV camera at the front of the property"*

We informed the officers that was not the case, and they had a CCTV camera at the back as well as the front. They said the Heads had told them they only had a camera at the front. The reason for that is clear, the Heads did not want the officers to see what had actually happened, not that NP would have cared anyway. The officers returned to the Heads to explain that it was just a coincidence that our daughter and Little Head had left their houses at the same time which resulted in our daughter being behind Little Head for a short distance, and to view the CCTV footage from the camera in the Heads rear garden.

A few minutes later, we heard Mrs Head shouting, *"Dick, get back in here."*

Shortly after that, we heard a siren. My wife said to me, *"That's coming here."* I said, *"No, it will be going to the A41."*

Again, the wife was right, as always. A few seconds later, a second Police car arrived via blue light. I can remember my wife and I saying to each other, *"Thank God, it's all over."*

How wrong we were. Little did we know, it was just the start of our troubles.

After about a further ten minutes, the initial two officers returned to our house. We opened the front door to let the officers in, the female officer looked very pale and was visibly shaking. We noticed another two officers standing at the end of our drive like they were on guard. The male officer then said, *"I suppose you heard all that"*

We said that we had heard Mrs Head shouting but that was it. He then told us that when they explained the reason our daughter was behind Little Head for a short distance along the road, they all went hysterical. The officers said they were so concerned for their own safety they had to call for emergency backup. That was why the other two officers arrived via Blue Light. The first two officers to arrive had called for emergency backup because of the hysterical and irrational conduct of the Heads.

They also said Mr Head ran out of his house to get to our house and break down our front door to attack me again. Mr Head had to be restrained in the street by the officers from doing exactly that. That was why the other two officers were standing at the end of our drive. They looked like they were on guard because that was exactly what they were, on guard to stop Mr Head from getting to our front door.

The officers then said they had recorded the behaviour of the Heads on their Body Cams and had managed to calm Mr Head down and they would return to the station to write the incident up.

So, even though Mr Head had already assaulted me once that evening, and Mr Head had then called NP via 999 telling them he was going to assault me again, and the officers needed to call for emergency backup due to the behaviour of all four members of the Head family, and these officers needed to restrain Mr Head in the street from breaking down our front door, and the other two officers who arrived via Blue Light needed to stand guard at the end of our drive, in case Mr Head tried to get to our front door again, and Mr Head had assaulted my wife just a few weeks before. They returned to the station to *'write the incident up'*, whilst leaving our family next door to a violent, out-of-control maniac.

At the very least, Mr Head should have been removed from the premises and in my opinion, he should have been arrested and detained overnight. What was to stop any of the Heads from carrying out further attacks on our family when the police had gone? Nothing, that's what. We could not call for emergency backup, we did not have battens, handcuffs, pepper spray or a taser. This left our family in a very vulnerable situation.

These officers were so concerned for their safety that they called for emergency backup, but they could not give a shit about our safety. To be clear, we were not even informed of the threats to break down our front door and assault me again made in the call by Mr Head to NP following the assault. But NP was, of course, fully aware of the content of the call by Mr Head to them but did not attempt to put any measures in place whatsoever to prevent Mr Head from carrying out his threats once they had gone. NP did not even have the decency to inform us of the content of the call made by Mr Head to NP so our family was at least aware of the threat and to protect ourselves from what might happen.

So, if you want to assault your next-door neighbour again after the police have just spoken to you about assaulting one of your next-door neighbours, again. Just tell them you have calmed down and they will go away, leave you alone and allow you to stay next door to the people you have assaulted and tried to assault again. What a joke.

We did not get a wink of sleep that night and in the morning, we were faced with the very real dilemma of whether to go on holiday and leave our daughter home alone next door to a family that was hellbent on harming any member of our family in any way they could. To be clear, this wasn't just harassment, this was targeted violence against our family by our next-door neighbours. It was a very difficult decision to make but our daughter insisted that we go on holiday as it was to celebrate my 50th birthday. Not that I felt much like celebrating. If anyone asked me what I did for my 50th birthday, it would not be, *'Oh, I had a lovely party, a meal with the family and a holiday in Portugal'* No. It would be, *'Oh, I was assaulted by my next-door neighbour'*

Holiday Woes

Before leaving for our holiday, I contacted NP to confirm the assault by Mr Head had been recorded by the attending officers. Remarkably, Force Control said the incident was on the system, but no offences have been recorded. So, even after the events of the previous evening, NP had failed to even record my allegation of assault against Mr Head or any other offences. Well, it was the Heads, so a little bit of crime didn't matter.

So, I informed Force Control that I wanted to make an allegation of assault against Mr Head. Before we left for our holiday, we asked our family and friends to keep a close eye on our daughter and to stay with her as much as they could until we got home. To be fair, all our family and friends did a great job in looking out for her while we were away, so thank you for that.

So, we went on holiday. I'm not saying I wish we hadn't gone, but I wish we hadn't gone. It was a complete waste of time. It was not like a holiday at all. We couldn't relax or enjoy ourselves. Not just because our daughter was at home living next door to a deluded, violent and dangerous family. But also, because I had just faced a man who seriously wanted to kill me. There was always this thought of what might be happening at home and that we were too far away to deal with whatever it was. Of course, the holiday was ruined, just like our daughter's birthday, my wife's birthday and all of what should have been a special summer for our family celebrating my 50th birthday.

While we were on holiday, PC Sloth called at our house. He knew we were on holiday so why did he visit when knowing we were not there? I don't know, probably because of the assault, I suppose. However, our daughter and the wife's sister were at home. PC Sloth informed our daughter that he had spoken to the Heads regarding the assault a few days earlier and Mrs Head had shown him a bruise on her chest and said that when I moved the pack of wood from our fence return, I hit her with it causing the bruise on her chest. This is a complete lie. PC Sloth went on to say that he knew Mrs Head was lying and asked our daughter not to tell me of the allegation because it might upset me.

Upset me, fucking upset me. Mrs Head had told a police officer that I had hit her with a pack of wood causing a bruise on her chest and PC Sloth thought it might upset me. If PC Sloth knew Mrs Head was lying, then why didn't he tell Mrs Head that it was an offence to make a false allegation to the police, instead of telling our daughter about this despicable and completely false allegation? PC Sloth knew our daughter would tell me about it.

Our daughter was very angry that Mrs Head had made this false allegation against me. They had once again reversed the truth. It was, of course, Mr Head who attempted to hit me with the pack of wood. Now, Mrs Head was claiming it was me who hit her with the pack of wood. And PC Sloth knew she was lying but did nothing. C U Next Tuesdays.

At least PC Sloth could see through the lie, for once. In any event, it is a serious offence to make a false allegation to the police, but that did not seem to matter to NP. Again, they let the Heads do what they wanted and get away with it. The Heads must have been laughing their socks off at us.

At the time of this visit by Sloth, the Heads, with the help of their relatives who lived around the corner, who I will call Mr and Mrs Hoperty, had also joined in with the harassment by doing things like threatening to throw things over the fence and making abusive comments when we were in our garden. Mr Hoperty was a big fat arrogant pig of a man, just like his brother-in-law Mr Head. Mrs Hoperty was just an ugly fucker, just like her sister-in-law Mrs Head. They were a good match to be fair, they must have got on like a house on fire.

Anyway, all four of them had started to erect the high-level fence between the two houses. PC Sloth told our daughter that he had again told the Heads not to erect any part of the fence on our land. The fact is, the Heads had already started to erect the part of the fence between the two front gardens on our land, and PC Sloth witnessed them doing so but again just let the Heads do whatever they wanted. Why tell our daughter he had told the Heads not to erect any part of the fence on our land when he had just witnessed them doing so but did nothing to stop them? To ridicule and pour scorn on our family, that's why.

If PC Sloth had done his job and prevented the fence from being erected on our land, it would have prevented the absolute nightmare that followed. I could not have cared less about how high the fence was, we didn't want to see the Heads as much as they claimed they didn't want to see us. But because of the other issues regarding the boundary and because Mr Head had assaulted both me and my wife, there was no way in the world I would allow them to erect the fence on our land. Even if I did let them get away with this, it would not be the end, it would just give them the green light to do something else to harass our family. Not that they were ever going to stop anyway. While they could harass, they would harass.

While they were erecting the fence, our daughter told us there was a great deal of shouting and swearing between the Heads and the Hopertys. It would appear the Heads didn't even get on with their own family. When they were erecting the fence between the two front gardens, they would look into the front window of our house and when they saw our daughter they would stare, point, laugh and do the hand gestures for *'fuck off'* and *'wanker'* to her. On another occasion, the Heads and the Hopertys shouted at a friend who had popped around to deliver a birthday card for my wife, not knowing we were on holiday. When we caught up with the friend, she said she felt very intimidated by their behaviour. It came as no surprise to me that all four of them would find it amusing to intimidate this elderly woman. C U Next Tuesdays.

A couple of days before the end of our holiday, our daughter phoned my wife to tell her the Heads had erected the fence between the two front gardens, and it was very high. Our daughter thought it would be better to warn us about the fence rather than returning from our holiday and seeing it there. It was dark when we returned from our holiday and although we had been warned about the fence, when we turned the corner and saw the height of the fence, it was still a shock. To be honest, I wanted to tear it down with my bare hands right there and then. I think I would have done so if my wife had not stopped me.

To think that the day before we went on holiday, I had been assaulted by Mr Head, and to return just a week later to see the height of the fence was very hard to swallow. It was clear, the Heads had no remorse for their actions, not just for the assault on me but also the assault on my wife, the threat to attack our daughter and all the other things they did for the previous two years. Anyone would have struggled not to lose their temper. But as always, I did the right thing.

The following morning, I went outside to have a look at the fence in daylight. As I had expected and told PC Sloth, the section of the fence between the two front gardens had been erected on our side of the boundary, not just by a little bit, but nearly half a metre at its worst. Also, the Heads had removed two sections of our fencing from our property, hacked down part of our privet hedge that runs along the front boundary of our property, and thrown the cuttings into our garden. Our front garden was a right mess. Before we went on holiday, we had a low-level fence on our property between the two front gardens, two sections of fencing at the front and back of our house which was sealing off our rear garden from the front and a lovely privet hedge on the front boundary. When we returned from our holiday just a week later, we had a seven-foot high fence in our front garden, our fence returns had been destroyed, and part of our privet hedge had been hacked down.

Due to the previous issues regarding the boundary and the Heads carrying out work on our property without our knowledge and permission, there was no way in the world they would not have known the section of the fence they had erected between the two front gardens, the two pieces of fencing they had removed and the part of the hedge they had hacked down, were all on our property.

To be clear, neither our two fence returns, nor the hedge were in the way of the Heads erecting the new fence, even though it was on our land. They had no right or reason to erect the fence on our land, remove our fencing and hack down our hedge. These acts were done out of pure spite.

The fence was horrendous. The height of the fence severely reduced the light in our front room. All we could see when we looked out of our front downstairs window, was the fence. It made our house feel even more like a prison than it already did. The psychological impact the fence had on our family was huge. It was like the Heads were closing us in. Further isolating, controlling and dominating our lives. Our daughter struggled with this.

The comments we had from many of our neighbours regarding the fence were unanimous, saying it was an absolute eyesore, and they would not be happy if their nextdoor neighbours erected the fence between their front gardens even if it was on their land but especially as it was on our land. It wasn't difficult for anyone to see the deviation in the fence, even PC Sloth who openly accepted the fence had been erected on our land, could see it, but would do nothing about it. Well, it's the Heads, so a little bit of crime didn't matter!

Most of the fence from the rear boundary, between the rear gardens and between the two side walls of our houses was largely erected on the boundary line. Which was fine, they could do what they wanted along the boundary line or on their side of it. But as the fence neared the front gardens between the two properties, the fence clearly dog-legged onto our side of the boundary. We now had a seven-foot-high fence stretching from the front to the rear boundary between our two houses, even between the two side walls. It was ridiculous and an absolute mess. There was nothing accidental and discrete about it, it was there for all to see, a seven-foot-high fence in our front garden.

It is still a popular misconception with many of our neighbours and indeed friends and family, that the issues with the Heads began with the erecting of the fence, which was understandable as the fence was the first obvious sign of the harassment. But that is not the case. Most of them were unaware of all the other stuff that had been happening for the past eighteen months since the Head's builder, Trigger, erected the retaining wall in our front garden, and the two recent assaults on me and my wife.

After a couple of days on from returning from our ruined holiday, I have never been so relieved to return home from a holiday as I was from this one, I am sure you can understand that. We received a visit from PC Sloth to discuss the assault by Mr Head. He asked me if I wanted to progress the allegation, a daft question I thought! I said that I did, and he said he would call back in a few days to take a statement from me and my family. We told him about what the Heads had done while we were on holiday, including erecting the section of the fence between the two front gardens on our property, even though he had told them not to and even though he had witnessed them doing so, the two sections of our fence the Heads had removed and the hacking down of our hedge.

I told PC Sloth that we wanted to make allegations of Harassment, Criminal Damage and Theft against the Heads for these acts. PC Sloth refused our request and told us, *"You cannot make any allegations against the Heads and I will not be recording any offences against the Heads for the erecting of the fence on your land."*

We asked him why that was and all he would say was, *"It would not stand up"*

What the fuck. He could see the fence was on our land, he could see our two sections of fencing had been removed and he could see our hedge had been hacked down as the cuttings were still in our front garden where the Heads had thrown them. All these offences were fully witnessed and evidenced. Why the fuck would these allegations *'not stand up'*?

I said to Sloth that I do not understand why this was the case, but Sloth would not explain or expand on what he had told us. Oh, I know why, because Sloth was a fat, lazy slob of a man who did not want to do anything and well, it's the Heads, so a little bit of crime didn't matter.

It is the fundamental right of any citizen to be able to make an allegation of criminal conduct to the police and it is the fundamental duty of all police officers to record, gather evidence, action and investigate any credible allegation that is made to them. Our allegations were not just credible, they were 100% irrefutable. I was not aware at this time that a police officer cannot deny a member of the public their right to make an allegation of criminal conduct to the police. I had no reason to be aware, I had not had any dealings with the police before this and as with most people, you assume the police will be telling you the truth. If I knew then what I know now.

The only possible reason PC Sloth refused to allow us to make these allegations was to protect the Heads and the Hopertys from their criminality. There can be no other reason. The question is, WHY?

Why would PC Sloth take this course of action, which amounts to gross misconduct, to protect not just the Heads and Hopertys, but clear offenders? Was it a liking of the Heads or a dislike of our family, or was there a darker force at work? It made no sense to me.

Before PC Sloth left, we both went into our front garden so I could show him where our fencing had been removed, our hedge had been hacked down, the cuttings in our garden and where the fence deviated onto our side of the boundary. Not that he didn't know that already and why I was wasting my time, I do not know. I suppose I was thinking that maybe he hadn't seen or understood what the Heads had done and if I were to show him, he might take a different view. It's that desperation for wanting the police to believe you and help you because there is no one else. PC Sloth agreed that the fence had been erected on our land, he could hardly deny it. So, I asked him what he was going to do about it.

PC Sloth said, *"I know it's on your land, you know it's on your land, the Heads know it's on your land, but that's just the way it is and the conduct of the Heads does not amount to any criminal offences"*

Absolute total bollocks.

It is unbelievable that after what the Heads had done to our family in just the two months since NP had been involved, the assault on my wife, the assault on me, the threat to attack our daughter, the removal of our fence, the cutting down of our hedge and the erecting of the fence on our land, that PC Sloth could say the Heads conduct does not amount to any criminal offences. Even if it did, he was not going to do anything about it. I think the penny started to drop and we were completely on our own with this.

The reason I called him PC Sloth was because that was exactly what he reminded me of, in appearance and attitude, a sloth. When he called at our house, he didn't just pop around for an update, he would stay for several hours sitting on our sofa listening to our family pouring our hearts out about what was happening and the impact it was having on our life and our health.

He would then leave saying he would do this and do that but in reality, he never intended to do anything at all. I suppose he would then visit some other poor family who were going through a similar crisis to ours, sit on their sofa for a couple of hours, listening to them pouring their hearts out and then leave, and do nothing. He could hardly muster the effort to get off the sofa. He was such an absolute waste of space and a considerable space at that.

How someone like that could be a police officer I do not know. Surely, police officers must go through some sort of fitness assessment to do their job. How the hell he could run after a thief or mugger is beyond me, he couldn't run a fucking bath.

I suppose it is not always a bad thing to be like him, I mean, he wouldn't struggle for work if he were to retire from the police force. He could always get a job at KFC as a gravy dispenser. When someone ordered gravy, the staff just needed to punch him on the nose and the gravy would flow. He was also like most of the officers we had the misfortune to encounter. They talked a good fight when they were face to face, saying they would do this and do that, but then they would leave our house and do absolutely fuck all!

Dangerous Delusion

A week or so later, some of my wife's friends came around for coffee. They were sitting in our front room. Mrs Head and her brother Mr Hoperty stood at the end of the Heads drive peering into our front window pointing and laughing at my wife and her friends. This, of course, made them all feel uncomfortable as well as my wife feeling embarrassed. It may seem surprising to some that one of the effects of the harassment was that we started to become increasingly isolated. Because of the conduct of our nextdoor neighbours, friends and family would stop visiting or not visit as often as they once did. We would not go out as often as we were concerned for our safety or too tired from trying to cope with the harassment. It was even difficult to have conversations with people. It was a topic I tried to avoid most of the time, but people would always ask and when you told or tried to tell them about it, it felt like they did not believe you. I don't blame them for that, it is not a criticism. Our family have lived through it, and we still cannot believe it has happened, so why would anyone else? For some reason, I felt a sense of embarrassment when speaking about it. The physiological impact of the drip, drip, drip.

Screw You

Towards the end of August, in one of the most blatant, mindless, reckless and dangerous acts of intimidation, provocation and Harassment Causing Fear of Violence it is possible to imagine. I went into our front garden one afternoon to put some rubbish in the bin and noticed numerous large screws were poking through the fence into our front garden. These screws were at various heights. I looked a little closer and noticed more screws were poking through the fence panels between the two side walls of our properties.

To be clear, these screws had been placed through the fence from the Heads side, meaning the sharp points of the screws were protruding through onto our side of the fence. These screws were grossly oversized and protruded some 30mm through the panels of the fence creating a very clear and real risk of causing serious injury to anyone who may have come into contact with them. They were so dangerous it was beyond my comprehension that a retired Safety Officer with the Fire Service would do something so reckless. There can be no doubt he would have known the danger these screws posed.

56

We had no idea that the Heads had done this. Surely, it would not cross any reasonable person's mind that your next-door neighbours would do something as stupid and dangerous as deliberately placing grossly oversized screws through a fence into your neighbours' garden. If we or anyone else came into contact with these screws not knowing they were there, the injuries would have been serious and even life changing. The various levels of the screws meant that they posed a risk to anyone of any age, some were at the height of an adult's face, and some a child. It would have been distinctly possible for anyone to have lost an eye on these screws. If you doubt what I am saying, I have numerous images of these screws so I can prove what I say. Everyone who either saw these screws or has seen an image of them has been horrified. Sorry, that's not quite accurate, there was one person who was not at all phased by them. Guess who? PC Sloth, of course.

As mentioned, these screws were not only placed through the fence panels between the two front gardens but also in the fence panels the Heads had erected between the two side walls of our properties.

The only way to gain access to our rear garden was via the narrow strip of land between the sidewall of our house and the fence the Heads had erected between the two properties. This gap was approximately 350mm wide. This would mean that if anyone needed to gain access to our rear garden in an emergency, for example, a paramedic or police officer who may have needed to attend an incident such as an assault! They would need to squeeze themselves between the side wall of our house and the fence. They would, of course, have been unaware of the screws protruding through the fence which could cause them serious injury.

Along with the assaults on me and my wife and the threat to attack our daughter, this is yet another clear act of Harassment intended to cause Fear, Alarm and Distress to our family. This was a mindless, callous, reckless, and extremely dangerous criminal act by the Heads that was beyond belief. And a clear indication of the irrational and delusional lengths the Heads would go to cause serious harm to our family. The Heads were clearly so blinded by their hatred of our family that they could not care less about the safety of anyone else either. Thank God, we discovered these screws before anyone was seriously hurt.

As PC Sloth was supposed to be our Dedicated Police Officer, I emailed him straight away to tell him about the screws. I did not get a reply!

A few days into September, we received a visit from PC Sloth. He said that he had interviewed Mr Head about the assault against me and NP would be offering him a Conditional Caution with the condition that Mr Head agreed to attend an Anger Management Course.

For those who may not be aware, for the police to offer you a Caution, you have to admit guilt for the offence, clearly Mr Head had admitted to assaulting me in his interview. I asked PC Sloth if he had received my email about the screws.

He said, *"I have read your email but you may as well show me the screws while I am here."*

His attitude was yet again a complete joke. He couldn't care less whether he saw the screws or not and clearly, he was not going to do anything about them. Anyway, I showed

Sloth the screws and his advice was, "Wait for it!"

"Why don't you just cut the ends off the screws and throw them over the fence?"

I could not believe my ears. Bearing in mind that only a couple of weeks ago, Mr Head had assaulted me, and Mrs Head had threatened to attack our daughter, and a few weeks before that Mr Head had assaulted my wife and now, they had placed these screws through the fence. For Sloth to tell us to cut the ends off the screws and throw them over the fence was totally ridiculous.

We were already living next door to a family that was hellbent on causing us serious harm. Surely, to any reasonable person, if we had done what PC Sloth advised, it would have antagonised the Heads even more and given them an excuse, not that they needed one in the first place, to continue their deluded quest to harass and harm our family. The primary aim of the police is to detect and prevent crime, not to advise people who are already victims of crime to antagonise and incite the offenders to commit further crimes.

Given what had happened before, just imagine what might have happened if we had done what PC Sloth advised. This advice from PC Sloth was stupidity of the highest order and summed up not just the attitude of PC Sloth toward the safety of our family, but the attitude of NP towards Harassment in general. They consider it to be petty and it must be both parties at fault, one is as bad as the other, and that way they don't have to deal with it. I am convinced this was a deliberate attempt by PC Sloth to get our family to retaliate to the Heads harassment, so he and NP could say we were as bad as them and wash their hands of us.

I am also sure, for the Heads to do something so dangerous and reckless as this and the consequences this would have for them under any other circumstances, by that I mean any other police force than NP, the Heads must have known before placing the screws through the fence that NP would do nothing about it.

'Why don't you just cut the ends off the screws and throw them over the fence?'

Why don't you just go around next door right now and tell the Heads to remove the screws from the fence immediately before they cause someone a horrendous injury, you absolute fucking moron.

I also informed Sloth that we were still unhappy regarding the fence being on our land, our missing fencing and the hacking down of our hedge. I also tried again to tell Sloth about the impact this was having on all of us but in particular our daughter. Since the assault on my wife, our daughter started to struggle with her anxiety again. The previous few years had been very difficult for her, she had lost many things including her relationship with her partner whom she was living with. She had also stopped attending University where she was studying Sports and Exercise Science. At one point, she got so low, that she was contemplating ending her life and needed intervention from the mental health crisis team. I will not go into any more detail than that, other than to say, that it is not a pleasant experience being on suicide watch for your daughter. However, in the few months leading up to the assaults, our daughter had made great strides in her recovery. She was holding down a full-time job at a local Garden Centre and had started to train with a ladies' football team.

However, the assaults on me and my wife by Mr Head, coupled with the threat to attack our daughter and the erecting of the high fence between the two front gardens, had a dramatic impact on her. Her anxiety led her to think that when she left the house one of the Heads would be hiding behind the fence and would attack her as she walked to her car. And why wouldn't she feel like this? I don't think you would have to suffer from Chronic Anxiety to think this might happen given recent events.

It was very difficult to see it becoming harder and harder for her to leave the house every morning to go to work. She was going backwards every day and after all her hard work to get to where she was, it was desperate to see her this way again particularly for the reason why.

So, desperate times call for desperate measures. I knew the fence had to go, if it did not, then our daughter would be in serious trouble sooner rather than later.

To resolve the issues with the fence, I informed PC Sloth that we were prepared to offer the Heads a compromise. The compromise was that we were prepared to let the fence remain on our land if they lowered the height of the three fence panels between the two front gardens. This would, of course, reduce the anxiety our daughter felt when leaving the house. As the fence was of larch lap panels, it would be easy to replace the high panels with lower ones or even cut the original panels down. I also told Sloth that if the Heads did not agree to the compromise, I would take these fence panels down myself. PC Sloth did not object to this. I would later find out why. I wasn't aware at the time, but I was playing straight into the trap being set by the Heads and Sloth.

Sloth said he would visit next door straight away to inform Mr Head of the offer of the Caution and to speak with them regarding the screws, the fencing they had removed and the offer of a compromise regarding the fence they had erected on our land.

I heard nothing from PC Sloth for about a week, so I emailed him to request an update regarding the compromise and to express our frustration at the lack of action by him to progress matters. I did not get a reply. Standard.

From Fence to Offence

A couple of days later, it was a Thursday. I had to walk my daughter from our front door to her car that was parked in front of our house. She was very distressed, and it was horrible to see. I knew I could wait no longer.

So, when I returned home from work that afternoon at approximately 1.00 pm, I removed the three high fence panels from the posts between the two front gardens. The only panels I removed were on our side of the boundary which were causing our daughter such distress. I did not remove any other part of the fence, and I did not remove any of the fence posts that were also on our land. The reason for this was so the Heads could easily fix lower panels to the same posts as per the compromise.

I did the minimum amount necessary to help our daughter cope with the problems the Heads had created, and a lot less than I was legally entitled to do. I am a qualified carpenter, so I know how to take a fence down, I properly used the appropriate tools to cause as little damage to the fence as possible. Before taking the fence panels down, I asked my son to stay in the garden with me in case of any hassle with the Heads. Although the Heads car was not on their drive, so I hoped they were not at home and there would not be any trouble. When I had finished removing the panels, I asked my son to take an image of the panels on his phone. This image clearly shows there was a minimal amount of damage to the side frame of one of the panels.

When I do something like this, I must be 100% sure I am doing the right thing. Not just for my family but legally. I had looked up the law regarding Trespass and Acceptance. Acceptance is a law that states,

'You have the right to remove any item from your property that has been placed there without your knowledge or permission by someone else and that does not belong to you.'

The longer you leave the offending item on your property, the less of a legal right you have to remove it. In other words, the person who placed it there can claim that you had accepted the situation and that the offending item could stay on your land.

I knew I was 100% within my rights to remove this fence from our land, both morally and legally. We had not permitted the Heads to erect the fence on our land. We had asked them to remove it, we had asked NP to tell them to remove it, and we had even offered the Heads a compromise where they could keep the fence on our land if they lowered the height of the three high panels between the two front gardens. We could do no more, we had exhausted every possible avenue to try to resolve the issues with the fence. If there was the slightest doubt in my mind that it was the wrong thing to do or that it could be an offence, I would not have removed the fence panels, regardless of the impact it was having on our daughter. I, or we, would have to find another way to help our daughter cope. I was 100% in the right to remove the fence from our land, and I will argue with anyone who tells me differently.

Later that day, I received an email from PC Sloth. The Heads had obviously contacted NP about me removing the fence. The content of this email I found to be very offensive. It also contained probably the most ridiculous statement we have heard in this whole debacle up to this point, regarding the placing of the screws through the fence by the Heads.

PC Sloth stated, *'I have certainly tried to action any relevant criminal offences applying an element of common sense to prevent the situation becoming vindictive from both sides.'*

Bollocks. PC Sloth had refused to even record the multiple criminal offences committed by the Heads and Hopertys when they erected the fence on our land without our knowledge or permission and while we were on holiday. There is no common sense in allowing a family who are clearly delusional, violent and repeatedly offending, to get away with clear criminal conduct. There was nothing vindictive about our allegations. They were legitimate allegations that were fully witnessed and evidenced. What Sloth was basically saying was that if you make any allegations against the Heads, then the Heads will make counter allegations against you and I can't be bothered to deal with that.

We felt deeply offended by this. Considering what this family had endured over just the past three months, the assaults, the threats, the erecting of the fence, the screws through the fence to name but a few. Despite all of this, we had not retaliated in any way towards the Heads, despite the immense provocation. We had done the right thing every single time and placed our trust in NP to help our family. For Sloth to even suggest we are simply being vindictive, is an insult to this family and the way in which we have conducted ourselves.

He also stated, *'It would be extremely time consuming to take action regarding the offences.'*

Well, there you have it in a nutshell. Clearly this comment confirmed that PC Sloth couldn't be bothered to do his job as it would be too time-consuming. If Sloth finds it too time-consuming to uphold the law, then why have laws, and why is he a police officer? The fact is, Sloth was a lazy slob of a man who would do as little as he possibly could and was a disgrace to the uniform. Also, Sloth clearly accepted that the Heads conduct did amount to offences. Shot yourself in the foot there, Slothy boy, tell me, did it bleed gravy?

So, just to confirm. If you want to break the law, just go ahead, nothing is likely to happen to you because the police find it too time-consuming to take any action against you. Brilliant.

Sloth also stated, *'As you are aware when there have been clear criminal allegations they have been investigated.'*

Bollocks. The assault on my wife, the threat to attack our daughter, the removal of our fence, the hacking down of our hedge, the erecting of the fence on our land, the screws through the fence, the false allegations to NP. Except for the assault on my wife, all these offences were reported to NP in the time Sloth was our Dedicated Police Officer, and all NOT INVESTIGATED.

Next is what I find to be the most ridiculous of statements contained in this email,

'I had discussed with Mr Head your issues about the siting of the fence, your offer to let it remain fixed to the old gate post if he lowered the panels out the front and also the issues of the screws, and the small piece of fencing that had been removed and you wished returning.

He instantly agreed to put shorter screws, return some fencing pieces and was considering the fence siting.' How ridiculous is that!

Firstly, what would be the point of placing shorter screws through the fence, the danger would still be there, there would still be the sharp points of the screws protruding through the fence into our garden on a fence that was already well on our side of the boundary. PC Sloth should have told the Heads to remove the screws completely, no ifs, no buts, remove them. Not to please us, but to remove the danger that these screws posed to anyone who may have come into contact with them.

The fact that PC Sloth did not tell the Heads to remove the screws was because he clearly did not want the harassment of our family to stop. As for Mr Head to be considering our offer of a compromise, firstly, this was not an offer for his consideration, he either lowered the fence panels between the two front gardens or removed the fence from our land altogether, or I would remove the panels myself.

Secondly, for Sloth to state that the Heads were considering the siting of the fence, they clearly admitted and accepted to Sloth the fence was on our land. So, why would PC Sloth not tell them at the very least, to agree to the compromise we had offered or remove the fence from our land altogether and if they do not agree to do any of these things, Mr Bean can and will remove the fence himself and he is perfectly within his rights to do so. The reason he did neither is because he wanted me to remove the fence so he could blame our family for the harassment and wash his hands of us as the next comment confirms.

PC Sloth finished the email by saying, *'It would appear however that you haven't awaited my response and have taken your own actions – as this may be subject to counter allegations it would not be right to comment further.'*

We never heard from PC Sloth again. His job was done. He had backed us into a corner where we had no choice but to take steps to protect ourselves and our property and then he abandoned us and his role in screwing our family over was done. C U Next Tuesday.

By the time I removed the fence, it had been in place for 6 weeks. In that time, we had done the right thing, we had done all we could to resolve the problem even to the point of offering the Heads a compromise where they could keep the fence on our land. That was something we did not have to do, we were perfectly entitled to remove the fence without the permission of anyone, including the Heads or NP, and without offering the Heads a compromise. The Heads had been *'considering'* the offer of the compromise for over a week. I emailed PC Sloth for an update on the compromise two days before I removed the fence, I did not get a reply. Time was up, the fence had to go, not out of spite, vindictiveness or vengeance, but out of desperation to protect the welfare of our daughter and to remove the danger that the screws through the fence posed.

As soon as I did something that PC Sloth could use against our family, and despite all of what the Heads had done to our family in the time PC Sloth had been our Dedicated Police Officer and which he refused to do anything about. Within a few hours of removing the fence panels, I received his email which left us at the mercy of the Heads yet again.

It was clear PC Sloth was never going to help our family. This was not the first time that NP had not only failed to help our family and protect us from the merciless harassment and criminality by our next-door neighbours. The conduct of PC Sloth while he was our Dedicated Police Officer, not only protected the offenders but also encouraged and facilitated the continued harassment of our family. Also, by deliberately failing to do his job, he was complicit to and actively joined in with that harassment. This left our family feeling totally alone, abandoned, isolated and desperate.

Chapter Four
They're Out to Get Me

Lies

That was it. I had fallen hook, line and sinker for the trap set by NP. Even though what I had done was perfectly within my rights and I was 100% sure of that. As far as NP were concerned, whether it was right or wrong, legal or illegal, did not come into the equation. Our family had finally done something that NP could manipulate to say we were as much at fault for the harassment as the Heads. And boy, did NP do that.

No word of a lie, I am sitting here shaking out of anger and dread because I know what happened to me and what I have to write in the next few pages.

The same day as I removed the fence, Mrs Head and her son Little Head, posted false and malicious comments on the Facebook page of Mrs Head regarding the removal of the fence.

These comments included, *'Our neighbour has KICKED the fence down.'*

And,

'The fence was well on our land.'

Little Head posted,

'I will upload a video of our neighbour pulling and kicking the fence. I feel like sending a link to the whole neighbourhood.'

To be clear. I did not kick the fence down. In fact, I did not kick the fence at all. And the fence was not on their land. Both Mrs Head and Little Head knew these comments were untrue and incited others to respond to these posts.

The way the fence had been erected, it was impossible to remove it without causing a small amount of damage to one of the panels, and I have never denied causing this damage. Under the law, it is not unlawful to cause damage when removing trespassing property from your land as long as you are not reckless when doing so. I am a qualified carpenter and joiner, so I know how to take a fence down. I properly used the appropriate tools to cause as little damage as possible. I was also aware before removing the fence that the area in question was covered by one of the Heads CCTV cameras. So, I knew I had to remove the fence in the best way possible or it would allow the Heads to make allegations against me. I need not have bothered as that was what the Heads did anyway.

The Heads alleged CCTV footage of this incident would prove to be a massive part of what was to follow and play a huge part in the next decade and counting, of my life.

In any event, as the fence had been erected on our land without our knowledge or permission and while we were on holiday, so we could not object at the time it was erected, and the refusal of our request to the Heads to remove the fence from our land, and their failure to agree to the compromise we had offered. My understanding of the Laws of Acceptance is that I could have removed the fence with a bulldozer and it would not be considered an offence.

That evening and the following day, friends and relatives of the Heads posted many replies to these posts which were threatening and abusive, such as calling our family Wankers, Bastards and Scumbags. These comments also included more threatening posts such as,

'I would KILL them.'

And

'I would put up an electric fence and electrocute the bastards.'

Considering the history of assaults and threats made by the Heads against our family, we had no reason to believe these were idle threats. And as they were from friends and relatives of the Heads, there was a high possibility that our paths would cross with these people. We found this to be very distressing.

Damaged

The next day, Friday, I took some more images of the fence panels as the previous events with the Heads made me realise that I needed to make sure I had the evidence to counter the false allegations I knew the Heads would make to NP against me. About 10.00 pm that night, I was in bed, my wife and daughter were downstairs in our front room watching the telly. We could all hear talking and rustling noises coming from the front garden area.

A little later, our daughter came upstairs and asked me if I heard the noise from outside. She looked out of the bedroom window and said to me that the fence panels had been moved slightly. I didn't get out of bed to look as I was feeling very low. In hindsight, I wish I had looked out of the window at the time we heard the noise. It would not have saved me from the nightmare that was to follow but at least I would have known exactly what happened.

The next morning, Saturday, my wife went into the front garden and noticed that not only had the fence panels been moved but a lot more damage had been caused to the panel than when I had removed it from the posts on the Thursday afternoon. Clearly, this was happening when we heard the noise the previous night. My wife came indoors and told me of this, so we took more images of this further damage.

To be clear. I did not cause this additional damage. As stated, the Heads have a CCTV camera covering the area where I had placed the panels after I had removed them. If I had caused this additional damage the day after I had removed the fence, then the Heads would have recorded me doing so.

Some years later, I made a Subject Access Request to NP for all the information they held about me on their local police system. I will go into this in more detail later. But, coincidently, I'm sure, the police logs of NP confirmed that when we had heard the noise coming from the front gardens on the night after I had removed the fence, an officer from NP was attending the Heads address. Now, I am not suggesting for a second that this officer, who I will call PS Giles, was in any way responsible or involved in further damaging the fence panel at the same time he was visiting the Heads, not for a second. I mean, an officer of the law would not be involved in fabricating evidence so the Heads could make a false allegation of Criminal Damage against me. Would they?

The fact is, the amount of damage that I caused to one of the fence panels was so minor, that it could not be considered criminal damage as the panel was easily repairable. That is one of the fundamentals of causing criminal damage in that the item removed or damaged must be damaged beyond easy repair. I could and would have been able to repair this panel within a few minutes. Although I would have repaired the panel if asked or requested, the fact is, I didn't need to as the panel was on our land when I removed it.

For NP to record, action and investigate an allegation of criminal damage made against me for removing the fence, the allegation would have to be credible. In other words, the damage to the panel would have needed to have been damaged far beyond the minor damage I had caused. And that was exactly what happened on that Friday night. I cannot say for sure who caused this damage whilst an officer from NP was visiting the Heads, because I did not see it happening. But what I can say for sure is that further damage was caused to the panel on the Friday night and it was not caused by me.

The next evening, Sunday, I returned home from the usual Sunday tea at the outlaws, sorry, in-laws! A calling card had been posted through our door from PS Giles, quite by coincidence again, I am sure. It was the same officer from NP who was at the Heads on the Friday night when further damage had been caused to the fence panel. Well, would you believe it, two coincidences in three days? Firstly, PS Giles was at the Head's address when further damage had been caused to the fence panel. And secondly, it was PS Giles who had visited my address on the Sunday afternoon, funny that! Was there something going on here, nah, just a coincidence!

The card asked me to give PS Giles a call. So, I called him straight away and guess what, he informed me that an allegation of Criminal Damage had been made against me by the Heads concerning the removal of their fence and I would need to provide NP with a voluntary interview under caution.

Excuse me, although I wasn't aware of it at the time. If the suspect had not been arrested for the offence in question, then the police need to investigate to establish the facts of the case (a credible allegation) before asking a suspect to provide a voluntary interview under caution. If that was not the case, the police would not be able to cope with the workload of interviewing under caution every single person who had an allegation made against them. So why was it different for me?

Why at this stage would PS Giles inform me I would be required to provide a voluntary interview under caution when there had been no investigation? In fact, no one from NP had even spoken to me regarding the removal of the fence. That was all they needed to do, just a simple conversation with PS Giles would have resolved the issue and it would not and should not have progressed to the unbelievable stage that it did. Within a few minutes, I would have been able to tell and show PS Giles that the Heads had erected the fence on our land without our knowledge and permission while we were on holiday, I had asked the Heads to remove the fence, but they had refused. I had asked PC Sloth to tell the Heads to remove it but he refused. And I had offered the Heads a compromise, but they failed to respond. I could also have told him of the further damage that had been caused to the panel on the Friday night at the same time he was at the Heads address. That would have been interesting, wouldn't it?

But that was not their plan, they didn't want to allow me to explain the situation, because if they did, they would not have been able to progress the allegation. No, PS Giles had decided that without even speaking to me, I would be required to provide an interview under caution. It was crystal clear, just like PC Sloth, PS Giles was not and never had any intention of treating me with equality and impartiality regarding this false allegation. This is what the Heads and NP had been planning for weeks. If you do not believe that now, by the time you have finished reading, I am sure you will be in no doubt. Make no mistake, I was set up to remove the fence panels and I was then screwed over for doing so. C U Next Tuesdays.

Just to explain. For anyone who hasn't experienced it. When you are asked by the police to provide a voluntary interview under caution, if you refuse, you face being arrested. So, for most people, being asked to provide the police with a voluntary interview under caution is a big deal and not voluntary at all, as there are serious consequences for refusing. You either provide the police with a voluntary interview under caution or face arrest, that is the actual term the police use, or they did against our family, multiple times. So, for most people, I'm sure, being arrested is an even bigger deal than providing a voluntary interview under caution. So, for most people, refusing is not an option.

Particularly for someone who has not been interviewed by the police, and has never been arrested and in fact, never been in trouble before. I never thought I would need to provide the police with an interview under caution or face arrest. Just to be asked was worrying, even though I knew I was innocent. But the experience of being interviewed by the police as a suspect for an offence, in a tiny little room with no windows and two police officers facing you on the other side of the desk is very intimidating. On top of that, of course, our family were the victims of the Heads Harassment, and this false allegation was part of that harassment. Because of that harassment, we were weak and vulnerable, and NP preyed on that vulnerability. C U Next Tuesdays.

Over the next few days, the Heads placed further screws through the fence panels between the two side walls of the houses. And why wouldn't they? They must have been laughing their socks off at us, I bet even they could not believe what was happening. In the past six weeks, they had erected a seven feet high fence on our land, removed and destroyed our fencing, hacked down our hedge, placed numerous grossly oversized screws through the fence, posted malicious communications via social media and made a false allegation of criminal damage to NP with absolutely no consequences whatsoever. And now I am being required to provide NP with a voluntary interview under caution or face arrest. You couldn't write it. Oh, I am!

I had not heard from NP for a week or so since the conversation with PS Giles regarding the voluntary interview. To be honest, I was finding the whole situation very difficult and stressful, which I am sure was the plan and I am sure you can understand. So, I contacted PS Giles for an update. Although the prospect of the interview was daunting, I wanted it to be done and dusted. I was sure I would be able to not only provide NP with the evidence that I had not committed the offence but also that the allegation was false, and the Heads knew the allegation was false. What I didn't know at that time was that NP also knew the allegation was false. So, I called PS Giles.

It was obvious from the very start of the conversation that he was not happy. It was a poor connection and after a couple of minutes, we were cut off, Giles called back and the first thing he said was, *"YOU ARE OBVIOUSLY DRIVING."*

What a twat, I was actually sitting in my front room. Obviously, this officer had already formed the opinion that I was a bad person. He must have assumed that because the Heads had told him so. If only we could all just tell the police that whoever we don't like is a bad person. But that is not the case for most of us, you must be one of the incrowd, a retired member of the emergency services perhaps.

Unfortunately, things did not improve as the call went on. I tried to explain the impact all this was having on our family and that I had the right to remove the fence as it was on our land and the reason I did so was to protect the mental well-being of our daughter due to the impact of the assaults on both her parents and the threat to attack her by the Heads. Giles replied, *"Your daughter's 'mental health issues' do not give you the right to take your neighbour's fence down and you should be pleased that your neighbours have put a new fence up as it makes your property more secure."*

What a twat, again. Firstly, I find it deeply disrespectful to describe our daughter as having *'mental health issues'*. To me, the word *'issues'* implies that the mental health condition that someone is suffering from is bad or wrong and they are a danger to themselves or others. I, of course, accept and fully understand that certain mental health conditions do cause some people to be a danger, there can be no doubt about that. Almost every day you can turn on the news and hear of a tragic event involving someone with a mental health condition such as paranoia or schizophrenia. I agree that those people could be described and considered to have a *'mental health issue'* because it can negatively impact them and others in their daily lives. My point is that when one of these events happens and is reported on the news, the newsreader will almost always say, *'The police describe the offender as having 'mental health issues.'*

Meaning those mental health issues are the reason for the behaviour of the offender. Not all people's mental health conditions cause them to be bad people or to do horrible things and they should not all be tarred with the same brush. Our daughter has a 'mental health condition' not a *'mental health issue'*. Sorry if that is a bit woke.

Secondly, regardless of our daughter's *'mental health issues'*, as PC Giles put it, I had the legal right to remove the fence. I did not need the Heads or anyone else's permission to do so. In any event, the deterioration in our daughter's mental health was caused by the Heads criminality. So, even in the warped world of PS Giles, I did have the right to remove the fence from our land! Twat.

That is another reason why NP should have investigated before telling me I needed to provide an interview under caution. If NP had established the facts at this early stage, it would have easily determined that I was within my rights to remove the fence from our land regardless of the impact it was having on our daughter, and that would have been the end of the matter.

Thirdly, the new fence had not made our property more secure, it was the exact opposite. The two sections of our fencing that the Heads had removed were sealing off our rear garden from the front. Now these sections of fencing had been removed, anyone who wanted to gain access to our rear garden could now do so by squeezing down the side wall of our house and the fence the Heads had erected between the two side walls virtually unhindered. Well, I say unhindered, anyone who attempted to do so may have ripped themselves to shreds on the screws the Heads had placed through the fence. But it's the Head's, so a little bit of crime didn't matter.

The attitude of this officer was typical of the attitude we had already become familiar with in the short time of our involvement with NP. Was there not a 'good cop' amongst them? He was only interested in progressing the allegation no matter what. He was totally biased towards the Heads allegation and didn't even want to hear my side of the matter, let alone consider it. He finished the conversation by telling me another PC would be contacting me to arrange the taped interview. Clearly, nothing I had said to him during this conversation had made the slightest bit of difference to his attitude and his prejudged opinion of me and my family. But, of course, that was their plan, I just hadn't clicked at that time.

NP had backed me into a corner until I was forced to do something to protect our family and our property and then they came down on me like a ton of bricks. Telling the officer that the fence was on our land and the reasons for removing it were never going to make the slightest bit of difference to him or anyone else at NP. They were not going to change course at this stage, not when they thought their job was nearly done. Unfortunately for NP, they did not count on the strength and resolve of this family to fight injustice and misconduct.

There's a storm coming that the weatherman couldn't predict.

Stitch Up

Due to the continued harassment and the failure and discrimination by NP, my wife emailed the Chief Constable of NP expressing the distress the situation was causing our family. We did not receive a reply from the Chief Constable. However, we did receive a reply from his Staff Officer, whatever position that is, confirming my wife's email had been received and read by the Chief Constable. We later received another email from the Staff Officer informing us the Chief Constable had asked another officer to review the problems we had been experiencing. Great, the Chief Constable had asked another officer of NP to look into the conduct of other officers of NP. That will sort it!

Just a couple of days later, we received a visit from another two officers from NP. They were not the typical police double act of *'good cop, bad cop'*. But they were a double act nonetheless, but this time they were both arseholes. But like great double acts,

Morecambe and Wise, Laurel and Hardy, the two Ronnies and, of course, the Chuckle. Brothers, to me to me, to you to you, classic comedy! They did bounce off each other well.

Unlike those double acts though, there was nothing funny about this gruesome twosome. They were the epitome of everything bad about the police. They are the reason why there are so many people out there like me, good, honest, law-abiding citizens who have absolutely zero trust or faith in the police. One of them for sure had a mental health condition known as Narcissistic Personality Disorder (NPD). The pleasure he got from abusing his position as a police officer to inflict as much pain and suffering on our family as he possibly could was clear for us, and others, to see. He didn't just do it once, but when his first attempt failed in convicting me of an offence, he knew I did not commit, he came back for another go but this time targeting our daughter. C U Next Tuesday.

This officer was in his twenties, I would say. He was the worst of all the officers of NP that we encountered; no, that is wrong, he was the worst human being I have ever encountered; no, no one can be worse than Mrs Head, but he did push her a close second. What he would go on to do to me and my family was despicable and I will never forgive or forget that. I will never stop pursuing him until he is held accountable for what he did. He may be Billy Big Bollocks when he is in uniform but that will not protect him in the end. Justice will be done and you will pay for your crimes. I will get you. Legally, of course.

The other officer was much older, in his sixties I would think. I wondered then why he was still a serving officer at that age. Most retire in their forties or fifties due to the demands of the job and the fact that they have accrued a huge pension that they no longer need to work. I also wondered why he was still a PC at that age. If you are still in the force at that age you are normally much higher up the ranks than a PC, or not in a frontline role. Had he done something wrong to have been demoted from a more senior rank or had he done something wrong to prevent him from being promoted to a senior rank, who knows?

Like all good double acts, they need a catchy name so I will call them PC's Pinky and Perky. No pun intended. I am not trying to relate police officers to pigs, that would just be downright insulting!

These two officers, in particular PC Pinky, would change the person that I had been for fifty years, and in so many ways. Pinky, in particular, put me through an ordeal that was the worst experience of my life and it was all unnecessary and wrong and he knew that. What these officers did to me made me feel for only the second time in my life, but also the second time in three months, that I might die. I knew that if Mr Head had got hold of me on the night of the assault, he would have killed me, or I would have had to kill him to stop him. This time, the stress these officers put me under was more than I had ever felt before, more than I ever thought I could cope with. Sounds extreme, but anyone who has experienced something similar to what you will read in the following pages will understand where I am coming from.

Pinky and Perky told me that they had been tasked with two assignments. Firstly, to discuss the ongoing problems with the Heads. Secondly, they had been placed in charge of dealing with the allegation of Criminal Damage made by the Heads against me for removing the fence.

They explained that as they were dealing with both issues, they would not be able to discuss anything to do with the allegation of Criminal Damage. Although we didn't object to this at the time because we had no experience of this sort of thing. In hindsight, we should have objected. At best, it is poor practice for these officers to be tasked with both issues as it created a conflict of interests. If Pinky and Perky could find I had committed an offence of Criminal Damage for removing the fence, they could also find that our family was as responsible as the Heads for the Harassment. Winner, winner, chicken dinner, so to speak.

I now know that it is or should be standard practice for the police to avoid any situation that could be perceived to create a conflict of interest as this may lead the public to believe that not all parties are being treated with equality. So, in almost their very first sentence, these two officers had failed to comply with the College of Policing Code of Ethics and correct investigative procedure.

Pinky and Perky said they could not discuss anything about the allegation of criminal damage until after I had been interviewed. They also said they cannot discuss the ongoing issues with the Heads until the allegation of criminal damage has been resolved. So, what was the point of their visit if they couldn't discuss anything about the two issues they had been tasked with? I suppose it was to request I attend our local police station the following day to provide my voluntary interview under caution. I do not think it needed two officers to come to our house to tell me that!

In any event, the above paragraph confirms the conflict of interest for these two officers in being tasked with both matters.

Anyway, as ignorance is bliss, I did not think this to be out of order as I thought the issues with the fence would be resolved as soon as I had provided my interview. However, that would prove not to be the case. The issues with the fence were dragged out for so long that Pinky and Perky never did deal with the ongoing issues with the Heads. In fact, they never had any intention of dealing with these issues from the very start of their involvement.

I would say that my ignorance was a big mistake on my part but. of course, I was not aware of what was to follow. Yet again, I wish I knew then what I know now. But that is what the police rely on, they know most ordinary citizens have not got a clue about correct police procedure, why would they? So, the police prey on the lack of knowledge and vulnerability of ordinary people to be able to follow their agenda regardless of the law and people's rights as citizens of this country.

Just before they left, the last thing that Pinky said to us was that we should not speak to any of our friends, relatives or neighbours about the harassment. Again, we just thought that is how it is meant to be. Of course, that was not the case. The reason was that Pinky and Perky already knew of their hidden agenda to incriminate me for removing the fence and therefore, blame our family for the harassment. If I knew then what I know now!

The following day, I attended the local police station for my voluntary interview with Pinky and Perky. I had a duty solicitor to represent me. Before I was called in for the interview, Pinky and Perky asked to speak to my solicitor alone and took her to another room. When she came back, she told me, *"You don't have anything to worry about, the CCTV footage does not show you causing any damage to the fence."*

To be honest, although I was very nervous as it was a daunting prospect and something I had not experienced before, I was not worried. I knew I had done nothing wrong and had nothing to worry about. I had a good idea something like this would happen even before I removed the fence, so I thought it was just a means to an end and my opportunity to put the record straight regarding the removal of the fence and the harassment by the Heads against our family. Of course, the interview is recorded so there would be a record of what was said.

I was taken into a pokey little room with no windows right at the back of the station. I do not know if this was a deliberate attempt to intimidate me, if it was, it worked. It felt like I was a criminal from the off. Before I sat down, the duty solicitor asked PC Pinky about the CCTV footage and the fact that it did not show me causing any damage to the fence. PC Pinky replied, *"There is another version of CCTV available but it is not in my possession at present."* Lie.

I was then placed under caution. Although Pinky and Perky made it clear I was not being arrested, it added to the feeling that I was a criminal. I am aware this is standard practice at the start of a voluntary interview under caution, there is a clue in the name. But I think it is only natural for most people to feel intimidated under the circumstances.

Pinky informed me of the allegation that I caused Criminal Damage to the Heads fence by kicking the panel loose from the post before placing the panel at the top of the Heads Garden. I was then shown the CCTV footage submitted by Mr Head to support his allegation and statement of Criminal

Damage against me. This was labelled Police Exhibit **PFC1**. It may be beneficial for you to remember the title of this footage moving forward as it may get a little confusing, Police Exhibit **PFC1**. The footage started after I had removed the first panel, which is the panel that it is alleged I caused criminal damage to by kicking it loose from the post. As I was informed by the duty solicitor, the footage did not show me causing any damage to the fence or acting in a criminal way whatsoever.

After about ten minutes of the interview, the duty solicitor questioned Pinky and Perky regarding their insistence that I had kicked the panel which caused the damage. The duty solicitor challenged Pinky and Perky by saying to them, *"The CCTV footage shows the gap between the retaining wall and the fence is only about six inches so it would not be possible for my client to have kicked the fence."*

Referring to the CCTV footage in question, PFC1, Pinky replies, *"There is another version available and it will be reviewed, it will have to."* Lie.

If there was another version of CCTV footage available before I was interviewed, why was I not shown this footage? If Pinky and Perky knew there was another version of CCTV available but did not have this footage in time for my interview, why did they not postpone the interview until they had the footage? The truth is, there was no other version of CCTV available at that time. And there would never be a version of CCTV showing me kicking the fence panel loose from the post because I did not kick the fence. End of.

To be clear. The allegation was that I caused Criminal Damage to the fence by kicking the panel loose from the post. As pointed out by myself and the duty solicitor at my interview, it would have been impossible for me to have kicked the fence at the place where the panel was damaged due to the position of the retaining wall as the gap between the retaining wall and the fence was too small for me to have even placed my foot there, let alone swing my foot with enough force to break a fence panel.

This is the same retaining wall that Trigger, under instruction from the Heads, erected in our front garden in February 2013. So, there can be no doubt that the Heads knew I could not and did not kick the fence causing the damage as they also knew it would be impossible for me to have done so due to the position of the retaining wall that they had instructed Trigger to erect on our land. The allegation by Mr Head was false, the statement by Mr Head was false and the evidence did not show what Mr Head claimed it did in his statement. The Heads and Pinky and Perky knew that from the start. C U Next Tuesdays.

How could Pinky and Perky continue the interview on the pretence that I had caused Criminal Damage to the fence by kicking it loose from the post when both my solicitor and I had pointed out that it would have been impossible to have done so and the CCTV footage did not show me causing any damage to the fence whatsoever. In fact, the CCTV footage started after the alleged damage had been caused. The whole interview was another stitch-up. It did not matter what I said, what evidence I was able to provide and the fact there was no evidence to support the allegation. The result of the interview had been decided before I even set foot in that room. And that decision was that I had caused Criminal Damage to the fence by kicking the panel loose from the post. C U Next Tuesdays.

However, the interview did continue and lasted for over an hour, which was incredible considering NP had no evidence to support the allegation. I was asked the same questions over and over and it felt more like I was being interrogated rather than interviewed. However, I was able to answer all their questions, just not in the way they wanted, so they had to keep asking me the same question in a slightly different way hoping I would slip up. But I didn't slip up because I was telling the truth. Being honest is easy.

I accepted that I did cause some minor damage to one of the panels, I have never denied this. But that the damage was unavoidable due to how the fence had been erected and I emphatically denied the allegation of Criminal Damage. As a gesture of goodwill, I even offered to pay for the damaged panel even though I had no obligation to do so, and it was still perfectly reusable after I had removed it.

During this interview, I was able to provide evidence such as the position of the retaining wall and the photos of the fence panels after I had removed them and after further damage had been caused to the panel on the Friday night. Therefore, it is Mr Head who should have been interviewed under caution for making a false allegation and providing a false statement. But none of my points were ever investigated or even listed in the written record of the interview. Well, it's the Heads, so a little bit of crime like making a false allegation and providing a false statement didn't matter. For me and you, it would be considered Perjury and Perverting the Course of Justice, but not for the Heads, not by NP at least!

Of course, Pinky and Perky could not do both. They could not continue with the *'due legal process'* against me and investigate my allegations against Mr Head at the same time, that would create a conflict of interests I believe, and that would never do. There was only one agenda that NP wanted to follow and that was to incriminate me at all costs.

Well, it just might cost you more than you think.

Also, at this interview, I informed Pinky and Perky about the false and malicious Facebook posts by Mrs Head and Little Head, and the abusive and threatening replies from their friends and relatives. I even provided them with a printed copy of the entire chain. Within ten minutes of returning home from my interview, Pinky and Perky visited the Heads house. By the time they left, the Facebook comments by Mrs Head, Little Head and the replies from their friends and relatives had been deleted and Mrs Head had blocked my wife and daughter from her Facebook page.

You may ask why we were looking at the Facebook Page of Mrs Head. Simple, we were not.

We were informed of these posts by a neighbour who was friends with Mrs Head on Facebook. In any event, we have a right and a need-to-know what people are saying about us, particularly when these comments pose a threat to our safety. As mentioned, we lived next door to the Heads at this time so there was a high chance we would encounter their friends and relatives who threatened harm to our family. And given the Heads propensity for assaults and violent and aggressive behaviour, there was no reason to believe that their friends and relatives would be any different. Trust me, we had to be always on our guard when we left the house.

To be clear, I feel very strongly about this. I made an allegation of Malicious Communications via Social Media against the Heads at this interview. I also provided Pinky and Perky with irrefutable evidence of this offence. Not only did Pinky and Perky fail to record, action or investigate this allegation, they instead visited the Heads straight after my interview and disclosed my evidence to the offenders. Do you need any more proof of the disgraceful misconduct of these two officers? Well, need it or not you're going to get it.

Pinky and Perky not only failed to record, action or investigate my allegation against the Heads, they also failed to investigate any of the points I raised in my defence of the allegation of Criminal Damage during my interview. Any police officer must carry out any investigation with impartiality and equality and investigate all lines of enquiry whether they lead to or from the suspect.

I know for a fact, that if Pinky and Perky had conducted a fair and impartial investigation into both the Heads allegation against me and my allegations against the Heads, what was to follow would and should have been avoided.

A few days after my interview, unbeknown to me, my wife contacted PC Perky to tell him of the impact this was having on my health. She shouldn't have bothered, PC Perky couldn't give a shit. In fact, I bet it pleased him to hear that I was struggling so much. And trust me, I was really struggling. As I have said, I understand that it may be difficult for some if not most of the people who read this book to comprehend the impact harassment has on its victims. But then to put the conduct of NP on top of that, it was hard, very hard, almost too hard. But we are only getting started.

Later that week, our son received a call from PC Pinky. He informed our son that an allegation of Criminal Damage had been made against him by Mr Head about the removal of the fence and that he would need to provide a voluntary interview under caution or face arrest. What a C U Next Tuesday.

It wasn't enough for Pinky and Perky to fuck me over, they were now coming for my son. Our son was only 18 years old and like the rest of our family, he had never been in trouble with the police before.

So, like me, our son had little choice but to attend the police station to give his taped interview to PC's Pinky and Perky or be arrested. The same Duty Solicitor as I had was present at my son's interview. This is where it might get a little confusing regarding the CCTV footage. At this interview, our son was allegedly shown a different version of CCTV footage. This version of CCTV was labelled as Police Exhibit **APC1** and not the version of CCTV I was shown at my interview which was labelled Police Exhibit **PFC1**. **APC1** was supposedly submitted by Mrs Head to PC Pinky a few days after my interview.

This also proves that for PC Pinky to tell the Duty Solicitor at my interview, *"There is another version of CCTV available but it is not in my possession at present"* and *"There is another version available and it will be reviewed, it will have to."*

To be untrue, Pinky would later confirm that he visited the Heads following my interview to request a further version of CCTV be produced and did not receive this CCTV until several days after I was interviewed, which he confirmed was **APC1**. So, to be clear, the CCTV footage labelled as Police Exhibit **APC1** was not available at the time of my interview. Clearly, PC Pinky lied to the Duty Solicitor at my interview. That is a clear act of Gross Misconduct, Perjury and Perverting the Course of Justice.

According to Pinky and Perky, this version of the footage, APC1, shows me causing Criminal Damage to the fence. In other words, according to the charge that I caused Criminal Damage to the panel by kicking it loose from the post, the footage would, of course, need to show me kicking the panel loose from the post. I knew it could not possibly have shown that and my son knew it could not possibly have shown that as he was with me the whole time when I was removing the fence. In any event, the position of the retaining wall would prevent the fence panel from being kicked. So, even though the footage shown to my son did not show me kicking the fence, Pinky and Perky claimed that it did by repeatedly asking my son, *"Is this where your dad is kicking the fence?"*

Even though our son had answered the question truthfully and, on several occasions,

"No, my dad did not kick the fence."

They kept asking him until the Duty Solicitor eventually had to intervene and tell Pinky and Perky that our son had answered that question several times and not to ask him it again.

Furthermore, our son did not help me remove the panels from the posts, he only helped me carry the panels to the top of the Heads Garden after I had removed them from the posts to help prevent any unnecessary damage being caused to the panels. To be clear, the only involvement our son had was to assist in preventing damage being caused to the fence panels – not to assist in causing damage to the fence panels. There cannot be any evidence to suggest our son caused damage to the fence and the decision to call my son in for an interview or face arrest was unnecessary, wrong and malicious.

The only reason our son was called in for an interview was to try to trip him up into incriminating me and according to the police logs that were later disclosed to me as part of my Subject Access Request (SAR), there was never an allegation of Criminal Damage made against my son by Mr Head. This was another fabrication on the part of Pinky and Perky to allow them to request our son provide an interview under caution or face arrest. Double C U Next Tuesdays.

To be perfectly clear, at my interview, I was shown the CCTV footage which was submitted by Mr Head to NP as evidence *'prior'* to my interview, to support his allegation and statement of Criminal Damage made against me for removing the fence panels. and did not show any damage being caused to the fence. This version of the CCTV was labelled as Police Exhibit **PFC1.**

At my son's interview, he was allegedly shown a different version of CCTV footage that had been submitted by Mrs Head to PC Pinky *'after'* I had been interviewed which the Heads, Pinky and Perky claim shows me kicking the fence panel until it comes loose from the post. This was labelled as Police Exhibit **APC1.**

So, there were allegedly two different versions of CCTV, **PFC1** and **APC1**. Although both my son and I have been interviewed under caution by Pinky and Perky, neither me nor my son were shown both versions.

When our son returned home from the interview, he was visibly distressed. He was trying to play the big man as if the experience hadn't bothered him, but it had a dramatic impact on him. He wasn't fooling anyone; he was no Robert De Niro. He told us that he was taken to the interview room and by the description he gave, it was the same room as I was interviewed in, right at the back of the station. He had to walk past all the people who were appearing in court as it was the day the Magistrates Court sat. He also told us that when he sat in the chair in the interview room, PC Pinky told him that a murderer had sat in that very chair. What an arsehole!

I will tell you something for nothing Pinky and Perky. I am like most men, husbands and fathers. I am fair game, if you want to have a go at me, that's fine, I can fight my own battles. I would rather not, but I will fight if I must. But you mess with my wife and children, you cross the line. If you want to know why I will never stop chasing you, this is why, you crossed the line. You can think what you want of me, but I am not stupid. I know that you think the best way to get to me is through my family, and you are right, but at the end of the day, it will be at your cost, not mine.

Sweet and Sour

It was the middle of October when I received a call from PC Pinky. First of all, he told me that there would be No Further Action taken against our son, which was a huge relief, of course, even though we all knew he had done nothing wrong. However, are you ready for this, I suggest you sit down.

PC Pinky then informed me I would be offered a Conditional Caution for causing Criminal Damage to the fence and the condition was that I would have to pay the Heads the sum of £205 for the cost of replacing the damaged fence panel and for the cost to have the fence re-erected back to the fence posts!!!! The fence posts that were on our land!!!!

I was absolutely devastated. I just could not believe what I was hearing. Never in my wildest dreams, did I ever expect to receive any sort of sanction for removing the fence panels, let alone a Conditional Caution where I would have to pay the Heads to effectively re-erect the fence back onto our land. I repeated my offer to Pinky to pay for the damaged panel and pleaded with him not to allow the Heads to re-erect the fence back on our land due to the impact it would have on our daughter who was already struggling to cope with day-to-day life. Pinky refused my requests point blank and hung up. Triple C U Next Tuesday.

As mentioned earlier in this book. For the police to offer a suspect a Caution, the suspect must admit guilt for the offence. At no stage did I ever admit I caused Criminal Damage to the fence. So, PC Pinky and NP should not have offered me a Conditional Caution at all. I was not aware of this at that time and as sure as hell, Pinky and Perky were not going to tell me. I wish I knew then what I know now.

I cannot emphasise enough the impact this had on my health. I, along with the rest of my family, were already struggling to cope with the non-stop harassment from the Heads. Bearing in mind what the Heads had done to our family over the past few months' and apart from the Conditional Caution offered to Mr Head for his assault on me, NP had done absolutely fuck all to protect our family from the Heads and their associates' relentless harassment and criminality.

To then be told by NP that I am being offered a Conditional Caution for removing three fence panels from my land, panels that we had exhausted every avenue to try to resolve to the point of offering the Heads a compromise where they could actually keep the fence on our land, that I would now have to pay the Heads £205 to erect the fence back on our land, was insulting, degrading, humiliating, wrong and unlawful. It made me feel physically sick.

If there ever was confirmation needed that the conduct of NP regarding this matter was a deliberate ploy by NP to incriminate me, then the above has got to be it. If you are still not convinced, then read on!

I received a quote for the cost of the replacement panel and the re-erecting of the fence, via an email from the Duty Solicitor who was present at both my and our son's interview, I thought it was very odd to receive the quote from her. The quote was from Trigger, the builder who in early 2013, erected the retaining wall in our front garden and in doing so destroyed my rose bush. I contacted Pinky to say that I thought it would be best for all concerned if Trigger did not do the work due to the history of him working for the Heads and carrying out work on our property. I also informed Pinky that the quote was wrong, it was for the erecting of four panels, and I had only removed three panels. Pinky's reply was, *"The quote is non-negotiable"*

So, if I accepted the Caution, not only would I have to pay for the re-erecting of the three panels back on our land, but I would also have to pay for the erecting of a fourth panel that didn't even exist. I do not think asking for a quote that is at least accurate was unreasonable. You wouldn't be expected to accept a quote from anyone else for work that did not need to be done, so why should I be expected to accept this one.

Furthermore, it is the responsibility of the police to maintain Public Order. Clearly, having Trigger to work for the Heads again and carrying out work on our property, would create the likelihood of a Public Order Offence being committed. I am sure Pinky and Perky would have loved that to happen so they could nail me to the floor again. However, there was a surprise coming that blew their little plan clean out of the water.

I received further contact from Pinky who informed me that his Inspector would like to meet with us to explore options that are *'proportionate and lawful'* concerning both parties involved with the case. Lawful, what the fuck would NP know about lawful!

Anyway, my wife and I attended this meeting the following week. We had taken a friend along with us for support as our trust in NP had started to wane, shall we say. The Inspector, who I will call Inspector Tool, was accompanied by the Deputy Head of the Force Justice Unit, a very grand title for a waste of space, whom I will not bother to name as her input at the meeting was largely insignificant. However, I do recall on entering the room the Deputy Head of the Force Justice Unit had her police officer's badge open and placed right at the front of the table in full view. It was clear to me this was done deliberately to make us feel intimidated by her and the situation. Pathetic.

We had been informed by Pinky before the meeting that he and Perky would be present. But for reasons unbeknown to me, they were not. Personally, I could not see how we could hold a constructive meeting regarding the issues with the Heads, without the investigating Officers (IOs) in attendance. However, we discussed the issues involving the Heads in depth. I told Inspector Tool that because of the conduct by NP towards our family, it felt like we were trying to fight the Heads with our hands tied behind our backs as NP would not do anything to help stop the harassment. And when we did do something perfectly legal to protect ourselves and our property, we were being punished by NP.

I then twigged why Pinky and Perky were not there, so we couldn't challenge them regarding their conduct and Tool could fulfil the intention of the meeting – to again apportion blame on our family. Tool stated that it would be beneficial to, *"Scope the use of Restorative Justice to try to mediate a solution."*

That being, if both parties agreed to Restorative Justice, then I would not receive my Caution for allegedly causing Criminal Damage to the fence (I would not receive a caution that I had not accepted at that stage anyway) and the Caution given to Mr Head for his assault on me, would be rescinded.

That brings me back to the word lawful. To my knowledge, I will stand corrected if I am wrong, but the police do not have the power to rescind a

Caution once it has been issued. I believe the reason is because of the admission of guilt by the offender. Clearly, if the police rescind a Caution after the offender has admitted guilt and accepted the Caution, it would not be fair on the victim and clearly lead to a lack of confidence in the police that they were taking crime seriously and protecting the public from criminality. Therefore, for NP to rescind the Conditional Caution already issued to Mr Head would be unlawful. Well, it's the Heads, so a little bit of crime didn't matter, even if it is an Inspector in the police force committing the offence!

During this meeting, Inspector Tool also referred to the Caution being offered to me for removing the fence as, *'TIT for TAT Justice, as Mr Head has been given a Caution for his Assault on you, you will be given a Caution for removing the fence.'*

Excuse me, but what the hell is *'Tit for Tat Justice'* and what basis has it in Law?

The police cannot issue you with a Caution just because the person who made an allegation against you already has a Caution because of an allegation you made against them. It is ludicrous, as well as a clear breach of British Law and the Police Officers Code of Ethics. Although that Code of Ethics is completely lost on most of the officers we have had the misfortune to meet. It is unbelievable that an Inspector with the police can have the audacity to even say that to someone, anyone, let alone the victim of the offence Mr Head had accepted the Caution for. Despite the fact whether it was legal or not, it was certainly not fair. Mr Head had admitted to assaulting me and accepted the Caution, I had not admitted causing Criminal Damage to the fence and had not accepted the Caution.

However, we agreed to take part in the Restorative Justice option as it seemed the only way to try to stop the harassment which at the end of the day was not just the main priority but the only priority. The harassment had to stop before there was a tragedy.

Before agreeing to enter the Restorative Justice process, we asked Tool to clarify two points. Firstly, if both parties agreed to take part in Restorative Justice, then I would not receive my caution and Mr Head would have his caution rescinded. Secondly, if the Heads did not agree to take part, then NP would investigate all the outstanding offences committed by the Heads and their associates against our family. I won't list them again as I am sure you are aware by now of what the main offences were.

If that was not going to be the case, then the Heads could refuse to take part in Restorative Justice and NP would wipe the slate clean so to speak and that was not acceptable.

I came away from this meeting thinking if this is the sort of policing NP endorse then no wonder they are consistently one of, if not the worst performing police force in the Country.

Once again, this is clear evidence that NP were determined to *'level up the score'* regarding Cautions and to apportion blame on both sides for the harassment. Guilt or innocence, legal or illegal did not come into their equation. This was why Pinky and Perky were so determined to issue a Caution to me. Not because I was guilty of an offence but to provide NP with a lever to use against our family in the Restorative Justice Process.

During the meeting, Inspector Tool took great pride in informing us he considered himself as an expert in mediation as he had worked for the British Government as a mediator during the Iraq war. Well, sorry to burst your bubble, Inspector Tool, but maybe you shouldn't be too proud of your achievements. You couldn't have been that good a mediator as the Iraq war was a complete fuck up and you are now working as a bent Inspector in a fucked-up police force. I mean, a bit of a come down, isn't it? Tool.

We later received an email from Inspector Tool to confirm what we had agreed at the meeting regarding NP investigating all the outstanding allegations against the Heads and their associates if the Heads failed to agree to the Restorative Justice option, the email stated,

'Numpty Police will assess allegations of criminal offences in line with the National Threshold Test if we are unable to implement restorative justice.'

At that time, the Heads still had to attend their meeting with Tool regarding the Restorative Justice option.

About a week later, we received another email from NP, informing us that the Heads had met with Inspector Tool and they had refused the Restorative Justice Option and they would not enter into any form of correspondence with our family whatsoever. And because of this refusal, I would be receiving my Conditional Caution from NP in due course.

This was another blow. Why would the Heads not want to resolve the issues? If they genuinely believed they were being harassed, they would explore every possible avenue to try to get it to stop. It is clear that yet again, our family was being punished for the Heads irrational and illogical behaviour. Surely, for the Heads to refuse the Restorative Justice option, this would leave NP in no doubt as to who was harassing who.

Looking at it now, I think it was all part of the plot to incriminate our family. The Heads and NP must have been working together. To be clear, if the Heads believed for a second that they would be investigated by NP for the multitude of serious criminal offences committed by them against our family if they refused to engage in Restorative Justice, they would simply not have refused as the consequences for them would be massive, especially as Mr Head had already accepted a Conditional Caution for Common Assault. They must have known NP would not be going to investigate these offences, no matter what the Heads decided.

I was left feeling devastated. Once again, I faced accepting a Conditional Caution or being prosecuted for an offence I knew I did not commit, and the Heads knew I did not commit, and NP knew I did not commit. The stress was unbearable.

Failure to Disclose

Obviously, the thought of the Conditional Caution was laying heavy on my mind. Even though I knew I had done nothing wrong, I was considering accepting the Caution because of the impact it was having on my health both mentally and physically. I then had a light bulb moment, I realised I had not seen the version of CCTV footage **APC1** that had allegedly been shown to my son at his interview and was being used by NP as '*KEY EVIDENCE*' to offer me the caution. So, I telephoned PC Pinky and told him the CCTV footage APC1 could not possibly show what Mr Head claimed and asked him if I could view this version of the CCTV footage. PC Pinky's reply was, **"OF COURSE YOU CAN SEE THE FOOTAGE, IF YOU GO TO COURT**."

I asked why that was, but he just repeated this line and would not say anymore. I could not understand this, why would Pinky refuse to show me this Key Evidence. Of course, for one reason and one reason only. PC Pinky and Perky knew as well as me and the Heads, this version of the CCTV footage APC1, did not show what was alleged and if I were to see it, it would not just expose Mr Head for making a false allegation and providing NP with a statement and evidence that he knew to be false. But it would also expose the misconduct of Pinky and Perky who also knew Mr Head had made a false allegation and provided NP with a false statement and evidence.

Again, something that I was not aware of at the time is that it is against the laws of disclosure for a police officer to refuse to show a suspect evidence that is being used against them for the purpose of issuing any form of sanction. PC Pinky was knowingly and deliberately wrong to deny me my right under law to see this evidence being used against me to offer me a Conditional Caution for Criminal Damage and the only reason he refused was to protect Mr and Mrs Head from serious criminal acts including Perjury and Perverting the Course of Justice and to protect himself and his colleagues Perky and Tool, from the same criminal acts as well as Gross Misconduct. I am 100% sure of this.

The only thing I am not sure about, as with the misconduct of PC Sloth, is why would PC's Pinky, Perky and Inspector Tool take such a risk? It does not make any sense. I suppose the reason was because they all knew they were not taking a risk as there was no one to hold them accountable. Even if they were somehow proven to have acted inappropriately, they would not face any sanction anyway.

Moving into November, we received a visit from Trigger, the builder who destroyed my rose bush in our front garden. My wife opened the door to him and he said, *"Can't you two just sort it out?"*

He was referring to the problems between ourselves and the Heads. We asked him in and explained that we had tried to resolve the matter through Restorative Justice but the Heads refused to take part and have told NP they will not engage into any form of communication with us whatsoever, so what can we do. He then said, *"Did the rose bush start the problems?"*

We said, *"No, it was Mr and Mrs Heads reaction to the rose bush that caused the problem."*

Trigger then said, *"I would not have even trod on your garden if it had not been so unkempt."*

The garden was not unkempt, it was February when he dug up and destroyed my rose bush, the garden was like most gardens at the end of a long winter. He may have come around with the best of intentions but he clearly did not have a clue on how to be respectful and considerate, he really was an arrogant and ignorant man. He went on to say that Mr Head had asked him to put the fence back up but he did not know whether to do the job or not but he felt he had a bond with Mr Head as he had offered him work.

We explained to Trigger some of the issues between ourselves and the Heads and in particular, the situation regarding the fence and that the part of the fence he had been asked to re-erect would be on our land and that he did not have our permission to do so. We asked Trigger not to erect the fence panels back to the existing posts and if he did there would be consequences. We talked for a short while longer and he left saying he did not know whether to do the job or not.

Extreme

It was the morning of the 12th of November 2014. I was upstairs preparing to leave for work when my wife shouted up to me, *"Trigger is putting the fence back up."*

We were like headless chickens for a while before deciding to go out and talk to Trigger. We said to him that we were very disappointed he had decided to put the fence back up. His reply in his usual arrogant fashion was, *"Well, its work en it, why can't you just grow a hedge and be done with it, you have got one there."*

And pointed to the hedge at the front of our garden. What our hedge had to do with anything is beyond me. Trigger was clearly on edge as he knew he was re-erecting the fence on our land, and he did not have permission to do so. We tried to reason with him for his own sake, but his arrogance and ignorance would not let him see sense. We returned indoors and Trigger continued to re-erect the fence.

We were watching Trigger erecting the fence from our bedroom window when as usual when there was an incident, the brother and sister-in-law of Mrs Head, Mr and Mrs Hoperty arrived on the scene. When Mr Hoperty saw myself and my wife, he started his usual behaviour of giving us the hand gestures for *'fuck off'* and *'wanker'* before beckoning us out for a fight. He and his brother-in-law really were like peas in a pod.

My wife phoned PC Pinky to tell him the Heads were erecting the fence back on our land and the conduct of Mr Hoperty. Pinky said, *"I know, the Heads phoned me this morning to tell me they were going to re-erect the fence today, but I am not going to get involved as it is a civil matter, and the police cannot get involved in civil matters."*

Bollocks. It was not a civil matter. To be clear, this was the second time NP had allowed the Heads to erect the fence on our land, even though they had prior knowledge on both occasions that the Heads were going to do so. PC Sloth told the Heads not to erect the fence on our land the first time and even witnessed them doing so and did nothing to stop it. PC Pinky knew the Heads were going to erect the fence back on our land the second time and would do nothing to stop it. This was a further and clear act of harassment by the Heads and Trigger. The Heads, Trigger and Pinky knew the erecting of the fence back on our land was a criminal offence and would cause our family great distress.

Furthermore, according to NP, when the Heads erected the fence on our land in August 2014 including removing and destroying two sections of our fencing and the hacking down of our hedge committing all manner of criminal offences, and when Trigger re-erected the three fence panels back to the posts in November 2014, again on our land, it was a civil matter.

But when I removed the three fence panels from the same posts in September 2014, it was a criminal matter, and I was charged and prosecuted for Criminal Damage. Answers on a postcard, please!

It was not just that. Pinky and Perky investigated the allegation against me with a level of inequality and discrimination that was beyond belief. It was as though I was Public Enemy Number 1. One rule for the Heads and another for our family. I wonder, if they knew the harm they were causing to our family, would they have done what they did. Of course they would, they are evil sadistic bastards. Shame on you, Pinky and Perky.

So, there we were, after a few weeks of freedom, we were back in prison. We once again had a seven-foot-high fence in our front garden.

I am sure I do not have to tell you that the re-erecting of the fence had a huge impact on our health, both physically and mentally. I had not accepted the Conditional Caution being offered by NP for removing the fence panels, so NP nor the Heads could claim that I had admitted I was in the wrong and therefore the Heads were within their rights to re-erect the fence. But there it was.

Due to the stress of the constant harassment, and in particular, the prospect of the Conditional Caution hanging over me. In the space of five days, I had two suspected heart attacks, and I was taken to hospital by ambulance on both occasions. I was later told by my daughter, on the first occasion when I left the house to get into the ambulance, Mrs Head was watching out of her front bedroom window, laughing. I assume she had seen the blue lights of the ambulance arriving and was waiting there to see what was going on. She really was an evil witch.

On the second occasion, I was admitted to the Coronary Care Unit where I was monitored overnight before having an Angiogram the following morning. Thankfully, the results of the angiogram were okay, and my condition was thought to have been stress related panic attacks believe it or not, and I was discharged later that day.

I had never had a panic attack before, and they are surprisingly scary. I am the last person in the world to make a fuss about anything, particularly my health, but I genuinely thought on both occasions I was having a heart attack and so did my wife and daughter and the paramedics to be fair, so I wasn't alone or exaggerating.

While I was in the back of the ambulance on the second occasion, our daughter phoned PC Pinky to tell him what had happened and that I was very unwell due to the stress of the harassment and the pressure being placed on me to accept the Caution. She asked Pinky to give me a little space and not to contact me for a couple of days. Although I had not suffered a heart attack, thankfully, I was still very poorly of course. Let's face it, to be admitted to hospital these days, you have to be seriously ill.

The stress was like nothing I have ever experienced, I couldn't eat, sleep or even function, so I took the remainder of the year off work. Being self-employed, this meant I had no income and so this placed further stress onto our shoulders, but it was definitely the right thing to do. I still feel to this day, if I had not taken that time off work, I would not have survived, particularly with what was to come in the very near future.

Bearing in mind what you have just read regarding our daughter contacting Pinky about my poor health, you may want to prepare yourself for what Pinky and Inspector Tool did next.

On the very same day I was released from hospital, and the day after my daughter had telephoned PC Pinky to inform him I was seriously ill, I received a telephone call from guess who, PC Pinky, requesting I attend the police station *to, "Discuss the Caution."*

Our daughter told Pinky just the day before that I was very poorly and had asked him not to contact me for a couple of days. Pinky was such a sick bastard that he even said to me in the call, *"I know you have been in hospital, so let's get this sorted."*

The only thought running through Pinky's head must have been, *'Ah, Mr Bean is vulnerable so let's see if I can get him to accept the caution or fuck him up completely.'*

The very next day, I received a letter through the post from guess who, PC Pinky.

This letter also requested that I attend the police station for the, *'Issuing of the Conditional Caution for causing Criminal Damage to your neighbour's fence.'* Those are the actual words he had written in the letter.

There is absolutely no doubt in my mind, PC Pinky was trying to tip me over the edge. He wanted to cause me serious harm and I do not hesitate in saying he would have taken great pleasure if his conduct had caused my death. Why else would he be doing this?

It wasn't because the Caution was the be all and end all of his career, he knew I was innocent anyway. Whether I accepted the Caution or not made no difference to him.

The Caution was just the tool he needed to try to destroy me for his own personal pleasure and to satisfy his Narcissistic Personality Disorder. And Pinky would not have been the only one to be happy at my demise. I am sure, Blankbrain, Sloth, Tool and Perky would have joined Pinky for a good old knee up to celebrate their success. And what about the Heads? I'm sure they would have got an invite to the knees up and they would have bought the first round.

It is clearly stated in the College of Policing Code of Ethics for Police Officers, that an officer cannot place any pressure on an individual to accept the offer of a Caution. I had not admitted any guilt, so I should not have been offered the Caution in the first place. And not only was Pinky placing the most incredible pressure on me to accept the Caution that it was making me seriously ill, he still did not stop. In fact, he increased the pressure on me with a phone call and letter when he knew I had been admitted to hospital.

To be clear on one point, for me to have received the letter on the day after I received the phone call, Pinky must have written and posted the letter on the same day that he made the phone call. That is not placing undue pressure on an individual, that is an out of-control dangerous obsession.

As with the conduct of Pinky and Perky regarding their investigation into the allegation made against me by Mr Head and the refusal by Pinky to show me the CCTV footage being used as *'Key Evidence'* to offer me the Caution. This conduct was yet another clear act of Gross Misconduct by PC Pinky and I am sure to any reasonable person, a deliberate and calculated attempt by Pinky to cause me serious harm, and my family great distress.

I realised later, why Pinky was so insistent that I accept the Caution. Because if I did not, the case would progress to court and his misconduct would be exposed due to disclosure of evidence, including the statement provided to NP by Mr Head, which I knew to be false, and the CCTV footage APC1, which Pinky refused to let me see and which I knew could not contain what Mr Head, Pinky and Perky claimed.

Abuse of Position

If things couldn't have got any worse. Also, on the same day as I received the letter from Pinky, we received an email from Inspector Tool. The content of this email was deeply distressing and insulting to our family. I am going to go on a bit now about the content of this email, some of you may find it rather tedious reading, others may find it very interesting. Personally, I feel it gives you an idea of how really fucked up NP are and the lengths they will go to protect their own and inflict suffering on not just the innocent, but on people who they know to already be the victims of crime.

It refers to a *'Strategy meeting'* Tool had arranged with a number of representatives, including Pinky and Perky, to have a holistic look at the current situation between ourselves and the Heads. We had no knowledge and were not invited to this meeting. Funny that!

Of course, if we had been there, they would not have been able to come up with the absolute bullshit contained in the email. The email was presented in a list of bullet points confirming the result of the meeting. I will only list the important ones below. *Bullet point 1,*

"The offer of a conditional caution to Mr Bean is the most appropriate way to proceed with this matter after the attempts at Restorative Justice have failed."

Tool is clearly referring to his idea of *'TIT for TAT'* justice being the most appropriate way forward. *'TIT for TAT'* justice was not and should never have been the most appropriate way to proceed. It is wrong and must be illegal, you cannot issue someone with a Caution just because you have issued someone else with a Caution. Tool also fails to mention the reason Restorative Justice had failed was because the Heads refused to take part. How many times does this family have to suffer due to the irrational behaviour of the Heads?

Before I list the next bullet point, you will need to know the following. Over the past few weeks, myself and my wife had been communicating with our local MP, the Police, Fire and Crime Commissioner and senior officers of NP including the Chief Constable regarding our situation, literally begging them for help. Although our MP did his best, it was to no avail, NP talked a good fight to our MP as they did with us. As for the Police, Fire and Crime Commissioner, what the fuck do they do apart from taking a stupid amount of money from the public purse to play golf with the Chief Constable.

Because of these pleas for help, we had received several emails from various officers of NP saying they had asked so and so to look into it and they had then passed it on to so and so to ask so and so to review the file. You know, pass the buck from one officer to another until it gets lost at some point along the way and therefore the end result is a big fat nothing. Standard!

Regarding these pleas for help, Tool states,

Bullet Point 5,

"That any attempt to seek interference from senior officers or external parties into disrupting the current investigation outcome could be construed as perverting the course of justice which is a criminal offence."

What The Fuck. Tool is clearly stating that it is a criminal offence for our family to seek help from anyone regarding our problems. This is a clear attempt by Tool to threaten and intimidate our family into silence and to accept what was happening to us. And if we do not, we may be charged with the serious criminal offence of Perverting the Course of Justice.

Sorry to get a bit technical but, Perverting the Course of Justice is an offence under the Criminal Law and Investigations Act 1996 and is defined as the following three acts,

- Fabricating or <u>disposing</u> of evidence

- Intimidating or threatening a <u>witness</u> or <u>juror</u>

- Intimidating or threatening a <u>judge</u>

Given the above definition of the offence of Perverting the Course of Justice, how the fuck could Inspector Tool consider our pleas for help to the Chief Constable of NP and our MP be construed as Perverting the Course of Justice. We were not fabricating or disposing of evidence, nor intimidating or threatening a witness or juror, nor intimidating or threatening a judge. But Inspector Tool was. He was clearly intimidating the witnesses by threatening them with committing the offence that he was actually committing against the witnesses. What a C U Next Tuesday.

Inspector Tool or any police officer, does not have the right to threaten anyone with criminal offences for exercising their fundamental and basic human right to seek help and advice from wherever and whoever they choose, whenever they choose to do so, particularly at such a distressing and difficult time for our family.

It is not as if we were asking a dodgy character to threaten or intimidate the Heads.

We had asked our MP, the Chief Constable of NP and the Police, Fire and Crime Commissioner for help. If that was an attempt to Pervert the Course of Justice then I think the Chief Constable of NP and the Police, Fire and Crime Commissioner were more able and better placed than Tool to tell us themselves. The fact is, they didn't, that tells me all I need to know. We had not done anything that could possibly be construed as a criminal offence, not even NP could wangle that one.

To be clear, if we were attempting to Pervert the Course of Justice, we would not ask our MP, the Chief Constable of NP and the Police, Fire and Crime Commissioner to help us do that, would we? On second thoughts, that's not such a bad idea. We only contacted these people to help ensure the course of justice was done, not perverted.

The clear, obvious and only reason Tool threatened and intimidated our family was because he knew if an external party or senior officer got involved in this matter, the misconduct of himself, Pinky and Perky would be exposed. Tool clearly chose to knowingly and deliberately bully, intimidate and threaten our family, who he knew to be the victims of crime, into not seeking help, or to stand up to NP or the harassers in any way. He was prepared and in fact determined to make sure our family continued to be the victims of the Heads harassment and his own and his colleagues' disgraceful conduct to the point of committing serious criminal offences himself.

For any police officer to tell any member of the public that it could be construed as a serious criminal offence if they try to seek help from senior officers and their MP is completely abominable.

I know I am going on a bit, babbling I suppose. But for an Inspector in the Police Force to have the confidence and audacity not just to say such a thing to a member of the public, but to actually put it in writing, to me, that is absolutely staggering. Yet again, it displays a total confidence that no matter what he was to do, say or write, there would be absolutely no consequence for him.

To be absolutely clear on this point, like the Heads, Tool is, in fact, reversing the truth.

It is not our family that were attempting to Pervert the Course of Justice, but Inspector Tool who was attempting to Pervert the Course of Justice and abusing his position as an Inspector with NP in order to do so.

Inspector Tool was completely aware of what our family were going through as we had recently met with him to discuss the *'ongoing issues'* with the Heads, yet he still sent this email. The sending of this email was not a mistake or an error of judgement, neither was it justifiable or appropriate, nor was it a slight infringement of the Code of Ethics for Police Officers or poor police conduct, it was sick and twisted. C U Next Tuesday.

This bullet point alone constitutes yet another clear act of Gross Misconduct. It is a disgrace and an absolute outrage and should be an embarrassment to all police officers, past and present. If you are a past or present police officer, you no longer have to wonder why the police have a bad reputation.

Bullet point 6,

"That historic allegations from the Bean and Head family will not be formally investigated."

This bullet point is in total contrast to the to the email sent by Tool less than a month earlier, when he stated,

"NP will assess allegations of criminal offences in line with the National Threshold Test if we are unable to implement restorative justice."

I would like to be absolutely clear on this point. NP were not able to implement Restorative Justice because the Heads refused to take part. Inspector Tool lied to our family regarding NP investigating clear criminal conduct to persuade our family to enter the Restorative Justice process. When the Heads refused to engage in that process, he again abused his position as a police officer by failing to investigate clear and repeated criminal conduct that was fully evidenced and witnessed to protect the offenders from the consequences of their actions.

No wonder the Heads did not stop their harassment; they had no reason to. NP had made it absolutely clear to them they could carry on and do whatever they wanted to our family and there would be absolutely no consequences for doing so. They must have been having the time of their lives, while we were struggling to stay alive.

Wow, that was a long chapter with an awful lot of information to absorb. But I hope you will agree that it raises some very important issues, especially regarding police conduct, or misconduct. Many of the officers we have met so far have been a disgrace to the uniform. They are liars, plain and simple, people pleasers who will tell you anything you want to hear to appease you and to keep you quiet and towing the line. Although some of you may be shocked and even sceptical of what is contained in this chapter, there is one officer you have yet to meet who takes lying to a whole new level than anything you have read so far.

Chapter Five
They Won't Catch Me

Under pressure

Due to the immense pressure PC Pinky placed on me and its impact on my already fragile health, I was seriously considering accepting the Caution, even though I knew I had done nothing wrong. It may sound silly, but I thought it was better to live to fight another day, than not to live at all.

My family were adamant that I should not accept the Caution as they knew I did the right thing for my family and the right thing by law. They could obviously see the impact it was having on me and, of course, they wanted me to do what I thought would be best for me. My daughter was taking this particularly hard as she thought it was her fault I was in trouble with the police as I took the fence down to protect her wellbeing. And she was right, selfish cow!

Sometimes, it can be a small world. Through life's rich tapestry, we knew someone who I would consider a friend, who happened to be a qualified barrister. Although he wasn't a practising barrister at the time, I asked him for some advice regarding our situation, and particularly the offer of the Conditional Caution from NP. I can remember his words as if he said them yesterday, his advice was, *"From what you have told me; you should not have been offered the Caution and you should not have been placed under the pressure you have to accept it. In all my years as a barrister, I have never heard of such pressure being placed on someone to accept what is or should be a voluntary option. I strongly advise that you do not accept the Caution, if you do accept the Caution, it will affect the rest of your life."*

Those words were like breathing air into my lungs. This advice had not just come from a random person or someone who just said what I wanted to hear. This advice came from someone who knew what he was talking about, a qualified barrister, and at the end of the day, confirmed what I already knew – I was innocent, and I should not accept the Caution. He was a friend before this, and a great friend after. I doubt if he is aware of the impact his advice had on my life, the strength it gave me to fight for what was right, and to kick through the door that was closing in on me. I will be eternally grateful to this friend, I hope he reads this and remembers our meeting. Thank you.

He had very kindly visited our house to meet me and offer this advice. When he left, I found the strength to call PC Pinky and tell him that I would not be accepting the Caution. I will not deny that it was a very difficult phone call to make, I was a wreck. Even though I knew I had done nothing wrong, it still felt like I had, it felt as though I was defying the police, which was alien to me for the fifty years I had lived. I was also aware of the consequences it would have for me, more stress, greater stress, but as mentioned, the right choice is often the hardest.

PC Pinky answered the phone and I told him that I would not be accepting the Caution. He was shocked, he must have been so confident that I would roll over and accept the Caution that he never thought that I would have the balls to stand up to him and NP. That is a mistake many people have made when it comes to our family, particularly over the time this book covers, they have mistaken our kindness for softness. We are not soft.

I wish I could have seen Pinky's face; it must have been a picture. His plan had failed and now what would he do? What could he do? The only thing that a scumbag like him can do, I suppose, heap more shit on me and tell more lies. After a not-so-brief pause, I assume while he picked himself up off the floor, he said, *"Due to your decision, I will submit the file to the Crown Prosecution Service (CPS) and you will receive a summons through the post to appear in court."*

And that was that. I was now being prosecuted for an offence I, the Heads, and NP all knew I did not commit. They had started a ball rolling along a path they now could not stop and because I refused to accept the Caution, they had lost control over. I now had the opportunity to fight. Not that any of them would have cared.

In all honesty though, this started the most difficult and stressful six months of my life. As mentioned, never in my wildest dreams, did I ever think I would be involved with the police. Never in my wildest dreams did I ever expect to be offered a Conditional Caution, and now, here I was being prosecuted by the CPS. The stress was unreal, and I knew it would get worse before it would get better, if it ever did get better. Now, due to one piece of advice and one difficult but correct decision, I could see a light at the end of a very long dark tunnel. Whatever happened from now on, I knew 100% that I had done the right thing. He who dares wins Rodney, he who dares wins.

After a few days, I received the summons through the post to attend the Magistrates Court on the 7th of January 2015, for my Plea Hearing. This is where the Charges are put to you and you give your plea, guilty or not guilty. Although this was expected, it was still distressing to see it in black and white, *'Mr Bean, you are charged with the offence of causing Criminal Damage to your neighbour's fence. You are lawfully required to appear at the town's Magistrates Court on the 7th of January 2015 to offer your plea. Failure to attend court on this date will leave you in contempt of court and a warrant may be issued for your arrest.'* All scary stuff.

Because I was now being prosecuted, I needed to have legal representation to defend myself. I looked into this and decided to try direct access to a barrister. This is where you can basically bypass a solicitor for many legal matters. It does have its restrictions as a barrister may not be able to do everything involved in legal proceedings, but for me in this case, it seemed the right option. It would prove to be another correct decision; I was on a roll.

It can also be a very cost-effective way of gaining representation as you are not paying a solicitor as well as a barrister, which was, of course, a major consideration due to our increasingly dire financial position. Most barristers work out of Chambers, which to my understanding is a place that can act as a base for usually several barristers to work from. It also allows them to gain advice from the other barristers in the Chambers, and also the administrators for the Chambers look after the day-to-day running such as appointments, enquiries, and invoicing. If you ever need legal representation and this option is suitable for you, I recommend it.

I enlisted the services of a barrister from a Chambers based in a neighbouring county who, like the barrister who gave me the advice not to accept the Caution, was very professional, supportive and adamant from the off that I had not broken the law and was even more adamant that this case should not have progressed to a prosecution. We decided on my defence and submitted it to the CPS, and we waited until the 7th of January.

Needless to say, Christmas was completely ruined. The prosecution was always at the forefront of my mind. No matter what I was doing and whose company I was in, the stress was literally suffocating me. Even though I and more so my barrister was confident that justice would be done, you never know. In the grand scheme of things, the charge against me was relatively minor and the potential punishment should I be found guilty reflected that, but the stress was still so intense. I cannot begin to imagine what it must be like for someone who had been wrongly prosecuted for something much more serious that they hadn't done and if found guilty they could lose their liberty for years.

Of course, it wasn't just the prosecution that we had to deal with. We had suffered the harassment from the Heads for a year and a half by now and it was getting rapidly worse. It started with little things like our bins going missing and progressed to assaults and false allegations to the police and now a prosecution against me.

And just because I was awaiting trial, the harassment did not stop. The Heads knew we were more vulnerable than ever and almost every day something would happen. Mostly petty and minor things but because of our situation, the impact of these acts of harassment was magnified. Drip, drip, drip.

Due to our communications with senior officers from NP regarding the issues with our next-door neighbours and their associates. We unexpectedly received an email from the Staff Officer to the Chief Constable. Contained in this email was a copy of an internal email sent to the Chief Constable by Inspector Tool which contained an update regarding the ongoing problems between ourselves and the Heads.

To be honest, I do not think I was supposed to receive this copy email as it was a lie from start to finish. Either the Chief Constable, or rather his Staff Officer had sent it to me accidentally or maybe even deliberately, who knows. The fact is, I do not think Inspector Tool ever expected I would have received it. Tool stated in his email, *'The dispute had been ongoing for over a year and surrounds civil matters in respect of a boundary dispute (although a number of issues have occurred from the back of this).'*

Completely untrue. As stated previously, there was a popular misconception within NP that the issues began with the fence being erected on our land in August 2014, but that was not the case. There had been many acts of

Harassment including several acts of Harassment Causing Fear of Violence before the fence was erected, the assaults on me and my wife, and the threat to attack our daughter, to name a few.

Tool also, again, confirmed his *'Tit for Tat'* justice approach by referring to my Caution by stating, *'This seemed appropriate as the other party in this dispute had previously received a conditional caution for a common assault on Mrs Bean.'*

Tool couldn't even get that right as it was the assault on me and not my wife that led to Mr Head receiving a Conditional Caution for Common Assault. NP had failed to even investigate the assault on my wife, let alone issue Mr Head with any form of sanction for it. Pillock.

Tool went on to say, *'The matter was brought to my attention when Mr Bean refused to accept a conditional caution and as such forced the OIC to proceed to court with the matter. (Mr Bean made admissions as to criminal damage during the interview to this offence).'*

Absolute total bollocks. At the time this email was sent by Tool to the Chief Constable, I had not refused to accept the Conditional Caution, and I absolutely did not make any admissions to criminal damage during my interview. I have a copy of this interview, and it did not contain any admission that I caused Criminal Damage to the fence when I removed it, in fact, it was the complete opposite. I categorically denied I caused Criminal Damage to the fence. Tool was blatantly lying to his Chief Constable.

He clearly felt he was able to do this as he must have thought I would never get to see the email. To be honest, I think the Staff Officer to the Chief Constable knew Tool was lying which was why he *'accidentally'* attached the email to his message. Dobbed in by his boss, how fucked up is that. I guarantee it wasn't done for my benefit, I bet the Chief Constable, or his Staff Officer had a grudge against Tool and wanted to fuck him up.

Tool went on, *'Myself and the Head of the Force Justice Unit, have met with both families and discussed Restorative Options at length. Unfortunately, the Head family were very hostile during this meeting and whilst initially agreeing to participate, later withdrew and made a number of complaints about the manner in which I conducted the meeting.'*

Surely, this paragraph had to tell NP all they needed to know. The Heads were even hostile to an Inspector from the police at a meeting to discuss Restorative Justice. Surely, this would give Tool and his colleagues some idea of what it was like living next door to these people every single day. But they still did nothing but kick our family in the head when we we're lying on the floor.

Tool then stated, *'As one of the parties does not consent to the Restorative Options this process cannot take place and the OIC for this case (PC Pinky has updated both parties that the Conditional Caution for Bean will ensue and if there is a failure to accept the Caution the case will proceed to Court).'*

Oh my God. Tool had told so many lies that he didn't even know what he had said earlier in the same email. Previously in this same email Tool stated, *'The matter was brought to my attention when Mr Bean refused to accept the Conditional Caution and as such forced the IOC (Investigating Officer in Charge) to proceed to court with the matter.'*

But, even on the same page Tool stated, *'As one of the parties does not consent to the Restorative Justice this process cannot take place and the IOC for this case (PC Pinky has updated both parties that the Conditional Caution for Bean will ensue and if there is a failure to accept the Caution the case will proceed to court).'*

These two statements were a complete contradiction to each other. One sentence stated that I had refused to accept the Caution, and the other sentence stated that I had not even been offered the Caution.

It is often the case that when you tell so many lies you end up forgetting what lies you have told, that's not uncommon. But to fuck yourself up on the same page in the same email to the Chief Constable, that's pushing it, even for a police officer. Pillock.

Next paragraph, *'The Beans have previously written to the Chief Constable, the PCC (Police and Crime Commissioner) and the local MP. During my meeting with them I have explained that they are engaged in a due legal process and that it would be inappropriate for any of these parties to intervene in the Justice process, yet Mrs Bean continues to write to ask for external involvement.'*

Untrue again. At no point during this meeting did Tool inform us that it would be inappropriate for us to contact third parties for help. Furthermore, it was not inappropriate for us to contact third parties for help, we were entitled to ask whoever we chose for help whenever we wanted. It is our fundamental right to ask for help and representation regarding criminal proceedings.

There's more, *'I have directed that the above action should take place as both parties are anecdotally stating that the police are working in favour of either party and have indicated a level of corruption. I have challenged both parties on this issue and have given reassurances in respect of our commitment to the code of ethics etc.'*

Fuck off. We have only ever told the truth regarding the way we have been treated by NP. If Tool was stating that our concerns were indicating a level of corruption, then that was his conclusion, not ours. Although he was clearly spot on. As for the *'Code of Ethics'* maybe police officers should try reading them now and again! How could Tool even mention the commitment to the Code of Ethics when he was knowingly breaking every rule in the book himself? C U Next Tuesday.

'I am satisfied that officers have acted correctly and we have looked at alternative options to try and have this dispute mediated.'

Bollocks. Maybe you will read this book, Inspector. If so, just read Chapter Four and then try and tell the Chief Constable that you and your officers had acted correctly. Prick.

'I am sure that we will not be able to satisfy the expectations of either parties involved in this dispute and that I expect a complaint against the Police to be levelled at some stage. However, the team continue to act professionally and put in place systems to manage this issue.'

I beg to differ. The team would not know what professional was if it slapped them around the face. And what systems do you intend to put in place to manage this situation, more threats and intimidation perhaps? And just one other point where I think you may be wrong, I think you will be able to satisfy the Heads expectations beyond their wildest dreams.

It had been ten weeks or so since I was interviewed under caution and we had not heard anything from Pinky and Perky regarding the allegation of Malicious Communications via Social Media I made against Mrs Head and Little Head during this interview. So, we contacted Pinky to ask him what was happening. We received an email from him saying, *'The Social Media comments placed by Mrs Head will not be looked into and that the matter had already been discussed with Mr Bean and that it was a civil matter, not a police matter.'*

Total bollocks. The matter had not been discussed with me at any time. The only communication with Pinky and Perky regarding these social media comments was when I made the allegation to them at my voluntary interview. At no time during this interview, did we discuss what was going to happen and that my allegation would not be looked into. I have a copy of this interview so I have the evidence to prove Pinky was lying.

Furthermore, how could Pinky possibly say this allegation was a civil matter, in no way was it a civil matter. There can be no doubt what Mrs and Little Head posted on social media amounts to Malicious Communications via Social Media. In fact, due to the increase in the use of social media platforms being used to spread false information and to incite others to commit criminal acts, it is considered to be a serious criminal offence. Just look at the punishments issued to many people for allegedly spreading misinformation via social media which allegedly incited the Southport riots.

For Pinky to claim this was a civil matter was a clear dereliction of his duty not just to protect the public and to allow them to feel safe in their own home, but also a deliberate attempt to protect the offenders and yet another clear act of gross misconduct. Well, it's the Heads, so a little bit of crime didn't matter.

Unless I am mistaken. This sort of crime is taken very seriously by most police forces. It must just be NP who considers this sort of crime to be a civil matter and not to be worthy of being investigated. Or was it just Pinky who thought that way? Or was it because it was the Heads who committed the offence? Or was it because our family were the target of Heads criminality, again? Whatever the reason, none of them were right, just or fair.

Rant alert! In my opinion, this is why in this day and age, on average two women a week are still being murdered by their ex-partner. Because the police still do not take Harassment and Stalking seriously. They fail to listen to the victims which empowers the offender not just to carry on with the harassment, but to escalate the severity. Clearly, for a male or female to Harass or Stalk their ex-partner, goes beyond being angry or upset that the relationship had broken down, whatever the circumstances and whoever was at fault.

They clearly have a *'mental health issue'* that allows them to think they have the control or power to destroy the life of the person they once loved. That *'mental health issue'* will not just go away if the police ignore it. It will manifest itself in the mind of the offender to the point that they are prepared to take the life of their victim. Although we may hear of cases where the victim has been murdered. Unfortunately, that is the tip of the iceberg. For every ex-partner that is murdered, there are a thousand men and women and families up and down the country that spend years and years being victims of this crime because they are ignored and abandoned by the authorities that should protect them. I remember watching a documentary about Stalking, it was about a woman who had been shot by her ex-partner. The woman, her parents and her sister had reported the Stalking to the police on dozens of occasions. They even told the police that he had threatened to shoot her and that he possessed a gun. Guess what, the police took no action, and he shot her dead.

The police gave the usual bullshit statement, *'We are sorry that we did not act on the victim's concerns, but we will learn from our mistakes, and we want to assure the public that due to the learning and changes we have and will make, this can never happen again.'* Bollocks.

The documentary also gave the statistic that in all cases of Stalking that had resulted in the death of the victim in the past twelve months, in 75% of those cases police failure played a part in the outcome.

The police will never learn and will never change until they are made to change. How that is done I have no idea. If that change ever does come, it will not happen overnight. The police have been left to their own devices for decade after decade with next to no accountability. So, these failures have become ingrained in the police force. I feel it will take as long to eradicate this failure as it did to become ingrained in the culture of the police. I am going to be in so much trouble when this is published. Not because I have done anything wrong, illegal or unjust, but just because I have challenged and exposed NP for what they are.

OMG

It was mid-December 2014. As if things were not bad enough. Remember I was awaiting my court appearance. We received a letter through the post from a local firm of Solicitors. The letter was titled, *RE: Harassment against Mr and Mrs Head.*

It started by informing us that they had been instructed by the Head family to act on their behalf regarding the Harassment of their family, by our family. The letter went on to list some points that the Heads had clearly told their solicitors that we were doing to harass them. It stated,

Our client specifically seeks that you desist from:

- *Videoing our client and visitors to their property,* (We were not)

- *Taking photographs of our clients and visitors to their property.* (We were not)

- *Looking out the window at our clients and visitors to their property.* (We were not)

- *Making false accusations.* (We were not)

- *Unnecessarily involving authorities.* (We were not)

The letter also refers to us using social media to accuse the Heads of criminal offences rather than going to the Police. Fuck sake, that was exactly what they had done to us with the Malicious Communications regarding the removal of the fence.

It was also, of course, a complete contradiction to the point above which states we are '*Unnecessarily involving authorities.*' We cannot be doing both, we cannot be '*Unnecessarily involving authorities*' and '*using social media to accuse the Heads of criminal offences rather than going to the police*'. Jesus, how can a supposedly reputable firm of solicitors write such shit. Money, that's why, some solicitors will do anything if they are paid enough.

Two things in this letter were familiar to the pattern of behaviour of the Heads that was by now crystal clear. The Heads were lying to their own

110

solicitors as well as to NP. Also, the Heads were reversing the truth again. They had told their solicitors that we were doing to them exactly what they were doing to us. For the Heads to go to the lengths of instructing a solicitor to act on their behalf regarding our family's harassment of them whilst being fully in the knowledge that it was them who were harassing us, was extreme, to say the least.

It was also further confirmation of the delusional fixation the Heads had in harassing our family. I know I have mentioned this before, but if the Heads genuinely believed we were harassing them, they would have agreed to take part in Restorative Justice. The fact that they refused to engage in that process but then instructed solicitors to act on their behalf regarding our harassment of them, was further confirmation that there was not going to be a quick fix to this and no happy ending for anyone. We were well and truly in the trenches and in a war that we did not want, ask for or deserve, but had no choice to fight.

I am sure of one thing though. The Heads were not prepared for the fight they were going to get. They thought we would bend, buckle and eventually break under the pressure of their non-stop bombardment. They had picked on the wrong family, not that we were special or different in any way. Like many or most people and families, we would much prefer to live a quiet life. Let's face it, enough shit will find you during life, there is no need to go looking for it. But when it's back-to-the-wall time, nothing gets me more fired up than protecting and fighting for my family.

I am most definitely not a hard man or a fighting man, but I will walk through walls to protect my family. I will take on anyone no matter how big they are, no matter what position they hold, I have no fear on that front. Don't get me wrong, I am not the all-guns blazing type, I am more the sniper, the sneaky little bastard that will wait for days, weeks, months, even years to get my one chance to even the score. And when or if I get that chance, I will blow your fucking head off. BOOM.

Not literally of course, I would not do anything illegal or underhand, that would just not be right would it? That would make me as bad as them. Anything I would do would be well and truly above board and beyond reproach. If I stoop to the level of my enemy or lose my temper, in my view, I would make my task a whole lot harder. I have to maintain the high ground, morally, ethically and legally, I believe that will serve me well in the end. It will also allow me to feel strong in the fight and not have to worry about being found out as being at least partly to blame for the predicament, whatever it may be.

To be honest, that approach did not help us in our darkest days, well, years, actually. We were still blamed by NP regardless of this approach. But I do believe it has helped at least myself, in surviving the past decade as intact as I am and also having the strength and determination to fight the injustice we have endured. Don't get mad, get even.

Over the past few months, we told NP on many occasions that this matter would not end well. The Heads not only had a delusional fixation with harassing our family, but they also believed it was our family that was harassing them. I suppose that goes hand in hand with the fixation, you have to believe one to believe the other. And with the level of reckless aggression the Heads had displayed on numerous occasions, someone would end up getting seriously hurt or even worse.

Just as with the Stalking incident mentioned earlier, that delusion will not simply disappear. If the Heads were left to continue their harassment, they would do so and it would escalate even further. I told NP on several occasions, that while the Heads could harass, they would harass and it would not end well. Did they listen, did they hell? Why? Because they did not care. By now, NP had not only condoned, facilitated and encouraged the harassment of our family, but they had on many occasions, actively joined in with the harassment.

I would not be surprised if it wasn't NP who advised the Heads to instruct solicitors in the first place. The only bright point I could find was that the firm of solicitors the Heads had instructed had a poor reputation in the area. They were regarded as a firm that would do anything for anyone. Cowboys.

The receipt of this letter further enhanced the feeling of isolation and indeed fear that there was no escape. Not only did we have the harassment of the Heads and their associates to deal with, along with the deliberate failure and what I had no hesitation in describing as the persecution of our family by NP, and the prosecution against me, we now had the threat of civil action being taken against us.

To be clear at this stage. By instructing solicitors to write to our family regarding the harassment, it was the Heads who started civil litigation against our family – not the other way around. The reason I say this will become clear later on.

Chapter Six
I'm Fucking Innocent

Guilty until Proven Innocent

After what seemed like an eternity, the day of my plea hearing finally arrived. I appeared at our town's Magistrates Court to face the charge of Criminal Damage. My barrister and I were provided with a small room to discuss what would happen. She explained the procedure would be that she and the CPS barrister would be in the courtroom, an Usher would call me in, and I would be shown to a seat behind her. She said I would not be required to stand in the dock for such a minor offence.

The CPS would make their submissions to the court and her submissions would follow. I would then be asked by the Magistrate how I plead, guilty or not guilty. Of course, I would plead not guilty, and the Magistrate would then announce a date for the trial and adjourn the hearing and we would meet up again in the same room as before to discuss what we need to do next.

When I was called into the court, the Usher directed me to the chair behind my barrister as I was expecting. After I had sat down, the Magistrate said to the Usher, *"No, not there, put him in the dock."*

The Usher got me by my arm and led me to the dock. So, there I was, standing in the dock in front of the Magistrates for an offence I and everyone concerned, knew I did not commit. It was one of the worst feelings of my life, so far! The Charge was read out to the court by the Magistrate and both sides made their representations. The Magistrate then asked me how I plead, guilty or not guilty. I replied, "Not Guilty." The Magistrate then said, *"You are now on Police Bail and if you commit another offence, you will be straight back in here. Your Trial is set for the 7th of June 2015."*

It may seem petty, but this really got to me. To me, for the Magistrate to say, *"If you commit another offence"* meant that she had already decided that

I had committed this offence, which was not the case as I had pleaded not guilty, and the Magistrate would have been fully aware of this. As the standard for British Law is innocent until proven guilty, I did not need to be told by the Magistrate, not to do something I have never done.

Putting this together with being made to stand in the dock, I felt something was amiss. I was being treated as though I was already guilty and a bad person before even being given a chance to defend myself. Maybe I was putting two and two together and making ten, but I did not think so, and neither did my barrister.

My barrister and I returned to the same room that we had used before the hearing.

The first thing my barrister did was to apologise to me for having to stand in the dock. She said she had never known that to happen before for such a minor allegation and for the Magistrate to tell me in such an abrupt manner that I am now placed on Police Bail was also very unusual.

This confirmed my belief that something was amiss, and I bet my bottom dollar, Numpty Police were behind it. Why would I have been treated this way by the magistrate if she did not believe I was a bad person, even though we had never met each other before? Whatever the circumstances or the reasons why, it was horrible, not as horrible as I thought it might have been at that stage but that was all going to change very soon.

Before the hearing, I had discussed with my barrister the evidence NP claimed to have of me causing Criminal Damage to the fence by kicking the panel loose from the post. The fact PC Pinky had refused to show me that evidence, which was the CCTV footage APC1, and telling me I would have to go to court if I wanted to see it. The only positive I could see before the hearing was that under the laws of disclosure, the CPS were legally bound to disclose any evidence they were relying on for the prosecution of a suspect. This would of course include the CCTV footage APC1.

So, while we were in the room, we went through the evidence that had been disclosed by the CPS to my barrister. Guess what, no APC1. There was a copy of the other version of CCTV footage, PFC1, which was shown to me at my interview, and did not show me causing any damage to the fence whatsoever. So, this meant the CPS had either failed to disclose this key evidence, or, they did not have the evidence. Whichever reason it was, it meant the CPS could not provide the court with any evidence of the alleged offence being committed. So, the case should never have progressed to court, and I should have been spared the trauma of appearing in court, being made to stand in the dock, making my plea and being placed on police bail awaiting trial in six months. Disgraceful.

My barrister said that I needed to contact the CPS directly and insist they disclose this Key Evidence immediately to allow me to make the strongest defence possible, that is my right under the law and it is a serious failure under the laws of disclosure for the police and the CPS to either fail or refuse to disclose this evidence to me. PC Pinky had no right to refuse to show me this evidence when I requested to see it before refusing to accept the Caution and the CPS cannot legally withhold this evidence from me.

So, who was really at fault? Was it PC Pinky and NP for refusing to show me this evidence? Or was it the CPS for failing to disclose this evidence? It must be both, and NP and the CPS must have been in on it together for it to have gone this far.

To be clear, NP could not provide me with any evidence that I committed the offence, so they had no right to offer me a Conditional Caution and no right to then forward the case to the CPS with no evidence to support the allegation. The CPS also could not provide any evidence to the court or my barrister of the alleged offence, so the CPS had no right to prosecute me. One thing is for sure, and no one could rightfully argue, it was not my fault, but I was the undoubted victim of this criminality and gross misconduct of the Heads, NP and the CPS.

I don't want to go down the route of slagging off the CPS because I am mindful that it will sound like I am criticising everyone all the time. But, over the next few months and on the advice of my barrister, I sent SIX written requests, all via Recorded Delivery, to the CPS requesting the CCTV evidence labelled as Police Exhibit APC1 be disclosed to me or my barrister. To be clear, APC1 was not just a piece of *Key Evidence*, it was the only *Key Evidence*. There was nothing else NP nor the CPS were relying on.

I received absolutely no acknowledgement from the CPS whatsoever to any of these six requests, not even an acknowledgement to say they had received the letters. After six months of waiting for a response from the CPS,

I eventually telephoned them and was put through to the case handler. I asked him about the footage, why they had not disclosed it to me at my plea hearing, and why they had not acknowledged any of my six written requests to them to disclose this evidence which is my legal right and their legal duty. The Case Handler would not answer my questions and told me that the evidence had been destroyed.

Bollocks. If the CPS had destroyed this *'Key Evidence'* it would not only have been an offence for them to have done so, but they would or should have a record of when and who authorised its destruction. The Case Handler could not or would not provide me with any information regarding the alleged destruction of this Key Evidence.

We think we live in a democracy, but my experience leads me to believe that is not the case. Just because we have offices and departments like the Professional Standards Departments of Police Forces, the Independent Office for Police Conduct (IOPC), the CPS, the Information Commissioner's Office (ICO), the Police and Crime Commissioner, the Data Protection and Freedom of Information Departments and Acts, we think we are protected from the type of events that were happening to our family.

We are living proof that we are not protected at all, no more so than someone living in a dictatorship. These offices are just Government quangos that are used by the powers that be as barriers to ordinary people like me and most of you gaining access to what they are entitled, require or need. A barrier to deny ordinary law-abiding citizens from gaining accountability against the wrongdoers, a barrier to prevent ordinary people from gaining their lawful right to provide the best defence possible to an allegation made against them – above all else a barrier to gaining justice.

My barrister also advised that I would need to enlist the services of professional Chartered Surveyors to draw up detailed plans of the properties, the exact line of the boundary, the exact line of the fence, and the deviation onto our property. I therefore employed a local firm of Chartered Surveyors and I have to say they were also very professional and supportive of my case. When they first visited our house, they were astonished that it was even a consideration that the fence in question was not on our land. The dogleg in the fence from the line of the boundary between the two side walls of the properties to where it started to trespass onto our property was not a minor discretion, but a significant diversion that was clear for anyone to see.

Anyway, they drew up the plans in as much detail as possible. They even went to the lengths of contacting the HM Land Registry to make sure they had all the information they could have and therefore be as accurate as possible in their drawings. These surveyors were very kind and sympathetic and went above and beyond what they needed to do to help as much as they could. Although these plans did cost me over £800, it was well worth it, particularly as I would later find out these plans were a significant factor in the decision by the CPS to discontinue their prosecution, which meant I could claim the £800 back anyway. I am very grateful for these two gentlemen, not just for their professionalism but also for the time they spent listening to me banging on about our family's plight. Thank you.

Back to the day of my Plea Hearing. Of course, it had been a very stressful and disappointing day. I had gone through all of that, not just this day but the past three months and the only bright spark was the fact that I would get a copy of the CCTV footage APC1. But of course, that did not happen.

That night I had the second of my horrific nightmares that would blight my life for years. The nightmare replayed the events of the morning when I appeared in Court. It started with me standing in the dock, the Magistrate asked me for my plea and when I said not guilty, a firing squad appeared in front of me and shot me. The shots blew my head off and I was walking up and down the dock with blood spurting from my neck saying, *"What's that all about, what's that all about?"*

Even though I no longer had a head on my shoulders, I did not fall to the floor, I just kept walking up and down the dock with blood spurting from my neck repeating the same words.

Although the day would have been very difficult anyway, the fact that I was treated as Public Enemy Number One by the magistrate and the evidence was not disclosed to me, which led me to believe something was not right, caused a difficult day to turn into a very traumatic few months, and years. It was this treatment that I believe at least to some degree, triggered the nightmare. The shooting of me equated to the extremity of the treatment, contempt and injustice by NP the CPS and the Magistrate. The nightmare may have happened anyway even if I had been treated as innocent until proven guilty as is my right. But the fact I was not, made it almost inevitable something like this would happen given the stress I was already under.

The difference with this nightmare compared to the previous one where my wife and daughter were killed by Mr Head using a chainsaw, was that it replayed an event that had actually happened to me earlier that day and was fresh in my mind. It wasn't an imagination of an event I hadn't experienced; it was real, and everything was identical to earlier that day. I was in the same courtroom, with the same people, wearing the same clothes and standing in the same dock. It was so graphic and disturbing that I still find it hard to put into words the impact it had on me. Maybe you can use your imagination to try to understand the impact, if you do, times it by ten!

Our lives were so difficult already that we were hardly able to cope as it was, and now this. Not just the nightmare, but equally as difficult was the fact I was now on Police Bail. It felt as though I might as well have been locked up by the Magistrate. It felt as though I could not do anything, go to work, go out for a walk or drive, or even out for a meal. If anything happened while I was out, no matter what it was, I would be found at fault and be back in court.

But even more scary, was the thought that the Heads would have known I was on Police Bail. All they would need to do was to make yet another false allegation against me to NP and I would be back in court and probably detained until my trial. In my mind, the odds of this happening were very high. To this day, I cannot believe that it did not happen, the Heads and NP missed a trick there, for once.

Or did they? If I was in jail, then the Heads couldn't harass me, and NP couldn't abuse me. So, was it a deliberate failure? Interesting!

Let's face it, I was in this situation because of a false allegation, false statement, false evidence, bent police officers and a useless CPS.

If anyone was wondering why I will never give up the fight for accountability and justice, hopefully, the above will help you understand. And I haven't even started to tell you the majority or by any means the worst of what was to happen to our family.

Black and White

Although the CPS failed to disclose the CCTV footage APC1 at my Plea Hearing, they did, however, disclose a copy of the statement provided to NP by Mr Head to support his allegation of Criminal Damage against me. Also, a copy of the Police Report and Witness Statement both completed by PC Pinky and submitted by him to the CPS to support the prosecution against me.

All three of these documents contained many entries that were not only misleading and false but also blatantly untrue. It dawned on me how easy it was for unscrupulous police officers to incriminate people. If I had fallen to the immense pressure being placed upon me by PC Pinky to accept the Caution, I would never have seen these documents and I would never have known the extent to which the Heads and NP had gone to fulfil their quest to incriminate me. Some of these entries are listed below.

The statement of Mr Head stated, *'We have had a dispute over the boundary fence, and to prevent further upset we deliberately had this new fence erected well inside the existing fence which was removed,'*

Bollocks. Mr Head confirmed there had been a dispute over the boundary in the past, so had no excuse to not be fully aware of the line of the boundary between the two properties. The Heads knew they had erected the fence on our land and had even told PC Sloth they had done so, and PC Sloth had even witnessed them doing so. The existing fence was not removed when the Heads erected the fence. *'The fence was erected by a local builder.'*

Bollocks. The fence was erected by themselves and their relatives the Hopertys.

'At 13:47 hours on the 11th September, the CCTV shows the bottom of one panel being broken by a foot from next door. It does appear that the bottom of the panel is being kicked several times before coming loose from the fence post.'

Bollocks. The CCTV footage cannot possibly show the panel being broken by a foot from next door as I did not use my foot to break the fence. Mr Head was fully aware that it would have been impossible to have broken the fence with my foot or kicked the fence, due to the position of the retaining wall which he had instructed his builder, Trigger, to erect on our land in February 2013. The panel was not kicked several times before it came loose from the post. The panel was not kicked at all. This is a blatant lie by Mr Head.

"*I have provided a copy of the CCTV on a memory stick which I have handed to PS Giles, Exhibit PFC1.'* (You remember PS Giles; he was the officer that was at the Heads house at the time further damage was caused to the fence panel).

Bollocks. Exhibit PFC1 did not show what Mr Head claimed it did in his statement. This was another blatant lie.

Mr Head finished his statement by saying, *'I am agreeable to a Conditional Caution on the understanding that my fence is made good.'*

What the hell is that all about? This clearly meant that PS Giles had already discussed with Mr Head that I would be offered a Conditional Caution for removing the fence, even before Mr Head had written his statement. Clearly wrong and clearly PS Giles had already decided at this stage that I had committed the offence, and I would be offered a Caution. The proof of the pudding is that I was, wrongly, offered a Caution. If this does not highlight the inequality and discrimination of this investigation, I do not know what will. Maybe the point I will make below!

In the Police Report submitted by PC Pinky to the CPS to support the prosecution against me, when referring to the evidence PC Pinky also submitted to the CPS to support the prosecution which was labelled as the infamous Police Exhibit APC1, he stated, *'BEAN was shown the CCTV footage at the beginning of the interview'*

Bollocks. At no time during my interview or ever, was I shown the CCTV footage Pinky submitted to the CPS as *'Key Evidence'* This was blatantly untrue.

In the Witness Statement also completed and submitted by PC Pinky to the CPS he stated, *'Following the interview PC 216 (PC Perky) and I visited Mr and Mrs Head at their home address to update them regarding the investigation. I explained to Mr Head that exhibit PFC1 was viewed and did not show how the damage to the fence was caused but did show Mr Bean dismantling the fence with some assistance from his son. From this Mr Head then showed PC 216 and me the CCTV footage of the damage being caused to his fence panel on his home CCTV system and informed me that he had organised an external company to copy the footage onto a USB drive.*

I informed Mr and Mrs Head that due to the exhibit PFC1 not showing how the damage was caused, a new copy of the footage needed to be produced.'

121

Clearly, the above paragraph from the Witness Statement of PC Pinky confirmed that I was not shown the CCTV footage APC1 at my interview which Pinky stated in his Police Report that I was. At my interview, I was shown Police Exhibit PFC1 which Pinky confirmed in his witness statement *'did not show how the damage to the fence was caused'.*

To be clear, I was not shown at my interview and to this day, I have never seen the version of CCTV footage labelled as Police Exhibit APC1 which Pinky stated in his Police Report that I was shown at my interview, and which he submitted to the CPS as *'Key Evidence'* to support the prosecution against me.

Pinky also fails to mention anywhere in his submissions to the CPS that following my interview and before I refused to accept the Caution, when this *'Key Evidence'* came to light he refused my request to view it by telling me, *'Of course you can see the footage, if you go to court.'*

There was nothing to stop Pinky from inviting me to see this new *'Key Evidence'* when it came to light. In fact, it was his duty to do so. It clearly states in the Code of Conduct for Investigators, *'If any new evidence comes to light and is in the interests of justice, it should be shown to the suspect.'*

Pinky not only failed to do this; he refused to do it. Further Gross Misconduct.

PC Pinky would have been fully aware that his submissions to the CPS were not just misleading and inaccurate, but knowingly and blatantly untrue. So, to be clear, PC Pinky knowingly and deliberately submitted information to the CPS to support their prosecution against me that he knew to be misleading, false and untrue.

If the above is not cast-iron proof of inequality, discrimination and Gross Misconduct, I do not know what is. It was not just Gross Misconduct; it was also several very serious criminal offences. We covered Perverting the Course of Justice regarding the email received from Inspector Tool. This was another clear act of Perverting the Course of Justice by PC Pinky as he had fabricated evidence.

Also, the Perjury Act states, *'If any person lawfully sworn as a witness or as an interpreter in a judicial proceeding wilfully makes a statement material in that proceeding, which he knows to be false or does not believe to be true, he shall be guilty of perjury.'*

As a police officer, PC Pinky was a sworn witness. Clearly, this was confirmed in the title of one of the documents in question, which was titled, Witness Statement. This made it clear that PC Pinky not only committed an act of Perverting the Course of Justice contrary to the Criminal Justice Act but also committed an act of Perjury contrary to the Perjury Act.

Some of you may consider this next point to be a little ironic. Some of you may think it to be beyond irony. And some of you, like me, may think it to be an absolute fucking outrage. At the same time, we received an email from Inspector Tool informing us that our pleas for help to the Chief Constable and our MP, *'Could be construed as attempting to pervert the course of justice which is a criminal offence.'*

Inspector Tool and PC Pinky were blatantly committing that same offence against our family. And Perjury on top! Unbelievable.

I don't think I need to list any more points regarding Pinky's Police Report and Witness Statement, but just for good measure, referring to my interview, Pinky also stated,

'7 minutes and 40 seconds BEAN stated being a carpenter he had the appropriate tools he did not kick the fence at all, he used a crowbar to lever the panel away from the concrete that caused an absolute minimum amount of Damage. The CCTV shows otherwise.'

Bollocks. The CCTV does not show otherwise. If APC1 existed at all, it would show exactly what I say it did. I used a crowbar to lever the fence panel away from the concrete which caused an absolute minimum amount of damage. I never denied that I caused this minimal damage to the fence panel, it was impossible to remove the fence from our land without doing so, and I was entitled to remove the fence from our land.

Pinky went on, *'The CCTV is key evidence as it shows the damage being caused and is of good quality.'*

Pinky stated the CCTV was *'Key Evidence'*, yet he refused my request to see it.

The Witness Statement completed by PC Pinky stated that the CCTV footage APC1 showed,

'From 13.46.00 hours you see movement in the middle panel of the footage.'

'At 13.48.20 you see a hammer being used.'

You may well see a hammer being used (I cannot say for sure because I have never seen the footage), but you would not see a hammer being used to damage the fence, or being used inappropriately. As stated, I am a qualified carpenter, I know how to remove a fence appropriately. I do not think there will be a carpenter or police officer, other than Pinky out there who would consider using a hammer when removing a fence panel from a post to be an offence or wrong in any way.

'At 13.48.31 hours you see force being used against the middle panel causing the bottom of the panel to break.'

Using force to remove the fence panel from the post is not an offence and is completely different to,

'At 13:47 hours on the 11th September, the CCTV shows the bottom of one panel being broken by a foot from next door. It does appear that the bottom of the panel is being kicked several times before coming loose from the fence post.'

Which was what Mr Head claimed in his statement.

You have to use a certain amount of force to remove a fence panel from a post. What did Pinky think I needed to do, just walk into my front garden and kindly ask the panel, *'If it wouldn't mind removing itself from the posts without causing any damage and stacking itself neatly at the top of the Heads Garden, please.'*

I did not use excessive force to remove the panel from the post and no version of CCTV footage could show otherwise.

Even more concerning was the fact that not once in the statement by Mr Head, nor my interview under caution, nor in the entire investigation, nor any of the submissions to the CPS by Pinky, did any of them anywhere mention the Heads had erected the fence on our land without our knowledge or permission and while we were on holiday, which was a fact that everyone involved knew to be the case. None of them can claim they were not aware of this fact. I had told NP on numerous occasions that the fence was on our side of the boundary. PC Sloth had even agreed with me because he had seen the Heads erecting the fence and the Heads had even told him it was on our land. But it was never mentioned at any stage by Pinky and Perky. And I was wrongfully prosecuted because of it.

To that end, this one simple, obvious and undisputed fact that was agreed upon by all parties including NP. but was ignored and omitted from any part of the investigation and submissions to the CPS by PC Pinky and Perky, would have been clear and irrefutable evidence that I had not committed the offence. And the huge impact this matter had on my life and will continue to have until the day I die, could and should not have happened. Not only that but this fact would also confirm that Mr Head had made a false allegation against me and provided NP with a statement he knew to be false. Well, it's the Heads, so a little bit of crime didn't matter.

This was a clear and deliberate failure by Pinky and Perky to ignore and omit crucial evidence that would prove I did not commit the alleged offence so they could proceed with their agenda to cause me and my family as much pain as possible. C U Next Tuesdays.

I knew the statement of Mr Head would be untrue. What I didn't know until this time was that the Police Report and Witness Statement completed and submitted to the CPS by PC Pinky were also untrue. Now, I had all three of these documents in black and white.

As you have probably guessed. I will never let this drop until those responsible for taking away huge parts of my life are held accountable. It may sound like an exaggeration, but as far as I was concerned, I was no longer clean. I had lived a life that I was very proud of until this point, the way I lived my life was my faith, my strength. From this point on, if anyone asked me if I had ever been interviewed under caution by the police, the answer would have to be yes; have I ever been offered a Conditional Caution by the police, yes; had I ever been charged with an offence by the police, yes; had I appeared in court as the suspect for an offence, yes; had I ever been prosecuted by the CPS, yes.

To some, that may not be such a big deal, some may even consider it to be a badge of honour. But not me, my name was tarnished, and I was not the person I once was and never could be again. Once these things have happened, they can never be taken away, no matter how wrong it was or what could happen in the future. The impact this had on my physical health, made my life extremely difficult. I could not be the husband and father I wanted to be and that I once was. I couldn't look after myself let alone anyone else. But also, around this time, my mental health started to seriously deteriorate, I am not embarrassed or ashamed to admit that. There is not a soul alive on this earth that could have coped better with what we were going through than our family, both individually and collectively.

But when I looked in the mirror, I was ashamed of what I saw – not because of anything I had done wrong but because of how others wronged me.

To be clear to the readers, over ten years on, I have never seen the CCTV footage labelled as Police Exhibit APC1. Over the past ten years, I have made multiple requests to NP for them to either show me or disclose a copy of this footage to me, but every single request has been refused. At one stage, the Head of the Freedom of Information Department of NP even accused me of harassing NP for requesting a copy of this evidence. Democracy, do me a favour.

I know I have banged on about this point a bit, well, a lot, okay okay, too much. But it is so important to me. I will not rest until I have a copy of the CCTV footage labelled as Police Exhibit APC1. End of.

Mind Games

At this time, I started to develop what I can only describe as a phobia. That is probably not the right word for it, but it is the best word I can think of to describe what was happening to me.

Basically, I am six feet tall, but whenever I was out in the neighbourhood, I felt as though I was only four feet small, hence the title and cover of this book. When I passed anyone in the neighbourhood, it was like they were towering over me, pointing at me and saying things like, 'That's him, that's him, the bastard'

I have always been a keen walker and would go for a walk around the neighbourhood almost every evening for a good hour. The phobia got so bad that I couldn't even do that because it was no longer enjoyable, in fact, it was distinctly horrible. Even if I was away from the neighbourhood, it would still be the same, but not as bad. It was like everyone in the world knew who I was and thought I was a bad person, someone who harasses pensioners and a criminal. This led to a deepening sense of isolation and indeed depression.

I wish I could expand on this, but I am no expert regarding the human mind. We are all different anyway so who can really be an expert in how we think and behave? All I will say is that I find the power of the human mind to be amazing, how it can convince you that something is not the way it actually is. Due to the complexity of the mind, it is not surprising most people will suffer some sort of mental malfunction during their lifetime. Our mind is an organ just like our heart, liver or lungs, only much more complicated. But also like any other organ, it can get ill. But it can also recover with time and treatment. It may never be the same as what it was before, but it can get better.

Although our mind has infinite capabilities and can solve the most complicated of mathematical calculations, the most puzzling combinations of words or numbers, or anything for that matter. The cracking of the Enigma Code is a prime example, how did they do that? It wasn't luck, it was solely down to the power of the human mind being able to solve the almost unsolvable. However, just like our body, our mind can also be fragile and in some cases, quite dumb, sometimes it can be the simplest of things, once we know the answer, that can send our mind into a complete kerfuffle. I am going to ask you a question, be honest with yourself for a few seconds and try not to look at the answer on the next page.

Question. Which side of a rabbit has the most fur?

Answer. The outside!

Be honest, how many of you struggled with that? You may have got there in the end, but I bet for some, it was much harder than you thought. And the reason is simple, our mind is like a computer and is programmed to think logically. When we hear the word *'side'* for most people, our mind will only think of left or right and not in or out.

Our mind is the most powerful thing we will ever have in our possession and most of the time it is our greatest ally, but occasionally it can be our worst enemy.

An indication of the state of body and mind I was in at this time came on the 25th of January 2015, just two weeks after my Plea Hearing. I was at a very low ebb, lower than at any point I can remember, unsurprising to me at least. I went to bed at the end of what was always a difficult day, I put my head on my pillow the thought went through my head, *'I might not make it through this.'*

I was scared to close my eyes that night and I will never forget that feeling of total desperation and despair. Not knowing if I would wake up or not, not knowing if I wanted to wake up or not. On one hand, I wanted to wake up because I enjoyed life before the harassment started and I knew I could again when it was over, but most of all, because of the impact it would have on those I left behind who would still have to fight the harassment and injustice but with my passing on top of all that, I could not do that to them. On the other hand, I didn't want to wake up because I knew it would be a shit day, so if I didn't wake up at least it would all be over, for me at least. I am sure my wife and children must have felt the same at times, but we all kept waking up and fighting on, thankfully. What doesn't kill you makes you stronger!

Bit dramatic? Of course it is but I have got to try to sell this book somehow!

I will go into this next point in more detail in the next chapter. But to cut a long story short for a change. On the 6th of March 2015, I received a letter from the CPS Discontinuing their Prosecution against me. **I'm fucking innocent.**

Chapter Seven
The Devil Lays Within

This is going to sound strange, maybe even a little mad. Okay, I will be honest, it's fucked up but hopefully, I will be able to explain to some degree. Because of what has happened in my life and more to the point, because of the way I am, and even more to the point, because of something that happened when I was in my late teens, nothing seems to really scare or phase me. Whatever the situation, I seem to be able to stay calm and composed and think clearly and rationally, even when everyone around me is losing their heads.

Why? Because I have seen the devil. No, not literally of course, because the devil doesn't exist, but we all have an image of what the devil looks like. I have seen that image up close, almost touching distance and it was horrible. It was a situation that I was not expecting, and it was one of the worst experiences of my life. I haven't told anyone about this except my wife, partly because it sounds ridiculous and partly because of the shame

I hold for not doing something about it. It may come as a shock to those closest to me to read this. Some of you may understand, some may not. Some may not even like me for what I am about to tell. C'est la vie.

It was an incident involving my parents. It was a Friday afternoon. I came in the front door from work and could hear my parents' upstairs in what used to be a bedroom but had been converted into a dialysis room for my mum who had chronic kidney failure. I knew my mum would be dialysing as she always did on a Friday afternoon, so I thought nothing of it. Dialysis does what the kidneys should do and cleanses the blood from impurities. To do this, the blood needs to come out of the patient's veins via a series of tubes, through a purifier and back into the veins. The flow of the blood is controlled by valves on the tubes, the opening and closing of these valves has to be done in the right sequence or air can get into the tubes and then into the patient with potentially fatal consequences.

What I didn't know is that on this particular afternoon, my dad had been drinking, there was only ever a problem with my dad when he had been drinking. Unfortunately, he would go through spells of drinking three or four times a week for months on end and then he wouldn't drink for months on end. However, on this occasion, he knew he would need to help my mum dialyse that afternoon as he always did but had gone to the pub anyway. Arse!

I went into the kitchen to put my work bag away and then started to walk up the stairs. I could hear my mother's voice, and it was clear she was distressed. I still did not know that my dad had been drinking. With all the things he had done in the past, it still didn't enter my head that he would be so stupid, selfish and uncaring. I approached the top of the stairs and peered down the hall into the room where my mum and dad were. My mum was more distressed than I thought, she was in total despair and terrified, sitting in her chair bawling her eyes out begging my dad to stop.

My dad was standing over her laughing and holding one of the valves in each hand and saying to my mum, *'Which one shall I open? This one or shall I open this one?'*

My dad literally had my mum's life in his hands knowing full well that one *'wrong'* move would almost certainly kill her, but he was loving it, loving the control and power he had over my mum – just like Pinky loved the control he had over our lives. My dad was teasing my mum with her very life, shall I let you live, or shall I let you die?

Right there and then, in front of my eyes, my dad morphed into the Devil. It was the classic devil image, naked, bright red, horns, tail, the lot. In fact, it was exactly like the image of the devil that you would find on the album cover of an Iron Maiden record (if you are not too young to remember Iron Maiden, 666 The Number of the Beast and all that). I have always been a fan of Heavy Metal music and Iron Maiden was one of the most popular Heavy Metal bands at that time, so I suppose that is where the image came from. This wasn't an imagination, or an album cover though, it was real. It was happening right in front of my eyes. The devil I was seeing was living, breathing, moving and doing exactly the same as when it was my dad before he morphed.

Why I am ashamed is because even though my mum's life was in danger, I turned and walked back down the stairs. To be fair, I was young and in shock and I hadn't been trained in how to work the valves anyway. So, what use I would have been, I don't know. Well, I do know, I would have been more useful than my dad. There are no excuses for what I did, it was a case of fight, flight or freeze, and I chose to fly away like a little yellow Canary because I didn't like what I was seeing. I let the person I loved more than anyone else in my life at that time down and I will be eternally ashamed of that. I was a coward. Sorry mum, I failed you.

Although both my mum and dad have now passed on, so it doesn't make any difference now. I am sure neither of them saw me at the top of the stairs. My dad was too pissed, and my mum was too scared to notice anything or anyone else. Not immediately, but a little later in my life, because of that moment, I promised myself and my mum, even though she had passed on, that I would never again let anyone I loved down. No matter what I faced, I would not fly or freeze, I would fight with every ounce of my body until I had done my best and I could do no more.

WOW. I cannot believe I have been able to write that, but there it is. I wish I could express to you all how I feel right now, but I haven't got a clue. I have stated that I believe you have to face your demons to defeat them and kick down the door to prevent them from restricting your life. But I have not been able to do that until now, over 40 years later. It is a door that has stayed firmly locked and bolted in my head and heart for 40 years. I was and still am so ashamed that I didn't do anything to help my mum at the time of her greatest need. I swore I would never be a coward again.

That is why nothing scares me or phases me. Nothing can come close to what happened on that Friday afternoon, but I would like to firmly lock and bolt the door again, thank you very much. So, to those who know me, please don't ask me about it, you know all I can tell you. I suppose despite my principles and beliefs some things are better left locked away. Sorry, if the above upsets anyone.

So, putting that experience together with several close calls from the Grim Reaper during my life, has made me very resilient to certain situations. My family has often asked me how I manage to stay calm under pressure, how I can keep my cool when everyone around me is losing theirs and how

I can keep my temper. I think the above is a big part of the reason why. Let's face it, when you have seen the devil, there is not a lot that can phase you.

We all experience many things in the course of life, good and bad. But I think it is only a few of those things that define who we are. We all have an input to the way we want to be, but I also think that our life experience moulds us into being who we are. Life chips away at our body, mind and soul like an artist working on a sculpture, but the sculpture is never complete until life is finished with us. Then we disappear while the artist starts again on the next piece of unmoulded clay. Bloody hell, where did that come from, Eric Cantona, move over.

There were the usual acts of harassment by the Heads carrying on over the next few months as always. But I will fast forward to the next significant event, however, for the first time in a very long time it was positive. I have touched on this in the previous chapter, but I cannot wait to share the full story with you.

I noticed NP were next door at the Heads. That in itself was not unusual by now, they often popped round the Heads for a cup of tea and slice of cake!

Although I was indoors and so were the Heads, I heard Mrs Head shout as clear as day, *"That's a fucking outrage"*

Really, although she was in her detached house and I was in mine, I still heard her shout so loud it was as if she was in our kitchen. Trust me, there was no mistaking her voice. She not only looked like a witch; she sounded like one as well. It was not going to be long before I could put two and two together and learn of the reason for the shouting from next door.

The next day, I received a letter from the Crown Prosecution Service regarding their prosecution against me for the allegation of Criminal Damage. I was alone when the letter arrived and to be honest, I was worried about what the letter might say, so much so that I decided it would be best to wait until my wife came home before I opened it, just in case I had another panic attack or something like that.

I assumed it would not be good news as having good news was a distant memory. At best, I thought it would be something like the CPS informing me that the date of the trial had been put back from June and I would have to live under the stress of being on Police Bail for even longer. At worst, it may have been the CPS informing me they had managed to find further evidence or a witness that had testified that they saw me causing Criminal Damage to the fence. Although I knew if it was something like that, it would be as false as the rest of the case.

Anyway, when my wife and children returned home, I told them that I had received the letter, but I hadn't opened it. We all sat in our front room, and I opened the letter, you could cut the atmosphere with a knife, the tension on my part, at least, was immeasurable. I opened the envelope and pulled out the letter, it was a single page and folded in the usual way. I unfolded the letter and the first thing I saw in big bold letters were the words, *'Notice of Discontinuance'*

It was good news, great news, the best possible news I could have wished for. The letter was to inform me that the Crown Prosecution Service had discontinued their prosecution against me for the offence of Criminal Damage, and I would no longer be required to appear in court and all restrictions placed on me by the court were now lifted and I was, therefore, no longer on Police Bail. The letter also stated the reason for the discontinuance was due to a *'Lack of Evidence'*.

Well, there's a thing, a lack of evidence, very strange! I thought NP had the case sewn up with the CCTV footage APC1 which showed me kicking the fence panel until it came loose from the post and using a hammer to damage the fence, funny that. Lack of Evidence. Hmm!

The relief was unreal, I could breathe again. Later that evening, I went into our back garden and popped open a couple of bottles of fizz. Unfortunately, the corks accidentally went over the fence into the Heads back garden, purely by accident, of course.

The next morning, I noticed the corks had been thrown back over the fence into our garden, fair enough I suppose. They must have been so pissed off their plot had failed. I picked up the corks and have kept them as a memento of that day. I was going to say it was a memento of my victory, but there were no winners, just not as many losers as there could have been. The Heads, Pinky and Perky had lost their blatant attempts to have me convicted of an offence they all knew I did not commit. It also dawned on me what the shouting was about the previous day when NP was at the Heads. They must have visited the Heads to tell them the CPS had discontinued their prosecution against me.

I'm fucking innocent. The Head's and NP's plan to issue their *'Tit for Tat'* justice had failed. Fuck you. Fuck you all.

This event breathed even more new air into my lungs. Something to make it worth opening my eyes for in the morning and I had something to fight with. It made me realise what fighting could achieve. I also knew from that point on that I had something in my armoury that was far more powerful than anything any of my enemies could ever muster. That something can be summed up in one word, honesty.

Throughout my life and particularly, throughout the harassment, I had, along with my family, been honest. To be honest with you now, it was easy, we had nothing to be dishonest about. But this honesty had defeated dishonesty, and I found that very empowering. It has to be the case in life, truth must win over lies, honesty over dishonesty, good over evil, right over wrong and most important of all for me at least, justice over injustice. It has to be that way, if not, we are one step away from mass anarchy and the breakdown of law and order and therefore society.

I knew from this point on that I would never stop fighting these bastards until I either won or drew my last breath. I would run a million miles to avoid trouble or aggression, but sometimes you cannot run. You have to stand and fight because the consequences of running are too great.

I knew this harassment was never going to stop by itself and if we did not fight, we would never be free. *'You could pack up and move away'*, I hear you say, and yes, we could, but that would mean defeat. We would have let evil win, and it would be a regret for the rest of our lives, that was not going to happen. Anyway, who in their right mind would buy our house? Nowadays, when you sell your house, you have to disclose if you have had any issues with your neighbours. When we disclosed to any potential buyer that the man next door had assaulted both myself and my wife, I think that might put most people off just a tad!

I knew the fight would not be easy; nothing was easy. But once again, the hard choice was the right choice and the only choice.

Chapter Eight
What Doesn't Kill You Makes You Stronger

When we first met with our criminal barrister and explained our situation to her, not just the harassment by the Heads, but also the conduct of NP, she told us that the police would never do anything against the Heads because they are pensioners, and you are not. So, in their eyes, it must be your family who are harassing them, blunt but accurate. She also said there was not a criminal court in the land that would impose any form of sanction on the Heads for harassment because they were pensioners, and we were not, blunt but accurate. So, she recommended we seek the services of a civil barrister.

So, through the same Chambers, we were recommended to a civil barrister who they thought best suited to our needs. We had an initial meeting with him, and he agreed to take on our case through direct access. We tried to progress the matter by appealing to the Heads more rational side by replying to their solicitor's letter we had received some weeks prior, explaining the truth of the matter and requesting mediation with the Heads to prevent the matter from escalating further.

Unfortunately, this attempt to resolve the issues was as unsuccessful as the Restorative Justice attempt in November 2014. There was just no getting through to the Heads. They were prepared to go to the lengths of employing a firm of solicitors to threaten our family with civil action if we did not stop doing what we were not doing in the first place but would not engage in any attempts to resolve those issues. If they did not engage in any attempt to resolve the issues between us, then there was no chance that these issues were ever going to stop. What could we do?

The Heads would not even liaise with us, or our barrister and NP just made matters worse. We even thought that the Heads might be being harassed by someone else, and the Heads thought it was us, but that was blown out of the water because both the Heads and NP claimed to have evidence of our family committing these acts of harassment. It was a hopeless situation and all the time the harassment of our family did not stop. The Heads knew they could do anything they wanted to our family, and it would not be considered harassment nor any other offence by NP. Surely, it could not be the case that the Heads genuinely thought that their conduct was legitimate. Surely, they must have known it was wrong.

But no, the Heads were so delusional that the thought they could possibly be mistaken, and we were not harassing them, would not even enter their heads for a second. Surely, when the Heads made these false allegations to NP and said they had it recorded on their CCTV, but when they looked at their CCTV it didn't show what they claimed it did, they would realise they were wrong. But no, they submitted it to NP as evidence anyway, allegedly!

When you consider that there were four of the Heads living next door, surely, one of them would realise something was wrong with their thinking. Surely, they all could not have been so deluded. More to the point, you would have thought at some point, the penny would drop with NP that something was amiss. But no, it just went on and on and on and nothing we could say or do would change the path the Heads and NP had chosen to take.

One thing I have learned about NP is that once they start a ball rolling, they will not stop, they will not look back or accept they got it wrong, not until it is too late and the damage is done. Their ego will not allow them to do that, they think they are above 'ordinary' citizens, and we just have to put up with being steamrollered into submission. And if they don't get you the first time, they will come back for another go. The Police constantly tell us that they have a difficult job, and they don't always get it right but when they do get it wrong, they will own up to it, be accountable and do what is necessary to put things right.

Bollocks. The police never own up to anything they get wrong. They will only come clean if they are forced to and if they can sweep it under the carpet, they will without a care for whoever they leave devastated in their trail. That is the whole purpose of the Professional Standards Department of the police force, to defend their own.

'If you are not satisfied with the service you have received from the police force, then please complain to the Professional Standards Department (PSD) of the police force that failed you.'

Great, that will sort it. Complain to the same police force that has already failed you. Come on, what police force is going to go against its own police force? In my opinion and experience, the PSD is a complete waste of resources and should be abolished. Let's be honest, when you are dissatisfied with the service you received from the police, initially, your point of dissatisfaction will probably be dealt with by an officer who was working with the officer you are complaining about, or even in a personal relationship with that officer, maybe even living with that officer, or even dare we think, have a child with that officer. You are probably wondering what that last sentence was about. Read on my friends, all will be revealed!

Anyway, another rant over.

We knew it wouldn't be long before the Heads got up to their tricks again. Sure enough, just a couple of weeks later, Mr and Mrs Head were working on a part of the fence between the two front gardens. I put my head over the fence and asked Mr Head what he was doing. He said he was moving the fence onto his land. Firstly, by saying this, Mr Head is clearly admitting yet again that he did erect the fence on our land in both July and November 2014, something he denied in his statement.

I knew full well Mr Head was lying, there is no way on this earth the Heads would voluntarily move the fence from our land after all the trouble it had caused. I informed Mr Head that he was yet again carrying out work on our land without our knowledge or permission and I asked him to stop. It was quite ironic, that if they were attempting to remove the fence from our land in April 2015, why didn't they do that in August 2014, and all that had happened regarding the fence and boundary would have been avoided.

The Heads were pissed off because the CPS had discontinued their prosecution against me and this was their way of getting back at me as in their eyes, I had got away with it. I suppose they also thought of it as an act of defiance and to let us know they had not given up the fight. In any event, Mr Head refused to stop, and he and Mrs Head then said to me, *"We are going to phone the police."*

137

Apparently, we were later informed by another officer from NP that the Heads actually did call the police. What on earth did they tell them this time? Whatever it was, we didn't hear any more about it so I could only assume that what the Heads' told NP was too bizarre for even NP to believe. Credit where credit is due though, if the Heads had thought up something that NP couldn't use against us, it must have taken some doing. So, well done too the Heads for that!

Because of this latest incident, our barrister recommended that we send the Heads a letter informing them that due to their latest trespass onto our property without our knowledge or permission, we require them to provide a written undertaking not to do so again. We also stated that we wanted all the trespassing items removed from our land including, and in particular, the retaining wall and concrete, and they must inform us when this was going to be done.

Our barrister made it clear that there must be evidence of anything that you may later raise in court and putting it in writing was at the very least confirmation that you had attempted to sort the matter before it reached court. Apparently, most Judges do not like civil cases as they think the matter should have been resolved before it got to court and if there had been no attempt at mediation by either side, even the winner of the case would be looked at unfavourably by the Judge.

In my opinion and experience, another thing I have learned about the justice system is that Judges, Magistrates and Chairperson of a tribunal panel for example, do not like it if you represent yourself. They look upon it as if you are demeaning the legal profession in that you think you can do their job, and you are just trying to avoid paying them your money. In all honesty, I have done it both ways and I would definitely recommend having legal representation. Firstly, for the reason above and secondly, because the law is an absolute minefield. British law can be twisted and turned to suit all cases both good and bad if you can afford a good enough lawyer! Justice is for the rich, it does not work for ordinary people, innocence or guilt does not come into the equation, some of the time anyway. I have also learned that the biggest difference between a barrister and a solicitor is that a barrister is interested in upholding the law and seeking justice, and a solicitor is interested in making money, as much money as they can, no matter where it comes from – money, money and more money. One thing is for sure, you won't see many solicitors riding a bike!

The Heads had really got the bit between their teeth now. The CPS dropping the case had clearly pissed them off big time and their fixation with harassing our family was in overdrive. To help them with their burning desire to destroy our family, they once again enlisted the help of their old friend and ally PC Pinky. The Heads were not the only ones who were pissed off with the decision of the CPS, PC Pinky would prove to be as determined as the Heads to make us pay for their failure to have me successfully prosecuted.

Not only that, but due to the disclosure by the CPS at my Plea Hearing, Pinky now knew I had the evidence to prove his misconduct and criminality and he was determined to yet again abuse his position as a police officer to try and intimidate me into not doing anything with this evidence by causing further distress to our family. This time, however, his target wasn't me, it was our daughter. He really was a maggot of a man.

Since late 2014, one of the things Mrs Head would do to harass us was to stand at her front downstairs window and every time a member of our family went past their house, she would stick two fingers up, do the *'wanker'* sign with her hand and mouth the words '*fuck off*', very mature. We had reported this to NP several times, but because PC Pinky had been appointed our '*Sole Point of Contact*' (SPOC) with NP, everything that we reported would be sent to him to deal with. But because he disliked our family, he repeatedly failed to do anything about it. He wouldn't even acknowledge our reports most of the time and when he did, he would tell us he would only log it, but he never did and what would be the point of that anyway? To be honest, if that was the worst thing the Heads were doing, we would settle for that all day long, so we had given up reporting this behaviour. Alas, it wasn't to be the worst thing the Heads would do, it never was.

It was nearing the end of March 2015, and our daughter and her friend left our house to go to the local shop. When they passed the Heads house, as usual Mrs Head was at the window, our daughter saw Mrs Head there and looked away but her friend then said to her, "*Your neighbour has just made the wanker sign to me and told me to fuck off.*"

Our daughter told her friend that Mrs Head always did that when we walked past and asked her friend to just carry on walking. When they returned from the shop, our daughter and her friend told my wife what had happened. Our daughter's friend said she was shocked and annoyed at this behaviour. My wife decided to call NP via 101 to report this incident as this behaviour was clearly escalating again, and visitors to our property were now being subjected to harassment. What this did mean, however, was that we now had a witness to the behaviour of Mrs Head. I assume this latest report had also gone straight to PC Pinky as yet again nothing was done about it.

Mrs Head had also sussed out the time our daughter would return home from work and every night Mrs Head would be waiting at her window for our daughter to turn the corner in her car and she would do the usual hand gestures and mouthing off. Due to the previous incident with our daughter's friend, we also reported this to NP as things were starting to get out of control because Mrs Head was not getting the reaction she wanted. Again, nothing was done about it.

Guess Who's Back, Back Again!

That evening, our daughter received a phone call from, guess who, PC Pinky. He said the two reported incidents had been passed on to him as he was still our SOPC. The attitude of Pinky was the usual mix of intimidation, inequality and bullshit. He told our daughter that he believed when our daughter turned the corner in her car, it was our daughter who was harassing Mrs Head by making hand gestures and mouthing off at Mrs Head and that it was our daughter's friend who had given the wanker sign to Mrs Head a few days previous. He would not listen to our daughter and 'advised' her to stop driving past the Heads house. As our daughter was again feeling distressed at the actions of the Heads and the attitude of Pinky, she asked Pinky not to call her in the future but to call her parents if he needed to contact her. Pinky refused this request and told our daughter that she was 22 years of age and that it would be against the Data Protection Act if he were to contact her parents.

Absolute Bollocks. Our daughter was a vulnerable adult. It was a failure in his duty of care for a vulnerable adult for Pinky to refuse her request not to contact her directly. He knew our daughter was vulnerable and he used this vulnerability to cause her distress and as a way to get to our family. Maggot.

To be clear. How could our daughter be harassing Mrs Head unless Mrs Head was standing at her window when our daughter came home from work? If she was standing at her window when our daughter came home, why? If she was standing at her window when our daughter returned home from work and our daughter was harassing her, why keep standing there every night?

Furthermore, at this stage, Mrs Head had not made an allegation of any sort to NP against our daughter, so why would Pinky decide it was our daughter and her friend who were harassing Mrs Head? This is another clear example of Pinky abusing his position as a Police Officer to incriminate a member of our family. Maggot. Also, it clearly states in the Prevention of Harassment Act,

'That if a person undertakes a Course of Conduct that causes another to change their normal day to day activities or routine, for example, their route home from work, that will be considered as an act of Harassment.'

For Pinky to advise our daughter to change her normal route home from work, he is acknowledging that Mrs Head was causing her harassment.

Knowing Pinky as I unfortunately do, it must have cut deep for his plan to punish me for removing the fence had failed. Someone who has NPD does not take kindly for their plan to control someone failing. But now he had the opportunity for revenge and to inflict further misery on our family. He wasn't going to pass up that opportunity come hell or high water.

Because of this phone call to our daughter by PC Pinky, we again contacted NP and informed them that we were not happy with the conduct of PC Pinky as he was again not treating our family with equality and we did not want him to deal with this matter or to continue as our SPOC as we had no trust or confidence in his ability to be impartial in his dealings with our family and the Heads.

I think this phone call may have touched a nerve with NP as the next we heard about these incidents was a couple of days later when we were visited by two officers of NP who we had not encountered previously. It was like chalk and cheese, these two officers were excellent, totally the opposite of Pinky and Perky and the majority of the officers from NP that we had encountered up to this point.

They listened to what we were saying, which was refreshing, and they were also very understanding and supportive of the situation being faced, not just by our daughter, but our whole family. That was all it needed from the start, someone from NP to actually listen to what we were saying instead of just disbelieving our every word and ignoring the irrefutable evidence. If they had just done those two things, all of this would not have happened. But it was too late for that now, NP had decided on the path this was going to follow and there was nothing we could say or do that would change their course. What happened next categorically confirmed that to be the case.

These officers took a detailed statement from our daughter regarding the two incidents we had reported which included the impact the extended issues were having on her. The senior of the two officers, I will call him PC Good, there and then contacted our daughter's friend who had witnessed the conduct of Mrs Head and arranged an appointment with her that evening to take a statement.

We expressed our concerns to these officers regarding PC Pinky not treating this family with equality or respect and that the history of the issues with the Heads and his involvement in those issues were not allowing him to look at the problems objectively or with equality. We again asked PC Good if it would be possible to change our SPOC to a different Officer as we had lost all trust in PC Pinky.

Before PC Good left our house, he voluntarily made several commitments to this family, including speaking to his Sergeant regarding changing our SPOC, arranging an appointment to see his Inspector regarding the ongoing issues with the Heads and arranging for a Victim Impact Statement to be taken from all members of our family. He also said he would be prepared to write a statement to our civil barrister regarding the obvious impact this was having on our family and that we could call him at any time. He also said he would call back later that evening with some leaflets regarding support for witnesses/victims of crime. True to his word, he did.

PC Good gave us his word that he would do all he could to help our family. We all felt reassured and confident that finally something would be done to stop the constant harassment by the Heads and the blatant and disgraceful conduct by the many officers of NP up to this point. We did not ask him to make these commitments, and he need not have offered to make them. The fact that he did so off his own bat, meant so much to us all. The relief we felt was immeasurable. At last, at long last.

By the time these officers left our house, for the first time in a very long time, we felt as though we had actually been listened to and that a member of NP had actually understood and believed what we were saying, and we had been treated with respect and equality. It was like a breath of fresh air and a huge weight had been lifted from our shoulders. At last, something was going to be done about the harassment, and it would stop. We could live a normal life again. However, our optimism was soon extinguished, by guess who, you guessed it, PC Pinky.

The day after this visit and whilst our daughter was at work, she received another phone call from PC Pinky, even though she requested him not to contact her directly. Pinky informed her that he had spoken with PC Good and told him that he was going to take the statement from our daughter's friend later that day as he was our SPOC. Need I say, this call took the wind completely out of our sails. Not only had Pinky contacted our daughter directly, but he had also made sure PC Good was off the case so to speak. We knew from that point on that we would not be treated with equality regarding the recent behaviour of Mrs Head but just how far Pinky would go to once again satisfy his desire to hurt our family was still shocking. All our optimism and hope that our nightmare might soon be coming to an end was gone and we were back in hell, well and truly.

A few days later, our daughter was returning home from work as usual. On the way home, she passed a neighbour who lived just a couple of doors away. This neighbour was one of the few who were still talking to us. So, our daughter stopped and asked her if she wanted a lift home. Our daughter warned the neighbour to be aware of Mrs Head being at her window and making hand gestures and mouthing off when she turned the corner into our road. The neighbour thought our daughter was joking so she was shocked to see that when our daughter turned the corner, sure enough, Mrs Head was standing at her window and as soon as Mrs Head saw our daughter's car, she started the usual hand gestures and mouthing *'fuck off'* to her.

Mrs Head was so obsessed with what she was doing that she obviously didn't even notice there was a passenger in the car. Our daughter had to give way to a car coming the other way, so the neighbour had time to record Mrs Heads behaviour on her mobile phone. The neighbour was stunned at what she had seen and told our daughter that she couldn't believe someone of that age would act in such a way.

143

However, this was gold dust to ourselves, or so we thought. Not only had another person witnessed the behaviour of Mrs Head, but she was also able to record Mrs Head in the act. Cast iron evidence, you would think! Little did we know this cast iron evidence of Mrs Head harassing our daughter would be turned and twisted by PC's Pinky and Perky and used as evidence by these two arseholes to incriminate our daughter. Maggots.

Our daughter and the neighbour came in the front door and told us what had just happened. I phoned PC Good straight away. Although he had just finished duty, he was still very supportive and said he would generate a couple of emails. I also mentioned that PC Pinky had informed us he was going to take the statement from our daughter's friend and we again expressed our concerns to PC Good that Pinky would not be objective in doing this.

The very next day, our daughter received yet another phone call from Pinky and again while she was at work. But this time the news was very distressing for her. Pinky informed our daughter that there had been an allegation of a Public Order Offence made against her by Mrs Head, and she was now the subject of an investigation by NP. Pinky went on to inform our daughter that the allegation was that when our daughter turned the corner into our road, our daughter made hand gestures and mouthed *'fuck off'* at Mrs Head as she was standing at her front downstairs window.

All in all, this was the eighth false allegation made to NP by the Heads and yet another reversal of the truth. It also confirmed that Mrs Head was so obsessed with what she was doing that she had not noticed the neighbour in the car. Not that she needed to bother anyway, the Heads knew they could say whatever they wanted to Pinky and Perky and that would be that. The Beans were guilty of whatever the Heads had alleged, job done.

Our daughter tried to explain to Pinky that there was a passenger in the car with her and that it was yet another false allegation and yet another example of the reversal of the truth and continual Harassment we were suffering. But as usual, Pinky would not listen and ended the call. Maggot.

This phone call caused our daughter great distress. As previously stated, Pinky had been asked not to contact our daughter directly due to the impact it was having on her physical and in particular, mental well-being.

144

Not only did Pinky ignore this request, but he also called her with such distressing news, whilst she was at work. Maggot.

To be clear. We had reported the conduct of Mrs Head to NP on three separate occasions over the past ten days and NP had not informed Mrs Head of these allegations, allegedly! Yet, Mrs Head made one allegation against our daughter, that was in any event false, and our daughter was informed by Pinky within hours of the allegation being made against her that she was now the subject of a police investigation. Worst of all, as Pinky was our SPOC, it would be Pinky himself who would be conducting the investigation.

In my opinion, PC Pinky had contacted Mrs Head regarding the three allegations that had been made against her, and they had together concocted the making of this false allegation against our daughter as a smoke screen to the truth. But as Mrs Head was not aware of the witness who had recorded her conduct, she was not able to tell Pinky of this. The blind leading the blind. I am not sure if maggots have eyes anyway!

As soon as Pinky ended the call, our daughter phoned the wife. She was very distressed and asked us if we could go to her place of work. Although of course, we did not know why, because of the past few days it did not take a genius to work out what the problem was. We left the house and started to drive to our daughter's place of work which was only five minutes away. Before we were halfway there, we received a call from Pinky who informed us he had just spoken with our daughter, and she was very upset and was calling us out of COURTESY!

Bollocks. Pinky wasn't calling us out of courtesy. He hadn't shown our family an ounce of courtesy since the day he became involved with us. He was only phoning us because he knew he had fucked up and was trying to make out he actually cared. Maggot.

I asked Pinky why our daughter would be so upset. Pinky replied,

"Due to the Data Protection Act, I cannot tell you!"

More bollocks, if he couldn't tell us what the problem was, why did he phone us.

Bang goes the courtesy straight away.

We were still on the phone to Pinky when we arrived at our daughter's place of work. Our daughter told us the reason for the call from Pinky was to inform her that an allegation had been made against her by Mrs Head. I told Pinky that Mrs Head had only made the allegation against our daughter because we had made allegations against her, and it was yet another false allegation and an attempt by Mrs Head to intimidate a witness. What I didn't realise at that stage is that, in my opinion, Pinky already knew that because he had put Mrs Head up to it. Maggot.

Pinky told us that it could not be considered as intimidating a witness as Mrs Head was not aware she was under investigation. Thank you for confirming that PC Pinky, as stated, our daughter was informed by Pinky of the allegation by Mrs Head and placed under investigation within hours of the allegation being made against her. But, as confirmed by Pinky himself, Mrs Head wasn't even aware of the allegations made against her a whole ten days after the first allegation was made. That could only have been because Pinky was our SPOC and he had not informed Mrs Head of the allegations against her because he was not treating both sides with equality, clearly.

Pinky also told us that when an allegation has been made to the police, they are dutybound to investigate. Thanks again for confirming that, it's a shame the shoe never fitted the other foot when we made allegations against the Heads, allegations that were fully witnessed and evidenced and NP failed and even refused to record, let alone investigate. Assault on my wife, screws through the fence, Malicious Communications via Social Media, Criminal Damage, False Allegations to the Police, Theft, Perverting the Course of Justice, Perjury, Intimidating a Witness, I could go on, **ALL NOT INVESTIGATED**

That evening, we received an unexpected visit from PC Pinky. He said he wanted to discuss the current situation. Initially, I thought he had visited because he knew he had fucked up and was shitting himself, but then I realised the real reason for his visit. Pinky wanted to see first-hand the impact his conduct was having on our family. He informed us he had just visited the Heads and they had agreed to mediation, I asked, why now? The Heads had refused mediation at every opportunity so far, what changed their minds?

I also said to Pinky. On the same day the Heads agreed to mediation, they made yet another false allegation against our daughter. That doesn't sound like people who want to meditate to me.

However, as there was no other way of moving forward and as reasonable people and despite everything that had happened to our family, we agreed to mediation. We told Pinky, if he could arrange it, we would take part in it. I knew it was just a ruse; the Heads would never take part in mediation; they were too far gone for that.

Pinky made clear his annoyance with us because we had spoken to other officers and in particular, PC Good regarding the recent problems. It appeared obvious to me that PC Pinky did not like PC Good at all. Pinky said that he had to go out of his way to find PC Good to tell him not to take a statement from our daughter's friend as he was going to do it. As with Inspector Tool, Pinky did not want any other officers getting involved because his misconduct would be exposed. Maggot.

In any event, it wasn't our fault, we had no choice but to contact Force Control to report these incidents as Pinky would not even log them or respond to us when we contacted him. The only reason he had done something this time was because other officers had become involved. In any event, it was Force Control who arranged for these other two officers to call. Before these latest incidents and despite reporting several incidents to him as we had been told to do, we had received no reply or contact of any sort from Pinky for at least four months. Anyway, we are free to contact anyone we choose regarding whatever we choose and why should Pinky be annoyed with us if we do? Exactly the same as Inspector Tool who threatened our family with Perverting the Course of Justice if we tried to seek help from our MP and senior officers of NP.

Pinky also informed us that he had spoken with his Sergeant regarding our request for him to be replaced as our SPOC but that it would not be happening and he and PC Perky would remain the investigating officers. Surprise, surprise.

Again, we are entitled to make NP aware of our dissatisfaction with the conduct of any police officer or member of staff, whether they are our SPOC or not. All police forces encourage the public to report their dissatisfaction with the police, to the police. Not to help or to investigate the dissatisfaction of course, but to pretend they care and do what is necessary to cover up the actions of the officer that led to the dissatisfaction in the first place and then rub the complainant's nose in the dirt.

This was a perfectly reasonable request under the circumstances and for NP to insist Pinky remained as our SPOC was a failure of their duty of care to allow the public to believe all parties are being treated with equality. The truth is, Pinky was desperate not to let another officer get involved because if they did and it was by some miracle, a decent officer, like PC Good, the misconduct of Pinky and Perky would be exposed.

Because Pinky would remain as our SPOC, we knew the investigation into the recent incidents would not be handled impartially, objectively or with any sort of equality.

So, there we were, it didn't take long for Pinky to poke his nose in and undo all the good work done by PC Good, one day in fact. We are sure PC Good left this house with the best of intentions, but we were also sure the odds of him being allowed to fulfil his promises to our family were very short. NP will simply not allow him to do what he said he would because of the fallout it would have for his fellow officers, the thin blue line as they call it. Well, let me tell you, the thin blue line is not thin at all, it is as thick as a solicitor's wallet.

Due to our concerns regarding Pinky remaining as our SPOC and conducting the investigation into the recent incidents, I phoned PC Good and asked if we could speak to him to express our concerns regarding the investigation by Pinky and Perky and that we knew this investigation would lead to our family being screwed over again. PC Good explained he was dealing with an incident and would call me back when he was free.

True to his word, again, he did. He said that he had finished duty, apologised for not being able to call back earlier and asked if he could call me the next day to arrange a visit. The next day, PC Good did not call, in fact, we received no further contact from PC Good whatsoever. Despite many attempts to contact him by phone and email, we did not receive a reply. We were correct in our concerns that PC Good would not be allowed to do what he said he would. NP had clearly got to him to the point he would not even serve us the courtesy of a reply to our messages. The thin blue line strikes again, they look after our own, always, no matter what.

Although disappointing, it was expected, so I do not blame PC Good for what he failed to do. I am sure the pressure placed upon him by other officers not to break the thin blue line was massive. I would not expect him to risk his career for our family, why should he? We are nothing to him, just another family who he knew were being destroyed by our next-door neighbours and discriminated against by his fellow officers.

Just a couple of days after agreeing to the latest attempt at mediation, we received another letter from the Heads solicitor containing yet more false allegations and requests that we stop doing what we were not doing in the first place. And threatened us with further legal action if we did not agree in writing to their demands.

What sort of mediation is that? Do what we tell you or we will sue you. Thanks, but no thanks.

After a couple of days had passed, our daughter received an email from PC Perky which stated he had been asked to arrange for our daughter to attend the Police Station to provide a taped interview under caution regarding the allegation of a Public Order Offence made by Mrs Head. I advised our daughter that due to my experience of being interviewed under caution by Pinky and Perky, it would not be good for her to attend the police station to be interviewed. I knew Pinky and Perky would try to make the ordeal as difficult as possible and I did not trust them to be in a room with our daughter.

So, our daughter replied to Perky and explained that due to her anxiety, she would not be able to attend the Police station. Our daughter made it clear that she was not refusing to be interviewed under caution as this could lead to her arrest, but that she did not feel able to be interviewed at the police station. To our surprise, Perky agreed to the interview being conducted at our house as long as our daughter could arrange for an appropriate adult to accompany her. Although we were relieved at hearing this, particularly as we were not expecting it, it does prove that Pinky and Perky were aware that our daughter was a vulnerable adult, and Pinky should have respected her earlier request for him not to contact her directly.

On the face of it, it may seem that Perky was being considerate, which he was, of course, and I am grateful for that, truly. But it also showed how desperate NP was to interview our daughter. However, the consideration was short-lived as Perky then told our daughter that due to previous incidents, no family member would be allowed to accompany her at the interview, or even to be in an adjacent room. To this day, I do not know why that was, I have found no guidelines or recommendations that do not allow a vulnerable adult to be accompanied by either of their parents at a voluntary interview, our daughter was not a criminal, and we were not criminals, but we were all being treated like we were. And we were being discriminated against by Pinky and Perky just because we were the Bean family. That discrimination would become even more evident in due course.

Neither myself nor my wife or daughter had committed any offences, so why should we not be allowed to accompany our daughter to this interview? What did Pinky and Perky think we might do? My wife and I are the two best people on the planet to be able to care for our daughter's needs during what will be a very traumatic experience for her. Why did Pinky and Perky insist that my wife and I not be present at this interview? What were they up to? We didn't have long to wait to find out.

Maggot Man

I hope you are sitting down for this bit. We received a visit from the neighbour that our daughter had picked up on her way home from work and who had witnessed and recorded the conduct of Mrs Head at her window. The neighbour appeared to be very pale and nervous, something was clearly troubling her.

She sat down and said, *"I don't know quite how to tell you this but I have just met with PC Pinky in the car park of the local Pub to sign my witness statement and to give him a copy of the footage from my phone, as Pinky passed me the pen to sign the statement, he said to me, **"You do realise you may be charged with entrapment so you may want to consider how involved you want to get in this"***

The neighbour then said that before coming to our house she went to another neighbour across the street to tell him what had happened and to ask what he thought of it. The neighbour told her that he thought it was a clear attempt to intimidate her into not signing her statement. I asked the neighbour what she thought about it and she said she thought the same and that was why she went to speak with the neighbour before coming to see us, to see if she was right to think that way.

We were as shocked as our neighbour at what she told us. It confirmed to us the lengths PC Pinky was prepared to go to cause pain and misery to our family. To go so far as to blatantly attempt to intimidate a witness into not signing a statement is an act of Gross Misconduct and indeed another clear act of Perverting the Course of Justice. Maggot.

That was why Pinky arranged for our neighbour to meet him in the car park of the local pub and not at the Police Station, so he could intimidate her without any witnesses. Clearly, it is not best practice for a police officer to arrange to meet a witness in the car park of the local pub to sign their statement. Pinky clearly had an ulterior motive for doing this, and this motive was witness intimidation. Maggot.

Hearing this was really scary and worrying. If Pinky would do something like this, what else would he be prepared to do? It is one thing being harassed by your next-door neighbour but being subjected to this level of misconduct and indeed criminality by an officer of NP that was our Sole Point of Contact, is a whole different ball game.

The police force is the only place you can go when you are the victim of crime. So, when they are so hellbent on hurting you, even more so than the offenders, what can you do, where can you go? The simple answer is nowhere. All we could do was never give up and basically, just hold on and hope things change.

But things never changed. As stated, once the police have decided on a course. They will never change that course; they will never accept responsibility unless they are forced to. It is in my opinion, the same for all government bodies, whether it is the police, the military, local authorities, the NHS or government-run or owned businesses. They will never change course or back down unless they are forced to.

In the present day, as I am writing this, it is the beginning of January 2024 and the Post Office Scandal is all over the news, and rightly so. What happened to the hundreds and hundreds of Sub postmasters who were wrongly accused, prosecuted, convicted and imprisoned for theft, false accounting and fraud and forced to pay back thousands of pounds they did not steal and did not have is an outrage and an embarrassment to the so-called justice system of this country.

I am in no way comparing what happened to our family to what happened to these poor people. Although I was wrongfully prosecuted, I was not convicted. I cannot begin to imagine the impact these convictions had on these poor people. What happened to them should not happen in a democracy. The Government only allows us to think we are living in a democracy when it suits them, to keep us calm and in line, but when something like this scandal blows up, the victims are treated with total contempt by the powers that be.

Their motto, deny any responsibility, accountability or liability, DENY, DENY, DENY. To make my point, while these Sub postmasters were losing everything they had ever worked for including their liberty and were so desperate and in the depths of total despair that some of them were even attempting to take their own lives – the powers that be awarded the Head of the Post Office the CBE. How sick is that!

The powers that be were clearly rewarding the Head of the Post Office for denying these people justice. They were basically saying to the victims of the biggest miscarriage of justice ever seen in this country,

'Well done Head of the Post Office, you have allowed these people to be treated with such a level of inequality and injustice that some of them have tried to kill themselves. Great job, as a reward for this excellent work, you are now a Commander of the Order of the British Empire.'

To be clear, other than a Knighthood or Damehood, the CBE is the highest award that can be awarded by the powers that be.

The fundamental difference between a democracy and a dictatorship is that all citizens are to be treated with equality and entitled to justice, no one is above the law. Would any of these Sub postmasters think they have been treated with equality or entitled to justice, have any of them been awarded the CBE?

Democracy, do me a favour!

Anyway, another rant over and back to the story.

Our daughter was subsequently interviewed under caution by Pinky and Perky at our home address. As well as the appropriate adult who we had asked to attend to support our daughter who was of course a close friend, we had also asked our civil barrister to attend the interview as her legal representative. Pinky and Perky were not happy that our daughter would have a legal representative present. They had not offered our daughter her right to a Duty Solicitor so they thought she would be a sitting duck for what they were about to do.

As I was supposedly not allowed to be present or in an adjacent room, I went for a walk. I knew our daughter would be well cared for and I could not bear to be banished to my bedroom like a naughty little schoolboy. I think in hindsight; it was a blessing that I wasn't allowed to be in the same room as my daughter for this interview. I think the appropriate adult and our barrister handled it much better than I could.

When the interview had finished, my wife gave me a call and I returned home. Pinky and Perky were still there when I returned. I was told by our daughter that Pinky and Perky had used the recording of the behaviour of Mrs Head taken by the witness when she was a passenger in our daughter's car, as evidence to support the allegation made by Mrs Head against our daughter.

Pinky and Perky stated that our daughter was stationary outside of the Heads house for six seconds and during these six seconds, our daughter had made hand gestures at Mrs Head. We had watched this footage several times before the interview, and it did not show our daughter making any hand gestures at Mrs Head whatsoever. Pinky and Perky were claiming and insisting the footage showed our daughter committing a criminal act when it did nothing of the sort. Sound familiar? APC1!

Our daughter explained to Pinky and Perky the reason she was stationary for six seconds was that when she turned the corner into our road, she had to give way to a car coming in the opposite direction as there was a car parked on her side of the road, that was why she was stationary for six seconds because she was obeying the Highway Code. She was actually abiding by the law, not breaking the law, this can clearly be seen to be the case in the footage. Our barrister then told us that Pinky and Perky asked our daughter at least six times,

"Why were you stationary in your car for six seconds?"

Even though our daughter explained the reason why they just kept on asking her until our barrister intervened and told Pinky and Perky that our daughter had answered their question and they needed to move on. Our barrister also told Pinky and Perky that in his experience they seem to have interviewed our daughter in a very biased way in favour of Mrs Head and he hoped the interview of Mrs Head would be conducted similarly.

Well, well, well, we needn't have worried about that one as Mrs Head was never interviewed at all during this investigation by Pinky and Perky. How can anyone consider it to be equality that our daughter was put through the trauma of providing NP with an interview under caution for one allegation made against her by Mrs Head with no witnesses and no evidence, but despite three separate allegations, three statements, two witnesses and video evidence taken by one of the witnesses which clearly showed the conduct of Mrs Head, she was not interviewed under caution, or at all.

In my opinion, if Mrs Head was not interviewed and no action was ever taken against her regarding our allegations, and I know that to be the case, it must also be the case that she was never under investigation by NP regarding this matter at any stage. To be clear, a 'voluntary interview', as well as giving the police the opportunity to interview the suspect regarding the allegations made against them, also provides the suspect with the opportunity to provide a defence to those same allegations. Both points would be considered as 'Key Evidence', so without either of these points of 'Key Evidence' how could Pinky and Perky have investigated Mrs Head?

It is clear inequality and discrimination and gross misconduct of the highest order, again, but why? We had never given Pinky and Perky or any member of NP any reason to treat our family in such a disgraceful and discriminative way. We were not criminals or bad people and had never been in trouble with the police. Why did they take the path that they did? I suppose that is something we will never know. Even if NP were to provide me with a reason, I wouldn't be able to believe them. In any event, they would only provide a reason if they thought it would help them out of their hole.

That was the final straw as far as Pinky was concerned. He can pick on me all he likes, but just like most men, when you pick on my wife or children you cross the line. Pinky had now started a war, a no-retreat, no-surrender, last-man-standing, fight-to-the-finish, backs-to-the-wall war. I will pursue this man until he has nothing left. I will take everything from him – his job, his career, his future, his money, his possessions, his relationships, every-thing. The only thing I will leave him with is his life and he can decide what he does with that. I do not care how long it takes me.

If you live in hell long enough, you get the devil in you!

Chapter Nine
I Feel a Change

Due to our concern regarding the conduct of PC Pinky and the fact he was and would continue to be our SPOC and we had absolutely no confidence in him. I emailed the Chief Constable of NP regarding the refusal by NP of our request to replace Pinky as our SPOC. Surprise, surprise, we did not get a reply from the Chief Constable.

So, this was the situation we were facing with Numpty Police. We have a SPOC, PC Pinky, who will not treat our family with any form of equality, he was also hell-bent on inflicting as much suffering as possible on our shoulders. He would not respond to any of our reports of incidents to him, but when the Heads contacted him, he was all guns blazing, but senior officers of Pinky would not listen to our concerns regarding the conduct of Pinky and refused to replace him as our SPOC.

The situation was as pathetic as it was hopeless. We could see no end to our nightmare. The Heads knew they could do whatever they wanted to our family, and nothing would ever happen to them. Our SPOC was as bent as they come and clearly on a mission to destroy our family. I would like to think it was because of the failure of his plot to have me prosecuted for removing the fence but of course, that was not the case as his discrimination had started way before that, from the moment we came into contact with him in fact.

Shortly after this, our daughter received notification from PC Pinky that No Further

Action would be taken against her for the allegation of a Public Order Offence made by

Mrs Head. Of course, this was an immense relief to us all but in particular our daughter. However, as mentioned, despite three separate reported incidents, three witnesses, three witness statements and the video evidence, PC Pinky also informed our daughter that No Further Action would be taken against Mrs Head. This was because Pinky and Perky had clearly not even investigated the allegations we had made against Mrs Head.

So, yet again, the Heads had got away Scott-free with their harassment, not just the Public Order Offences committed by Mrs Head but also the false allegation of a Public Order Offence made by Mrs Head to PC Pinky against our daughter.

The Heads must have been on cloud nine. All they had to do was contact PC Pinky and he would do whatever they said, and Pinky would do whatever he wanted. It was like another double act, but again, not funny. We had provided NP with witnesses and evidence of the conduct of Mrs Head, and not only had Pinky failed to use this evidence against Mrs Head, but he twisted this evidence to incriminate our daughter. Pinky didn't even interview Mrs Head, so how could he have ever intended to take any action against her? Another nailed-on stitch-up.

Not surprisingly, shortly after receiving this news, we were informed by Pinky that the Heads had now changed their minds and were not prepared to engage in the mediation process that was proposed by PC Pinky just a week or so previous. Of course, the Heads were never going to engage in this process, they were deluded in their fixation with harassing our family and now they had further confirmation from NP that they could continue with that harassment without fear of any repercussions or consequences for them. Why would the Heads engage in mediation which would prove they were the ones at fault when they were having the time of their lives in destroying ours? What incentive did they have to mediate a solution to end something they wanted to continue and were at fault for?

In any event, the proposed mediation just like the false allegation against our daughter was just another smokescreen concocted by the Heads and Pinky to allow the Heads not just to escape any sanction for the conduct of Mrs Head but to provide Pinky with the opportunity to lay the blame for the harassment at the feet of our daughter. Maggot.

As I have no physical evidence that Mrs Head and Pinky conspired regarding the allegation and mediation, I have to stress this is just my opinion. Whether they conspired or not, the above events did happen, and I can prove that.

ABBA

It was early May 2015 by this time, and due to this latest failure by NP to protect our family from the harassment and the fact we had not received a reply to the letter sent to the Heads requesting a written undertaking from them that they would not trespass onto our property again. Our civil barrister advised us that in his opinion, and ours, NP was never going to help our family and therefore the only way to try to get the harassment to stop, would be to take civil action against the Heads. He also advised that we need to enlist the services of a solicitor as he would not be able to do all of what was required regarding civil litigation.

Taking on board the advice of our barrister, our case was taken on by a local firm of solicitors and we were allocated a solicitor they deemed most suited to our needs. We met with our solicitor at our home address to discuss the problems with our next-door neighbours and for him to see for himself the issues surrounding the fence and to assess the likely cost of civil litigation to the point of resolution. Our solicitor advised that his first act should be for him to write to the Head's solicitors. The letter contained the basis for our complaint regarding the boundary dispute and the harassment.

With this letter, we enclosed a copy of the detailed plans of the properties that had been drawn up by the Chartered Surveyors and used as evidence in the criminal prosecution against me. These plans included the correct line of the boundary between the two properties and the line of the fence between the two properties that the Heads erected in July 2014, and highlighting where the fence deviated from the line of the boundary onto our land. The plans also detailed the encroachment of the retaining wall that was erected in February 2013. We also enclosed a statement from the previous owners of the Heads house which they had kindly agreed to provide, confirming the true line of the boundary had not changed.

We also included several examples of harassment committed against this family by the Heads, over the past three years. They included the assault by Mr Head on my wife, the verbal abuse from Mrs Head towards my wife, daughter and visitors, including the four-year-old child in June 2014, the assault by Mr Head on me in July 2014, the false allegation made to NP that our son had harassed the Heads in June 2014. and the involvement of the brother and sister-in-law of Mrs Head (The Hopertys) in the harassment of our family. The letter informed the Head's solicitors they had 14 days to agree to an undertaking that they would stop the harassment and remove the fence and retaining wall they had erected on our land.

You can bet your bottom dollar the Heads had not been honest and open with their solicitors regarding the harassment. This letter would at least give the Head's solicitors an idea of the real situation and who was at fault for the harassment. Not that this firm of solicitors would care about that.

Our solicitor also advised us of the likely cost of the civil litigation against the Heads would be (are you sitting down again), between £60,000 and £70,000. Bloody hell, our chins hit the floor. We did not expect it to be in this region, maybe it was naive of us having never been involved in civil litigation before, we did not have this sort of money, and not many people do. It added more pressure and stress on our shoulders. We already had to cope with the nonstop harassment and the failure of NP to protect us from this criminality, and now we had the financial burden of trying to find up to £70,000. Life was so tough.

Desperate Times

We also knew that things were never going to improve with NP while Pinky remained as our SPOC. So, rather than continuing with the softly, softly approach which we had tried but had failed. I contacted the Sergeant of PC Pinky and told him that we had requested that Pinky be replaced as our SPOC but this request had been refused so we now want no further contact with him. It is alien to me to be forceful, particularly to the police, but we had no choice. We had to get Pinky off our backs so he could not cause any more harm to our family. We also hoped at least this might make NP think a little harder about our concerns regarding PC Pinky.

Our solicitor received an email from the Head's solicitors informing him they are currently not instructed to act on behalf of the Heads, but they have sent the letter directly to them. Maybe the letter from our solicitor did have an impact after all. Although throughout the litigation, this would become yet another familiar pattern, the Heads would enlist a firm of solicitors to represent them who would write a letter to our solicitor making all sorts of crazy claims and stating the Heads wanted to mediate a solution, only for our solicitor to reply to the letter to be told by that firm of solicitors they no longer represented the Heads.

This is another reason why I think the Heads had done something like this before, they always seemed to be one step ahead. They knew how to play everyone involved including their solicitors and of course, NP. They knew exactly what to do and when to do it. All I can think of is that the Heads underestimated our family and maybe they thought we would break like their previous victims, perhaps.

It was at this time that I contacted the CPS regarding the CCTV footage APC1 that should have been disclosed to me at my Plea Hearing in January 2015, to ask why they had not replied to my six written requests for this evidence to be disclosed, we were now in June 2015. As stated earlier, I was told by the CPS they had destroyed the evidence. They advised me that I should contact NP to request a copy of the footage from them. Of course, if NP were ever going to disclose this evidence to me, I wouldn't need to contact the CPS to request a copy of it. Neither the CPS nor NP can disclose something that doesn't exist, or that incriminates a police officer!

But, as advised by the CPS, I contacted NP to request a copy of the footage. I was informed by the Police Information Department of NP that the only way the Police would release a copy of the footage was via a Court Order as part of a civil case. Total rubbish, this footage was used by NP as 'Key Evidence' to offer me a Conditional Caution and then allegedly submitted to the CPS and used as 'Key Evidence' to prosecute me. I was entitled to a copy of this footage then and I was entitled to a copy of this footage now. I did not need a Court Order or take civil action against NP to gain access to this alleged evidence.

The Case Handler from the CPS also informed me that I should make a complaint regarding their failure to disclose this footage at my Plea Hearing and also the fact that they had failed to respond to my six written requests for this footage to be disclosed to me. To be clear, if the CPS had acknowledged any of my requests for this evidence, clearly, they would not have been able to destroy it. The CPS deliberately ignored these requests to be able to deny my right to this 'Key Evidence'.

Taking the advice of the Case Handler, I made a complaint to the CPS regarding the above. To be fair, I received a response from the Deputy Chief Prosecutor of the CPS upholding all aspects of my complaint, offering an apology for the stress it would have caused and stating they will adopt any learning that can be made to prevent this from happening again.

Mmm, they should have stopped after the apology, that would have been enough; to say they will learn lessons from their failure is absolute bollocks, in my opinion. If they were ever going to learn lessons from their failure we wouldn't be where we are. This is clearly not the first and definitely not the last time the CPS has or will fail to disclose evidence to a suspect. The CPS are just like the police and the rest of the criminal justice system, their failures and conduct are systemic and engrained, that is just how it works and has worked for decades. It will not change unless it is made to change. The criminal justice system is so resistant to change because it is just the way they like it. Thank you very much. They can do what they want, when they want and to whoever they want, why would they want to change that.

Well, well, well, unbeknown to us, a neighbour who lived just across the road, worked in the Planning Department at the Borough Council. We were talking to her, and she told us that a while ago, two police officers had visited the council offices and requested to see the Plans of ours and the Heads properties. The timing of their visit coincided with the investigation by Pinky and Perky into the allegation of Criminal Damage made against me by Mr Head for removing the fence panels. This would mean that Pinky and Perky did investigate the line of the boundary between the two properties, but when these investigations confirmed the fence was on our land and would therefore confirm I had not committed the offence, they completely ignored and omitted this crucial evidence from any part of their investigation and submissions to the CPS.

This was further confirmation that I should never have been interviewed under caution, offered a conditional caution, charged with the offence of Criminal Damage and prosecuted by the CPS. I should not have endured the immense stress this caused, including two suspected heart attacks, being admitted to hospital, the horrendous nightmare and the huge impact this had and will always have on my life.

I have made several references to PC Pinky being a maggot of a man. That was wrong of me, it was unnecessary, uncalled for and extremely derogatory and if in the writing of this book I have caused any offence, I sincerely and unreservedly apologise, to maggots.

It really was non-stop; it had been for the past two years and would continue to be for years to come. Although we did not talk much to our other neighbours about it, word was beginning to spread, largely down to the fact the Heads were spreading all sorts of malicious rumours around the neighbourhood. Rumours that incited several more of our neighbours to join in with the harassment of our family, harassment that would have just as big an impact on all of us, but in particular myself. From now on, I would be a particular target of the harassers, not the only target, the harassers would still target other members of the family but as was often the case in this sort of crime, the harassers target another member of the family or group to get to their main target.

Another neighbour that I had seen many times before as he would often pass our house when walking his dog and we would say hello and maybe have a little chat. This particular day, I was in our front garden when he came past with his dog, he asked me how things were with our next-door neighbours. To be honest, I didn't know that he knew anything about it. He went on to tell me that he had seen Mr Head being restrained in the street by the police officers on the night Mr Head had assaulted me. He said he was shocked at the behaviour of Mr Head and the level of aggression being displayed and the police officers were really struggling to restrain him. I told the neighbour that just before that Mr Head had assaulted me with a piece of wood when I was in my back garden. The neighbour was not aware of this and was even more shocked, he said to me that he couldn't imagine what it must be like living next door to someone like that. He was right, you cannot imagine what it was like! The neighbour gave me his best wishes and said if there was anything he could do to help to please let him know.

This also made me think back to the assault. During our conversations with PC Sloth after the assault, he said he could not consider any other action than offering Mr Head a Conditional Caution as there were no witnesses to the conduct of Mr Head. Of course, this chat with our neighbour confirmed that not to be the case. The fact is, that NP did not conduct any investigations or enquiries to determine if there were any witnesses.

Desperate Measures

I had not heard back from NP when I informed them we did not want any further contact from PC Pinky. I, therefore, discussed with our barrister the option of making a complaint against him. Our barrister advised that it was the right thing to do but also advised that making a complaint against a police officer often makes the situation worse as the police will discriminate against our family for making a complaint against one of their own. I took this on board but decided that doing the right thing was the only option. We had to get PC Pinky out of our lives, I also thought things couldn't possibly get any worse for our family, could they?

So, in early July 2015, I submitted a complaint to Numpty Police regarding the conduct of PC's Pinky and Perky. If I knew then what I know now, would I have still made the complaint? Yes, yes, I would, but I would have been better prepared for what was to follow.

My barrister was, of course, spot on. The level of discrimination and misconduct we were to suffer from this point on was horrendous. Unbelievable in fact. Complaining to the police about the police is never going to work. But just how the police treat people who dare to complain about them is a complete disgrace, and again, what happened to our family is a drop in the ocean compared to what happens to some, some people who make a complaint against the police end up in prison. Their lives are completely ruined, some even worse. I often wonder how many innocent people are locked up in our prisons. I bet if we knew the true figure, it would be shocking. There is always going to be the odd miscarriage of justice, but just how many innocent people have been framed or set up by the police because they made a complaint or had evidence of police misconduct, I dread to think. Of course, this might still happen to me now I have made a complaint and written a book, who knows! However, I was in fight mode. No more being intimidated by the police, been there, done that, got the kicks in the head to prove it.

I also contacted NP and informed them that the statement by Mr Head that had been disclosed to me at my Plea Hearing as evidence to support the prosecution for Criminal Damage against me was knowingly and deliberately false. I was contacted by a Sergeant from NP regarding this, I will call her PS Quack, and she informed me that she had tasked PC Perky to investigate my concerns.

Hang on a minute, that would mean PS Quack had tasked the joint investigating officer, along with PC Pinky, of the allegation by Mr Head to which the statement I have alleged to be false and untrue relates. Also, I had recently submitted a complaint against Pinky and Perky. Conflict of Interests, maybe!

I expressed my concern to PS Quack that as PC Perky was the joint investigating officer to which this allegation relates, for PC Perky to be tasked with investigating this matter would create a clear conflict of interest. In effect, Perky would be investigating himself as well as his joint investigating officer, PC Pinky, and of course Mr Head. However, Quack insisted Perky was the appropriate officer and that he would conduct the investigation. I made it absolutely clear to PS Quack that I was not happy with that as it was completely inappropriate and went against all correct investigative procedures.

I would later find out why Quack was so insistent Perky conducted this investigation. But if that wasn't bad enough, I would later find out how wrong it was for Quack to have any involvement in this matter whatsoever. Even more important and relevant, was that she would be the officer who would make the determination of the investigation by Perky. I could tell you now what I was to later find out, but I hope you don't mind hanging on for a bit. I'm sure it will be worth the wait.

About a month later, I received a Report from PS Quack regarding my allegation to NP that the statement of Mr Head was knowingly false and untrue. Not surprisingly, the report was a complete exoneration of Mr Head, therefore putting both Pinky and Perky as well as Mr Head in the clear as far as any wrongdoing in the investigation was concerned. Quack stated in her report,

'There is no evidence that he (Mr Head) has intentionally told any lies or given any false facts and the evidence provided by Mr Bean (me) is "hearsay evidence" and is not possible to be proved to court. Based on the above investigation and conclusion no further action will be taken in this matter.'
Absolute bollocks.

There is not one part of my evidence that is *'hearsay'*. The evidence was all there in black and white in the statement of Mr Head and the fence and concrete retaining wall were still in place which was cast iron evidence that the content of the statement by Mr Head was knowingly and deliberately false. For Quack to state that my evidence was in any way *'hearsay'* was extremely derogatory and completely wrong.

As if PS Quack could not be any more derogatory, she also stated in her report that the statement of Mr Head was based on his,

'Assumption, presumption and interpretation.'

Any evidential statement used in any criminal proceedings as *'Key Evidence'* must be based on the evidence that was available and could be supported and confirmed as fact. There was a clue in the name, an evidential statement. You cannot use a statement that was based on *'assumption, presumption and interpretation'* as *'Key Evidence'* to prosecute someone, particularly when this statement was the only statement. It was not as if it was one of several witness statements and could be considered as supporting evidence. And the only other piece of *'Key Evidence'* was the CCTV footage APC1, which Pinky refused to let me see and the CPS failed to disclose.

This is further undeniable and irrefutable evidence that this prosecution against me should never have happened, and it was a complete and utter set-up by the Heads, Pinky and Perky from the start. And now PS Quack had joined in with this gross misconduct and criminality. I wonder why that was!

I know I have banged on about this point probably too much, but it is one of the most significant points not just for this book or with regards to the harassment and police misconduct and criminality, but one of the most significant events in my entire life. The impact this had on me has been mentioned earlier, but words do not do it justice. I hope you understand but I don't blame you if you don't.

PS Quack also stated, *'PC Perky has conducted a thorough investigation into the points you raise.'*

Bollocks.

Clearly, my concern that PC Perky was not the appropriate officer to conduct this investigation was fully justified.

I cannot wait to get to the point where I tell you what I was to learn regarding PC Quack! See if you can guess what it is before I mention it! Good luck and don't be afraid to let your imagination run wild.

Towards the end of August, our solicitor received a letter from a different firm of solicitors informing him they had been instructed to act on behalf of the Heads. The letter stated that the Heads denied trespass and that we had not shown any adequate evidence they had trespassed onto our land!

Urr, the Chartered Surveyors Plans maybe! For the Heads to go to the lengths of employing a second firm of solicitors to inform us they disputed the fact the fence was on our land, which was something they admitted to NP at the time they erected the fence, was absolutely crazy. Also worryingly, it confirmed that this matter was never going to be resolved mutually, with this letter the Heads had confirmed they were not interested in a resolution but were intent on fighting to the bitter end. Even though they must have known they were in the wrong, they knew the fence was on our land, so why fight a battle you know you cannot win? It doesn't make any sense; it didn't make sense then and it still does not make sense now and I guess it never will. The letter also stated that the Heads denied they were harassing our family, and it was our family who were harassing them, but they did not want to particularise their claims.

Bollocks. They did not want to particularise their claims because there was nothing to particularise, because we had not harassed them. Surely, their solicitors can see that. As far as I am aware, any reputable solicitor should always act in the best interests of their clients, including informing them when they are on a loser. Apparently not, unless this new firm of solicitors is as disreputable as the last.

The letter is complete nonsense, the Heads have clearly been as dishonest with this new firm of solicitors as they had with their previous, that comes as no surprise as the Heads are incapable of telling the truth.

The letter proposed a cross undertaking that both parties refrain from harassing each other. Our solicitor advised that this was a common and manipulative method used by less ethical solicitors to try to get our family to admit we had harassed the Heads by making an undertaking not to harass them. This could then be used as evidence that we had admitted we had harassed them or why else would we have signed an agreement not to. Our solicitor advised us to resist this as we have simply not harassed the Heads, and we did not need to agree not to do something that we had never done.

Finally, and after all that was contained in the letter, it stated that the Heads would be prepared to mediate this dispute and asked for us to confirm whether this would be something we would be prepared to consider.

Fuck sake, not again, the Heads did exactly the same with their previous solicitors and with NP. They instructed them to act on their behalf and the first thing they did was tell their solicitor they wanted to try and mediate a solution in an attempt to make their solicitor think they were reasonable people and the victims.

Our solicitor again said this was a common course of action. A firm of solicitors would write a letter that was intimidating and threatening and then offer a way out in the form of some sort of resolution. Basically, the side that was in the wrong would attempt to bully the victims into providing the wrongdoers with a way out.

That said, we felt it was an opportunity to at least progress matters. If we could make the Head's solicitors aware of the truth, they may encourage the Heads to be serious about mediation. We had nothing to lose, so we agreed. Our solicitor replied to this letter stating that we agreed in principle to mediation and set out some proposals as a starting point.

At the beginning of September 2015, we met with the officer from the Professional Standards Department (PSD) of NP who had been tasked with investigating my complaint against Pinky and Perky. He requested we provide him with a statement concerning our allegations and he would tweak it if necessary. Tweak if necessary, totally change to suit their purpose of protecting their own more like.

Making a complaint against the police is a big undertaking, our barrister made us fully aware of that. It was not something we did on a whim; it was something we were forced to do out of desperation. We had no experience of the procedure, how to word statements or how to exhibit evidence for example, rather than helping us to do this, NP used our naivety against us, of course, we were none the wiser back then and had no idea what NP was up to. We stupidly thought the PSD of NP would treat us with equality and respect and would want to see misconduct exposed and bent officers held to account. What an idiot, what was I thinking?

It's obvious when you think about it, that these officers would not behave the way they did if they ever thought they would be held accountable. They knew if anyone complained about them it would be dealt with by their colleagues and they would have their back, obviously. If I knew then what I know now!

No Escape

The next event was not necessarily an act of harassment but was quite shocking and difficult for our family to accept or fathom. One of the neighbours that were still speaking to us, called around to tell us that Mr Head had become a member of our Parish Council.

Excuse me, but how can a man who had assaulted both his next-door neighbours, received a Conditional Caution for Common Assault for one of those assaults and be a suspect in an investigation by NP regarding his family's harassment of his next-door neighbours, become a Parish Councillor. Not just a Parish Councilor but a Parish Councilor for the Parish in which he and we lived.

To become a Parish Councillor, you have to be nominated and elected by the Committee. I wonder if Mr Head declared on his nomination form or even mentioned to the Committee that he had a Conditional Caution for Common Assault against his nextdoor neighbour and was a suspect in a criminal investigation for the harassment of the entire family who lived next door! Perhaps not, I think. Or maybe he did, maybe the Parish Council were fully aware of the situation, maybe Mr Head had friends on the Parish Council!! Remember that, friends on the Parish Council!!

It may not seem like a big deal to anyone other than us, but to us it was huge. Obviously, the situation with the harassment by the Heads and the conduct of NP had made us feel very vulnerable. For Mr Head to become a Parish Councillor meant to us at least, that he was now in a position of power in the community. There was no way in the world someone like Mr Head should be allowed to become a Parish Councillor and there is no way in the world someone like Mr Head would become a Parish Councillor to help the people of the Parish. He clearly could not care less about anyone, and he clearly had an ulterior motive. Whether that was to make us feel even more vulnerable, isolated and intimidated or to make it look as though he was a pillar of the Community. Whatever the reason, it had a huge impact on our family.

Around the same time, our daughter was at her place of work in the Pet Shop Department of a local Garden Centre when the husband of Little Head, Sponger, entered the pet shop where our daughter was on the till. It appears Sponger was the carer for a disabled person. They hadn't noticed each other until Sponger walked past the till and said hello to our daughter. They looked at each other and, of course, instantly recognised who the other was. Sponger was fully aware of the situation with the rest of the Head family as he was one of them and lived next door with them. Even though he had clearly recognised our daughter, he continued to walk around the pet shop for a few minutes before leaving without further incident, which was fine, just a coincidence.

Unfortunately, this now meant the Heads knew where our daughter worked, and they did not waste any time in using this knowledge to harass our daughter at her place of work as well as at home. There really was no escape for our family, particularly our daughter. The harassment of our daughter at her place of work by Sponger and the Hopertys that was to follow, coupled with the incitement of many of our neighbours to not only stop talking to us but just like NP, to actively join in with the harassment, was causing a net to close ever tighter around us. More like a python than a net, slowly but surely, squeezing the very breath from our lungs, crushing our soul, spirit and will to live. Drip, drip, drip.

Chapter Ten
In the Trenches

Workplace Woes

I cannot properly explain the feeling of being the victim of harassment as I have nothing to compare it to. I have never experienced anything like it in my life that was even similar. Only others who have suffered the same experience could truly understand. We had lost control of our lives, what happened in our lives depended on the actions of the harassers and NP, and we had no say, no voice and no hope. What power did the Heads have that made not only some of our neighbours who we had known for years but also NP turn against us, what hold did they have?

The power of lies that was what. A liar is worse than a thief as the saying goes and the Heads were not just liars, they were pathological liars in that they must have believed at least some of the lies they were telling. They must have genuinely believed that we were harassing them when we were not, and they were not harassing us when they were.

We are not just talking about an individual though, but a whole family. How could all four of them believe their own lies? You would have thought that at some point one of them would have come to their senses. For example, if Mr and Mrs Head were pathological, you would have thought that their son would have realised this and said to his parents, *'Hang on a minute, mum and dad, I think you have got this wrong and you are going to get us all into a whole load of trouble if you do not stop.'*

Particularly, when the Heads started to get solicitors involved, but no, they all just kept on lying, not just to our neighbours and NP but even to their own friends, relatives and solicitors.

Just a few days after Sponger had recognised our daughter at her place of work, surprise, surprise, Mr and Mrs Hoperty visited not just the Garden Centre but the Pet Shop Department. Mr Hoperty spent several minutes in

170

the Pet Shop repeatedly glaring at our daughter before leaving without buying anything. Clearly, the only reason Mr Hoperty visited the Pet Shop was because he now knew our daughter worked there.

Just a week later, Mr and Mrs Hoperty were again in the Pet Shop. This time our daughter managed to see them before they saw her as she was returning to the Pet Shop from her break, so she waited for them to leave before returning to work.

It can be no coincidence that these visits had happened within the two weeks since the visit by Sponger. Our daughter had worked at the Garden Centre for several years before this time and she had never seen any member of the Head family or their relatives in the Garden Centre before Sponger's visit. If that had been the end of it, we could have dealt with that. In any event, there was nothing to stop the Heads or anyone else visiting the Garden Centre. Trying to get NP to see these visits were clearly an attempt to harass our daughter at her place of work, we knew would be a waste of time.

However, as always, that was not to be the end of it, not by a long chalk. You had probably guessed that anyway, or maybe not. Even when the harassment was at its worst, we always felt as though the latest act of harassment would be the last act of harassment. We would think, that's got to be it now, they must stop now, what else can they do? But, of course, it never stops, that is why it is harassment, it never stops. I knew deep down and had told NP on many occasions, the harassment will never stop unless it is made to stop, until measures are put in place to make it impossible for the Heads to continue their harassment. If the Heads could harass, they would harass. They were deluded and dangerous, there was clearly no lengths they wouldn't go to. Nothing would be too severe, too irrational, too dangerous. Nothing was off the table as far as they were concerned.

Just a week after this second visit by Mr and Mrs Hoperty, our daughter was working in the Pet Shop of the Garden Centre as usual. Sponger again entered the Pet Shop, and he again seemed to be the carer for a disabled person. Sponger spent several minutes in the Pet Shop constantly glaring at our daughter. After Sponger had been in the Pet Shop for several minutes, our daughter managed to record Sponger glaring at her on her phone, this recording lasted for three seconds and clearly showed Sponger glaring at our daughter.

Our daughter was in the Pet Shop on her own, so she couldn't leave the till unattended or report the presence of Sponger to her work colleagues. She was basically trapped in the Pet Shop, not that Sponger would have known that to be fair. After a few minutes, Sponger left the Pet Shop without further incident and our daughter felt relieved that he had gone. Just another visit by a member of the Head family to her place of work to harass her and that was the end of it. It was just something else we had to get used to, just another way the Heads and their relatives had found to harass our family whether we were at home or away, but that was the end of it. Oh no it wasn't, but this was no pantomime, not by a country mile.

Later that afternoon, the Garden Centre Manager received a phone call from a man making a complaint that earlier that day he had visited the Garden Centre and was constantly stared at by the girl on the till in the Pet Shop (our daughter) and it made him feel uncomfortable. Also, that this girl was using her mobile phone to record the disabled person he was caring for.

The man refused to give his name but said he would be making a statement to his manager who would be in touch. This man was, of course Sponger, and, of course, Sponger would have known at this stage the girl he was complaining about was our daughter. C U Next Tuesday.

It gets worse. The next day, the owner of the Garden Centre received an email from the manager of Sponger making a formal complaint against our daughter that when Sponger had visited the Garden Centre the previous day, our daughter had harassed him and used her mobile phone to take recordings of the disabled person that he was the carer for at the time of his visit. Sick bastard.

I absolutely guarantee you; our daughter did not take any recordings of a disabled person. As stated, the recording lasted for three seconds, and you couldn't even see the disabled person in the recording. Clearly, if Sponger wasn't glaring at our daughter, he would not have seen her using her phone.

Sponger knew our daughter worked in the Pet Shop Department of the Garden

Centre as he had seen her there before. He did not need to visit the Garden Centre; he certainly did not need to visit the Pet Shop Department, and he certainly did not need to spend several minutes wandering around the Pet Shop if he felt uncomfortable and harassed.

Since Sponger discovered where our daughter worked this was the fourth visit in less than a month by the Heads and their relatives the Hopertys. Before that first visit, in the years that our daughter had worked there, she had never seen any member of the Head family anywhere in the Garden Centre, let alone in the Pet Shop. It was a blatant act of Harassment and Stalking. If you are in any doubt, look on the Government Legislation website and the CPS Guidelines for Prosecutors at the Prevention of Harassment Act. Under the law set out in these documents, you cannot have a clearer act of Harassment and Stalking than what Sponger and the Hopertys were doing to our daughter.

Sponger knew exactly what he was doing and that his visit would cause our daughter fear, alarm and distress. But to then make a formal complaint against our daughter to his manager, who in turn made a formal complaint to our daughter's employer, was evil.

This visit was planned, deliberate and calculated. I can just see the Heads sitting in their front room hatching their little plan like witches around a cauldron,

'Oh, I tell you what Sponger, why don't you visit the Pet Shop tomorrow where the girl next door works.'

'Yea, I will, what a great idea, then I will make a complaint against her that she harassed me, that should really wind-up next door, how funny.' Total fucking arseholes.

Our daughter was still very concerned about the threat made by the Heads to attack her if they saw her. Now the Heads knew where she worked and had made it obvious, they would use this knowledge to their advantage. This latest incident had a very big and immediate impact on her. Our daughter said that if any member of the Head family visited her place of work again, she would leave, and who could blame her. If it was not bad enough being harassed in our home and neighbourhood, it was now happening to our daughter at her place of work, there was no escape. The Heads claimed they wanted to mediate a solution but continue to harass, it was a ridiculous situation, and it had got to stop.

The Garden Centre did what they could to help our daughter feel as safe and protected as they could. They provided her with a Walkie Talkie and told her that if she was to see any member of the Head family anywhere in the Garden Centre, she should report it to other staff members and leave the shop floor immediately. She, and we were very grateful for their care and understanding. Thank you.

This latest visit and complaint by Sponger were a clear and deliberate attempt to harass our daughter while she was at work. Could anyone possibly disagree? Oh yes, Numpty Police, of course! No, really, they did disagree, totally!

The harassment was clearly escalating yet again and if past experience was anything to go by, if something wasn't done to stop it, it would continue to escalate until the Heads were satisfied they had got what they wanted, whatever it was. To force our daughter to leave her job, perhaps!

Due to the clear escalation again, we reported this latest incident to NP, not out of choice but out of desperation, again. What would the next visit to the Pet Shop bring? Would it be another member of the Head family visiting the Garden Centre to carry out their threat to attack our daughter? Would they manage to incite one of their friends to attack her? Would they even pay someone to do it? It may sound far-fetched, but I tell you, nothing was out of the question.

That is one of the main reasons people harass others, to cause that fear of never knowing what is going to happen, never knowing if you are safe. And the Heads had got this down to a tee, with the help of NP of course. We were very concerned and indeed scared that our daughter was in danger while she was at work. The Heads were clearly dangerous, aggressive, violent and deluded people. When our daughter was away from the house, we were unable to protect her. Mr Head had already proven that he did not have a second thought about assaulting a woman. All in all, not a good mix, I am sure you will agree. How our daughter must have felt I cannot imagine.

Thanks for That

When we reported the incident to NP, we made it absolutely clear that we had submitted a complaint against PC Pinky which was being investigated and that we did not want him to have any involvement in this matter whatsoever. The next we heard about this from NP was that the investigation had been completed, and the report had been forwarded to PS Quack for her to make a determination. Remember PS Quack? She was the officer who created the clear conflict of interests by tasking PC Perky to investigate my allegation to NP that the statement of Mr Head was false and untrue, which she somehow determined was not the case.

A while later, we received an email from PS Quack containing her determination regarding the attendance of Sponger at our daughter's place of work and the subsequent complaint to our daughter's employer.

PS Quack started her email by addressing me as Dear Mr Head!

Not a good start but completely accidental, I am sure!

Anyway, it went downhill from there. I won't bore you with the whole content of the determination as that might be deemed as babbling and I don't want to babble. The wife and kids are always telling me I babble but I don't think I do. I mean, I don't go over the same thing time after time or say the same thing over and over. I think I get straight to the point and move on, perhaps. So, to prove them wrong I will not babble, I will not repeat myself or say the same thing in a slightly different way, now that would be babbling, and I do not babble. Do you think I babble because I don't think I do? Am I babbling, maybe they have a point!

PS Quack stated, *'I am satisfied that no offences have taken place and Mr Sponger did not deliberately harass your daughter and is a case of 'he says she says.'*

Fuck off, you condescending twat. There was nothing about this matter that was *'he says, she says'*. Sponger attended our daughter's place of work, FACT. NP had the three second recording of Sponger staring at our daughter, FACT. NP had the letter sent to our daughter's employer making a formal complaint against her, FACT. How the hell was any of that *'he says, she says.'*

Quack went on to say that Sponger,

'Admits to attending the Pet Shop and spending several minutes wandering around the Pet Shop, he admits to staring at your daughter and to making the complaint to the Garden Centre Manager and then to his Manager. But he says it was because your daughter was filming the disabled person he was caring for and felt it

175

was inappropriate for her to do this. Neither party made any comment or approached each other. This does not constitute harassment or intimidation.'

Fuck off, you condescending twat. Sponger clearly made far more than a comment by telephoning the Garden Centre Manager making a complaint against our daughter and then making a complaint to his manager.

Considering the situation regarding the Head family and that NP was aware of the *'neighbour dispute'* as NP preferred to call it, including the assaults against me and my wife, the threat to attack our daughter, and the fact Sponger knew our daughter worked in the Pet Shop, according to the Prevention of Harassment Act, the actions of Sponger constitute a clear *'course of conduct'* for the offences of both Harassment and Stalking. Whatever defence Sponger may give for his actions, he clearly admitted to the offence, but Quack still concluded it was all okay.

Quack also stated in her correspondence that as part of the investigation she had spoken with the manager of the Garden Centre where our daughter worked. But when our daughter asked her manager if he had spoken to the police about the incident, he told her he had not spoken to any police officer whatsoever. Funny that.

So, not only had Quack arrived at a totally ridiculous and unacceptable determination regarding the incident, but she has also lied to us regarding her investigation, and we would later prove that to be the case, and we would later find out why. PS Quack finishes her email by stating,

'The investigating officer for professional standards has also been copied in on this response so he is aware of the current situation'

Why would PS Quack state this? I will tell you why, but not yet.

We absolutely could not believe the content of this email. To be clear, Sponger had discovered where our daughter worked. Over the next three weeks, there had been multiple visits by Sponger and the Heads relatives the Hopertys, having never been noticed in the Garden Centre before in the years that our daughter had worked there. On the last visit, Sponger attended the Pet Shop of the Garden Centre when he did not need to and had no obligation to and in full knowledge that our daughter worked there. He then spent several minutes in the Pet Shop constantly glaring at our daughter who was on the till, even though he said he felt uncomfortable and harassed. So why didn't he leave?

He then left the Garden Centre, phoned the Garden Centre Manager, and made a complaint against our daughter that she was staring at him and recording images of disabled people on her phone. He then made a formal complaint to his manager that our daughter harassed him and was taking recordings of a disabled person on her phone. His manager then contacted the owner of the Garden Centre, our daughter's employer, making a formal complaint against our daughter for harassing a member of his staff and recording images of a disabled person.

PS Quack concluded this conduct did not amount to any offences and did not constitute an act of Harassment or Intimidation.

So now, our daughter couldn't escape the harassment and did not feel safe even when she was at work. Thanks for that PS Quack.

I do not like to be derogatory, especially towards women, but I will make an exception on this occasion. What an absolute fucking bitch.

It was inconceivable given the history and the fact that Quack was fully aware of this history, that she or any police officer could genuinely come to this conclusion. There must be a reason for her blatant discrimination and dereliction of duty. I know what that reason is, but I am not telling you, yet! Hold on, not long to wait.

This meant that the Heads had yet again got away with their blatant harassment of our family, they must have thought there was nothing they could not do to us. No matter what it was they choose to do, they would not be held accountable. There was only one way this was going to go, and it would not be good, for anyone. Thanks again, Quack.

It was my firm belief by this time that NP must be in on it, they must be working with the Heads. For the Heads to do something like the above, they must have known before the event that NP would do nothing about it. I suspect it wasn't just the Heads and Hopertys sitting around the cauldron!

I have always thought the Hopertys had more to do with things than would appear. It was just a gut feeling I had that either one or maybe both had some sort of power or influence. I suspect they are or have been involved in the justice system, either with the police or I just have this feeling it has more to do with the courts. Maybe one of them was a Judge, Magistrate, Usher or maybe worked in the court system as a secretary for instance. I am probably completely wrong, but it is a strong feeling that I have had from the very start. It's a shame I cannot use their real name then someone might be able to tell me if I am correct, or not.

Our solicitor received a letter from the Head's solicitor in response to our proposals for mediation.

The letter stated, 'Following the offer of mediation made by ourselves and the obvious time and expense in replying to this offer with our proposals, the Heads have now decided mediation is not an option as the likely cost of mediation cannot be justified.'

Same old, same old. Anyway, this sentence does not make any sense to me, it is clearly contradictory. The sentence clearly stated that the Heads replied to themselves with their own proposals to their own offer of mediation. This was no surprise; we knew the Heads were not and never would be serious about mediation. If they had been, we wouldn't be where we were as there had already been several attempts at mediation which the Heads had either refused to take part in or used and manipulated to avoid any consequences for their harassment. All in all, this latest false offer of mediation was an absolute disgrace. Yet again the Heads have exploited the opportunity to resolve the issues through mediation to harass this family further. This time, we had the financial consequences of having our solicitor deal with this matter and at a cost of £250 per hour plus VAT, nothing comes cheap, especially when it comes to civil litigation! C U Next Tuesdays.

Arsehole, Arsewipe.

Due to our ever increasingly desperate situation, we contacted the senior officer of PS Quack, Inspector Arsewipe, that is not his real name by the way, to request an appointment with him to discuss the ongoing situation.

Arsewipe was what I would call a career cop; all he was interested in was climbing the ladder as fast as he could, and he did not care who he trod on to get there. You know the sort of person, young, arrogant and ignorant, typical copper you might say. He agreed to this meeting and said PS Quack would be in touch to arrange this as she was now our Sole Point of Contact to replace PC Pinky as we had made a complaint against him. You may want to remember that,

Inspector Arsewipe confirmed **PS Quack** was now our **SPOC** to replace **PC Pinky** because we had made a complaint against him.

That may be a bit of a clue as to what we would discover about PS Quack. Not long to go before all is revealed. Don't skip any pages to find out what it is, will you?

Before being told this by Arsewipe we had no idea Quack was now our SPOC, you would have thought that at some point during the contact we had with her, she would have mentioned it. Maybe when she was assigned as our SPOC might have been a good time. Could she be hiding something?

It was mid-November 2015 by now and we met with PS Quack and Inspector Arsewipe at our home address. This meeting was recorded on the Body Cam of Quack of which I have a copy so I can confirm what I write.

Before we could sit down around the table in our dining room, and before Quack turned on her Body Cam, Inspector Arsewipe said,

"If you want to make allegations of harassment against your neighbours, you may find yourself being investigated for the same offence as these things have a habit of backfiring." Clearly inappropriate and clearly an attempt to intimidate us into not making any allegations against the Heads, not the best way to start the meeting I thought. I suppose it's the only way the police know, intimidate and threaten those who they perceive to be the weakest link and make the victims feel as though they are the villains. NP was fully aware of the level of aggression displayed by the Heads on several occasions, not just towards our family but towards the police as well. So, it would be much easier for the police to pick on us rather than the Heads regardless of who was at fault.

I told Arsewipe that in the interests of equality, we were open to any investigation NP wanted to conduct into any allegations the Heads wanted to make against this family. Given the way NP had treated us so far, that was probably a bit rash, but I knew we had done nothing wrong and thought we had nothing to fear. I knew that if the Heads did make any allegations against us, they would be false, and we would be able to prove they were false.

I also wanted Arsewipe to know we were not afraid or intimidated by him. We were in the trenches, and we had to fire back when under attack. I think it may have worked as he definitely changed his tune so to speak. He then went on to say that NP would not be able to put anything in place to protect this family as the Heads had not been convicted of any offences. Bollocks, although he already knew, I informed Arsewipe that Mr Head had a Conditional Caution for Common Assault, so did that not count as an offence? Arsewipe did not answer. Prick!

Could this have been because the Conditional Caution issued to Mr Head for his assault against me had been rescinded by NP?

The meeting lasted for almost two hours and a lot of points were discussed at that time, too many to detail all of them in this book, you would die of boredom I would think. It was basically a Merry-go-Round; we would tell them what had happened, and they would come up with some bullshit reason why they believed it was not an offence and did not amount to harassment. It was more like having a meeting with a pair of defence lawyers for the Heads than a couple of supposedly impartial police officers. I knew it would be a waste of time judging by the comment by Arsewipe at the very start of the meeting.

However, one point that was discussed in detail was the biased investigation and determination by PS Quack into the incident when Sponger attended our daughter's place of work just a month earlier. We made it absolutely clear to both officers that we regarded this incident as very serious as it clearly marked an escalation in the harassment. Both officers disagreed that this was the case!

In the letter we received from Quack regarding the investigation, she made several claims that we knew were false. She claimed to have spoken to the manager of the Garden Centre as part of her investigation, we knew this to be untrue. She claimed to have visited the Garden Centre and viewed the CCTV footage of the incident, we also know this to be untrue. Also, why she had only investigated lines of enquiries that would provide Sponger with a defence to the incident and ignored everything that could possibly be used against Sponger, such as the CCTV footage from the Garden Centre and the letter sent to our daughter's employer by Spongers manager.

It was eventually acknowledged by Arsewipe that PS Quack not only failed to conduct a reasonable and proportionate investigation, but she failed to investigate with any sort of equality and impartiality. It was also acknowledged that Quack deliberately misled us regarding her investigation by claiming to have investigated lines of enquiry that she had to admit at this meeting, she had not done.

Why would she do that? She must have known we would find out about these false claims as our daughter still worked at the Garden Centre with the people Quack falsely claimed to have spoken with and viewed the CCTV footage with.

Arsewipe and Quack also brought up the matter of our complaint against PC's Pinky and Perky which was ongoing. Get this, Arsewipe informed us that there may be a conflict of interest between the investigation into the harassment and the investigation into our complaint being live at the same time, so our complaint may have to be put on hold. So, there was a conflict of interest when it suited NP, but not when we raised concerns regarding officers investigating themselves and their colleagues. Little did we know at this time, that there was a much more pressing reason why NP did not want the investigation into our complaint against **Pinky** and Perky to be progressed.

You may want to remember this. At this meeting, we discussed the complaint we had made against **PCs Pinky** and Perky with Inspector Arsewipe and **PS Quack.** Have I put the names of PC Pinky and PS Quack in bold print, I wonder why I have done that! Surely, you have guessed by now.

As stated, I have a recording of this meeting and I am sure anyone who knows anything about police misconduct would have a field day with this footage alone, especially with what I was about to discover and the real reason NP wanted to put our complaint against Pinky and Perky on hold.

At the end of the meeting, Inspector Arsewipe said he would order a review of the determination by PS Quack regarding the attendance of Sponger at our daughter's place of work to be carried out by a senior officer.

Really! What's the point of that? A senior officer was never going to go against their fellow officer in favour of us. At least this showed Inspector

Arsewipe who was Quack's senior officer, had no choice but to accept the original investigation and determination by Quack was floored.

Arsewipe asked us to provide PS Quack with a list of witnesses to the entire harassment by the Heads and their associates and he would order an investigation into the harassment issues and task an officer to conduct a full, thorough and impartial evidence-gathering exercise to include speaking with and taking statements from these witnesses. Oo, very posh words for

'We are going to screw you into the dirt for daring to challenge our authority and expose our wrongdoing'

To be fair, we did feel a little more optimistic following this meeting. Surely, now NP had seen the light, and we would be treated with fairness from now on. However, we didn't know what these two officers knew.

The hardest thing I have ever tried to do in my life is to try to be something I am not;

I find that very stressful. I am not a forceful person by nature, but not only did I have to be a forceful person, but I had to be a forceful person to the police. Even though and despite all they had done up to this point, they were still the police, they were the authority that you are supposed to be able to trust and respect. This made it doubly hard for me to stand up to them, but I also knew it had to be done. If I was not forceful and made it clear we would not be walked all over, that is exactly what they would have done, and did anyway, but at least I knew I was fighting.

NP had mistaken our family's kindness for softness, we are not soft either individually or collectively. We have proved that by managing to survive the hell our lives had become for this long. Sometimes, you just have to stand your ground, because the consequences of not doing so are too great. It was like something changed in me, probably because it had to. Even though I was still broken from the events of the past year, I knew I had to fight back, it was now or never, sink or swim, and as the head of our family I had to take the lead, I had to demonstrate the ability to keep on fighting, not just for their sake but also for mine. That was why this was so important to me, I needed to feel I was the General, the one that had to take on the fight and the one that ultimately had to stand or fall.

To me, this fight would determine who I was as a husband, father and person. This fight will define my legacy if you like. If a family could move in next door and become hellbent on destroying our lives and I was not strong enough to prevent it from happening and if NP could treat our family with such a level of disdain and contempt to the point that on many occasions rather than protect our family from the harassment, they actively joined in with the harassment, and I was not able to expose them and hold them accountable, then what was the point of being a husband and father? To me, there would be no point.

For me, this was one of the principal roles of the head of the family, the silverback. You protect your women and children. You show them right from wrong and lead by example. You put your head above the parapet and take the hits. Once a husband, always a husband. There will never be another woman in my life, no matter what. Once a parent, always a parent. I have always been okay with my children growing up, flying the nest and finding their way, including making mistakes along the way but hopefully, learning from those mistakes. Although my children have grown up, they are still my children and I feel the same level of responsibility and duty to protect them as I always have, not from anything and everything. But in this case, from wrongdoing and injustice. That feeling of responsibility, duty, and love for my wife and children will be with me till the day I die.

Three things helped me find the mental and physical strength to be able to take on the harassers and NP head-on. Firstly, quite simply my mum. Secondly, honesty, I knew we had been honest from the start, I did not have any fear or worry, honesty is the best policy, or so they say. Although it hadn't done us any good so far, in fact, just the opposite, the Heads lies were definitely winning the day, but I would put that right come hell or high water.

Thirdly, I knew it was the right thing to do. As stated, when I do something, anything, I have to be 100% sure it is the right thing to do, if I am not 100% sure then I will not do it. I was 100% sure it was the right thing to do to remove the fence from our land in September 2014 and I was 100% sure I did not commit an offence in doing so. When I am 100% sure and decide to do something, I am unshakeable. I have an unwavering determination, and I will see it through to the bitter end. I will not stop until the war is won or lost, no surrender.

I have always lived by a policy that if I have done my best and it is not good enough then it is someone else's problem. You can never do better than your best. So, I didn't go into this blind, I knew what I was up against, and the chances of success were remote, to say the least. Billy Bean versus Numpty Police, David versus Goliath, what chance do I stand, really? So, if I can see this through to the end and I am still not successful, as long as I know I have tried my best, I will be okay. I will know I could do no more.

There is the saying *'Nothing is impossible'* and whilst it would be nice to believe that, the fact is I don't believe that. Some things are impossible to many if not all of us. I remember listening to a top British tennis player being interviewed and he was asked what makes him so good, his reply was, *'I train really hard'*. Of course, he was right, no matter how good you are, you cannot do your best if you do not try your best. However, if it was a case of just training hard and you would become a Grand Slam-winning tennis player, then we would all train hard and win a Grand Slam.

The truth is, we cannot all achieve this, it is impossible for most. To become a Grand Slam-winning tennis player or an elite-level athlete or sportsperson, you must have a very high level of natural ability. Then training hard enables you to make the most of that natural ability. It is the same in most areas of life not just sports, of course, you can say, *'I'm going to be the best brain surgeon I can be.'*

But you cannot say,

'I'm going to be the best brain surgeon in the world, ever.'

Because you just do not know if you can be. Someone else might want to be the same and just be better at it than you. I cannot imagine the stress some people put themselves under when they have that burning desire or desperation to not just be the best they can be but to be the best, full stop. That may suit some, but not me. The best that I can be is good enough for me, thank you very much.

I knew what was likely to be in store for me if I was to take on NP, I knew it would be a war. NP would never admit their failings unless they were made to, and I would have to dig deep to find the strength that I hoped would lay within. The harassers and NP had awoken something in me that I didn't know was there and my beliefs, values and above all, my family new and old, gave me the determination to fight harassment, discrimination and injustice until I achieved victory or could fight no more.

Chapter Eleven
Don't Tread on Me

The title of this Chapter is also the title of a song by Metallica, the lyrics include, *'So be it, threaten no more, to secure peace is to prepare for war.*

So be it, settle the score, touch me again for the words you will hear evermore,

'DON'T TREAD ON ME.'

There are also other links to bands, solo artists or songs in this book. See if you can get them all. I will give you a clue to one of these. Three consecutive Chapter titles are linked to the lyrics of a track by a legendary Rock Band. Guessed what it is yet?

Over the past few months, our solicitor tried to liaise with the Head's solicitor without any success. Both the Heads and their solicitor were being as awkward as possible, proposing a way forward, waiting for our response and then saying, *'Na, we have changed our minds'*, not just but in particular the latest attempt at mediation. So, unable to see any other way forward, in December 2015, we issued our pleadings to the Royal Courts of Justice (inappropriate title). This involved providing the Heads with a court-approved and stamped copy of our Pleadings.

Just a few days later, we received an email from Inspector Arsewipe stating that a Detective Sergeant from CID had investigated the incident where Sponger attended our daughter's place of work and then made a formal complaint against her. Arsewipe stated the DCI agreed that this act alone does not constitute harassment but also agreed that this incident should be looked at as part of the wider review. He also informed me that he had tasked an officer with the *'impartial evidence gathering exercise'* who I will call PC Clueless, and she would be in touch in due course.

Oh my God. We had never said that this act alone amounted to harassment, even though it does. The first visit by Sponger, the two visits by the Hopertys and then the second visit by Sponger followed by the phone call by him to the Garden Centre manager and the formal complaint to our daughter's employer amounts to a clear *'course of conduct'* for harassment. We reported the second visit by Sponger not as an isolated incident but as yet another act of harassment by the Heads as it amounted to a course of conduct of harassment against our family. No one incident in isolation can be considered harassment as there needs to be a course of conduct, which means on more than one occasion. Furthermore, if the DCI and Arsewipe both agree that this incident should be looked at as part of the wider review (for harassment), then they are clearly agreeing the conduct of Sponger did amount to an act of harassment. Do NP think we are completely stupid? No, they don't, they just do not care.

Of course, we expected nothing else from NP regarding this, however disappointing it was.

However, something we were not expecting to receive from Arsewipe was the following,

'Following receipt of papers from your civil solicitor the Heads have made allegations of harassment to the Police and that these allegations will be joined up with the investigation being carried out by PC Clueless and at some point, in the future you may be required to provide the police with interviews regarding your suspected involvement in harassment'

For fuck sake, here we go again. As soon as the Heads made an allegation to NP against our family, we were told by NP that we were once again suspects in an investigation by NP and we may be required to provide NP interviews regarding our suspected involvement in harassment.

In any event, how the fuck can the issuing of civil papers to the Heads possibly be considered as an act of harassment or any other criminal offence? NP had now stooped so low as to tell us that our attempts to stop the harassment by the Heads through the civil courts, could in itself be considered by NP as an act of harassment against the Heads. More threats, intimidation, incrimination, discrimination, inequality, misconduct and abuse of power and position by yet another officer of NP against our family. C U Next Tuesday.

Because of the failure by NP to protect our family, or just to treat our family with any sort of equality and just the tiniest amount of respect, we were exploring the only avenue left open to us to get the harassment to stop. Arsewipe was now clearly telling us that we should not pursue this route and if we continue with civil action, we will potentially be committing a criminal offence.

Arsewipe was clearly pissed off that we had done this and this email was a clear and deliberate act by Arsewipe to try to intimidate our family into not taking any form of action against the Heads through the civil court, leaving us nowhere to go and totally trapped and at the mercy of the Heads and NP. Arsewipe nor any other police officer has the right or authority to inform us that the issuing of civil papers against the Heads or anyone else for that matter, is in any way a criminal offence.

It is as ludicrous as it is disgraceful. By informing our family of this Arsewipe was not only attempting to bully, threaten and intimidate us into not taking civil action against the Heads but also clearly attempting to bully, threaten and intimidate our family into remaining victims of crime and police misconduct. He was trying to isolate our family, so we had nowhere to go, no one to turn to and no one to ask for help, not even from the civil justice system.

Again, this was another classic example of an officer of NP attempting to Pervert the Course of Justice. How many times were NP going to threaten us with committing criminal offences, we must be up to half a dozen already.

We tried our best and remained patient and tolerant of both the Heads and NP, hoping against hope that things would change. I think it is fair to say, most families would have cracked by now. How many men would have reacted to their wife being assaulted by their next-door neighbour? Most people would have taken matters into their own hands for that one incident, let alone all the other stuff.

We did the right thing every single time in the forlorn hope that NP would finally see the truth and help bring the harassment to an end. But NP could see the truth as clear as day, they knew exactly what was happening. They knew the Heads were responsible for the harassment, they knew the Heads were the offenders and we were the victims. We could see it, our friends could see it, or relatives could see it, and our solicitor and barrister could see it, in fact, everyone and anyone could see it. So, NP could also see it!

There was no great mystery to be solved, no major complex investigation needed. Everything was fully evidenced and witnessed. The only way that you could not see what was happening was if you deliberately failed to see what was right before your eyes.

Following the meeting with Arsewipe and Quack, we were a little more optimistic that the inequality and discrimination against our family by NP would at least ease and hopefully stop but no, it is getting even more obvious and severe. The reason is our standing up to PS Quack for one and our complaint against Pinky and Perky for another.

And no wonder, these two reasons would have a connection we could not possibly have imagined at this time. Sometimes it is still hard to believe even now. I hope you haven't guessed what it is yet, that would spoil the surprise!

The warnings I received regarding making a complaint or standing up to the police were true, not that I doubted them for a second. This was our punishment for standing up to PS Quack at our meeting and exposing her failings, this was our punishment for making a complaint against PC's Pinky and Perky. Clearly, NP was never going to back down or accept they got it wrong or made a mistake, they couldn't, they had travelled too far down the path they had chosen from the very start of their involvement. Maybe, some of them even at this stage wished they had never started down this path, but I doubt it.

NP was in it for the long haul and would fight to the bitter end. Why would they do anything else? What have they got to lose? The likelihood is they will never be held accountable for their actions, so why not inflict as much pain and misery as possible along the way?

Not so long ago, receiving an email like this from an Inspector with the police, would have achieved the aim of intimidating me and I would never have dared to question the content. I would have thought I had better do what they say because they are the police. Of course, it still had an impact, no one should have to deal with this. But I somehow had the strength, if not the knowledge, to fight back, and fight back I did.

I am not going to lie, of course, the conduct of the Heads and NP were having a huge impact on our family. I haven't spoken of this much so far, maybe I will put a Chapter in at the end detailing some of the huge impact this has had on our lives and in many ways. But for now, I'm sure you can imagine the stress we were under every minute of every day.

Regarding the threat by Arsewipe, *'At some point in the future, you may be required to provide the police with interviews regarding your suspected involvement in harassment.'*

We were more than prepared to be interviewed if necessary, as long as there was equality for both sides (fat chance of that). Being interviewed would at least allow each member of our family to defend ourselves against the allegations that had and would continue to be made against us by the Heads and, of course, NP, but I feel NP have set themselves a bit of a precedent.

I made it very clear to NP about the seriousness with which I regard the incidents and determinations regarding Mrs Head repeatedly making hand gestures and mouthing obscenities through her front window at our daughter and her friend on three separate occasions, and the incident where Sponger attended our daughter's place of work. In both incidents, the Heads were clearly targeting our daughter because they thought she was the weak link in our family chain, but NP did not consider it necessary to interview either Mrs Head or Sponger regarding these incidents.

So, in the interests of equality and impartiality, it would take some pretty serious allegations by the Heads with some pretty strong evidence to support for NP to justify requesting our family to provide the police with interviews regarding our suspected involvement in harassment!

Also, Inspector Arsewipe went on to say in the email,

'The Heads have been advised not to have any unnecessary contact with your family in order to prevent them inadvertently incriminating themselves.'

'Unnecessary contact, inadvertently incriminating themselves', do me a favour. They had assaulted both myself and my wife, threatened to attack our daughter as well as numerous other serious offences and NP had done nothing about it! As far as NP was concerned, the Heads couldn't inadvertently incriminate themselves if they hung, drawn and quartered all four members

of our family in the middle of the street. *'Unnecessary contact, inadvertently incriminating themselves'*. TWAT.

In any event, just two days after receiving this email from Arsewipe, the Heads fitted Christmas lights to the fence they had erected in our front garden. So, the Heads had clearly not heeded the advice given to them by Arsewipe. No surprise there then!

You know, looking back at what happened to our family, not just the harassment which I am nowhere near finished telling you about, but also the conduct of NP, which I am only just getting started on. I often think our family were and still are an experiment by NP and probably by other, greater powers. How long can we allow a family to be the victims of crime before they break? How far can we push a family until they break? How much misconduct and criminality can we commit and still get away with?

I haven't even introduced you to many of the officers and members of staff of NP who failed our family. So, in my opinion, this must have been a group effort. For the misconduct and criminality to go on for so long, to be so severe and obvious and by so many members of NP, it must have been a collective effort. I know that is a bit radical, things like that don't happen in real life, do they? Maybe wait until you have finished reading before you make up your mind.

The beginning of the new year began the same as the old had ended, more shit. Just a few days into January 2016, our solicitor received a letter from the Head's solicitor in response to our Civil Court Pleadings. The letter stated that they were no longer instructed to act on behalf of the Heads but even so, requested a 28-day extension for a response to be issued. As the letter stated they were no longer instructed to act on behalf of the Heads, they were not legally entitled to request a delay in civil proceedings. Our solicitor thought it to be very strange. However, an extension was agreed.

As the year ticked on, we had a couple of meetings and exchanged several emails with the PSD Investigator regarding my complaint against Pinky and Perky. I was informed by him that due to the investigation being carried out by NP into the allegations of harassment, my complaint has been split into Part One and Part Two and the PSD investigation would be restricted to investigating Part One only which was regarding the investigation conducted by Pinky and Perky into the allegation of criminal damage made by Mr Head against me for removing the part of the fence they had erected on our land. The rest of the complaint, Part Two, would be investigated once the investigation into the allegations of harassment had been completed.

This was a tactic that I would become very familiar with over the next few years. When you first make a complaint to the police about the police, the first thing the PSD tries to do is to water down the complaint. They will use every trick in the book to say that parts of your complaint cannot be investigated, or in some cases when they cannot find an excuse not to investigate or cannot find an excuse for the conduct of the officer you have complained about, they will refuse to consider your complaint as a *'Recordable Complaint Matter'*. That means your complaint will not only not be investigated, but that your complaint will not even be recorded as a complaint against the police so there is no record of the complaint ever being made.

Another tactic used by the police is to eliminate any witnesses you may have to the misconduct. That is what NP did here, Part Two of the complaint would include the time PC Pinky intimidated our witness to the Public Order Offence by Mrs Head against our daughter by arranging to meet her in the car park of the local pub and saying to her, *"You do realise you may be charged with entrapment so you might want to consider how involved you want to get in this."*

Of course, this is a very serious allegation of gross misconduct, and the fact NP were investigating the harassment by the Heads was no reason for not investigating this very serious matter. In fact, there is not or should not be any valid reason why an allegation of this nature should not be investigated as a matter of extreme urgency.

As mentioned, the reason NP failed to investigate this matter was because there was a witness to the allegation, our neighbour. Other than this incident, all the other matters contained in my complaint involved the treatment of our family members only. However, if this point of my complaint was to be investigated that would no longer be the case, there was, of course, not only a witness to this gross misconduct but also a victim. And more importantly, a witness and a victim who was not a family member.

By eliminating witnesses, the Police can keep you isolated and vulnerable. If they cannot eliminate a witness, they would come up with some bullshit reason why they cannot or will not investigate the matter, no matter how serious it might be. Isolation is the key to their success, as soon as a third party becomes involved their job becomes much harder, even impossible.

Remember when Pinky told us not to speak to anyone about the harassment and when Inspector Tool sent us that email informing us that if we continue to seek help from third parties it could be construed as Perverting the Course of Justice and when Arsewipe told us the issuing of civil papers to the Heads could lead to us being interviewed for our suspected involvement in harassment. Those are a classic example of police pressure and intimidation to eliminate any witnesses and to keep you in isolation. You will read more examples of this later in this book.

If you are in isolation, it is like you are cut off from the world. We even got to the point of not telling anyone what had happened just in case NP found out that we had told someone they didn't want us to tell. When the isolation goes that far, the police can do what they want, they have got you. Very much the same as a domestic abuser who uses the same tactics to isolate their victim. What NP did to our family was a form of coercive behaviour, repeated threats, intimidation, incrimination, allegations and the elimination of any third party or witnesses. Let's face it, the police do not just practise this sort of behaviour, they are trained in it. And in some circumstances and situations, I can imagine it to be a very good tool to use. But like all good things, put it in the wrong hands and it will be abused.

Whether you are NP or a domestic abuser, once they have got you, they can or think they can do what they want, they can bully you, intimidate you and threaten you. They can also make you feel as though you are the criminal and not a victim or that you have mental health issues and what you believe is happening to you is a figment of your imagination, despite what evidence you have and can provide. NP did this to our family on more than one occasion, one officer even recorded me onto the local police system of NP as having *'mental health issues'* for reporting an act of harassment by another neighbour of ours even though this neighbour had been convicted of harassing me, TWICE! And was on a two-and-a-half-year suspended prison sentence for those convictions. Oh, I haven't mentioned that yet have I? Boy, you've got a treat in store.

To be honest with you, I did agree to the second part of my complaint being put on hold until the investigation into the harassment was concluded. I thought that was what had to happen because NP told me so, but that was

193

not correct, it was just an excuse and they thought I wouldn't know any better, and they were right, I didn't know any better, but I do now.

By this time, PC Pinky was not involved in an active role in the investigation into the harassment and he was not to have any direct contact with our family and he was no longer our SPOC, PS Quack was. There was no reason why these two matters could not be investigated at the same time. The only reason NP did this was to protect Pinky from his misconduct and they took advantage of my lack of knowledge of correct police procedure to do this.

This was blatant discrimination against me because I had made a complaint. Although I was unaware at this time, this wasn't the first time I had been discriminated against because I had made a complaint. However, there was an even more pressing reason why NP did not want to investigate this part of my complaint that I also wasn't aware of at the time. All will be revealed!

To be clear. The reason given by NP why Part Two of my complaint could not be investigated at that time was because of the ongoing investigation into the harassment, although that investigation finished in 2019, to this point in time, April 2025, Part Two of my complaint has still not and never will *due to the passage of time* be investigated by NP.

Another tactic used by NP to fudge the outcome of an investigation, whether that is a criminal investigation into an allegation made by an alleged victim of crime or a complaint against the police, is to use every trick in the book to delay matters. So, on top of deny, deny, deny, you have to cope with delay, delay, delay. I will give you two examples of this tactic now, but I will detail them later in this book.

Firstly, the investigation by NP into the allegations of harassment made by ourselves and the Heads took TWO AND A HALF YEARS to complete and when it was finally complete, it was a total and deliberate fuck up. So much so that the investigating officer, a Detective Inspector, openly admitted that he failed our family in his investigation. What he did not mention, however, was that this was a deliberate failure.

Secondly, I made several complaints to NP regarding the conduct of various officers and members of staff, not through choice, well, in a way it was through choice, no choice. I had to do something to get these bent bastards off our backs before they caused one or all of our family serious harm.

When you make a complaint against an officer, if it manages to get through the first hurdle of the Professional Standards Department refusing to record your complaint, it is then investigated by an officer from the PSD. Once this investigation is complete, the officer compiles a report which is then passed to a senior officer from the PSD for what is called a determination which decides the outcome.

The determination of this particular complaint took SEVEN months. When I finally received the outcome, it stated that the officer in question had since retired from the Force! In other words, NP had deliberately delayed the outcome to allow the officer in question to retire with a huge pension, no doubt, a pension that you and I have funded through paying tax on our hard-earned wages! I am sure some of you can recall hearing similar examples on the news when a more high-profile investigation into misconduct allegations has concluded.

The reporter finished their report by saying,

'The officer in question has since retired from the Force'

It's that thin blue line again. The police will protect their own, no matter what. It is their law.

Chapter Twelve
Wheelie Bin Woes

Once a week, we and every other household in the neighbourhood, would put our waste bins out for collection. We would place our bins on the grass verge in front of our house. However, in mid-January 2016, the Heads also decided to place their bins on the grass verge in front of our house. The Heads knew our daughter parked her car there and that placing their bins on the verge would prevent our daughter from doing so. Just another of those little things the Heads would do to wind us up. But for one day of the week, it was no big deal, and compared to the more serious acts of harassment, if this was the worst thing they were doing it was a relief, and we would take it every day of the week.

It's a good job we could take it because it wasn't just one day of the week or even every day of the week, it turned into every week of the month. This meant that our daughter could not park her car on the verge in front of our house because the Heads bins were permanently camped there. Still, compared to some of the incidents, it was still relatively minor, but as with all the other minor acts of harassment, because the Heads did not get the re-action they wanted – it didn't stay minor for long.

For some reason, the Heads had two blue recycle bins, a black bin for general waste and a grey bin for garden waste. Not the small lift-up lid ones with the swing handle, but the big wheelie bin type. We had weekly collections, one-week general waste, and the next week recyclable waste, but from this point on rather than take their bins in after collection, they would leave at least one of their bins on the verge in front of our house for the next three months. Although it might sound a bit petty, in our borough all residents are instructed by the local council to put their bins out for collection by 6 am and bring them in after they have been emptied, standard and sensible stuff. Too sensible for the Heads though, why take your bins in after collection when you can leave them on the verge in front of your neighbour's house to annoy them. So, that was what they did for three months. Not the sort of behaviour you would expect from your Parish

Councillor though, is it, to defy local council guidelines? Well, it's the Heads so a little bit of breaking the local council guidelines didn't matter.

To be clear, rather than bringing their bin or bins in as they had done for the past four years, the Heads went to the extreme lengths of carrying their waste from their front door to put it in the bin that was on the verge in front of our house, just so the bin could stay on the verge. Deluded or what?

On several occasions, over the time the bins were on the verge, often because they were empty, they would sometimes blow over in the strong winds. Rather than bring the bins in they would stand them back up on the verge only for the wind to blow them over again. On one occasion, we had a bad storm, the wind was so strong that it blew the bin over when it was full of rubbish. Of course, the rubbish blew all over the neighbourhood but still rather than bring the bin in the Heads stood the bin back up and placed a bag of sand against it to try to prevent it from blowing over again. Crazy.

This is how stupid, dangerous and deluded the situation with the bins on the verge became. Maybe it is hard for you to imagine a situation regarding a bin on a grass verge becoming dangerous, but you haven't met the Head family!

Just a few weeks into our Wheelie Bin Woes, the Heads recycle bin was emptied. As usual, instead of taking their bin in after collection, the Heads placed the bin back on the verge. Later that afternoon, I walked to the post box to post a letter, funnily enough. This meant walking past the bin camped on the verge of our house. When I walked past the bin, I noticed the base of a broken bottle half hidden under the bin. The bottle had been embedded in sand, so the jagged edges of the bottle were pointing upwards.

It wasn't the base of a small bottle like a bottle of lager, but the size of a wine bottle if you get the picture.

Not too bad you might think, or maybe not. The broken bottle was hidden under the bin so it wasn't causing much of a danger to anyone or anything while the bin was there you might think, just stupid, reckless and intimidating!

However, this was at the time of the storms that I mentioned earlier, and again, I assume because the Heads had used the bag of sand to embed the base of the bottle, it was no longer there to prevent the bin from blowing over. So due to the strong winds, the bin that was hiding the bottle blew over again. Instead of placing the bin back on the verge as they had done earlier the same day to hide the broken bottle, the Heads brought their bin in, this left the broken bottle totally exposed. The jagged edges of the bottle were lethal and posed a serious risk of harm and injury to people, their pets that often walked on the verge and to any vehicles that may drive or park on the verge such as visitors to our house or delivery drivers. But and yet again, our daughter who always parked her car on the verge in front of our house. When the bins weren't there!

To be clear, this bottle was on the verge that bordered the pavement and the road. If a dog were to tread on this glass, it would cause a horrendous injury. If a car or van were to drive over this bottle, it would cause serious damage to the tyre.

There was no way in the world the Heads would not have been aware of the danger this broken bottle posed, in any event, they must have placed it there in the first place. Even if they didn't, they obviously would have seen it when they moved their bin off the verge but made no attempt to remove it. They just left it there fully exposed without a care in the world for the harm it could cause, not just to ourselves but to anyone or anything. You probably think I am exaggerating or even completely lying. I don't blame you if you do think that, maybe I would think the same, even at the time I thought it was unbelievable, so I took a photo of the broken bottle.

This made the situation very dangerous and was another clear example that the Heads would go to any lengths to harass our family, even to the point of causing serious harm not just to ourselves but to anyone and anything, including innocent animals. They even had two dogs themselves so they would have been fully aware of the risk posed to other pets. The Heads delusional fixation with harassing our family had clearly not abated, in fact, it was the opposite. They were thinking of new, more extreme, more reckless ways to cause fear to our family.

I was, of course, very concerned regarding the danger the bottle posed. I knew that the area of the verge where the bottle was placed would probably be covered by the Head's CCTV. I knew if I removed the bottle, the Heads would make yet another complaint to NP that I had committed some sort of offence, even though the bottle was on the verge in front of our house. I also knew that if they did, NP would come down on me like a ton of bricks.

How stupid is that? I felt so scared of what the Heads and NP would do if I removed a broken bottle from the verge in front of our own house, I even doubted myself as to what was the right thing to do. That is another impact of harassment, it chips away at every area of your life, some are obvious, others, not so. Drip, drip, drip.

I knew the bottle could not stay there until it was dark. To be clear, the bottle was green, so it matched the grass verge. It was easy to spot in daylight but when it was dark it would be next to impossible to see, particularly as you would never expect it to be there. I decided it would be too irresponsible to leave it exposed so I had the brainwave to place a bucket upside down over the broken bottle. Clever, I thought.

By this time, we had been contacted by the officer who would be conducting the impartial evidence-gathering exercise regarding the investigation by NP into the harassment and informed by her that she was now our SPOC and we should contact her with any concerns, this was PC Clueless. So, I contacted her and informed her of the bottle, she said she would log it and speak with her supervisor!

Really, if this officer needed to speak with her supervisor about such a serious risk to the public then what was the point of her being a police officer? In any event, we needn't have bothered, the bottle had also been spotted by our next-door neighbour on the other side of the Heads, and he removed the broken bottle from the verge, job done, danger removed, and injury averted. It was a good job our neighbour did remove the bottle as we did not hear anything back from NP for over a week and when we did it was total bollocks, again. It was PS Quack who emailed me to say, '*Inspector Arsewipe does not consider the glass to be in the scope of the harassment investigation as it has not been done to you directly and we will not be contacting the Heads about this matter.*' Remember that, **PS Quack** failing our family again!

Unreal! The Heads had embedded the base of a broken bottle in sand on the verge in front of our house and left this bottle totally exposed causing an incredibly high risk of serious harm to the public, pets and property. It is hard to imagine a more reckless, dangerous and targeted act of harassment than this. If this act was not targeting our family, then who was it targeting?

Even more importantly, just because Arsewipe, *'Does not consider the glass to be in the scope of the harassment investigation as it has not been done to you directly.'*

Does not mean the bottle does not constitute an offence or risk to the public. Would Arsewipe be okay if every homeowner in the County placed the base of a broken bottle on the verge in front of their neighbours' house? I think not. Would Arsewipe consider it okay if his neighbour placed the base of a broken bottle in front of his house? I think not. What would happen to our family if we had placed a broken bottle in front of the Heads house, would Arsewipe have the same attitude? I think not.

For Arsewipe and NP to consider this act by the Heads did not constitute any offences was completely ridiculous. Furthermore, NP was not even prepared to talk to the Heads about this unbelievably stupid, reckless, deluded and dangerous act, leaving the Heads to think they could do whatever they wanted with no consequences whatsoever. NP were not just failing our family, but the whole community, what was going on? If this happened anywhere else the police would do something about it, but not in this instance, not when it was the Heads at fault. Well, it's the Heads, so a little bit of crime didn't matter. What hold did the Heads have over NP?

Anyway, it wasn't quite as straightforward as our neighbour removing the bottle, job done, as you might expect where the Heads and NP are concerned. What we later, much later, discovered was that because the bottle had been placed on the verge in front of our house and not the Heads, several of our neighbours and NP had either concluded or been told by the Heads that we had placed the bottle there! This led to several more of our neighbours joining in with the harassment. Believe me, our troubles were only just beginning!

Over the following few months, the Heads had one, two and on some occasions three of their Wheelie Bins on the verge in front of our house. This was despite two notices placed on the bins by the Borough Council instructing the Heads to take their bins in after collection. For a Parish Councillor to not only leave their bins on the verge, which is against local regulations, but to ignore the instructions of the Borough Council to return the bins to their property after collection, demonstrates a complete lack of respect for anyone and any authority. Clearly and yet again, this was not the sort of behaviour you would expect of your Parish Councillor.

Eventually, in early April, almost THREE months since the Heads first started to leave their bins on the verge, they finally brought all their bins in. However, the ridiculous behaviour of the Heads didn't quite end there. When the Heads had brought their bins in, Mrs Head sprinkled something on the area of the verge where their bins had been and performed what I can only describe as a war dance or some ritual ceremony to summon up the Gods of the Wheelie Bins. This was in the middle of the afternoon; it was one of the most bizarre scenes I have ever witnessed. The woman was not only deluded and fixated but clearly deranged and mentally unstable. To witness this event in other circumstances would have been hilarious but this woman was living next door, and her husband, son and his husband were all as bad as she was. We were not living next door to a normal family, or even a horrible family, but a freak show.

Anyway, this brought our Wheelie Bin Woes to an end. The only question was, what would be next?

Chapter Thirteen
Civil War

Going back to early January, our solicitor received a letter from yet another firm of solicitors informing him they had been instructed to act on behalf of the Heads. This would be the third firm of solicitors the Heads had enlisted in less than a year. The Heads were clearly using these solicitors to either delay or prevent any civil proceedings from progressing.

The letter requested a further 14-day extension for the Heads to respond to our issuing of civil proceedings. We, of course, agreed to this further extension, what choice did we have, they were clearly not going to respond any sooner.

A couple of weeks later, our solicitor received a response to our civil proceedings. This response was a complete and utter pack of lies, no surprise there then. However, some of these lies were beyond belief and very distressing. It was crystal clear that yet again, the Heads had been as dishonest with their latest firm of solicitors as they had with the previous two.

A few examples of their lies were,

'The Heads claim they informed the Beans in December 2012 that they were going to relay their drive and that they informed the Beans that they were going to replace the wooden gravel boards on the low-level fence with concrete ones.'

Urr, there were no wooden gravel boards on the low-level fence and they most certainly did not discuss it with us prior to or even during the work being carried out. It goes without saying, that if they had we would not have let the rose bush be destroyed. According to their builder, Trigger, even he was not aware that the Heads wanted him to erect the concrete gravel boards (these concrete gravel boards turned out to be the retaining wall between the two front gardens), even Trigger, as dumb as he was, could not quote to replace the timber gravel boards with concrete ones when the timber gravel boards did not exist. When this incident happened in February 2013, Trigger told us himself that the Heads asked him to erect the retaining wall as an extra only after he had started the job and that it was not part of the original quote.

'The Heads deny they have carried out any acts of trespass or harassment at all.' Urr, the fence is still on our land to this day.

'The Heads deny they have threatened or assaulted any members of the Bean family.'

Urr, Mr Head admitted guilt and accepted a Conditional Caution for Common Assault against me in July 2014.

'The Heads deny they have made any false allegations to the Police about the Beans.'

Urr, the Heads know they have made multiple false allegations to the police about all four members of our family, including the one to follow! And most disturbing of all.

'The Heads claim that on the 24th of July 2014, (the day Mr Head assaulted me), **it was in fact Mr Bean who had assaulted Mrs Head.**

Regarding the above claim, the letter stated,

'When Mr Bean forcefully removed the timber, it struck Mrs Head on the chest. As a result, Mr Head, having seen his injured wife, lost his temper and attempted to pull down the reed fence which he had erected. He then rang the Police in an effort to stop the provocation and harassment being caused by the Beans.'

This is total bollocks. I did not assault Mrs Head. Mr Head did not mention this alleged assault by me against his wife when he phoned the police after he had assaulted me. The Heads did not mention this alleged assault to the police officers who attended the incident. It was an absolute despicable lie for the Heads to make this allegation against me. For them to go to the lengths of telling their solicitors that I had assaulted Mrs Head was sick beyond words and a clear indication that yet again there were no lengths the Heads would not go. Nothing is out of bounds or too low. The impact an allegation like this could have on not just my personal life but also my business life would be devastating. And as you would expect, it would prove to have exactly that.

I could go on and on about the lies contained in this letter, but nothing could top the above. How could it? Being accused of assaulting a female pensioner is about as low as it can get. As for their solicitors, how could they write a letter containing such an atrocious lie? Surely, a solicitor needs to verify what they are being told by their clients before containing it in a letter which at the end of the day is part of legal proceedings.

Another letter from their solicitors was received shortly after this one. The same solicitor for two letters in a row, believe it or not. It contained a request that we discontinue proceedings against all four members of the Head family. Also, in a separate letter from the same solicitor but this time solely on behalf of the Little Head and Sponger, it stated,

'It would appear the issuing of proceedings against Little Head has merely been done in an attempt to cause further harassment and stress to Little Head. In light of this, we invite your clients to discontinue proceedings against Little Head upon payment of his costs.'

Yep, you read right, not only did Little Head want us to discontinue proceedings against him, but he also wanted us to pay his costs. TWAT.

Little Head and Sponger are clearly trying to say they have not harassed our family, which, of course, is again total bollocks. The Malicious Communications via Social Media and the posting of videos of me on YouTube falsely claiming I was committing criminal offences by Little Head and the harassment of our daughter at her place of work by Sponger. No, they had harassed our family alright, and they were not going to be let off the hook.

This letter signified a shift in momentum though. The Heads were clearly worried that they were in trouble and that we were not going to be bullied by them or NP into giving in to the harassment. Mr and Mrs Head clearly wanted their mummy's boy to be left out of our civil proceedings, that was not going to happen. If you can't do the time, don't do the crime.

To be honest with you, I knew Little Head was their weak link, he was a coward and a snake. He would have stabbed his own mum, dad and husband in the back if it would have benefited him. No, I was going to keep him in the loop at all costs.

Like the Heads and PC Pinky used our daughter to get to us, I will use their son to get to them. In any event, he wasn't innocent, he was as bad as the rest of them, and he would deserve all he would get. That might sound a bit mercenary, but we were at war, a no-holds-barred, fight-to-the-finish, last-man-standing, backs-to-the-wall war. A war that we did not start or want, but a war we will win, at all costs, no matter what. Right over wrong, innocence over guilt, good over bad, justice over injustice.

Our family as we knew it and I personally, depended on it. There is no way in this world that I would let a family of scum like the Heads beat me and my family. Oh no, Little Head, you are in it up to your neck my son and I will drown you, metaphorically speaking, of course!

Even when the harassment is over and you think you have moved on, probably to your next victim, I will still be in the shadows, like that sniper, waiting for my one opportunity to blow your fucking head off. You will never be free from the shadow that will hang over you. You may think that your time at Brit School taught you to be a good actor, how to play the victim, threatening to commit suicide or self-harm to deflect any action being taken against you when you were exposed as the prick that you are. You don't fool me Little Head, you never did. See you soon!

Over the same time period as the above, we received an email from PS Quack who informed us that the investigation into the case for harassment was about to start and that PC Clueless would be in contact to start the evidence-gathering exercise in due course.

Quack also requested that we provide her with an update regarding our civil case against the Heads. Why Quack needed this, I have no idea as we had been told on several occasions by NP the police cannot get involved in civil matters. It would appear they cannot get involved in civil matters only when it suits them.

I also received an email from the PSD Investigator regarding my complaint against Pinky and Perky. He informed me that he had concluded his assessment as potential Misconduct, and he would now serve Notice to the officers concerned and await their response. Wow, that's a rarity. An email from NP that wasn't completely offensive and derogatory, but it was bullshit.

We also received a flying visit from PC Clueless to introduce herself and inform us she would be in touch soon to start her investigation. We appreciated this initial contact; it made us feel NP were at least going to progress matters. Although we still knew, in the back of our minds, it would not progress how it should have done. And we were right, in fact, it didn't progress at all. Not for two and a half years anyway.

During those two and a half years we were subjected to relentless harassment by even more people and when we finally did have the result of the *'investigation'* it was a complete fuck up.

About a week later, we met with PC Clueless to discuss the investigation into the harassment by the Heads. This initial meeting lasted for four and a half hours. I am sure Clueless thought she would just pop around for an hour, talk about what was happening, and leave. I bet she didn't have a clue as to the extent of the harassment, not that that was going to make any difference to her or NP.

PC Clueless requested that we all write a separate statement in as much detail as possible and provide as much evidence as possible regarding the various incidents. We asked PC Clueless about the allegations of harassment the Heads had made against various members of our family, PC Clueless said she was unaware of the specifics, but she would be meeting with the Heads regarding their allegations. We asked Clueless if she could inform us as soon as possible as to the specifics of these allegations due to the stress it was causing us all and to allow our family to be able to provide statements to NP with as much detail as possible as she had requested. Clearly, a big part of the Heads harassment was to make multiple false allegations to NP. It was only fair we knew what all these allegations were to be able to detail them in our statements.

Going back to the allegation of Criminal Damage made against me by Mr Head for removing the fence, again. I knew the CCTV footage APC1, provided to NP by the Heads could not possibly contain what the statement of Mr Head claims it did which would therefore be evidence that it was a false allegation. I knew the PSD investigator had a copy of this footage, so I emailed him and asked if he could forward a copy of the CCTV footage APC1 to me to allow me to compile my statement for PC Clueless with as much detail and evidence as possible. The PSD Investigator replied saying he could not forward a copy of the footage to me, but he did not provide a reason why!

Because it was either fake, did not even exist or would drop Pinky right in it up to his tiny little knackers, that's why.

I emailed the PSD Investigator back expressing my concern that I would never get to see this footage and the distress that would cause due to the impact this *'evidence'* has had and would continue to have on my life. I basically pleaded with him to keep his copy of this footage safe. He replied stating the content of my email had been noted!

What the fuck does that mean? Was he going to keep a copy of the footage safe or not? Why can't NP just answer a question? Every little thing is like a quiz show with them. It wastes so much time and money, but it's not their money so why should they care?

So, as I was not going to get a copy of the footage from the PSD Investigator, I emailed PC Clueless and asked her if she could forward a copy of the CCTV footage APC1 to me to allow me to be able to compile my statement containing as much detail and evidence as possible, as she had requested. I also emailed the Data Protection Department (DPD) of NP to request a copy of the CCTV footage APC1 from them for the same reason.

After a week or so having not heard back from Clueless or the DPD regarding my request for a copy of the footage, I emailed the Freedom of Information Department (FID) of NP to request a copy from them. That must have jumped them into action as the very next day, I received an email from the DPD informing me, *'Numpty Police no longer hold a copy of the footage as we have returned it to the Heads.'*

Total bollocks. I knew this to be untrue as the PSD Investigator had confirmed that he had a copy of the footage on file just a week before. NP knew as well as I did that this footage did not show what the Heads, Pinky and Perky claim and if they released it to me, I would have the evidence to prove the criminality of Mr Head and the misconduct of Pinky and Perky. NP would never voluntarily disclose this footage to me come hell or high water, even though I am fully entitled to it.

This so-called Key Evidence caused so much damage to me that I would never stop until I had this footage and the officers responsible for failing to disclose it to me were held accountable. NP would rather continue to lie their heads off regarding this footage causing further unnecessary stress than own up to their failings and protect their own yet again. They do not care or even give a second thought to the victims of police misconduct or people like me, my family and most of you. We are cannon fodder with no right to equality, impartiality or justice. Democracy, do me a favour!

To recap, during the investigation into the allegation of criminal damage made by Mr Head to which this evidence was related. The investigating officer, PC Pinky **'refused'** to show me this Key Evidence, the CPS then 'failed' to disclose this Key Evidence to my barrister at my Plea Hearing, and the CPS then **'failed'** to even acknowledge my six written requests sent via recorded delivery to them to disclose this evidence to either me or my barrister, when I eventually did get a response from the CPS, they said they had destroyed it.

Since the CPS discontinued the case against me, I have made many requests to NP to either disclose or retain this footage. To now be told by NP clearly untruthfully, that they no longer have a copy of this vital piece of evidence because they have returned it to the Heads was beyond belief and it didn't take Einstein to work out why!

We were now in a situation where NP had requested all four members of our family to provide NP with detailed statements regarding the harassment by the Heads with as much evidence as possible, but NP would not disclose the evidence that would allow our family to do exactly that. Of course, if we were denied our right to submit this evidence with our statements, then it proved the *'investigation'* was a complete sham from the very start.

How can NP investigate with any sort of impartiality and equality when they deny one party their right to provide the best evidence possible not only to support our allegations against the Heads but to provide the best defence possible to the allegations the Heads had made against ourselves?

At this point, we did not know the specifics of the allegations the Heads had made against us. We had asked NP for these specifics, but they had again refused to tell us what they were, surprise, surprise. This was because both the Heads and NP knew the Heads could not make any specific allegations against our family because we had not harassed them, so they would have no evidence to support these allegations.

When any evidence that is relative to a criminal offence or allegation is destroyed or not retained, the Force is required to keep a detailed record of who authorised the disposal, for what reason, what method of disposal was used and when the evidence was disposed of. So, I asked both the Freedom of Information and the Data Protection Departments of NP for this information.

I received a reply which stated, *'Unfortunately, I cannot disclose any information about a third party.'*

So, this tells me they do have a record regarding the disposal of this evidence but will not disclose that information to me when they are legally required to do so. NP was so desperate to prevent me or anyone else on the other side of the thin blue line from seeing this footage that they would come up with any excuse, no matter how ridiculous it was.

To be clear, as this footage was evidence of an alleged criminal offence it should not have been disposed of at all by this time. It is my understanding that according to the College of Policing regulations regarding the retention and disposal of evidence, this footage should have been retained for a minimum of ten years. So, for NP to have admitted to disposing of this evidence within just two years of the alleged offence, NP had clearly failed yet again to abide by their standards.

NP might think they are being clever in denying me access to this CCTV and I am sure it amuses them to keep coming up with excuse after excuse, but I absolutely guarantee that one day I will get to see this footage if it even exists, and when I do, all those officers and members of staff from NP that placed all of these hurdles in my way causing so much needless stress when we were already going through the most stressful time of our lives, will pay the price. So, laugh loud, laugh long, but he who laughs last laughs longest.

I knew NP were never going to release this footage to me, but I did not give up asking for it as I knew I was being lied to by NP. It was one of those rare occasions when I knew I was 100% right and guess what, I was eventually informed that miraculously NP did have a copy of this footage after all. YEY, but they will not release it to me without a court order, BOO.

So, I may not have gained a copy or a viewing of this footage, but I had at least forced NP to admit they did hold a copy. This was a lesson I had to learn very quickly, if you know you are right, never give up. Authorities like the police will never make life easy for anyone who dares to challenge them but if you bang on the door hard enough for long enough, even tiny fish like me can win the odd battle, or even a war, maybe!

As the civil case progressed, very slowly, we were informed by our solicitor that the Heads were going to issue a Counterclaim against our family. This came as no surprise as we had been forewarned by our solicitor that due to the Heads failure to mediate and refusal to accept any wrongdoing, they basically had nowhere else to go. The Heads latest solicitor tried even more strong-arm tactics by telling our solicitor that if the case were to go to Court the Judge would throw the case out and we would then be liable for the Heads costs as we had brought the case against them and that mediation should have been used as a way of solving the issues.

We were and always had agreed to mediation but with all the previous attempts, the Heads had either refused to take part, manipulated or exploited these opportunities for their own benefit. Although we would always opt for mediation, it was never going to work in this case. You cannot mediate a solution with people who cannot tell fact from fiction and who are incapable of telling the truth. The only way the Heads would consider mediation to be successful was if we were to agree to all their demands, including not only admitting to harassing them but also admitting they had not harassed us. That was never going to happen.

I was very concerned as to the content of the allegations that would be made against our family in the Heads Counterclaim. Although we knew the allegations would be false and they had no evidence to support them, that had not made any difference so far.

Somehow, the Heads were able to not only convince NP that they had not harassed our family, despite the irrefutable evidence we were able to provide time and time again, but it was our family who were harassing them.

I was sure that one of the allegations contained in the Counterclaim would be that I assaulted Mrs Head in July 2014. Although I knew this allegation would be false. It was, of course, very distressing to have an allegation of that nature made against you. It would be unforgivable for the Heads to make this allegation against me again, not just to our solicitor but as it would be contained in a Counterclaim, this allegation would be made to the Court. God knows what other allegations would be contained in it.

I met with PC Clueless to start to compile my statement. She was accompanied by another officer who was one of the rare *'Good Cops'*. This officer didn't do our family any favours, he just did his job the way it was supposed to be done. He treated our family with equality and impartiality, that was all. I think he could also see through the Heads lies and understood what was really going on with NP. To be honest, it didn't take a genius to see through the Heads, it was only because the officers we had dealt with so far from NP were deliberately turning a blind eye, well, both eyes actually. This *'good cop'* was the same officer who had originally dealt with the assault on my wife by Mr Head before he suffered a serious hand injury and was placed on long-term sick leave, PC Willis. I am sure, if PC Willis had been able to continue dealing with the issues with the Heads, our lives would never have been destroyed.

After a couple of hours of what seemed more like an interrogation by Clueless rather than taking a statement from a victim of crime, Clueless was clearly bored, she said that it would be better if she took the copy of the notes I had written with her and she would continue to write it up into evidential format herself. On several occasions during this meeting, PC Willis was visibly embarrassed to be there due to the attitude of Clueless. He often looked at her with a puzzled look on his face as if to say,

'What the fuck are you saying that for?'

It was clear to me; we were not going to get any change out of Clueless.

The very next day, PC Clueless visited the Heads. Nothing strange about that, other than Clueless parked her police car on the Heads drive!

It may have been the harassment affecting my view, you know, the paranoia that can start to twist your mind into making every molehill into a mountain, but that is what Harassment does. Drip, drip, drip.

We thought this to be at best, a bit *'pally'* with the Heads. After all, they were the suspects in a live police investigation regarding the harassment of their next-door neighbours which Clueless knew had included at least one assault by Mr Head. She should also ensure her actions were to be seen as impartial, clearly, parking her car on the Heads drive would not give all parties that impression. At worst, it is against all correct police investigative procedures for an officer to park their police car on the drive of a family who were the suspects in a police investigation, particularly, as the officer who had parked their car on the suspects' drive was the same officer who was conducting an *'impartial evidence gathering exercise'*. Paranoia? I don't think so!

When Clueless visited our house, she didn't park her car on our drive. The parking of her police car on the Heads drive was a deliberate act by Clueless to cause our family great anxiety and distress. Not just because NP had decided it was our family at fault for the harassment but also because we had made a complaint against her colleague PC Pinky. If we had any doubts whether that was the case, those doubts were well and truly dispatched with what Clueless would go on to do.

Shortly after this, I received an email from Inspector Arsewipe. The email informed me that I was not entitled to a copy of the CCTV footage APC1 and would not be provided with a copy as the Heads were using it as evidence for their criminal allegations against our family.

Hold on a minute. So, NP will not allow me to use this CCTV footage as evidence against the Heads to support our allegation of harassment against them, but NP will allow the Heads to use the same CCTV footage as evidence to support their allegation of harassment against our family. Work that one out.

To be clear, this would be the second time NP would allow the Heads to use the same false evidence against me to support another false allegation. Slight lack of equality maybe!

NP were clearly shitting themselves regarding this footage, they knew what I knew, the footage was false. And if I got hold of a copy, it would fuck them up and blow their investigation as well as their careers clean out of the water.

Due to the above and the fact the civil case was progressing, we decided it would be best to suspend providing NP with our statements. We were of the view that providing NP with statements regarding the criminal investigation whilst at the same time trying to resolve the matter through civil mediation, was counter productive. What was the point anyway? It wasn't going to be fair.

Chapter Fourteen
Civil Shenanigans

Our solicitor had received correspondence from the Head's solicitor. Contained in this correspondence was a Notice to Admit Facts (NAF) for each member of our family. The Head's solicitor requested we each sign our relative document.

An NAF is a document used in civil cases such as ours when one side requests that the other side accept and admit that the facts contained in the NAF are true. That way those facts do not have to be contested, and the case can concentrate only on the facts that are contested, sort of streamlining if you like. Our solicitor could not understand how the Heads could serve us with a NAF before they had served their Counterclaim. In normal practice, it would be the other way around, the Counterclaim would be served before the Notice to Admit Facts.

Of course, the Heads did not have a Counterclaim so the issuing of the NAF at this stage was an underhand way of trying to get our family to admit to certain things so the Heads could then include it in their Counterclaim. Basically, the Heads and their solicitors were trying to pull a fast one. Why our solicitor didn't twig this God only knows, I'm sure it didn't have anything to do with the fact he would be able to charge thousands of pounds for his part in dealing with these NAFs!

If we had known better at the time, this would have been one of the first red flags that our solicitor may not have always been acting in our best interests. One of any solicitor's responsibilities is to protect their clients and the other side from unnecessary costs and to prevent costs from spiralling out of control. This is to try to make the civil justice system work for everyone, in that if one side has more money than the other, that side cannot price the other out of the market, so to speak. Sounds good, doesn't it, it doesn't work! Money talks, end of.

So, as the Heads had issued the NAFs before their Counterclaim, our solicitor maybe should have told the Heads that we would not be dealing with the NAFs until we received their Counterclaim, but he didn't. He told us that as the NAFs had been issued via the Court, we were legally obliged to complete and return them. Whether that's right or wrong, I am not sure. Anyway, at a cost of several thousand pounds as well as countless hours of our time, we did as we were advised.

However, looking on the bright side, this made it clear to us that the Heads did not have a Counterclaim as they were trying to trick our family into giving them one.

Needless to say, the NAFs were a complete lie. The allegations contained in them were so ridiculous it is hard to believe that their solicitor could have believed them. I will list just one of the facts from my NAF that I was expected to admit to below. There are many more I could list but just this one will tell you all you need to know, I'm sure.

Just to explain for those who may not have been involved in civil litigation. As we took civil action against the Heads, we are referred to as the Claimants and the Heads are the Defendants. The NAFs can be rather confusing to begin with because of the way they are written. What this document is requesting is for our family to admit to the facts as they are written, not as it may appear that we have already admitted to the fact. So, when it is written as below 'It is admitted by the first claimant', it does not mean that I have admitted to the fact already, but that if I sign the document, I will then be admitting to the fact. I hope that makes sense and I am not insulting your intelligence, but I think it is important to be clear on this point as it could give the reader the completely wrong impression if they were not sure.

Contained in my Notice to Admit Facts was,

'It is admitted by the First Claimant (me) that on the 29th July 2014, he did push a wooden fence post that was situated on the Defendant's property so as to collide with the Second Defendant (Mrs Head).'

The answer is NO, I did not do this. Yet again, the Heads are making the despicable claim that I assaulted Mrs Head. Absolute bastards.

Oh, one small point about the above allegation,

ON THE 29TH OF JULY 2014, I WAS ON HOLIDAY, IN PORTUGAL

What the fuck. I assume this was the same assault as they had previously stated happened on the 24th of July 2014 and not another allegation regarding another assault that didn't happen! Either way, it is clear the Heads told so many lies they did not know whether they were coming or going, in fact, they did not care whether they were coming or going. They know that right from the very start they have been able to say and do whatever they like and it will be okay. Lying through their teeth had got them exactly where they wanted themselves, and us, to be.

I hope I do not need to, but I would like to make it clear that I nor any member of this family have ever hit or tried to hit or assault any member of the Head family in any way, shape or form. For the Heads to make this allegation against me again is despicable, the damage this could do to me is beyond words.

I was extremely concerned that the Heads will include this allegation in their statements to NP regarding the harassment and that NP would treat me with the same level of inequality and discrimination that they did regarding the false allegation by Mr Head that I caused Criminal Damage to the fence and between them, try to destroy my life again.

This allegation even now is very hard to take. Being falsely accused of assaulting a female pensioner was one of the worst things I could imagine to be accused of. If the Heads do make this allegation to NP, whether they formally investigate it or not they can still record it on to the Local Police System. This information could then be disclosed in a Disclosure and Barring Service (DBS) check. As I work as a self-employed Sports Coach mainly in Care Homes for the elderly, this would also have a massive impact on my business. No Care Home in their right mind would let someone who was even suspected of assaulting a pensioner through their doors, and rightly so.

To be clear, the police have no obligation to inform an individual of any information they have entered onto the Local Police System or even the Police National Computer. So, if this was to happen, I wouldn't even know about it. Imagine that, NP wouldn't do something like that though, would they? I know they are bent and incompetent, but that would be just plain evil!

By this time, we had just entered into the fifth attempt at mediation that had been suggested by the Heads through their latest solicitor and agreed by ourselves. Clearly, it was not the best way to start the mediation process by making further despicable allegations against our family, or was it? Was this a sneaky way of trying to put us on the back foot, to intimidate us into meditation for fear of what the Heads would do next? Whatever our thoughts were, we were more determined than ever to mediate a solution.

To facilitate this latest attempt, both sides had agreed to employ the services of a firm of Mediators. This company has a panel of mediators that are totally independent of any authority or body.

Both parties agreed on a mediator and the process began. Like all things legal, it doesn't come cheap, although compared to the costs of taking the matter to court it was a drop in the ocean. The idea is not that one side admits to anything as such, it is that both sides agree to a compromise regarding events up to that point and how to move forward, forgive and forget so to speak. Although we were and always had been willing to try mediation, we were sure this latest attempt would end the same way as the previous four attempts with the Heads either refusing to compromise or as before, exploiting and manipulating the opportunity for their own gain.

I know that sounds very negative and may appear as though we were not giving mediation the best chance of success. I can assure you that was not the case. There was not a family alive that wanted the harassment to stop more than us, we would have tried anything and everything and given it our best shot. I make no bones about it; this was the worst experience of our lives by a million miles. You could add up all the shit that happened in our lives up to this point and it wouldn't come close to what we were going through. Hard to believe I know, but true.

In any event, we would have our barrister present at the mediation so he would be guiding us through and advising on what was agreeable or not. Also, one reason why we were unsure that the Heads were serious was that whilst they said they wanted to mediate a solution, they were at the same time providing NP with their statements regarding our alleged harassment of them. We, on the other hand, had suspended providing NP with our statements to give mediation the best possible chance of success. Hardly a good basis for successful mediation, however, after a few weeks of back and forth, we had agreed on a mediator.

Chapter Fifteen
The Hand of God

Deranged

Although both parties had agreed to mediation, the harassment did not stop. The next incident worth mentioning happened in mid-June 2016. We live very close to the local Theme Park and on this particular day, they were holding a Britain at War event, and I was looking out of our rear bedroom window watching a Spitfire and Hurricane flying around.

I could also see Mrs Head at the back of her garden pruning a bush with a pair of shears. My wife came into the back garden with our grandson, he was only four months old, so my wife was carrying him in her arms. When Mrs Head heard my wife in the garden with our grandson, she stopped pruning the hedge and moved to a position immediately behind the fences between the two back gardens. Mrs Head then stooped down behind the fence and to my astonishment, I saw her hand come under the fence into our garden. Mrs Head repeatedly grabbed at the soil and the fence with her hand. I don't know if any of you can remember a film called 'The Hand' which was a film about a hand funnily enough, it was a horror film where just a hand would creep along the floor towards a person that might be sleeping in bed or a chair, the hand would stealthily crawl onto the person and strangle them. The hand of Mrs Head was exactly like that, the way she was grabbing at the soil was just like the hand creeping along the floor in the film, it was very creepy. My wife was not aware that Mrs Head was doing this as she was facing the other way. In fact, my wife wasn't even aware Mrs Head was in her back garden at this point. So, when she heard the noise behind her she turned to see the hand grabbing at the soil and fence. My wife stood there looking at the hand for about thirty seconds or so, she, like me, could not believe what she was seeing. She initially thought it was a rat and was scared and thought the best thing to do was to keep still. When she realised it was a hand, she became even more scared. She said it was like she was frozen to the spot for a short time, just like when I was assaulted by Mr Head also in our back garden. Mrs Head continued to grab at the soil and fence for at least a minute or so until my wife came inside. Sometimes a minute can seem a lot longer than you think. A few seconds later, Mrs Head reappeared from behind the fence, returned to the back of her garden, and carried on pruning the bush.

I didn't think I would ever see anything more bizarre than the war dance performed by Mrs Head on the verge in front of our house after they eventually brought their Wheelie Bins in, but the actions of Mrs Head on this occasion topped even that.

We already had concerns about taking our grandson out the front of our house due to the harassment. Now and yet again, due to the actions of Mrs Head, we couldn't even take our four-month-old grandson into our own back garden without being harassed. This was the very first time we had taken our grandson into our back garden and this was what happened. It was a horrendous situation to be in and no way to live a life.

This was also another clear example of the delusion the Heads had for harassing our family. If the Heads could harass, they would harass, in any way they could, and they couldn't stop. When you consider that at this point, we had agreed to mediation and had even appointed a mediator, it confirmed to me that the Heads had no intention of mediating a solution. We found the behaviour of Mrs Head regarding this incident to be deeply disturbing.

What NP would go on to do to our family regarding this incident turned the horrendous situation into an absolute debacle. NP and in particular, PC Clueless heaped so much shit onto our family regarding this blatant act of harassment, it was beyond our belief and imagination. Even after all that had gone on before, what NP would do was as low as it was pathetic.

It would have been great to have this incident recorded as it would again allow us to prove to NP beyond any doubt that we were telling the truth, and the Heads were harassing our family and not only that but that they were truly deranged, deluded and dangerous.

Well guess what, by this time we had installed our own CCTV system, so we had this entire incident recorded from start to finish. When we played the CCTV footage back, it clearly showed the hand of Mrs Head coming under the fence into our garden and grabbing at the soil and fence, even though we could see it with our own eyes, again, it was still hard to believe.

Mrs Head was so fucked up, she was the driving force behind the harassment, she dictated what happened and controlled Mr Head. She must have lied to him as much as she lied to NP, and he, like NP, believed every word and did whatever she said. She really was evil.

Mr Head was a horrible man. He was abusive and aggressive and had no respect for anyone including and especially women. There are not many men that I have met that would assault a woman, but clearly, he would, and he did, and then lied about it. He was so old school, he thought women were the weaker sex and should know their place and if they stepped out of line, he would put them back in line, unless it was Mrs Head and then he was her lap dog obeying her every command. He also suffered from the red mist, when there was a situation that could have been sorted calmly and rationally, he just could not do it. He just resorted to type and used abuse and aggression to sort it his way. When that red mist descended there was no going back, he did not know what he was doing or saying, and he lost all control of his body and mind. He could cause serious harm or even kill someone when he had lost it.

Little Head was just a wet sponge, a drip and a coward,

'Oh, mummy, mummy, mummy, the girl next door tailgated me along the road, and I was really scared. Call the police.'

He was a grown man for God's sake. He would portray himself as a victim and that we were harassing him because he was gay and had mental health issues. What a prick.

And Sponger, he was just that, he was only with Little Head for a free ride, milking them for all they had. He too claimed to have mental health issues and that both he and Little Head would self-harm due to the stress that our harassment was causing.

In fact, and it is a fact as I have the evidence to prove it. The Head family repeatedly contacted NP and told them they were suicidal due to our behaviour. They would go so far as to detail an incident that had caused them to contemplate taking their own life, knowing full well the incident they described had not even happened. To be clear, both Mr and Mrs Head were retired, and both Little Head and Sponger were adults, so for all four of them to have reached the age they had, their suicidal tendencies could not have been that strong, could they?

During the criminal and civil case, when the Heads lies got them into a situation where they couldn't tell an even bigger lie to get them out of the shit they had caused, their go-to plan was to claim Mrs Head had attempted suicide. This happened on several occasions, even during the civil trial. Honestly, I am not joking, this really happened, on several occasions, one or another of the Head family falsely claimed to have attempted suicide to escape from the hole they had dug for themselves.

I am in no way belittling self-harm or suicide, just the opposite. My point is that the Heads were not and never had been suicidal and in all the time of the harassment and the involvement of NP and in the civil case. None of them provided any evidence of attempting suicide or self-harming, no doctor's letters, no evidence of admissions to hospital following an attempted suicide, no evidence of attendance at Accident and Emergency to have their wounds stitched, no psychiatric reports or mental health assessments. My point is that all the Heads were so fucked up that they would even stoop to the level of feigning self-harm and suicide to convince others including NP, that they were the victims of our harassment. So, it is not me that is belittling suicide and self harm, but the Heads. They were a sick family beyond belief.

I cannot imagine what life was like living in that house with all of them being so fucked up. No wonder they focused on fucking up our family to deflect from their own chaotic life.

Once we had viewed our CCTV footage of the incident to confirm the 'Hand of God' had been recorded. I also realised that the behaviour of Mrs Head would also have been recorded on their CCTV as well as ours and that this footage may well be even more compelling than ours. I tried to contact PC Clueless to report the incident as she was now our SPOC, but could not get hold of her, so I left a message informing her that I think it to be vital that the Heads CCTV footage of this incident, as well as our own, should be looked at as a matter of urgency and in particular before the Heads have the opportunity to delete the footage.

Both ours and the Heads CCTV footage of this incident would be Key Evidence in proving the harassment of this family by the Heads and that every effort should be made by NP to obtain this. I did not hear back from

Clueless, so I called 101 and reported the incident to Force Control. They informed me that PC Clueless was not on duty for several days, but another officer would call me back.

Later that evening, I received a call from a PC Luck (that was his real name or the name he told me anyway). I explained the incident to him as best I could and not for the first time an Officer NP made me feel like I was a pathetic little man who was wasting their time over an insignificant incident or an incident that hadn't even happened. His attitude was a disgrace. Standard.

Because of this and the fact I knew by now that if you are ever going to get anywhere with NP, you must keep banging on the door, I called PC Willis, the *'good cop'*. I explained the incident to him along with some of the other incidents that had happened recently such as Mrs Head manicuring the verge in front of our house and the *'war dance'*, which were also recorded on our CCTV. PC Willis was more understanding, probably because he was more aware of the history between ourselves and the Heads, he said he would contact his Sergeant to see if anything could be done and would call back tomorrow.

PC Willis also asked what we thought of the attitude of PC Luck when he called us. I told him it was a disgrace, but I also wondered why PC Willis asked me this question. It may be my mind working overtime, but I got the distinct impression PC Willis knew PC Luck was a wind-up and that there wasn't an officer called PC Luck at all and whoever it was on the other end of the phone when I spoke to *'PC Luck'* was deliberately taking the piss.

A couple of days later, we received a visit from PC Willis. We showed him the CCTV footage of the *'Hand of God'*, and he provided us with a memory stick to download the CCTV footage onto. PC Willis said he would speak with his Sergeant again and call back the next day with an update as far as viewing the Heads CCTV footage and collecting the memory stick.

Well, well, well can you believe it? That was the last we heard from PC Willis regarding this incident. He, just like the other officer who threatened to show our family the slightest bit of respect and equality, PC Good, suddenly disappeared off the face of the earth.

Stupidly, I knew PC Clueless was back on duty the next day, so I expected her to call as she was our SPOC. As expected, the next day came and went without any contact from Clueless or anyone else from NP. It had now been one week since the '*Hand of God*' and no attempt had been made to gain or even view the Heads CCTV footage of the incident. This could be no accident, if it was the other way around and the Heads informed NP that we had CCTV footage to confirm we had harassed them, NP would be around our house like a police officer after a BOGOF on Dinky Doughnuts at ASDA.

We were told by Inspector Arsewipe in our face-to-face meeting with him and PS Quack, that we were to report all incidents to NP, no matter how trivial or insignificant we think they were, and they would be included in the investigation. However, when we reported an incident that was much more serious than that, we were treated like something you would scrape off the sole of your shoe.

As expected, a further week went by without any further contact from NP. No one had called to collect the memory stick with our CCTV footage, no one had attempted to even view, let alone gain a copy of the Heads CCTV footage. It was now two weeks since the incident and our SPOC, PC Clueless, had made absolutely no attempt to even contact us.

About ten days later, the first day of July, in fact, PC Clueless called at both ours and the Heads houses but neither of us was at home. PC Clueless then called at one of our neighbours, the same neighbour that witnessed the Public Order offence by Mrs Head against our daughter.

Our neighbour told us of this visit and informed us that Clueless asked her if she had witnessed anything between ourselves and the Heads and whether she would be prepared to make a statement. Our neighbour told Clueless that she had witnessed several incidents, and an officer of NP (PC Pinky) attempted to intimidate her into not signing her witness statement regarding one of these incidents.

Our neighbour asked Clueless about the incident where Mrs Head put her hand under our fence. Clueless said she was aware of the incident, and she had spoken to Mrs Head about it and Mrs Head said she was weeding!

We had previously shown the footage to our neighbour, so our neighbour asked PC Clueless if she had seen the CCTV footage of the incident, PC

Clueless said she hadn't. Our neighbour suggested to Clueless that she should see the footage.

Needless to say, our neighbour never heard from PC Clueless again. Not regarding the '*Hand of God*' incident or with regards to making a statement detailing the other incidents that she had witnessed, even though PC Clueless had been tasked with taking statements from neighbours and witnesses as part of her '*impartial evidence-gathering exercise*'!

Anyway, why would PC Clueless have spoken to Mrs Head about the incident when she had not spoken to us or seen the CCTV footage? We report a blatant act of harassment by Mrs Head and the first and only thing Clueless did before speaking to the alleged victims and viewing our evidence, was to speak to the suspect. We had been told on many occasions by NP that a suspect was not informed that an allegation had been made against them before it had been investigated and evidence secured. This is to help prevent witness intimidation by the suspect against the victim and to not allow the suspect to create a false defence or alibi. Clearly, those rules do not apply to the Heads or PC Clueless. Well, it's the Heads, so a little bit of crime didn't matter!

I hope you are ready for this bit. You may not agree with me, but I find this sickening. While PC Clueless was at our neighbours' house, the Heads arrived home in their car. I did not know if it was a coincidence or whether Clueless saw the Heads arrive home but within a minute. PC Clueless left our neighbours' house and walked up the road towards the Heads house. The Heads had the doors of their car open and were carrying what looked like shopping into their house.

PC CLUELESS WALKED ONTO THE HEADS DRIVE, LEANT INTO THEIR CAR, PICKED UP THEIR SHOPPING FROM THE BACK SEATS AND CARRIED IT INTO THE HEADS HOUSE FOR THEM.

CLUELESS THEN RETURNED TO THE HEADS CAR AND CLOSED THE DOORS BEFORE RETURNING INSIDE OF THE HEADS HOUSE. ALL THE TIME, MR AND MRS HEAD AND CLUELESS WERE LAUGHING AND JOKING AS IF THEY WERE BEST FRIENDS RETURNING FROM LUNCH OR A SHOPPING TRIP.

To be clear, by this time, the Heads had assaulted me, for which Mr Head had been issued with a Conditional Caution for Common Assault, assaulted my wife, threatened to attack our daughter, verbally abused all members of this family, made numerous false allegations to NP, provided false statements to NP, submitted false evidence to NP, destroyed our property, taken our land, made Malicious Communications via Social Media and harassed our family to the point of destruction and they are the suspects in a live police investigation for their relentless harassment of our family. And PC Clueless, who was supposed to be carrying out an *'impartial evidence-gathering exercise'* into the harassment,

CARRIED THE HEADS SHOPPING IN FOR THEM, LAUGHING AND JOKING WITH THEM WHILE SHE DID IT.

I hope I do not have to say anymore as I am lost for words. This is one time I cannot babble!

Over the following few days, we arranged several meetings with PC Clueless to discuss the *'Hand of God'* incident. PC Clueless cancelled all of these appointments at short notice. She said she would call us the next day to rearrange the appointments, but she never did.

It was blatantly obvious that PC Clueless did not want our CCTV footage of the incident. If NP did have a copy of the footage, even they would struggle to find an excuse for the behaviour of Mrs Head. Clueless was using the delay tactic to avoid gaining the evidence from ourselves and the Heads.

The way it was at that time. if PC Clueless had not seen the footage, she could accept the excuse by Mrs Head that she was weeding. If PC Clueless were to see the footage, she could not possibly conclude Mrs Head was weeding, no one in their right mind could view this footage and determine Mrs Head was weeding. Even a Numpty Police officer would struggle.

Finally, a whole month to the day since the incident, Clueless called to collect our CCTV footage. We now know why Clueless had left it this long, most CCTV systems run on a 28-day cycle or less. So, by this time, the Heads CCTV system would have recorded over the *'Hand of God'*, so the Heads recording of the incident would have been lost. Clueless also informed us that the Heads had provided her with their statements regarding the allegations of harassment against our family but that she was unwilling to inform us of the specifics of these allegations and that we would have to be interviewed under caution if we wanted to find out.

We told her that we would love to be interviewed under caution regarding these allegations. Despite the stress it would cause, we knew the allegations would be false and we would be able to expose the Heads for the bare-faced evil liars they were. Not that it would have made any difference to NP, but at least we would know what we were being accused of.

This visibly shocked Clueless. She clearly expected us to shit ourselves at the thought of being interviewed under caution by NP, again. She didn't know what to say so came up with some bullshit excuse why we could not be interviewed under caution until her *'impartial evidence-gathering exercise'* had been completed. So, I told her, okay, you let me know when that was done, and I will attend for interview.

There was no way in the world that I would let this excuse of a police officer think she could intimidate me. Although I knew being interviewed again would be a traumatic experience, it was an experience I needed to go through to do my best to bring the harassment to an end.

I knew deep down though, that NP would never allow our family to expose the truth. If they did, they would be as deep in the mire as the Heads. Furthermore, for Clueless to inform us that the Heads had provided her with their statements, meant she must have been in contact with the Heads since the *'Hand of God'* incident but had failed to gather the Heads CCTV footage as evidence. Convenient!

Beyond belief

Just three days after this visit, we received an email from Clueless regarding the *'Hand of God'*. Again, the whole email was so demeaning and as expected, equated to a complete exoneration of the conduct of Mrs Head. It stated,

'Dear Mr and Mrs Bean

'I have viewed the footage you provided me with on 11th July 2016 (AP1) regarding Mrs Head poking her hand under the fence; 11-06-2016, in the rear garden whereby Mrs Head puts her hand under your fence, no offences – it is clear from the

footage that Mrs Head is gardening and pulling weeds from between the fences. I will speak with Mrs Head. I will not be investigating this matter any further.'

Oh my God, she actually went and did it! PC Clueless concluded that the CCTV footage of Mrs Head poking her hand under the fence into our rear garden clearly showed that,

'Mrs Head was gardening and pulling weeds from between the fences.' That was beyond belief, crazy.

Firstly, there were no weeds between the fences, it was solid concrete. Secondly, there were no weeds in the area of our back garden where Mrs Heads hand appeared under the fence and even if there were, Mrs Head would not have been able to see them from her garden. Thirdly, whether Mrs Head was weeding or not, she did not have the right to weed our back garden. This was the clearest possible act of harassment by Mrs Head you could possibly imagine with the strongest possible evidence to support, and NP still concluded it amounted to no offences. Mrs Head was not weeding, this conclusion by Clueless was so insulting to our family. It again confirmed to us and the Heads they could do what the hell they like to our family, and it would be okay as far as NP was concerned and it would not amount to any offences. The letter also stated,

'I have spoken with Inspector Arsewipe regarding the issues you discussed on Monday 11th July 2016, in relation to your complaint, (and lack of feedback and communication), previous incidents and the need for a taped interview.

Your complaint is still under investigation by our Professional Standards Department (PSD) and is ongoing and I cannot make comments regarding this, nor can I disclose the allegations made by Mr and Mrs Head against you, these allegations as I explained will be put to you via voluntary taped interview, which you are not happy to proceed with Total bollocks.

I never discussed my complaint against Pinky and Perky with Clueless on the 11th of July 2016. I would not discuss this matter with another officer, particularly one who works with the officer who was the subject of my complaint. I am not stupid (well maybe a bit), I had been warned by my barrister that it was likely I would be discriminated against for making the complaint, so I was not going to brag about it or hand myself on a plate to NP. This was Clueless's way of telling me she was going to discriminate against our family regarding her investigation into the *'Hand of God'* and her *'impartial evidence gathering exercise'* because I had made a complaint against her colleagues.

She also stated I was not happy to proceed with a voluntary taped interview, total bollocks. It was the exact opposite; I told Clueless that I desperately wanted to be interviewed to find out what the Heads had alleged against us and to defend our family from the allegations that I knew would be false. It was Clueless who had come up with the bullshit reason I could not be interviewed at this time.

Clueless had deliberately lied in this letter regarding the content of our meeting to portray our family in a bad light and to appear as though we were not willing to partake in the investigation into the harassment. Nothing could be further from the truth, if we were going to be treated with equality that is!

We were absolutely disgusted at the content of this email. We did not think it possible for NP to treat our family with a greater level of inequality, discrimination, disrespect and disdain than we had already been subjected to by NP. But fair play to PC Clueless, she managed to achieve the almost impossible. For anyone to conclude that Mrs Head was weeding the area between the two fences, was a total insult to anyone with an ounce of intelligence, and particularly this family. We would challenge anyone to watch the CCTV footage of this incident and come to any other conclusion than this was a blatant act of harassment. We showed this footage to many people and Clueless and NP stood alone in their conclusion that Mrs Head was weeding.

This obviously compounded our already strong suspicion that Clueless was never going to help this family and indeed would do all she could to assist the Heads and NP in their continued and unrelenting harassment of our family.

Due to the content of the letter from Clueless, I emailed Inspector Arsewipe to tell him what I thought of the content of the letter and how disrespectful and insulting PC Clueless had been. I asked Arsewipe to ask himself this question,

'When was the last time you repeatedly poked your hand under your neighbour's fence to weed their back garden?'

I also asked Arsewipe if he would come and see the CCTV footage we have of this incident.

I did receive a reply from Arsewipe but he chose not to answer my questions. He instead decided to write the most derogatory email I have ever received. I could list the entire email here but I think that would be a bit of an overkill, I am again mindful that parts of this book may be a bit tedious, but also necessary to be able to give you enough of the picture for it to make sense, I hope I have got the balance right, if not, I suppose you will not be reading this book by now anyway. If you have stopped reading, I do understand, but you are going to miss out on what I have been dying to tell you for ages.

Never mind, your choice.

However, the main points stated by Arsewipe in his email were as follows. Regarding the '*Hand of God*' Arsewipe said,

'The actions of Mrs Head do not constitute a criminal matter – any person is perfectly entitled to act in this manner.'

Bollocks. No person is perfectly entitled to weed their next-door neighbour's garden without their permission, particularly when they are under investigation by NP for the harassment of the same next-door neighbours.

'No element here is tantamount to a criminal offence or would be constrained as harassing behaviour.'

Bollocks. It was the most blatant act of harassment you could ever see. And what the fuck does the word '*constrained*' mean in the context of the sentence. Twat.

'PC Clueless is empowered to use her discretion in order to keep the peace. In this instance seemingly acting on your behalf at your exception over weeding.'

Bollocks. Mrs Head was not weeding, Arsewipe was basically telling our family that Clueless used her discretion not to consider the actions of Mrs Head as harassment because Mrs Head would kick off.

'I cannot see how putting hands under your fence can be seen as unnecessary contact.'

Bollocks. Mrs Head didn't have to poke her hand under the fence into our back garden, whether she was weeding or not. Mrs Head did not need to do this, it was unnecessary, uninvited and deliberate contact with our family. In any event, it was Arsewipe himself who told us that he had instructed the Heads not to have any unnecessary contact with our family. If he did not believe this to be unnecessary contact, then what was? Assaulting us again maybe!

'Again, I will re-iterate that there is no clear indication at this stage that the evidence provided will meet the threshold for a criminal offence of harassment to be formally investigated.'

Fuck off. They have assaulted me, assaulted my wife, threatened our daughter, stolen our property, stolen our land, caused criminal damage to our property, made false allegations to the police, used social media to incite others to harass and threaten our family, all of which were fully evidenced and witnessed and Arsewipe stated there was no clear indication that the Heads conduct would meet the threshold for a criminal offence of harassment to be formally investigated. What an insult to our family. Excuse my French but, FUCK OFF YOU C U NEXT TUESDAY.

'Crimes that have been investigated will not be re-investigated – this was not promised to you in November.'

Bollocks. That was exactly what we were promised in November by him and PS Quack in our face-to-face meeting with these two officers of which I have a recording of the meeting to prove it.

'I am proud that Kettering has seen some of the best crime reduction figures within the county which has come about by utilising this proactive approach.'

Bollocks. This proactive approach is to tell the victims of crime that they are not victims at all, and that no crime has been committed against them, so NP do not have to record a crime, so the crime figures drop, and he gets a promotion. Arsewipe is a career cop who does not care about the public or the victims of crime whatsoever. If he, as an Inspector in the Police Force is proud of that, then God help us, because NP won't.

'To be clear – people are lawfully entitled to carry out activities / past times that are not prohibited, weeding, DIY, mowing lawns, interment festivities and parties. The fact that someone might take offence or find these activities annoying or in your terms 'harassing' does not necessarily make them so.'

To be clear. The Heads are prohibited from weeding our back garden without our knowledge or permission. Dick Head.

Arsewipe finished the email by warning us about the angle of our CCTV camera as our footage of the '*Hand of God*' showed part of the Heads garden. I understand that, I wouldn't want the Heads CCTV recording our property, although they clearly were as the CCTV footage of me removing the fence from our land clearly shows me in my front garden!

Anyway, we were doing exactly what NP had told us to do to gain evidence of the harassment. How could we gain evidence of the harassment if our CCTV was confined solely to our property? The Heads and their associates conducted their harassment from outside of the boundaries of our property. In any event, you are allowed to use CCTV to detect and prevent crime, that was all we were doing, detecting crime. Let's face it, somebody had to as sure as hell NP were not going to.

This is not just typical of Arsewipe, but of the attitude of NP towards our family from start to finish and the attitude of NP towards harassment and stalking, not just in our case. Ask the thousands of other families that have been the victims of harassment and stalking for decades.

The police do not take harassment, stalking and domestic abuse seriously. Their attitude is the victim must have done something to deserve it, or in our case, must be the offenders. Incriminate the victim and you have no crime as one is as bad as the other. It is an age-old tactic used by the police to not have to deal with certain crimes as they consider them to be petty or two-way offences where both parties are as bad as each other

How many women will it take to be murdered by their ex-partner before the police realise it is a serious matter? How many victims of a stalker will have their lives ruined before the police take it seriously? How many people will take their own lives because they cannot take the harassment any more before the police take it seriously?

The attitude of the police towards these crimes is outdated and things will never change until their attitude changes. And that attitude will not change until it is made to change. If I were a bigger man, I would start a movement, peaceful protest you might say, to highlight these failings, to draw awareness that more has to be done to help protect all of society, not just the ones the police feel are worthy of their protection, you know, like offenders.

But I am not a big man, I am old and very tired. But I am sure if a bigger man does come along and start this movement, they will have an army behind them in no time. So many people are desperate to be able to live a happy life but are unable to do so because they feel threatened or intimidated by other people and even more threatened and intimidated to report their problems to the police. Democracy, do me a favour.

We provide NP with cast iron evidence of multiple acts of harassment by the Heads, and all that happens is we get a warning from Arsewipe regarding the angle of our CCTV camera. The email is not merely threatening and extremely derogatory to our family, but also inaccurate regarding the law. I wasn't as clear on the Prevention of Harassment Act then as I am now. I now know Inspector Arsewipes *'interpretation'* of the law was as ridiculous as he was, and he knew it then and he knows it now. Trust me, I could go on and on adding stuff to the above, but this is the best, or worst of it. One day, he will answer my questions.

NP had an absolutely golden opportunity to gain evidence to prove the harassment of this family by the Heads, but they deliberately failed to take this opportunity. NP did not want this evidence, they did not want anything that would get in the way of what they had already decided, the path they had chosen to take, which was our family were harassing the Heads, no matter what. Yet again, we now have to sit back and let the harassment continue knowing no matter what the Heads choose to do, NP would not help us.

The way I was spoken to by PC Luck and the failure by NP to view or to gain a copy of the Heads CCTV footage, was a deliberate failure and an absolute joke. The Heads and NP disgust me.

Every time we had contact with NP, we thought it could not possibly get any worse, but somehow it did, much worse. We struggle to think what will happen next; I am sure we will not have to wait long to find out!

It had got to the stage long ago, but this matter consolidated our feelings towards NP. We really wished we could have no contact with them as each time we do, it causes so much pain and distress. Often, reporting an incident to NP causes more stress than the incident itself and it shouldn't be like that. You should be able to report an incident to the police with confidence that you will be treated with not just equality, but respect and dignity.

That is not the case for our family. I am sure it is not the case for many other families up and down the country that the police have decided to target with their discrimination and prejudice. These officers didn't just treat our family badly, they loved doing it. They loved the thought of inflicting pain and distress on a family they already knew was really struggling, an innocent family who was already the victim of crime. You could see it in their eyes.

But what choice do we have? Do we just sit back and let the Heads continue their non-stop harassment until we are destroyed? There is no one else to turn to for help, not unless you want to be threatened by an Inspector with Perverting the Course of Justice that is. The only choice we have is to keep on contacting NP and hope that one day the penny drops or we are fortunate enough to find the needle in a haystack – that is an officer who is honest enough and strong enough to put their head above the parapet and call out the *'mistakes'* of their colleagues. I think there is less chance of that happening than this book becoming a bestseller!

NP are never going to help us. It is a matter of trying to survive for now, fighting back when I am strong enough, and then doing my very best to hold NP accountable for their actions. And I will do that, or try at least. I will not waver; I will be strong and resolute. I have something in my arsenal that is more powerful than anything NP could ever muster, and it can be summed up in one word, honesty and honesty must prevail.

And if I do manage to do that, NP should not blame me, they should blame PC Clueless. When I saw her carrying the Heads shopping in for them it made me so angry, and I don't do anger. That one thing may seem quite small compared to some of the things that NP have done to this family, but it really got to me. It showed me the level of disdain NP had for our family and that they wanted us to know about that disdain. There is no way Clueless didn't know what she was doing and that it would distress our family. She wanted us to know that she was going to screw us over, just like her colleagues had done. The fact that it amounted to misconduct was neither here nor there to her, what would happen anyway.

It also confirmed to me what I was up against. Taking on an authority not just like, but in particular, the police, would be a huge undertaking and I would not do it lightly. I would go into it with eyes wide open, but not until the time was right. It is hard to explain, but seeing Clueless carrying the shopping in for the Heads should, logically, have made me feel worried, scared and fearful of what was happening. I do not deny, it did, very much so, but it also gave me the strength and determination to keep going against all the odds and to eventually come out the other side stronger than ever with my head held high and my family vindicated. Clueless awakened a beast in me I didn't know existed and NP are going to hear me roar!

I have made my views clear on my feelings towards the word hate, it is a horrible word. But I am very sad to say that I hate NP as much as I hate the Heads for what they have done, and what they continue to do to this good, law-abiding family.

Chapter Sixteen
Mediation, My Arse

It was decided between all parties that it would be better for all concerned if the agreed mediation was to take place at our home addresses. The Heads had again raised an issue regarding the fence and again claimed the fence between the two front gardens was on their side of the boundary, I know, I know, here we go again. So, if the mediator attended the properties, he could see the lie of the land for himself so to speak.

More interesting is that our solicitor had informed us of a telephone call he received from the Head's solicitor. Their solicitor confirmed that the Heads Counterclaim was being *'worked on'* and we should be in receipt of it by the end of the following week, that was the end of June 2016.

Also in this conversation, the Head's solicitor stated that she had visited the Heads property the previous day and took lots of photographs and she believes the boundary fencing to be on her clients' property.

Excuse me love, but you are a solicitor and a shit one at that, but you think you know better than a qualified Chartered Surveyor, HM Land Registry and the CPS! I don't think so love, jog on. This solicitor was clearly as dodgy as the others the Heads had lied to in the past. All would become clear regarding this solicitor later.

Although we knew the content of any Counterclaim by the Heads would be false and easily defended, it was, of course, still very stressful for all members of our family. We just didn't know what allegations it would contain and going by past experience, they would be very unpleasant.

Up to this point, I haven't mentioned much about the impact this was having on our health, I hope that speaks for itself. I do not think many families could have gone through what we have without it having a huge impact on every area of their lives. I also think that there are not too many families that could have coped better than we have. How we had managed to get to this point and stay as intact as we were, really was a miracle.

However, just to give you an idea of what it was like. This particular evening, I was preparing to leave the house to do an individual coaching session with a very promising junior rugby player. She was a lovely girl from a lovely family, and I hope they are all doing well. Suddenly, I started to shake and twitch uncontrollably, I hoped it would soon pass but unfortunately, it did not. I asked my wife if she could phone and cancel the session, and I went to bed. I was unable to function and remained in bed for three days solid.

It had been the weekend, so first thing, Monday morning, my wife made an appointment for me to see my GP. I told my GP what had happened, and she thought I had a mini nervous breakdown. My GP was aware of our situation because the impact on the health of myself and my wife over the past two years had led to us needing medical support on many occasions. I had also accessed support for my mental health which I had been struggling with since being prosecuted for Criminal Damage in 2014.

It came as no surprise that my GP thought it was a nervous breakdown; the symptoms were unmistakable. Unfortunately, this was the first of several breakdowns over the next few years but at least now I knew what was happening and what was causing the shaking and twitching, which made it a little easier to cope with when they happened. The worst thing about them was that there were no warning signs or none that I could see or feel. They would happen suddenly and without warning and each time they happened, I knew it would mean at least three days of being unable to function and at least a week of work, yet more pressure onto our shoulders.

Although we were still in the early stages of the civil case, the costs were starting to mount up. We had already used all our savings and assets, which to be fair wasn't a huge amount. We were already having to take out personal loans to pay our legal fees which didn't help with our situation.

By the time the civil case went to court in March 2018, we had taken out personal loans totalling £55,000 and had borrowed a further £25,000 from a very good friend. In November 2018, we could no longer afford the repayments on our debts, so we had no choice but to remortgage our home to consolidate these debts.

Like most families of our generation, we had spent the past 30 years paying off our mortgage and in 2017, we finally owned our own home, only to have to remortgage in 2018 because of the harassment and the failure of NP.

Right at the end of June, our solicitor received further correspondence from the Head's solicitor. This correspondence contained yet another false allegation by the Heads that we had harassed them. The Heads had not provided their solicitor with any evidence of this allegation, because it was false, but stated that due to this latest act of harassment by our family against the Heads, any attempt at mediation would be fruitless.

So, there you have it. The games had started and yet again the Heads were exploiting and manipulating the opportunity of mediation to make further false allegations against our family. They will just not stop. However, our barrister was strong with the Head's solicitor and told them that if the Heads pulled out of mediation at this stage, they would be liable for our costs so far, which I can assure you was not a small sum of money. This did the trick. The allegation was never mentioned again and mediation continued as planned and a date was set for mid-July. We were extremely hopeful that this round of mediation would at least resolve some of the issues. Doh, wrong again!

Also over this time, due to the failure of PC Clueless to take any action against Mrs Head for the '*Hand of God*' and the other acts of harassment we had reported. Mrs Head had developed an obsession with manicuring the verge in front of our house. Yes, our house, not theirs. This had been going on for months and was steadily getting more and more of an obsession. She repeatedly manicured this area of the verge to within an inch of its life. By the time she had finished, our verge made Centre Court at Wimbledon look like a forest, it was unreal to see. But did we care, did we hell, we had the best-kept verge in the village, and we hadn't had to lift a finger. Brilliant.

As an aside, one of my claims to fame is that I have actually been on the Centre Court at Wimbledon. As a junior, my son was a very good tennis player and qualified to play in a tournament at Wimbledon for two years on the trot. One day, he, I, and our daughter were wandering around the tunnels that ran around the show courts when we came across a big green roller door. I slid the door open slightly and there was Centre Court, we all walked through the door and there was a big sign saying, 'KEEP OFF THE GRASS'.

I thought fuck that, this was my only opportunity to step onto Centre Court, one of the most iconic sporting arenas in the world. I wasn't going to pass up the opportunity, so I walked just a little way onto the court and then done a runner. Yippee, I had been on Centre Court, and no one can ever take that away from me, Cliff Richard, eat your heart out.

At the beginning of July, we received an email from our solicitor stating that the Heads could not meet the proposed mediation date in July due to holiday plans!

Here we go again, again! The Heads had agreed to mediation to take place on this date only two weeks ago. If they had booked a holiday for mid-July, they would have known that at the time they agreed to mediation. The Heads either booked the holiday after agreeing the date to avoid mediation taking place or they were not going on holiday at all. This was just the latest trick in trying to prevent mediation from taking place. The Heads knew they had nothing to mediate with, so they had nothing to gain and a lot to lose if it was to happen. This act was a clear indication of the Heads attitude to mediation.

Through protracted communications between the relevant solicitors, a new date for mediation was set for mid-August. This communication didn't come for free and every email to and from the solicitors was costing us £150 a time, so the costs of trying to mediate a solution were mounting up. It wasn't just the cost of these communications, there was the cost of our barrister to attend the meeting as our legal representative and the cost of the mediator, which was to be split 50/50 with the Heads.

I think this was part of the Heads plan to try to make the cost of continuing with mediation and the civil case so expensive that we were unable to continue. We would later discover that in the early stages of the case, the Heads costs were being met by an insurance policy they had but the upper limit of the policy had been reached, so they were now funding their case themselves. That might have had something to do with why the Heads had employed the services of their latest solicitor. If I am right in what I think could have been happening, it is no wonder the Heads were running us around in circles with mediation, the Notice to Admit Facts and their Counterclaim.

By this time, one thing that we had received from the Head's solicitor was a list of witnesses the Heads were relying on in their civil case, not just to defend themselves from our allegations against them, but also as witnesses to acts of harassment by our family against the Heads. Most of these witnesses were either our neighbours or relatives of the Heads and some were both.

It was a Sunday afternoon; I had taken our grandson for a walk in his buggy. As I was nearing home, one of the neighbours the Heads had listed as a witness was in his front garden. As we neared each other, I wasn't sure what to expect, he then said, *"Hello, how are you?"* in the usual friendly way, we had greeted each other for the past decade that we had

been neighbours, and I responded with the same. We started to talk to each other as we had done many times before. After a while, I said to him I was surprised he had said hello to me as he and his wife were listed as witnesses for the Heads in the civil case.

He told me he had no idea that the Heads had listed them as witnesses. He also said that he could not think what the Heads would have been referring to regarding acts of harassment by our family against the Heads as they had not witnessed anything.

It may not sound like a big deal in the grand scheme of things but to us, it opened a whole new avenue of harassment by the Heads. For the Heads to falsely list our, and their neighbours as witnesses without their knowledge and to claim these neighbours had witnessed our family harassing them when they had not, was very wrong and very worrying.

What else had they been saying about us, what lies had they told our neighbours. If it was anything like what they had told NP and their solicitors, no wonder some of our neighbours turned their back on us and no wonder some of them actually joined in with the harassment, particularly if they had been told I had assaulted Mrs Head. They must have thought we were the scum of the earth, I mean, who would doubt the word of a couple of pensioners? I can just imagine the neighbourhood gossip.

'Poor old couple being harassed by their younger next-door neighbours. I've never liked them anyway, they look the sort, let's tell Sharon next door, she will spread the word."

239

This was a deliberate attempt by the Heads to make this family even more alienated and isolated in the neighbourhood. We had no idea at this stage how successful this tactic would become. However, it also made me think, how many others on the Heads list are not aware they have been listed as witnesses? I think this point became clear in the leadup to the civil trial!

Just a word to those neighbours who did turn their backs on us. The neighbours who used to say hello when we passed each other on the way to and from the shop but now crossed the road to avoid us or simply turned their back when we passed, the neighbours who no longer waved when we saw them in their front garden.

Don't think we don't know who you are. You're not as clever or as subtle as you think and if you ever find out the truth, don't think you can just start to say hello again. You had a choice, and you chose to believe the gossip and the lies. We do not need people like you in our lives, we have had enough of people like you to last us a lifetime. Bridges burned.

One of our neighbours went far beyond turning his back on us. He became as obsessed as the Heads in destroying our lives. He was not the only neighbour who joined in with the harassment though, this was why what we endured was sometimes referred to as Community Harassment – word spreads around the neighbourhood and then into the wider community. The gossip starts to snowball out of control, and it cannot be stopped like a runaway train and before you know it, the whole community has become involved. Once the original harassers have managed to convince others that they are the victims it feeds right into their hands. They no longer have to do the harassing themselves; all they have to do is incite others to do it for them and the Heads seem to be masters of incitement. It is more common than most people think, occasionally, it makes the news.

To those few and far-between neighbours who stood by us and even became firm friends, you cannot imagine what it meant to us to have your friendship. You rose above the lies and the gossip that you must have heard just like the rest of the neighbourhood, but you did not jump on the bandwagon and did not take the soft option. We will never forget that. Thank you.

Going back many years, a man was wrongly accused of being a paedophile by a neighbour. This neighbour spread these rumours around the neighbourhood, and it ended up with another man who lived in an adjacent flat to the person labelled as a paedophile, breaking into his flat and beating him to death. The man wasn't a paedophile at all. He had learning difficulties and lived alone, that's all. He was a vulnerable man living his life in peace until someone decided to label him a paedophile and someone else killed him because of it.

I remember it well as it was reported that the victim had called the police to report the harassment on many occasions, but the police failed him to the point that they would not even respond to his pleas for help when he was being attacked. The news article even played a recording of a conversation between a police call handler and a police officer who was asked to respond to the 999 call from the man and the officer said he wasn't going to attend as the man was a time waster and a complainer. You got the usual bullshit from the police afterwards.

'We have made mistakes but we have learned from these mistakes and made changes so this sort of thing can never happen again.'

Absolute rubbish. We must have heard that a hundred times over the past decade and nothing has or will ever change, end of.

Red Flag

Anyway, back to the civil case for a while. Finally, after excuse after excuse, on the day in July when we should have had civil mediation, we instead received the Heads Counterclaim. I am not sure why their solicitor decided to issue the Counterclaim on this day and while the Heads were supposedly on holiday, but nevertheless, we had this document, at last.

Although our solicitor informed us it was not worth the paper it was printed on as their solicitor had failed to either sign the document or submit it to the civil court, so it was not a legal document. Accidental? Call me sceptical but I think not.

I wasn't up to speed with civil proceedings back then, so I was not aware that as this document was not signed or submitted to Court, there was no requirement for it to be responded to as it was not a legal document. As previously stated, it is the duty of any solicitor to always act in the best interests of their clients, therefore, in my opinion, our solicitor should have told the Head's solicitor that as the Counterclaim was not a legal document, it would not be responded to until a signed copy had been received and submitted to Court.

The Counterclaim consisted of two parts, a **Particulars of Counterclaim** and a **Schedule of Complaints,** standard stuff in civil cases. The Particulars of Claim particularised the incidents, clue in the name, and the Schedule of Complaints is basically a list of the incidents in chronological order.

These documents were basically a lie from start to finish, no change there then. They had clearly been made up from the Notice to Admit Facts we had been advised to complete by our solicitor. So, in effect, and thanks to our own solicitor, we had actually paid for the Heads to issue a totally false Counterclaim. These lies include,

Particulars of Counterclaim

'The Head's claim we have been monitoring and recording them for 4 years.'

Untrue, the only recordings we have ever taken were of the Heads committing offences and/or harassing us. This was on the advice of NP to gain evidence.

'The Head's again claim the fence they had erected between the two front gardens is within the boundary of their property.'

Untrue. End of. They have accepted and admitted the fence between the two front gardens is on our side of the boundary. The only reason the Heads are continuing to dispute this can be because they have dug themselves into such a hole regarding the fence, they cannot now accept and admit the fence is on our land, or they have a trick up their sleeve.

'In spite of the defendant's (the Head's) new fence being located within the defendant's boundary, the claimants (us) have removed this fence causing damage.'

Untrue, the fence is not located within the Heads boundary. I did say you would be sick of hearing about the fence, but that is not our fault, the Heads just kept bringing it up at every opportunity, but why? They must know by now they were on a loser every time they do. I suppose it was the only thing they could call on, that and the false allegation that I assaulted Mrs

Head. The Heads and Pinky invested so much time and energy into the allegation I caused Criminal Damage to the fence, the fact the CPS discontinued their prosecution against me must have cut the Heads and Pinky so deep that they just could not let it go. It's pathetic.

'The first claimant also trespassed onto the defendant's land to pour concrete into the defendant's drain.'

What! Where the fuck has that come from!

'The 1st and 2nd defendants have both suffered a personal injury and physical injuries as a result of the claimant's wrongdoing.'

Absolute bollocks. No member of our family has ever acted in a way which could or would have caused any member of the Head family any injury of any sort. Any injuries they might have suffered were because of their actions, not ours. Bastards.

'The Head's claim the 1st claimant (me) has assaulted the 2nd defendant (Mrs Head).'

Oh my God, here we go again. The Heads were again claiming that I assaulted Mrs Head. This is a total and utter lie. At this point, the Heads had given three different versions of the alleged assault on two different dates, none of these versions' had a shred of truth about them. On one of the dates they alleged I assaulted Mrs Head; I was in fact in Portugal. This false allegation again demonstrates the depths the Heads would go to harass this family which showed no sign of abating. To falsely accuse someone of assaulting you was sick beyond belief. Clearly, this does not bode well for the civil mediation that is due to take place in just a few weeks. How were we supposed to mediate with a family who was making such despicable allegations against us?

'The claimants have made false allegations to the Police of criminal conduct by the defendants.' Untrue, we never made any false allegation to the Police.

'The claimants (our family) *have all made witness statements in support of their allegations to the Police which contain statements which are untrue and which the defendants have known to be untrue.'*

This gets very interesting!

Firstly, as stated earlier, we had suspended providing NP with our statements to give mediation the best chance of success, so we had not made witness statements to the police at all.

Secondly, and even more important. If we had provided witness statements to NP at this stage, how the hell would the Heads know what our statements contained unless NP had disclosed the content of our statements to the Heads?

If you recall, PC Clueless did take a copy of my detailed notes away with her so she could continue to write up my statement in evidential format.

You don't think, no, she wouldn't, would she! PC Clueless wouldn't have written up our statements herself and then provided the Heads with a copy of these statements, not during a live police investigation to which the statement would relate, would she? No, that was too far-fetched, surely not, I mean, that would be an act of gross misconduct, wouldn't it? No, out of the question, I know NP were fucked up and would do anything to screw our family over, but not that, surely! There must be another explanation, yea, that's it, another explanation. But just imagine if I were to get evidence that NP had in fact disclosed our statements that we hadn't even written to the Heads. But that was never going to happen, was it?

I bet you're glad you are still reading now.

Defendants Schedule of Complaints

'Early 2013

The defendants claim the fourth claimant (our son) drove his vehicle at the second defendant (Mrs Head), her brother and sister-in-law (The Hopertys) in a fast and excessive manner causing them alarm.'

Oh dear, the Heads have fucked up again. In early 2013, our son could not drive, had not passed his driving test and did not own a car.

This is yet another outrageous lie. Clearly, the Heads were so fucked up and obsessed with their harassment that it would not have crossed their minds that our son didn't have a car at the time they said he drove at them. They had told so many lies that they didn't know fact from fiction anymore.

To make a false allegation against me was one thing, to make one against my son was another. Bastards.

'13th June 2014

The defendants claim the fourth claimant (our son) drove his vehicle at the second and fourth defendants (Mrs Head and Sponger) who were standing on their drive swerving away at the lastminute causing both the second and fourth defendants alarm and to feel intimidated by the fourth claimant to put them in fear of an impact with the fourth claimant's vehicle.'

This incident did not happen. The Heads had CCTV installed at the front of their property, the same CCTV that had recorded me removing the fence, so would have a record of this incident if it had happened. Once again, the Heads were making a false allegation against our son, again claiming he used his car to harass them. Bastards.

'24th July 2014

The defendants claim that as the second defendant (Mrs Head) was walking along her fence in her garden the first claimant (me) reached through the fence in an attempt to remove the timber striking the second defendant as he did so.'

Yet another different version of events of the way the Heads claimed I assaulted Mrs Head.

'24th July 2014

The defendants claim the above action was witnessed by the first claimant (that should state defendant not claimant) *who attempted to pull down the reed fence which he had erected between the two properties. The first claimant (me) walked back onto his own property so that the first defendant (Mr Head) would not have been able to have made contact with him but later advised the Police that the first defendant had physically assaulted him a fact that was impossible and untrue.'*

Jesus Christ. The first defendant (Mr Head) was offered and accepted a Conditional Caution for Common Assault by NP for this incident to include a course of anger management. To be clear, to be offered a Conditional Caution by the Police, the suspect must admit guilt for the offence. For Mr Head and their solicitor to now claim it was impossible and untrue

for him to have assaulted me, is diabolical and obviously untrue. Their solicitor would have known that unless NP had actually rescinded the Conditional Caution given to Mr Head!

'*28th July to 1st August 2014*

The defendants state, following the above events the defendants erected a fence on their side of the boundary so as to try and prevent further harassment by the claimants. This fence was erected within the defendant's boundary as had been communicated to them by the claimants.'

Not the fence again. It would be funny if it wasn't so fucking boring. When were the Heads going to stop going on about the fence when they knew they were lying? Never, that's when.

'*11th September 2014*

The defendant's state that following a confirmation from the Police that the first defendant (Mr Head) had been issued with a caution (for assaulting the first claimant) and so as to incite a response from the first defendant, the first claimant (me) confirmed to the Police that as he knew that the first defendant had the caution, that he was going to remove the fence between the claimants' and defendants' properties. The first claimant then proceeded to forcefully remove the August 2014 fence erected by the defendants without their permission and using a hammer and his foot to kick it down. During this action, the first claimant caused damage to the fence and both the first and fourth claimants trespassed onto the defendants' land to remove it. This act of damage was reported correctly by the Claimants to the Police. CCTV'

The above paragraph confirmed the Head's solicitor was fully aware that Mr Head had accepted a Conditional Caution for his assault on me, an assault that the Heads and their solicitor stated in the previous paragraph to have been impossible. When were the lies ever going to stop, even the Head's solicitor was as bad as them.

I wonder if the Head's solicitor would consider it an offence for every carpenter to use a hammer when removing a fence panel from a post, or was it just me? I sure as hell did not use my foot to kick the fence down. The Head's solicitor stated at the end of this claim. *CCTV.*

So, if you had the *CCTV* showing me using a hammer and my foot to kick the fence down, then disclose it to our solicitor, but you wouldn't, because you couldn't, because it did not exist. TWAT.

As with all the Heads documents and statements, there was so much more I could add to the above. These two documents confirmed to me that the Heads were in it until the bitter end. They were prepared to put everything on the line for this. They were so obsessed and deluded that they couldn't or refused to see the truth.

There was no way on this earth that their solicitor did not know the Heads were lying, so should have advised them to think again about what they were doing and the risks involved. Instead, the Head's solicitor decided to join in with the lies. Clearly, the Head's solicitor was after their money, or was it the Heads money?

As this was the fourth different solicitor the Heads had used, maybe these other solicitors had advised the Heads to consider their position, but the Heads refused to listen to their advice and got rid of them or as I suspect, their solicitor refused to represent them any further.

To be fair, the Heads wouldn't listen to anyone, they were completely unapproachable. Right from the start, if anyone did or said anything they didn't agree with or even like, they would resort to type and use verbal and physical aggression until they thought they had won the argument. For them to still be that way at their age, that approach must have served them well up to this point, but not this time. There was still time for them to come to their senses and see the truth that was slapping them round the face. If not, they would lose and lose big, their choice.

Pointless

16th August 2016, big day, it was the day of civil mediation. We hoped that this day would see a resolution to many if not all the issues between ourselves and the Heads. In the time leading up to this day, the Heads had been in overdrive with their harassment, not a day had gone by in the last two weeks without something happening. They were clearly trying to get us to snap and retaliate either to give them some ammunition to barter with or an excuse to cancel mediation altogether. That was never going to happen.

But we might well have snapped their fucking necks as what an absolute fucking waste of everyone's time mediation turned out to be.

The Heads and their solicitor, (this is the same solicitor who submitted the Particulars of Claim that stated Mr Head did not assault me!), spent the whole day disputing the line of the boundary between our two properties and the fact the fence the Heads had erected in July/August 2014 and again in November 2014, was on our land. They just would not budge and refused to move on until this matter was resolved but only resolved in the way they wanted it to be. They would only move on if we agreed the boundary line between the two properties was where they said it was and that the fence they had erected in the summer of 2014 was on their land. It was an absolute joke.

We would make a proposal to the mediator, and then our barrister and the mediator would go around the Heads house to put the proposal to the Heads and their solicitor. They would then return an hour later with our proposal being refused. To be clear, the Heads were refusing to accept what they had already accepted. They had previously confirmed to us exactly where the boundary was between the two properties and the said fence was on our land, but now, on the day of mediation, they are again disputing their own confirmation regarding the boundary and the fence.

In an attempt to find a solution to the above and to be able to move on and deal with some of the other matters, we again offered the Heads the same compromise we had offered them in September 2014, which was that the Heads could keep the fence on our side of the boundary as long as they reduced the height of the three high panels between the two front gardens to a reasonable height. This offer was again turned down point blank by the Heads and their solicitor.

We then offered the Heads a revised compromise where they only needed to lower the height of the two high panels nearest the road to allow light into our front window and for our daughter to feel a little safer when leaving our house. This revised compromise was also refused. Our family was the only side trying to mediate. The Heads would not budge or give any ground or concessions whatsoever, that was no surprise, but their solicitor was just as bad as them. When our barrister returned from the Heads, he would be exasperated at the conduct and attitude of the Heads and their solicitor. I would have loved to have been a fly on the wall.

248

Eventually, after SIX hours of back and forth, our barrister and the mediator returned from the Heads and the mediator said,

'The fence is on your land. I have just put a string line up on the line of the boundary in accordance with the land registry plans, and the fence to the front of the properties is clearly on your side of the boundary. I have informed the Heads of my findings and rather than reducing the height of the panels between the two front gardens as you have offered, they would rather remove the fence from your land completely and keep it the same height.'

Our barrister then drew up a document stating that the Heads would remove the fence from our land and that if the Heads were to re-erect the fence it would be entirely on the Heads side of the boundary. This document was signed by ourselves and the Heads and witnessed by our barrister, the Head's solicitor and the mediator, thus making it a legally binding document.

We had a little time left so we continued with the mediation. The mediator informed me that the Heads had made an allegation to him that I had intimidated one of their witnesses. This witness was the neighbour who had said hello to me when I was returning home from a walk with my grandson about a month earlier. I assume this neighbour had spoken to the Heads regarding our chat, probably to ask them why the fuck they had listed him and his wife as witnesses without their knowledge or permission. The Heads had then twisted this into an attempt by me to intimidate this witness. I informed the mediator of the true version of events and with that the mediator said, *'I give up.'*

And that was that. Mediation was over and not a single thing had been resolved, in fact, we were further away than ever to finding a resolution. The Heads had yet again manipulated and exploited the opportunity of mediation and spent nearly the entire day disputing what they had already agreed and accepted and then finished the day off by making yet another false allegation against me to the mediator. It was clear from the conduct and attitude of the Heads, that they were not interested in resolving the issues between us and were intent on continuing their delusional fixation in harassing this family, and their solicitor was as much to blame. To be clear, this mediation cost us in the region of £10,000, and it achieved absolutely nothing. That was down solely to the Heads and their twat of a solicitor. As far as the Heads were concerned it was mission accomplished, again.

Chapter Seventeen
Short but Not Sweet

Well, here we are. I am about to reveal what I have been teasing you with for ages, if you haven't guessed already that is. If you haven't, I hope it doesn't disappoint you when all is revealed. So, sit down, strap yourselves in, and get your popcorn. It's one hell of a ride.

Firstly, let me recap, just so you are up to speed for what I am about to tell you all. Sorry if I babble a bit.

Well, you remember PC Pinky, the officer in charge of the investigation into the allegation of criminal damage made against me by Mr Head for removing the fence from our own land, the same PC Pinky who failed to conduct a fair, reasonable and proportionate investigation into that allegation, the same PC Pinky who failed to investigate all lines of enquiry in that investigation whether they led to or from the suspect, the same PC Pinky who requested I provide an interview under caution for an offence he knew I did not commit, the same PC Pinky who required my son to provide an interview under caution for an offence he knew our son did not commit, the same PC Pinky who refused to record or investigate our many reports of criminal conduct by the Heads including the Malicious Communications via Social Media by Mrs Head and Little Head, the same PC Pinky who refused to show me the Key Evidence being used by NP to offer me a Conditional Caution, the CCTV footage APC1, the same PC Pinky who claims to have submitted this same evidence to the CPS to support their prosecution against me, the same PC Pinky who included inaccuracies and blatant lies in his Report of Crime and Witness Statement also submitted to the CPS to support their prosecution against me, the same PC Pinky who was asked by our daughter not to contact me because I was seriously ill, the same PC Pinky who phoned me the day after I was released from hospital after suffering my second suspected heart attack in a week, the same PC Pinky who falsely recorded me onto both the Local Police System of NP and the Police National

Computer as an offender, the same PC Pinky who interfered with another police officer's investigation regarding our three reports of Public Order offences against Mrs Head, the same PC Pinky who had been asked not to contact our daughter directly because of the distress he caused her, the same PC Pinky who phoned our daughter while she was at work to inform her she was the subject of a police investigation for an allegation of a Public Order Offence that had been made against her by Mrs Head, the same PC Pinky who put our daughter through the distress of being interviewed under caution by Pinky and his sidekick Perky, for this one allegation, which had no evidence to support, the same PC Pinky who despite three allegations of Public Order offences and Harassment made against Mrs Head with two independent witnesses who had both made statements to Pinky, and the video evidence of Mrs Head committing one of these acts, did not require Mrs Head to provide an interview under caution, the same PC Pinky who attempted to intimidate our witness to one of these Public Order Offences into not signing her statement, the same PC Pinky who I had made a formal complaint against due to his conduct and treatment of our family which was being investigated by the Professional Standards Department of NP. Okay, okay, I will stop there.

Well, you also remember PS Quack, the same PS Quack who tasked PC Perky to investigate my report to NP that Mr Head had lied in his statement to NP in support of his allegation of Criminal Damage against me, of which PC's Pinky and Perky were the investigating officers, so Quack tasked Perky to investigate Mr Head as well as himself and his joint investigating officer PC Pinky, the same PS Quack who denied the tasking of PC Perky to investigate this matter would create a conflict of interests, the same PS Quack who wrongly determined Mr Head had not told any lies in his statement and that the statement of Mr Head was based on his *assumption, presumption, and interpretation'*, the same PS Quack who stated my claims that Mr Head had lied in his statement were *'hearsay'*, the same PS Quack who failed to conduct a reasonable and proportionate investigation into the attendance of Sponger at our daughter's place of work, the same PS Quack who concluded Sponger had done nothing wrong, the same **PS Quack** who replaced **PC Pinky** as our SPOC following the submission of my complaint against PC pinky that at that time was being investigated by the PSD of NP, the same PS Quack who sat across a table from us in our dining room with Inspector Arsewipe where we discussed the ongoing harassment issues with the Heads and also my complaint against PC Pinky, the same PS Quack who wrongly told me at that same meeting that my complaint against PC Pinky may have to be put on hold due to the Harassment investigation and to investigate both matters at the same time would create a *'conflict of interests'*. Okay, okay, I will stop there.

Well, you have probably guessed anyway but just in case. We discovered through social media that PS Quack and PC Pinky were in a personal relationship with each other, they were living together and had a child together.

WTF. I could go on and on, as often as I do, about what this means, regarding openness, transparency, honesty, conflict of interests, equality, impartiality, respect, deceit, disdain, consideration for victims of crime, and conducting yourself in a manner to allow the public to feel all parties are being treated with equality, etc, etc, but it does not need to be explained, the evidence is clear. All I will say is the following.

Inspector Arsewipe, PS Quack, PC Pinky and PC Perky, and the organisation, which means senior officers of NP, all knew about this personal relationship between Quack and Pinky from the very start, but none of them ever mentioned a single word about it to any member of our family at any stage of their involvement. Even when we sat across our dining room table from Arsewipe and Quack and actually discussed the complaint I had made against Quack's personal partner, PC Pinky, neither of them made any attempt whatsoever to mention this relationship to us. Even when Arsewipe confirmed that Quack was now our SPOC, they still did not mention this to us.

I have the Body Worn footage of this meeting and when we are discussing my complaint against PC Pinky, PS Quack is an absolute nervous wreck. Of course, I didn't know why at the time, I didn't even notice at the time. And just a few minutes after Arsewipe confirms Quack is now our SPOC to replace Pinky, Arsewipe and Quack have the nerve to tell me my complaint against Pinky cannot be investigated due to a *'conflict of interests'*.

It was crystal clear. PS Quack on multiple occasions had the opportunity to inform our family of her relationship with PC Pinky but deliberately failed to do so. It is also crystal clear, PS Quack abused her position as a police officer and our SPOC to discriminate against our family because I had made a complaint against her personal partner. The level of Gross

Misconduct by Arsewipe, Quack and Pinky in particular and NP as a whole, is staggering.

Because of this discovery, it was crystal clear we were not being treated equally by NP. But also, if any reader was in any doubt about the conduct, or misconduct to be more accurate, of NP, surely this has removed that doubt. When you put the conduct of these three officers together with that of the likes of Blankbrain, Perky, Sloth and Clueless, surely, any possibility that the conduct of these officers against our family was in any way a mistake, accidental or coincidence, is eliminated.

NP had deliberately targeted and discriminated against our family from the very start of their involvement, and, just like the harassment, the longer it went on, the worse it was getting. Our barrister had warned me that NP would discriminate against us for making a complaint against one of their own, but to discover the level of discrimination, deceit and the lengths these officers would go to hurt our family, a family that had done absolutely nothing wrong and nothing to deserve it, was still shocking.

Furthermore, get this for irony. At this time, and probably still to this day, PS Quack was the Chair of the Numpty Police Black Officers Association and regularly spoke out about the impact of racism and all forms of discrimination. Yet, here she is blatantly discriminating against our family because I had made a complaint against her personal partner. All the above, but particularly PS Quack, are a disgrace to the Police Force and a discredit to everyone who either fights against or is a victim of all and any form of discrimination, prejudice, and injustice. Shame on you Quack, shame on you all.

Chapter Eighteen
The Only Way is Down

Soft Option

The very next day after mediation, we received a call from our solicitor who informed us that he had received correspondence from the Head's solicitor stating that Little Head was now making a claim against our family for personal injury due to a mental health condition caused by our harassment of him and his parents.

Really? On the day of mediation, the Heads made yet another false allegation that I intimidated one of their witnesses. The very next day after mediation, Little Head made a false claim for personal injury because we harassed him and his family, causing him a mental health condition. Please, give us a break. This wasn't drip, drip, drip, this was tsunami, tsunami, tsunami. Honestly, it was relentless.

Our solicitor also said that he had spoken with our barrister regarding the allegation made at mediation that I had intimidated the Heads witness. Our solicitor advised us not to speak with any of our neighbours that the Heads had listed as witnesses.

Hang on a minute. It was the Heads alleged witness who had spoken to me, he initiated the conversation. He wasn't aware that he had been listed as a witness by the Heads, if he had been aware, he more than likely wouldn't' have spoken to me. Also, as I was aware he had been listed as a witness, I definitely would not have spoken to him, so it wasn't my fault or the neighbour, but the Heads, again.

But well done to our solicitor, you just tell your clients (us) not to speak to our neighbours and make us feel even more alone in our fight against everyone and their dog. Don't you go fighting our corner and telling the Heads to stop making false allegations against us will you? No, you do exactly what NP has done and blame us because you think we are the soft option. Thanks for your support, mate. If things weren't bad enough, now our own solicitor was being a dick.

The Heads had listed as witnesses, the neighbour who lived directly opposite our house, the neighbour who lived directly opposite the junction at the top of our road, their relatives who live around the corner, and the neighbours who lived in the house that backs on to our rear garden. What the fuck are we supposed to do? Never leave our house just in case one of these neighbours who probably had no idea that they had been listed as a witness by the Heads, speaks to us. Talk about feeling isolated, we couldn't feel more isolated if we lived on the moon.

This is one of the main impacts of Group or Community Harassment and one of the main aims of the harassers. You become isolated and everyone in the neighbourhood or community is against you. It may not be too bad for some people, who may not care what others think of them, unfortunately, that is not the case for me, I have always cared very much, too much, about what others think of me.

This made it very difficult to deal with and was the main contributory factor to the phobia I had developed of feeling only four feet small when I left the house. It was such a strange feeling to walk past someone knowing I was taller than them, but feeling and visualising them towering over me, scowling, pointing, and calling me all the names under the sun, especially as they nor I were doing anything wrong. It would even happen when I was miles away from home and passing people I had never seen before and would never see again, it was as though everyone on the planet thought I was a bad man. The power of the human mind!

So, this is the result of the past two days. On the 16th of August 2016, we attempted mediation. The only thing that was decided on the day, again, was the exact line of the boundary and that the Heads had erected the section of the fence between the two front gardens on our side of the boundary, rather than except the compromise we had offered, the Heads elected to remove their fence from our land completely, which they probably have no intention of doing anyway. During mediation, they made yet another false allegation that I had intimidated their witness. The following day, Little Head made a personal injury claim against us because he had suffered a mental health condition due to our harassment of him and his parents. And our own solicitor kicks us while we are down. Brilliant!

255

After living at this address for over 18 years and having a great relationship with all our neighbours, we are now in the ridiculous position that we cannot even speak to these neighbours because of the harassment and the spreading of false and malicious rumours into the community by the Heads, and a toothless, but wealthy solicitor!

No wonder some people turn to crime. It must be a fucking ball. Just ask the Heads!

Course of Conduct

It was a Friday morning in mid-October 2016. I returned home from work to see, to my surprise, that the Heads had started to do some work on repositioning the fence to the front of the properties onto their side of the boundary as per the agreement reached at mediation.

The builder and neighbour who had previously excavated the trench, erected the retaining wall, destroyed my rose bush in 2013, and re-erected the fence back on our land in November 2014, Trigger, was doing this work for the Heads. This was despite the agreement reached at mediation on our request that Trigger should not do this work due to the previous issues with him.

Our barrister was of course more experienced in this sort of thing and knew the pitfalls and risks of Trigger becoming involved again. This would be another person in the neighbourhood that the Heads could again manipulate and use to continue the harassment of our family, and boy, was our barrister spot on. The course of conduct Trigger was about to embark on was beyond what even we could have imagined, despite what we had already been through. He became as deluded as the Heads in harassing our family and he almost lost his liberty because of his delusion, the Heads played him like a fish on a line.

On this particular morning, I returned home from work and parked my van on our drive as usual. When I got out of my van, I heard a voice say, *"Are you happy now?"*

I looked up to see Trigger looking at me over the low-level fence panel nearest the pavement.

The following is the conversation between me and Trigger. Trigger is in *italics*.

'What do you mean?'

"You need to come to your senses."

"I don't know what you mean."

"You need beating up."

"Are you going to do that then?"

"No, not me I am far too old, you would batter me, absolutely batter me."

"No I wouldn't there is not an aggressive bone in my body."

I then came indoors. I was not surprised that Trigger had spoken to me, but I was shocked at what he said. Why would he think I need beating up? Even if he did think that why would he need to tell me if it wasn't to intimidate, threaten and harass me? There could only be one reason, because of the despicable lies the Heads must have told him about me. Including I had assaulted Mrs Head, no doubt.

After a while, I decided to phone my solicitor to inform him of what had just happened and the fact that the Heads had employed Trigger to do the work on the fence when they had agreed at mediation not to do so. My solicitor advised me to report the incident to NP.

So, against every brain cell I had left working, I then reported the incident to NP as advised and to be fair to my solicitor, I am so glad I did as this was only the start of what Trigger would go on to do.

I could not believe or understand why Trigger said I needed beating up. That is not something you just say to someone without reason, or believing you had a reason. I do not think it takes a genius to guess where that belief came from. The Heads had managed to incite another neighbour to harass our family.

And just like the Heads, Trigger was in his late sixties or early seventies. I am not too sure on this point, but I think I may be right in saying that

Trigger had a serious illness a few years previous and nearly died, he also had a pronounced limp. Why would he want to fight the Heads battle for them? Okay, fair enough, do the work for the Heads if he wants, but just keep his head down and do the work. It must have been some pretty bad stuff he had been told about us by the Heads for him to have developed the level of hatred he had for our family and me in particular. Why would he just not want to live a quiet life?

It may not seem like a big deal, someone telling you need to be beaten up and if it happened in isolation, it wouldn't have been, I suppose. But in our circumstances at that time, it had a huge impact on me, more than I ever thought it could and should, but definitely more than it would have done if it wasn't for the events of the past few years. To me, it was our worst fears realised, the Heads malicious lies had incited yet another person to become involved in the harassment, but unlike the friends and relatives who stated on social media that they wanted to harm us, this was another neighbour, someone else from the community who clearly thought we were the family from hell.

It wasn't so much the impact on my physical health, but the impact on my mental health that was surprising, worrying in fact, and I am not ashamed to say, distressing. I was really confused, anxious and concerned for my safety. I had felt confused and concerned before, but I had never felt anxious or had anxiety before. The feeling of my stomach constantly being tied up in knots, my heart pounding and racing, panicking over everything all the time, thinking everything was going to end badly and there was no hope that things were ever going to change.

As stated earlier, I had not been afraid of anything for decades. Now, I feared everything all the time, even things that had not happened and were not likely to happen. Feeling like this was alien to me. Why was this happening to me? How was this happening to me? What was happening to me? I really felt so close to losing the plot.

The next morning, I received a visit from two officers from NP regarding the incident with Trigger the previous day. Unfortunately, due to the impact of the previous day, I was feeling very unwell and was unable to talk to them. My wife spoke with the officers briefly but became very upset. The officers were very understanding and advised my wife that if I felt better later in the day, I should call 101 to arrange another visit.

So later that day, I called 101 to arrange another visit, and to their credit, later that day, another two officers called. My wife said it was a different two officers than had called earlier, but they were officers all the same and I was very surprised they had called a second time. I was very surprised they had called the first time to be fair.

I gave the officers a brief history of the harassment issues with the Heads and the involvement of Trigger over the past few years. I then explained in detail the incident the previous day. The officers said they would go and speak to Trigger straight away. The officers then left our house and returned about ten minutes later. They informed me they had spoken to Trigger and he had admitted to them that he had said to me *"You need beating up,"* and that he was sorry, he did not know why he said it and he did not bear any animosity towards me or any member of my family and he had no intention of carrying out his threat.

The Police said that Trigger had recalled the incident almost word for word as I had told them, and they had advised him not to carry out any more work on the fence. Before they left, they gave me the same advice as we had been given at the start of the Heads harassment, *'That if anything else happened, to report it to NP no matter what it is and how insignificant it might seem and to record the incident in as much detail as possible as soon as possible after the event.'*

Sound advice, you see, I don't hate all police officers, and they don't all hate me, allegedly!

Thank God for that we thought, it was just a one-off. Trigger had either lost the plot for a moment or just wanted to look like a big man in front of the Heads. Whatever the reason was for the conduct of Trigger, we were wrong, totally, completely and utterly wrong to think it would be a one-off. This would be the start of a prolonged *'Course of Conduct'* by Trigger that would end with severe consequences for him and for me!

Over the next few days, the incident with Trigger started to have a massive impact on me. My anxiety grew and I could not stop thinking that Trigger was going to arrange for someone to carry out his threat that I needed *'beating up'*. I was convinced that if I left the house I would be attacked.

I started to have a horrific vision that played over and over in my head. I can't call it a nightmare as I was fully awake. The vision was that I was taking my grandson for a walk in his buggy around the block when a car pulled up next to me. Two men jumped out of the passenger side and started to kick the shit out of me until I was on the floor barely conscious. They stopped beating me up and as they went back to the car, they picked up the buggy with my grandson in and took it into the back of the car with them and drove off. The next moment, it was like I was in the car, watching what was happening, it was as if I was a camera fixed to the rear window of the car looking forward. The two men were sitting in the back seat with the buggy between them. They were arguing and shouting at each other, *'What shall we do with the buggy, what shall we do with the kid?'*

Then, the man sitting on the passenger side opened his door and threw the buggy out with my grandson still in it. I was then out of the car and back on the side of the road. I had just managed to get to my feet to see the buggy bouncing along the road until it came to a stop on its wheels. I could see that my grandson was still strapped into the buggy so I started running as fast as I could but when I reached the buggy my grandson was dead.

There were loads of people walking by and I was shouting for help. My grandson and I were covered in blood, but everyone just kept walking past looking at me and my grandson. Some stopped and pointed, some couples spoke to each other as they passed, one man even stopped so his dog could have a wee on the grass verge while he looked at us and then when his dog was done, he just carried on walking. They could all see what had happened and what a state we were in, but they just ignored us and carried on walking their dogs or taking their kids to the park. No one stopped to help or even asked how we were, they simply did not care, and we did not matter.

First thing Monday morning, I made an emergency appointment to see my GP. I told her about the incident with Trigger and the vision I was repeatedly having, and I was prescribed a course of Diazepam.

I was unable to work for the whole of the following week and I was very mentally unwell. I was really struggling to cope with the effect the incident with Trigger was having on my health.

Just a word on anxiety before I move on, and I know some may find this controversial, but I do not mean it to be. It is just something I have been thinking about for a while that might even help someone, who knows? I think anxiety has become a modern word, a goto for how we may be feeling, and I think social media has played a part in that. Many people now use social media, particularly the younger generation, so many people will use social media to exploit and control them. Many children may not be aware of how many bad people are out there, waiting for an opportunity to exploit their vulnerabilities. It is also the younger generation, particularly children, that has seen anxiety jump to epidemic levels. Why? Anxiety has always been around, so why now has it become so common?

When I was younger, I got nervous. For example, when I was a child, I was very nervous about my first day at school. I can remember crying like a child in the front room of our house saying I don't want to go; I don't want to go. Oh, I was a child. I was very nervous about going to the dentist or doctor's, I was nervous about taking an exam, I was nervous about going for a job interview or my first day in a new job, I was nervous about getting married and becoming a father. I was nervous when I appeared in court, and so on and so on. We all get nervous or anxious on occasions.

Today, no one seems to get nervous anymore. Those same things that made my generation nervous, now make this generation anxious. Obviously, today's children and young adults look to social media for answers, which can be a good thing. Don't get me wrong, it is probably better than in my day when we didn't look for answers at all. If you told anyone including your parents that you were anxious, they would look at you as if you had told them you were an alien from Mars.

But social media can also be a bad thing. There are plenty of people using social media who look for vulnerable people of all ages to exploit. If someone were to ask Google, *'Why am I feeling nervous or anxious?'*

They would find as many sites that are good as well as bad. Many of these sites would take advantage of the way these vulnerable people are feeling and drum into them, *'You're not nervous, you're anxious and you need to do this, or you need to take this medicine I can give you'*

It can even be worse than that, but I do not want to give such sites any publicity. Please, please, please, do not misunderstand me. I know real anxiety exists and it is a serious and genuine illness or even disability. However, I think the line between anxious and nervous has become very blurred for many. My daughter has chronic anxiety, I can remember taking my daughter

261

to her first day of work in a new job. As we arrived my daughter said to me, *'I'm anxious.'*

Me being the understanding dad that I am, said to her, *'You're not anxious, you're nervous, it is perfectly normal to be nervous about your first day in a new job.'*

This is something that has stuck with my daughter since that day and I hope has helped her cope on many occasions. Being nervous and anxious is usual, common and normal in all of us, it lets you know you are alive, heightens your senses and alerts you to risk or danger, we would all be like zombies without it. Sometimes, when you are feeling nervous or anxious, it is not necessarily abnormal, unusual, or different to anyone else, and not necessarily a bad thing, maybe.

Strange Encounter

I will chronicle the next bit as I think it might help you to understand what happened.

31/10/2016

08.10 am. My wife leaves for work in our car as usual. When she stopped at the junction at the top of the road, which is directly opposite Trigger's house, he was standing on his drive staring at my wife. My wife looked both ways to check for traffic, she then looked back at Trigger and he was aggressively mouthing off towards my wife and pointing towards our house. My wife could not hear what Trigger was saying as she was in her car. The road was then clear, so she pulled out of the junction and continued her journey to work.

8.20 am. I noticed Trigger was once again working on the fence to the front of the properties. After the incident just ten days ago when Trigger said I needed to be beaten up, despite being spoken to by the Police and advised not to do any more work on the fence. I was very concerned that Trigger was once again working on the fence.

Following the advice of the Police to report each and every incident, I called 101 to have this incident logged, sounds sad I know, but that is what you have to do. If you are being harassed, you must establish a '*Course of Conduct*', without a course of conduct, it cannot be considered as harassment. Although the Prevention of Harassment Act has been refined since its introduction in 1997, it is by no means watertight, some loopholes can be used by offenders to escape sanction, which is partly the reason harassment is still so common today. It is very easy to do and very difficult to stop, legally. The other part of the reason is that the police either fail to enforce the laws on Harassment and Stalking or do not even know the law, take your pick, I think it is a bit, well a lot, of both to be honest.

I also texted my wife to tell her that Trigger was once again working on the fence. My wife was very concerned for my safety and in particular, my mental wellbeing so much so that she telephoned a neighbour and asked the neighbour to keep an eye on the situation in case Trigger started anything.

09.30 am I heard a knock on the front door. I went into our hall and looked through the glass to see it was Trigger. I could clearly see Trigger was holding a claw hammer in his right hand.

I told Trigger several times to go away but he just kept knocking on the door.

Trigger then shouted, *"Why don't you just come outside, you fucking coward?"*

So, here was Trigger just ten days after being warned by the police for his conduct and advised not to do any more work on the fence, standing outside our front door holding a claw hammer and telling me to come outside.

My heart is thumping and racing just writing this, just nerves though, not anxiety, maybe!

This incident caused me a great deal of distress and once again, I was scared for my safety. What was Trigger intending to do with the hammer if I did, stupidly, go outside? If I didn't go outside, was he going to smash the glass in the door and enter our house? What if I had not seen him holding the hammer? I know our paths had crossed previously so I knew he was a bit of a dick, but other than that I did not know what he was capable of, he could have been a total psychopath for all I knew.

It was wise that my wife had called the neighbour to keep an eye on things as she was watching from her bedroom window, so of course, witnessed the entire incident. Although we did have it recorded on our CCTV anyway and the camera doesn't lie, unless it was our camera of course, then our camera, according to NP, showed Mrs Head weeding an area of our back garden, when there were no weeds in that area of our back garden. Funny that!

Once again, I called 101 to have the incident logged. The call handler said she would log it under the same incident number as the earlier call and inform her Sergeant as there was a clear escalation in the situation.

I phoned my wife to tell her what had happened. I don't really know why, I suppose it was because I was so concerned about the situation, I was in a bit of a state, to be fair. It is not every day someone knocks on your front door holding a claw hammer and says, *'Why don't you just come outside, you fucking coward?'* It's only ever happened to me well, once, actually!

My wife came home as she was naturally worried about me. She had seen the state I had been in for the past ten days and she, like me, did not know how much more either of us could take. About an hour later, my wife decided to return to work, so we went out of our front door together. As my wife started to reverse off the drive, Trigger, who was clearly still next door and must have heard our car, peered over the low-level fence panel again and the following conversation between Trigger, my wife and I happened. Trigger is again in *italics*,

"Can I come round and put this in?"

Trigger was holding a long Coach Bolt in his hand.

"No, you can't"

"Why?"

"Because you threatened to have my husband beaten up."

"I didn't threaten to have him beaten up. I just said he needs a good hiding and that's exactly what he needs, a good hiding."

"The Police have already spoken to you about what you said."

"Yea, and do you know what they said, they said if Billy calls the Police again, they will come and Taser him."

Trigger then looked at me and said,

"You need a good hiding, I want to tell you a little story, I will tell you when your missus has gone."

"No, tell me now, we have no secrets."

"You need to come out of the closet and get a good hiding, a good hiding is what you deserve."

"Why do I need a good hiding, explain, what have I done?"

"Why does Billy need a good hiding, are you saying my husband is gay?"

"You need to come out of the closet and take your beating, what you have got is hereditary, you are your wife's puppet, she controls you, you do whatever she tells you."

Trigger then leaned over the fence and was again holding the claw hammer. He then said to me, "You look seriously ill."

"I am seriously ill, I am on Diazepam, Beta-blockers and Statins."

"Yea, I know."

Almost schizophrenically, as though suddenly, we were best mates, Trigger then said,

"How are you going to maintain your chimney breast with that fence there?"

He then said to my wife,

"Can you put this in for me?"

And held out the Coach Bolt towards my wife.

"No."

Trigger then lost his temper and said,

"Then I am coming round to do it myself."

"No, you're not."

Trigger then said to my wife in a threatening and intimidating manner,

"Then you will have to stop me."

Trigger then started to walk down the path towards our driveway, still holding the claw hammer.

We both rushed indoors, and I again called NP but this time via 999 instead of 101. We simply did not know what Trigger was going to do. He was clearly mentally disturbed and unstable in our *'conversation'* with him, changing from being aggressive, to calm and then back to aggressive.

This caused us both great distress. On top of everything else, we now had another clearly deranged and deluded neighbour who was not only intent on harassing us but clearly wanted to hurt us. Trigger was as fucked up as the Heads. Could this really be happening? It must be quite rare to come across one neighbour in your life who developed a delusional fixation with harassing their next-door neighbour, but we had four living in the same house next door! And now we had a neighbour who lived opposite the junction, less than 50 metres away. What are the odds of that, I wonder. I am not a celebrity, but get me the fuck out of here, please!

Talking of schizophrenia, I received a Valentine's card from a schizophrenic a few years ago. She had written a lovely little rhyme in the card, it went,

'Roses are red, violets are blue, I'm a schizophrenic, and so am I.'

I never found out who sent the card, it could have been any number of people I suppose!

Later that day, we were visited by two officers concerning the incidents we had reported earlier in the day. They must have looked at the police logs as the first thing they said was that the conduct of Trigger amounted to Hate Crime due to the references to,

266

'Coming out of the closet.' And the threat of violence, *'You need a good hiding.'*

However, the officers were not aware of the incident ten days ago. When we informed them of this, they said it was clearly harassment as the two separate incidents amount to a course of conduct. Fucking hell, an officer from NP actually knew something about the Prevention of Harassment Act!

They informed us that they will speak with Trigger to inform him not to have any further contact with any member of our family, but they will not mention anything about the earlier events as it may hinder a later charge of harassment. They asked us if we were satisfied with that. Although we said we were not entirely satisfied as we did not feel safe to leave our house, we understood their reasoning regarding the harassment issue. The officers then left saying they would speak to Trigger.

If you are spoken to by the police regarding an incident, it may present difficulty later in including that incident as part of a Course of Conduct for Harassment. It does not mean it cannot be used, just that it might be a hurdle. For example, Mr Head was given a Conditional Caution for assaulting me, this was at the start of the involvement of the police, so NP would not know at that stage, that it would develop into harassment. In that case, the assault can be used as part of a course of conduct as it would be reasonable at that stage to expect that the harassment would not have occurred. On the other hand, if Mr Head had received the Caution for the assault after the Course of conduct had been established, then it might not be able to be considered in the course of conduct for harassment.

My wife and I found the behaviour of Trigger on this day to be totally irrational and abnormal. Being very abusive, aggressive, intimidating, insulting, threatening, and homophobic one minute, to acting like we were best friends the next. It was one of the strangest *'encounters'* if you can call it that, in our entire lives.

For Trigger to behave like this less than ten days after being spoken to by NP, displayed a total lack of remorse for what he had already done and a lack of respect for the police. I get that! Clearly, for Trigger to tell the police he was sorry for the first incident and that he did not bear any animosity towards our family, was complete bullshit.

Some of the comments made by Trigger were totally ridiculous and illogical. Saying the Police were going to Taser me if they needed to attend our property again and inferring I was gay and needed a good hiding because of it, were completely ridiculous.

I am a heterosexual male and have been married to my wife for far too long! I have no problem with people being gay or whatever people want to be, but I am straight. Because of a medical condition, I have great difficulty in getting my poop to go downhill, let alone letting someone push my poop uphill! No thank you very much.

This incident had a really big impact on me and my wife. We were both already on the brink. The last few years had taken so much out of us that there was no pleasure left in life. Even if we got the chance to do something we used to enjoy, I certainly did not find it enjoyable anymore. Even going for a walk around the neighbourhood, which I used to do almost every night, was just not enjoyable. We were so desperately tired all the time; we hadn't had what anyone could call a good night's sleep for months and months. The only time I fell asleep was from complete exhaustion and even then, it wouldn't last longer than a couple of hours due to the nightmares. If you believe just a fraction of what I have written so far, I am sure you can have some idea of what our lives were like and how difficult things were.

02/11/2016

At approximately 08.45, I left the house to attend an appointment with my GP to discuss how I was coping with the impact of the last act of harassment by Trigger and the prescribed course of Diazepam. As I turned the corner of our road, I heard Trigger say,

"Oi, I want a word with you."

I looked in the direction of the voice to see Trigger standing by his van on his drive. He was staring at me, I ignored him. Trigger then shouted, *"Oi, I want a word with you man to man, or should I say girl to girl"* Trigger then laughed loudly.

I again did not respond and turned around to walk home. Trigger then said, *"Are you going to call the Police?"*

He laughed again, it was a real belly laugh, like Father Christmas. There was nothing funny about what Trigger was doing, so the laugh was purely for my benefit, his way of letting me know he knew what he was doing and was enjoying it. I wonder if he ever thought of the impact it was having on our family. Personally, I think he was fully aware of the impact, and was glad of it, he clearly hated me. The only reason for that hatred would have been because of the lies the Heads had told him. There were no excuses though, Trigger was a grown man and capable of making his own decisions. I wonder if he was man enough to take the consequences for those decisions, the way he was at this time, he clearly didn't give a shit.

This is how bad the situation was. I couldn't even leave my house in broad daylight to attend an appointment to see my GP regarding the chronic state of my mental and physical health due to the harassment, without being subjected to further harassment before I could even turn the corner of our road. This was the first time I had left the house on my own in over two weeks since Trigger knocked on our front door holding the claw hammer. It was an unreal situation to be in.

I didn't go to the doctor's appointment, instead, I returned home. I did not know if I carried on walking, would Trigger follow me on foot or in his van, and if he did, what would he do if he confronted me when I was away from my house?

When I got home, I called 101 to report the incident. The call handler said there were other incidents on the log regarding Trigger and he asked if I could explain them. He informed me he would log it as a Hate Crime and Harassment, and he would forward the record of the incident to an Officer who would contact me later in the day.

I then phoned my GP Surgery to explain why I would not be able to attend my appointment and rearranged it for later that day. When I attended the appointment with my GP, we talked about the recent encounters with Trigger and how they had affected me. I had just finished the course of Diazepam a couple of weeks ago, so my GP advised me to start a course of more long-term Antidepressants and asked me to see her again in two weeks.

Clearly, Trigger had again totally ignored the advice of NP not to have any contact with this family. He had become exactly the same as the Heads, totally obsessed, if he could harass, he would harass. Our family was so low, so beaten down, there was no light at the end of the tunnel that we could see. What could we do, the situation felt totally hopeless.

As if I was not in a difficult place already, the harassment by Trigger caused me great distress, it had seriously affected my day-to-day activities. I often took a neighbour's dog for a walk around the neighbourhood, but now I didn't feel safe to even do that or even to walk down the street. I also took great pleasure in taking my grandson out for a walk in his buggy, but due to the *'vision'* I was unable to do this on my own.

09/11/2016

At approximately 10.00 am, I left for work in my van. As I approached the junction at the top of our road, I could see Trigger was again on his drive staring at me. When I stopped at the junction, I looked at Trigger and he was still staring at me. It was one of those situations where I was telling myself not to look and not to allow Trigger to do anything, but as hard as I tried, I had to look. I am sure you have experienced the same sort of thing, like walking past a dead bird on the side of the road, you know it is not going to be a pretty sight, but you have to look. It is another way in which our mind works. We often need to have absolute confirmation that something is real or that something has actually happened or is happening, just believing or thinking it is the case is not enough to get closure.

Trigger then tried to entice me over to him by waving his arm at me and saying, *"Come here."* I did not respond to the enticement of Trigger. I looked both ways to check that the road was clear, as I started to pull away, Trigger repeated the hand gesture and said *"Come here"* again. I again did not respond to Trigger and continued my journey to work.

I was shocked that despite the previous incidents and warnings from NP, Trigger was still trying to have contact with me and due to the recent threats of violence in his harassment, I did not think he was inviting me over for a friendly chat.

This incident caused me to feel very anxious, the level of anxiety was disproportionate to the nature of the incident, it indicated the impact the previous incidents had on my mental wellbeing. I wouldn't have normally been bothered too much by this incident if it had happened as a one-off. I would normally have looked at it as just one of those things that happens in life and brushed it off. I may even have blown Trigger a kiss, me being gay and all! Although I knew I was struggling mentally and physically, the way I reacted to this incident was a clear indication that I was on the edge, everyone has their limits.

The behaviour of Trigger over this time has caused our family and in particular myself, an unimaginable amount of stress, worry, anxiety, alarm, fear, and distress. We were afraid to leave our front door out of fear of what might happen, and it had a major impact on our health. I have suffered threats, abuse, homophobic, and transphobic allegations and harassment at the hands of Trigger on four separate occasions in 18 days. In that time, he had totally ignored the warnings of NP and continued his harassment unabated.

I was a 52-year-old man living in a quiet village, I was and still am, a law-abiding citizen who wouldn't hurt a fly. I should not have to feel scared or worried to leave my front door. But due to the actions of the Heads, their friends, relatives and now Trigger, that was exactly how I felt.

Trigger was fully aware of the history between us and the Heads. We were aware that NP had spoken to him regarding the criminal allegations of Harassment made to NP by the Heads in December 2015, he may also be a witness for the Heads and may also have provided NP with a statement regarding these allegations and he was definitely listed by the Heads as a witness in the civil case. From the criminal case point of view, the Heads should not have employed Trigger to work for them while he was a witness for them to avoid any unnecessary contact with our family. Trigger should not have agreed to do the work for the Heads at this time, and even if he did do the work, he should not have made any unnecessary contact with our family. Trigger not only failed to do this, but he also harassed and threatened me and my wife at every opportunity. Yet NP only warned him about his conduct, twice.

Just as concerning to us was not what Trigger said, but WHY he said it.

The comment by Trigger, *"What you have got is hereditary,"* Was of particular concern to other members of our family, what did he mean by this? Was it just a wind-up? I was certainly not aware of any skeletons in our family's closet. Did he know something I didn't? I don't think so, but he was the same generation as my dad, so we could not be sure. There may have been something in my dad's history that Trigger knew about, he definitely knew my dad as I think they both played football for the same Sunday League team back in the day.

It was just another uncertainty that whirled around my head, another impact of the harassment. I never doubted for a split second that I could have done something to harass or upset the Heads, what was happening was solely down to them and no one else. But when other people started to get involved, it made me wonder what was going on, why did so many people have this deep-rooted hatred of our family? Under the circumstances, I think even a Saint would start to doubt themselves.

Reversing the Truth

Oh my God. We were informed by our solicitor that he had received an allegation from the Heads that I had verbally abused Trigger while he was working for them. Yet again, the Heads were reversing the truth. The Heads will not have been able to provide their solicitor with any evidence of this verbal abuse as it did not happen. Surely, there must be some sort of legislation or Code of Conduct whereby a solicitor should not forward any allegations made by their clients against another party if they are unable to substantiate the claim. In any event, it had been agreed at mediation that the Heads would not employ Trigger to do the work on the fence, and here we have the Heads alleging that I verbally abused Trigger when they had employed him to work on the fence.

Unfortunately, our solicitor thought it prudent to respond to this allegation by writing a letter to inform us of the allegation at a cost of £150 and also sending a letter to the Heads solicitor at a cost of another £150. Winner, winner, chicken dinner, if you are our solicitor, again!

Surely, if the allegation was unsubstantiated, it does not need to be responded to. If it is necessary to respond, then it is a money-making machine for the legal profession.

Talk about making a fortune out of our misfortune.

Shortly after this, I received a call from an officer of NP who was dealing with the incidents we had reported against Trigger. He advised me that he wanted to issue Trigger with a Police Information Notice (PIN). This is basically not worth the paper it is printed on; it means that the suspect has not done anything wrong, and there is no evidence to suggest they have, but they have been informed that certain conduct could be considered as a little bit naughty and if they do anything like it in the future, they might be sent to bed with no supper.

I told the officer that I was not happy with that due to the severity of the harassment and Trigger had already been warned about his conduct by NP twice and totally ignored those warnings, so a PIN would have no great effect on his conduct.

To be fair, the officer said he would gain further advice regarding this and contact me again. A couple of days later, I received another call from the officer, and he requested that I and my wife attend the Police Station to make a statement regarding the incidents with Trigger. A couple of weeks after that, I received another call from the officer who informed me our statements had been submitted to the Crown Prosecution Service for advice, and they recommended that Trigger was to be prosecuted for Harassment and Homophobic Hate Crime.

WOW! NP were actually going to do something. Well, no, it was only because of my unwillingness for NP to issue Trigger with a PIN and only on the advice of the CPS that Trigger was now facing prosecution. If it was left to NP, they would have issued Trigger with less than a slap on the wrist and no doubt the harassment would have carried on unabated, but I wasn't complaining, for once I hear you cry. At least now Trigger knew he was being prosecuted; he would stop the harassment. Wouldn't he?

Over the next few months, there were the usual relatively minor acts of harassment by the Heads like shining lights in our windows, leaving their bins on the verge, again. In the lead-up to Christmas, the Heads installed a landscape light projector in their front garden, the type that projects Christmas patterns onto the front of your house. Which would have been fine, except for the fact that they angled the projector to point directly into our bedroom window! Our bedroom was like a winter wonderland. My wife is only five feet tall, the amount of times I walked into our bedroom and thought she was one of Santa's little helpers was ridiculous.

Anyway, as an aside. It was nearing Christmas, and I was really struggling to think of a present for my wife, so I went down to the local town to look for a present for her and ended up in a Sex Shop. The man behind the counter said, *"Hello Billy."*

He asked me what I was looking for and if I had remembered to bring the DVDs back from my last visit! I told him that I was really struggling to find a Christmas present for my wife. He said, *"Have you ever thought of a blow-up doll?"*

I said,

"No, I hadn't thought of that."

He said, *"We have three types, Ian Botham, Kevin Keegan, and Father Christmas."*

I asked him what the difference was, and he said, *"Kevin Keegan, scores a lot, but he dribbles, Ian Botham, once you get him in you can't get him out, and Father Christmas comes but once a year but when he does, he fills your stockings."* I got her one of each!

Every hour of every day

With the rip-roaring success of mediation out of the way, we had informed NP that we were able to continue to provide them with our statements for the criminal investigation, and on top of everything else, we had spent many, many hours over the past two months or so working on these. PC Willis had now been tasked with dealing with this instead of Clueless.

NP identified 38 pieces of evidence they required to support just my statement alone and over 50 in total. These were in the form of images, CCTV recordings, letters, emails, etc. I am not joking; this took me and my wife hundreds of hours. Each exhibit had to be listed, numbered, dated, and a written description of what was shown, who was in the footage, etc. It was a painstaking task, but one that had to be done. We would have done anything to help get the harassment to stop, we hoped it would be worth it, what idiots we were. Despite the hundreds of hours spent by us and the time PC Willis spent collating our statements and evidence, this evidence was never used in the investigation. In fact, there was no investigation, it was all more bollocks by NP.

NP must have been laughing their socks off knowing what we were spending every spare hour of every day, night and weekend doing, knowing full well it would be a complete waste of our time, and theirs come to think of it, but at least they were being paid for it, with your money!

For a police officer to deliberately waste they're and the public's time is called *'Misfeasance in Public Office'* which is defined as, *'Acting negligently or improperly while performing a duty causing harm or loss.'* At the end of the day, I suppose it doesn't matter what it is called as it is just another law that is not enforced against police officers.

Our statements and evidence were finally ready to be submitted to NP for the purpose of the investigation by mid-January 2017. This was already FOURTEEN months after Inspector Arsewipe had instructed PC Clueless to conduct her *'impartial evidence gathering exercise'*. To be fair, it wasn't just the fault of NP, we had asked NP for a delay in submitting our statements to prepare for civil mediation in August 2016, but I will blame them anyway. They have blamed me for enough things I hadn't done.

Also, Trigger attended Court for his plea hearing regarding the prosecution for his harassment. I was informed that Trigger had pleaded Not Guilty, and a date had been set for his trial which was scheduled for February 13th. It came as no surprise that he had pleaded Not Guilty. He was clearly a complete idiot, and he must have been aware of the evidence against him, but it is his choice and right to plead how he likes. Of course, this meant there would be a trial and my wife, daughter, and I would all have to appear in Court and give evidence. I will fast forward to the trial.

On 13th February 2017, we attended Court for the trial of Trigger for Harassment and Homophobic Hate Crime. The attitude of Trigger in Court was the same as what had got him there in the first place. He was arrogant, ignorant, argumentative, and displayed a total lack of remorse for the harassment and respect for the Court. In fact, while I was giving my evidence, he continued to insult me from the Dock with comments such as, *"You need to man up,"* and, *"You're a big girl's blouse and you hide behind your wife and walk three paces behind her."*

When it was his turn to give evidence, he proved his stupidity. As well as shooting himself in the foot so many times, it's a wonder he could walk out of the Dock, he made many ridiculous statements. Rather than trying to defend himself, he chose to attack our family further and go down the route of claiming we were the harassers and he and the Heads were the victims.

It will come as no surprise to you that at one point, Trigger stated that Mr and Mrs Head were suicidal due to our harassment of them. The most bizarre thing was, Mr Head spent the whole day at court supporting Trigger! Not the sort of thing someone would be able to do if he were suicidal due to our harassment of him. I know Trigger was as thick as shit but even he must have known his attitude was going to go against him. After a very long and obviously very stressful day, Trigger was found guilty of both charges of Harassment and Homophobic Hate Crime. He was a total twat.

Before the trial started, the CPS barrister assured us that due to the locality of our addresses, the magistrates would issue Trigger with a Restraining Order that would prevent him from having any contact with our family under any circumstances and if he broke the terms of the Order, he would be arrested. Guess what, no Restraining Order, the magistrates deemed it not necessary as Trigger knew that if he was to continue his harassment, he would be back in Court. Trifik!

I suppose the magistrate had a point. I mean, I know Trigger is stupid, but even he was not that stupid that he would continue his harassment having been found guilty once. Would he?

Chapter Nineteen
Pathetic PSD

Towards the end of November 2016, some sixteen months after submitting my complaint to NP regarding the misconduct of PC's Pinky and Perky, I received a report from the Professional Standards Department of NP regarding Part 1 of my complaint. As you may recall, Part 2 of my complaint, which included the very serious allegation of witness intimidation by PC Pinky, was put on hold due to the live investigation by NP into the ongoing harassment.

I wasn't expecting too much from the report, the police do not take kindly to being criticised, let alone a complaint being made against them. They feel they should be beyond reproach and allowed to do whatever they want, whenever they want, and to whoever they want. All I was hoping for was to be treated with a little respect and acknowledgement that NP had made mistakes. What a fucking idiot I was, again.

The way it works is that when a complaint is made, the police firstly consider whether it is a Recordable Complaint Matter. So, in effect, the first hurdle to equality is that the police can consider a complaint not to be within the remit of a recordable complaint matter and if so, they do not even have to record that the complaint was ever made. If the complaint does pass the first hurdle, the second hurdle to equality is that an officer from the Professional Standards Department of the same police force as the police officer that you are dissatisfied with, is tasked to investigate the complaint. This officer is the IO, who in this case, I will call PC Yellow. The third hurdle to equality is that the IO then investigates the complaint and compiles a report which is forwarded to a senior officer from the same police force as the police officer you are dissatisfied with, who then makes a Determination as to whether any misconduct has taken place, who in this case, I will call DCI Sheep. I think it is called a *'Closed Shop'*.

Anyway, and as expected, the report was not only a complete exoneration of PC's Pinky and Perky, but it was also overly defensive towards the two officers and unnecessarily derogatory and demeaning to our family. The report worded the individual allegations regarding the conduct of Pinky and Perky in a way that was not reflective of the statement I had provided to PC Yellow.

Notably and specifically, my allegation regarding the refusal by PC Pinky to show me the CCTV footage APC1 that was used as Key Evidence to offer me the Conditional Caution and submitted to the CPS by Pinky as Key Evidence in the prosecution against me.

The report stated,

*'You believe that you should have been shown CCTV footage APC1 **after** you had been reported for summons."*

This is knowingly and deliberately wrong.

It is crystal clear from the correspondence between me and Pinky, and the statement provided to PC Yellow for this complaint that I requested to be shown the CCTV footage APC1 **BEFORE** I had been reported for summons. To state that I requested to see the CCTV footage **AFTER** I had been reported for summons, is wrong, knowingly and deliberately wrong and a clear example of my allegation being worded differently to facilitate the conclusions of the report which could not have been reached otherwise.

The substitution of the word after for before makes all the difference for this point of my complaint. If I had made my request to see the CCTV footage after I had been reported for summons, then Pinky may have some grounds for his refusal. But as I requested to see the footage before I had been reported for summons, Pinky had no grounds to refuse my request.

The conclusion in the report for this point stated,

'PC Pinky's interpretation of the relevant PACE Code C 16.5, as detailed in the Investigating Officers Report, prevented him from showing APC1 to you."

Total bollocks. There is absolutely nothing in PACE Code C 16.5 that would prevent Pinky from showing the CCTV footage APC1 to me.

In fact, it is the complete opposite as PACE Code C 16.5 states,

16.5

A detainee may not be interviewed about an offence after they have been charged with, or informed they may be prosecuted for it, unless the interview is necessary:

to prevent or minimise harm or loss to some other person, or the public;

to clear up an ambiguity in a previous answer or statement;

in the interests of justice for the detainee to have put to them, and have an opportunity to comment on, information concerning the offence which has come to light since they were charged or informed they might be prosecuted. Before any such interview, the interviewer shall: (a) caution the detainee in the terms of paragraph 10.5 above.

This makes it clear that even if I had been charged or reported for summons.

When this *"new evidence"*, the CCTV footage APC1, came to light after I was interviewed, *'In the interests of Justice'* Pinky should have contacted me to arrange for me to view this key evidence to provide me with the opportunity to comment on it. And he should have done this before offering me the Conditional Caution.

Not only did Pinky fail to do this, but he also point-blank refused my request to see this evidence and told me, *"Of course you can see the footage, if you go to court."* And the PSD of NP concluded Pinky acted appropriately. Absolute wankers.

To be clear. I have been to court, and despite a multitude of requests to both the CPS and NP, to this day I have still not seen this footage.

To be absolutely clear, if PC Pinky's or any police officers *'interpretation'* of PACE Code C 16.5, led them to believe it was in any way correct police procedure to refuse my request to see this evidence, then they should not be a police officer as they are clearly not of a level of intelligence necessary to conduct their duties to an acceptable standard.

And if the IO, PC Yellow, and the reviewing officer, DCI Sheep, considered the conduct of Pinky to be correct procedure either they are deliberately lying to protect Pinky from his misconduct or they too are clearly not of a level of intelligence necessary to conduct their duties to an acceptable standard. I would opt for the former. If the above wasn't bad enough. At the start of PACE Code C 16.5 it states,

16.5

A detainee may not be interviewed about an offence after they have been charged with, or informed they may be prosecuted for it, unless the interview is necessary.

I was not and never have been a detainee, so PACE Code C 16.5 appears to me to be irrelevant. So, in effect, NP had no defence to the allegation of misconduct, so this point of my complaint should have been upheld. The fact is, NP could find no other way to attempt to excuse the misconduct of Pinky other than to deliberately misuse this piece of the *'Rules of Investigative Procedure'*, to find some way to defend Pinky from the indefensible. Pinky, the PSD Investigator and the Decision Maker, were all fully aware I was not a Detainee and therefore, PACE Code C 16.5 was irrelevant. They are not stupid, just bent.

They must have thought I wouldn't have the sense to pick up on this. That was why they even had the nerve to include the description of PACE Code C 16.5 in the report, knowing it was a complete contradiction to what they claimed it stated. To be fair, they couldn't care less if I did pick up on it, they would only find some other piece of bullshit to cover up their previous piece of bullshit.

This is the level of disdain the PSD have for a complainant, and this is why I am of the firm belief the Professional Standards Department of all Police Forces should be abolished. They are dishonest and unfit for the purpose for which they are intended, which is to uphold the professional standards of the police and to hold officers and members of staff of the police force that fall below this standard, accountable for their actions, whether that is accidental or deliberate. That is clearly not the case.

Their only aim is to defend officers who are the subject of a complaint, no matter what, even if that means knowingly lying to the complainant. Honesty, equality, impartiality, fairness or justice, do not enter their equation. This will never change or improve when a complainant must complain to the police about the police, and the police complaints system is constantly abused to protect the subject of the complaint.

Furthermore, when a complaint is made against a police officer, that officer gets support from the Police Federation. They have the benefit of a representative to give them support and to help provide a defence to the complaint, often working with the PSD to do that.

What does the complainant get? A big fat nothing, that's what. No help, no support, just discrimination and disrespect from the police for having the audacity to make a complaint against one of their own. The PSD goes far beyond not treating the complainant fairly but abuses the complaints process to heap further misery on the individual or family who are already the victim of police misconduct.

Although the police will not admit to it, once an individual makes a complaint against the police in any form, they are flagged on the local police system. This flagging leads to that individual being targeted by the police. They are harassed, mistreated, abused and discriminated against. I was aware this might be the case before making my complaint as our barrister had warned us about this. However, I was not aware of how blatant and disrespectful that discrimination would be. All that said, we just had to do something, anything that might help our situation. I thought it couldn't get any worse, and not all police officers and members of staff can be bent. Fucking idiot, again!

I know many of you will have a different opinion to mine, but this is just my first encounter with the PSD of NP, and it is by no means the last or even the worst. So, if you are still in disagreement with my opinion, that is fine, but I am confident that by the time you have finished reading this book, at least some of the sceptics may have changed their minds.

The report also concluded,

'Mr Head did not tell any untruths or make any inaccuracies in his statement.' Bollocks. I have his statement to prove that he did.

'PC Pinky did not make any inaccuracies in his Witness Statement and Summary of Key

Evidence Forms submitted by him to the CPS.'

Bollocks, I have both forms to prove that he did.

'PC Pinky was correct to offer you the Caution even though you had not admitted guilt and he had refused to show you the evidence.'

Bollocks. The police cannot offer a suspect a caution unless they admit guilt for the offence. The police cannot refuse to show the suspect the *'Key evidence'* being used to offer the suspect a caution.

Furthermore, and very importantly, to me at least. This determination makes it clear that I had not admitted guilt for the allegation of criminal damage made against me by

Mr Head for removing the fence in the summer of 2024. But in the email sent to the Chief

Inspector by Inspector Tool in December 2014, stated,

'The matter was brought to my attention when Mr Bean refused to accept a conditional caution and as such forced the OIC to proceed to court with the matter. (Mr Bean made admissions as to criminal damage during the interview to this offence)."

This was yet more stonewall evidence that this was a malicious prosecution by NP. And the fact that Inspector Tool lied to his own Chief Constable regarding my admission of guilt for the offence, was further stonewall evidence of Perjury and Perverting the Course of Justice.

The above was something that just dawned on me after all this time, some ten years after the event. Writing this book has brought to light many things that I hadn't previously realised. The reason for that is when the events actually happened, they were over a time frame of several years, and I was also unable to deal with them or give them as much attention as I can now. At the time these events happened, we were just trying to survive and did not have the strength, mentally or physically, to deal with them. Writing this book has allowed me to have many of the issues fresh in my mind and able to put two and two together, so to speak. Even for me, it has been quite eye opening to see the extent of the lies, misconduct, discrimination and criminality of NP against our family.

Regarding the allegation that Pinky and Perky disclosed evidence provided to them of the Heads criminality while I was being interviewed under caution (the Facebook posts by Mrs Head and Little Head), to the suspects of my allegation, the Heads. The report stated,

'PC's Pinky and Perky cannot remember what was said when they visited the Head's following my interview.'

Oh, that's alright then. So, if a police officer discloses evidence to the suspects of criminal allegations, all they have to do is say they cannot remember doing so and everything will be okay. What a joke.

And to finish, probably, no, definitely one of the most insulting comments made to our family during the whole decade of police discrimination and misconduct.

"PC Pinky did not place any undue pressure on you to accept the Caution as you did not accept the Caution."

What an absolute C U Next Tuesday. The undue pressure placed upon me by Pinky to accept the Caution that I should not have even been offered in the first place, put me in hospital, and even though Pinky knew this, he still did not stop his obsession in trying to force me to accept the Caution.

I find this determination not only to be wrong but also unnecessarily and extremely derogatory and a clear failure to treat this complaint with equality and impartiality. There can be no doubt in anyone's mind that Pinky placed extreme, undue and unnecessary pressure on me to accept the Caution, even though he knew I had not committed the offence nor had I admitted guilt, even to the point of phoning me when he knew I was seriously ill and had been admitted to hospital, and that he had been asked by our daughter just the day before, not to contact me. Pinky even said in his phone call to me,

"I know you have been in hospital so let's get this sorted."

For the PSD to conclude that because I did not accept the Caution, I was not placed under undue pressure by Pinky to do so, is disgusting and so degrading. Both PC Yellow and DCI Sheep have deliberately taken the wording of my complaint out of context to yet again facilitate their conclusion that Pinky did not do anything wrong. Bastards, the lot of them.

The PSD of NP had taken sixteen months to conduct their investigation into just Part 1 of the complaint, and the investigation and determination is a complete and utter sham. I consider it to be in itself, an act of gross misconduct by all the officers involved.

The IO and the Determining Officer have clearly abused their position to protect one of their own from multiple serious acts of Gross Misconduct and possible criminal conduct. It was such an insult to our family, I cannot express the impact this report had on our already extremely fragile health.

This deliberate failing by the PSD not only allowed Pinky and Perky to get away scot-free with their disgusting conduct but also facilitated the continued harassment by the Heads and their associates, and the misconduct by NP against our family. If our complaint had been treated with equality and the correct determination reached, it would have opened the eyes of NP to what was happening to our family and would have brought a swift end to the hell we were living. The PSD deliberately chose not to do that, and our hell continued for many years to come.

This was the first but by no means the last time we would be treated with utter disdain by the PSD of NP. With this report, the PSD had not even started with their level of disrespect for our family. I suppose they thought we would just roll over and accept the findings. To be honest, that was what we did, not because I thought the report was in any way correct or fair, but because we simply did not have the strength to go through the procedure of complaining about the complaint.

If I wanted to appeal the decision, I would have to do it within 28 days of the date on the report. There was no chance on this earth that we could have dealt with that on top of everything else. I had no choice but to put this matter on the back burner, but I will return to it when I am able. There is no way Pinky is going to escape being held accountable for what he has done to our family.

No way Pedro!

Chapter Twenty
Friends in High Places

Since we found out Mr Head was on the Committee of the Parish Council, I had been looking at the minutes of their monthly meetings that were posted online. A bit sad I know, but I wanted to know what the Parish Council was doing. As stated, there was no way Mr Head had joined the Parish Council for the benefit of the Parish, so it seemed sensible to keep an eye on things. There was also another reason for this that I will cover later.

On looking at the Minutes for the Annual General Meeting of the Parish Council, they confirmed that Mr Head was no longer on the Committee of the Parish Council. No, he had been elected to the role of Vice Chair. The regular monthly minutes of the Parish Council also confirmed that the officers who were involved in the police investigation into the harassment, were attending the monthly meetings of the Parish Council to provide the Crime Report.

How ironic was that, officers of NP were providing the Crime Report to the Parish Council when one of the most prolific offenders in the Parish was the Vice Chair of the Parish Council. What a pantomime.

I also discovered that the firm of solicitors used by the Parish Council for their business, was the same firm of solicitors the Heads were using to represent them in their civil case against us. Coincidence, surely!

Coincidence or not, at the very best, it clearly created a conflict of interests for the Parish Council, Mr Head, and the firm of solicitors. At worst, Mr Head was abusing his position as Vice Chair of the Parish Council to advance his personal interests. Maybe, this firm of solicitors was on a retainer for the Parish Council and representing the Heads was part of that retainer! In other words, was the Parish Council funding the Heads legal fees in whole or in part??

I cannot see the Parish Council and their solicitors taking the risk of a conflict of interests for no reason. There was clearly something underhand going on. Could it possibly be the case that the Parish Council, their solicitors and Mr Head were all acting inappropriately?

To be clear, at this time we were submitting evidence for the civil case to this firm of solicitors, who were perhaps working on a retainer for the Parish Council of which Mr Head was Vice Chair, that cannot be correct practice for any of the parties. Maybe an expert in this field might like to let me know, I would be very grateful.

As an aside, as I have stated earlier, I have always had the suspicion that someone in a high or influential position was assisting the Heads, even to the point of being able to influence NP to discriminate against our family. The Chair of the Parish Council was a *'Knight of the Realm'*, in other words, a Sir. Clearly an influential person, hmm, could this be where the Heads were getting their help? It makes sense when you think about it. How was Mr Head able to become a Parish Councilor when he was harassing his next-door neighbours and had a Conditional Caution for Common Assault? How was he able to be elected to the role of Vice Chair of the Parish Council? Why would the Chair allow the conflict of interests between Mr Head, the Parish Council, and their solicitors to happen? The Chair of the Parish Council and the Committee have to allow this to happen, they must approve and endorse everything the Parish Council does, so why would he and they do this? Why would a Knight of the Realm risk bringing his *'good name'* into disrepute for Mr Head? There is more to come on this.

We also continued to receive correspondence from this firm of solicitors making yet more false allegations against our family without providing any evidence of these allegations. To be clear, if these allegations were in any way true, our conduct would have been recorded on the Heads CCTV system, but they were not, because they did not happen.

We found this continued conduct by the Heads and their solicitors to be wholly unprofessional and very distressing. We informed our solicitor that we felt it to be pointless to correspond with them anymore as they were incapable of accepting facts and telling the truth. Our solicitor informed us that if an allegation was made, he had no choice but to respond. I was not sure that was entirely accurate. I think,

'If an allegation is made, I have no choice but to milk it for all it is worth. 'Might be more accurate!

For the past six months, following the failure of civil mediation in August 2016 to resolve any of the issues with the Heads, our solicitor had been chasing the Court for a date for the Case Management Conference to take place to progress the case. We were informed by our solicitor that the Court has "LOST" our Case File, but they were searching for it every day to see if they could locate it.

Absolute bollocks. The court had not lost our Case File, how could they lose an entire file? Did they take the File out for a walk, and it got off the lead and ran away? Were they having a game of football with the File and they accidentally kicked it over the fence, and they couldn't find it? Of course not, you might lose a dog or a football, but you do not lose an entire Case File from a building where the Case File never leaves. To be clear, if the Case File was not where it should have been, then someone who should not have access to it, had it. Wouldn't it be ironic as if by magic, the Case File reappeared again at some point in the future!

This was another of the reasons why I strongly believed the Heads had friends in high places. For the Heads to have NP in their pocket, and now it seemed the Parish Council and even the County Court were prepared to lie and help them, something or someone very powerful must be at play. Maybe I was being a bit paranoid, but I don't think so.

This didn't give us any hope that the civil justice system would be any more impartial or efficient than the criminal justice system in holding the Heads to account and getting the harassment to stop. I cannot put into words how we were feeling, we were not just taking on the Heads, but also NP, the Parish Council, and now the County Court. And it seemed on occasions, even our own solicitor. How could we possibly compete against all of that?

Around this time, at around 11 am one morning, our daughter returned home in her car and parked on the verge in front of our house as usual. As she pulled onto the verge, she noticed there was some broken glass in the road, she got out of her car and noticed that there was also broken glass on the area of the verge that she had parked her car. Our daughter came indoors and told me about the glass.

We looked at our CCTV footage and it showed that when the recycle bins were emptied earlier that morning, a bottle had fallen out of the bottom of the collection lorry and smashed on the road. We continued to watch to see how the glass was also on the verge and to our astonishment the footage showed that when Mr and Mrs Head left their house, when Mrs Head spotted the broken bottle, she walked into the road and picked up some pieces of the bottle, she then walked back to the side of the road and threw the pieces of broken glass on to the verge in front of our house. Mrs Head then returned to the road, picked up some more pieces of glass and again scattered them on the verge in front of our house. Then she did the same again for the third time, before getting into their car and driving off.

To be clear, the Heads recycle bins were on the pavement at the time. There was absolutely no reason why Mrs Head could not have put the broken glass in the recycle bin. In fact, it would have been easier for her to do that than to walk back and forth into the middle of the road to pick up the glass and then scatter the glass on the verge.

For her to scatter the glass on the verge in front of our house was a deliberate act of harassment and yet again placed the many pets that walked on the verge in danger of injury as well as the possibility of damaging the tyres of any vehicles that may park on the verge, in particular, our daughter's. After we had watched the footage, our daughter went outside and took some photos of the glass before picking up the pieces from the verge and disposing of them safely.

This incident reminded me of the previous occasion when the Heads had left the base of the broken bottle exposed on the verge in January 2016. And, when the Heads placed screws through the fence between the two front gardens in the summer of 2014.

All three of these acts were so reckless, dangerous, and inconsiderate. It is difficult to understand what the Heads were thinking when they committed these acts. What I found to be most disturbing was the amount of time from the first incident of this kind being the screws through the fence in the summer of 2014, to this latest incident in November 2016, well over two years. This proved the Heads still clearly had their delusional fixation with not only harassing our family but a determination to cause our family fear and harm in any way they could.

If it wasn't clear to us before, this incident confirmed in no uncertain terms that the Heads were as obsessed as ever and would never have any regard for the safety of ourselves or anyone, or anything. They will stop at nothing to continue their harassment of our family. Nothing was off the table, and they would risk causing harm to even neighbours' pets if it meant there was the slightest possibility that their act would impact our family.

This incident left us feeling shocked and alarmed that after this length of time, we were still at the mercy of the Heads harassment and that we were alone in our fight. We could have reported this incident to NP, but what was the point, it would only have led to more stress as by this time NP had failed to protect us from the harassment by the Heads on almost every occasion. Not only that, but NP had actively encouraged and joined in with the harassment, so reporting this latest incident would only give NP a further opportunity to do the same again.

Chapter Twenty-One
Outof the Blue

It was the 21st of February 2017, I was sitting in our front room when I saw a removal lorry pull up outside the Heads house.

I could not believe what I was seeing, and I did not know what to do. I was running around the house, and I noticed our cat was going crazy wondering what the hell I was doing. As I continued to watch the removal men carry the Heads possessions into the lorry, it slowly started to sink in. After 4 years of total hell, it seemed there was finally some light at the end of the tunnel. It was really happening; the Heads were moving out of next door.

Finally, it was over. The Heads were no longer living next door, and they could no longer harass our family. What a relief, and totally out of the blue. We didn't take anything for granted though. We had our hopes dashed on so many occasions over the past four years. We had thought on many occasions that a particular incident would be the last incident, but it never was.

The first time we felt like this was on the 24th of July 2014, when I was assaulted by Mr Head and the police who attended the incident needed to call the police for emergency back-up to protect them from the behaviour of the Heads. But nothing was done then by NP to stop the harassment, and nothing has been done since, even when NP had the many cast iron opportunities and evidence to do something, anything about the harassment by the Heads, they somehow managed to find a defence for the Heads ridiculous and dangerous actions.

The amount of opportunities NP had to stop the harassment but failed to do so, knowingly and deliberately failed to do so, meant that we had lived our lives in such a way for so long that we had learned not to trust anyone, believe nothing and definitely not to think that we were out of the woods. That would prove to be the right approach, although the Heads were no longer living next door, their harassment did not stop. Far from it, they just could not help themselves.

Although they had moved out of next door, they returned on an almost daily basis. We did not have a problem with them returning to their former home if they chose to, of course, but it soon became clear that on many of the occasions they did return next door, they only did so to continue their harassment in any way they could. I will detail some but not all the incidents that happened when they returned to next door in the next few paragraphs. To start the ball rolling:

28th February 2017

Just one week after moving out and even though they were no longer living there, the Heads still placed their Wheelie bin on the verge in front of our house even though it wasn't due to be emptied for several days, and even though it was empty, of course. A few minutes later, and for no other apparent reason other than to antagonise us, Mrs Head moved the Wheelie bin further along the verge in front of our house, so there was not enough room for our daughter to park her car without moving the bin and we knew what that would cause. No problem, another neighbour who was aware of what was really happening offered our daughter to park her car on their drive. The only downside to that was that it pissed the Heads off big time that their little plan to cause a problem had failed and they would return with a vengeance.

6th March 2017

The Heads were again next door. Just before they left, Mrs Head came out of their front door and walked to a position next to the fence between the two front gardens. She then ducked down behind the fence out of sight. About 30 seconds later, Mr Head came out of the front door and stopped in his tracks when he saw Mrs Head next to the fence, they argued with each other briefly before getting in their car and driving away.

I knew Mrs Head would have been up to something when she was behind the fence, and the reaction of Mr Head when he saw her confirmed that to me. So, when they had gone, I went into our front garden to see what, if anything, Mrs Head had been up to. Sure enough, Mrs Head had gathered up a pile of twigs and small branches that must have been on their drive and pushed them under the fence into our garden. How pathetic and annoying, but after the previous four years, this was something we could handle. It was just so childish.

There was no point in saying or doing anything about it as that was exactly what they wanted. They wanted a reaction so matters would escalate again, and they could call NP and tell them we were harassing them even though they had moved out of their beloved home, and they were once again suicidal due to our behaviour and the whole cycle with NP siding with the Heads would begin again. The only trouble was, as our experience had taught us, if the Heads did not get the reaction they wanted, they would escalate the harassment anyway.

One of the things I am most proud of in the way I and the rest of our family handled the incredible stress and strain of the harassment was that we never succumbed to the sometimes immense temptation of just wanting to get hold of the Heads and shake them to their senses and just ask them why they were doing this, why would they just not want to live their lives in peace. Most of all, to ask them what they think we have done to deserve their undoubted and undiluted hatred of our family. I know my wife, son and daughter all felt the same as me on occasions, but we were all strong enough both individually and collectively to resist that temptation, even though we had nowhere to go, no one to turn to and were completely abandoned by those who should be there to help and protect us from crime.

The very next day, Mr and Mrs Head returned next door. Clearly, because they did not get the reaction they had wanted the previous day. They had to do something else to harass. Mr and Mrs Head were talking to the neighbour who lived exactly opposite our house, this was one of the neighbours we had lived alongside for many years and always had a good relationship with. In fact, this neighbour couldn't drive, so I would occasionally give her a lift to the town if I passed her in the street or waiting at the bus stop. Yet again, the Heads somehow managed to incite her with their poison and our friendship counted for nothing.

After a while, Mrs Head and the neighbour walked towards the Wheelie bins that the Heads had put on the verge in front of our house over a week ago. Both Mrs Head and the neighbour were egging each other on like a couple of naughty school children. They each grabbed a Wheelie bin and moved them even further along the verge in front of our house.

How pathetic they both looked, giggling and poking each other in the ribs with their elbows. I wouldn't't have given a second thought to this if it wasn't for the fact that the Heads had somehow managed to incite yet another neighbour to join in with the harassment. It was only a few months ago that another neighbour, Trigger, had been convicted of harassment against me, and now this. I was now aware this was a classic harassment tactic. The harassers somehow manage to incite others to carry on where they left off. The Heads would have been fully aware of the impact their incitement of another person to join in with the harassment would have on our family, particularly, when the latest harasser was like Trigger, yet another neighbour.

To be fair to this neighbour, she was in a very vulnerable position and the Heads exploited that vulnerability, them being the arseholes that they were. She wasn't the brightest or prettiest light on the Christmas Tree, her partner had just left her for a younger, prettier woman and she had developed a severe drinking problem. She was clearly very sad and lonely. I suppose she was glad of the attention and excitement that becoming involved in trying to destroy the family she had lived opposite to for ten years, without any issues, would give her. But at the end of the day, she was an adult and capable of making her own decisions, when she was sober anyway, so there were no excuses. I wonder if she ever regretted doing what she did, probably too pickled in white wine to even remember!

Over the next week or so, the Heads visited next door on many occasions, and almost every single time Mrs Head would do something to try to get a reaction. Things like poking her hand under the fence between the two front gardens, picking up a stone from our garden and then throwing it back over or under the fence. Stupid, pathetic, and childish things like that. But it was still the effect of the drip, drip, drip.

16th March 2017

Mr and Mrs Head were again next door. Mrs Head, as usual by now, ducked down behind the fence between the two front gardens. I know it was a bit sad, but I knew Mrs Head would do something to harass. So, I wanted to see what she was doing in case it was something dangerous. I was watching on our CCTV when I saw Mrs Head poke her hand under the fence into our front garden. Previously, she had only poked her hand under the fence far enough to grab a stone or something close to the fence. But this time, Mrs Head pushed her arm further and further under the fence until she was almost up to her shoulder. She then grabbed a wooden ornament from our garden and started to pull it towards the fence. The ornament was too big to fit under the gap between the fence and the ground, so Mrs Head tried to yank the ornament under the fence. She eventually lost her grip, and the ornament rolled back into our garden even further away from the fence than it was before.

If it had ended there, it would have been one of the most blatant and disturbing acts of harassment by the Heads I had witnessed. Right up there with the war dance on the verge and the '*Hand of God*'. But this was the Heads and as usual, it didn't end there.

Oh my God, what the fuck was she doing. To my absolute astonishment, Mrs Head pushed her arm even further under the fence into our garden until she could grab the ornament again. She must have been literally lying on the ground to be able to get her arm so far under the fence. This time, Mrs Head kept a tighter grip and managed to yank the ornament under the fence. When she had done this, she and Mr Head, who had been watching Mrs Head the whole time, got into their car and drove off. I went into our front garden to find that Mrs Head had smashed the ornament and put the pieces of the ornament back under the fence on top of the twigs and branches that she had pushed under the fence on the 6th of March.

This act was not only proof that the Heads were as deluded as they had ever been and a clear act of Harassment, but also Theft and Criminal Damage of our property, again.

And we had it all recorded on our CCTV, as plain as day.

The Heads were no longer living next door, but their harassment was just as bad, and just as fucked up. From past experience, I knew the Heads delusion equalled danger. If they didn't get the reaction from this, what would be next?

The Heads knew we had CCTV covering this area of our garden, so they would have been fully aware the actions of Mrs Head would have been recorded. But she did it anyway. How could Mrs Head be so brazen with the harassment? How, that was obvious by now, at least to me.

As we had the irrefutable evidence of this incident and despite everything that had happened before, we reported this incident to NP. Even NP could not find an excuse for the conduct of Mrs Head this time, could they?

Not with the CCTV footage as evidence, could they? The camera doesn't lie as they say. Does it?

Well, you've guessed it, according to NP, when it comes to Mrs Head, the camera does lie, again, just as with the '*Hand of God*' in June 2016. We were informed via a telephone call by an officer of NP that he had viewed the footage and spoken to Mrs Head, and she said,

'She thought it was her ornament in your garden, so she was just retrieving it, but when she yanked it under the fence the ornament became broken, and she then realised it wasn't hers, so she put the pieces back under the fence.'

The officer said although he thought Mrs Head was lying (fucking brilliant detective work, I thought), this was a legitimate reason for Mrs Head to take the ornament from our garden, so NP would not be taking No Further Action. C U Next Tuesday.

That was another tactic the police used. When they want to tell you something they know is untrue or too ridiculous, they phone you to tell you, so there is no record of what was said. If I ever have the misfortune to receive a phone call from the police for whatever reason, I will ask the officer to put it in an email and hang up. That way, there's a paper chain, the police don't like a paper chain, a paper chain equals evidence, the police don't like evidence.

This phone call was the absolute pits, it was so degrading and insulting. To once again be told by NP that the Heads were yet again going to get away with several blatant criminal acts against our family was very distressing. Of course, by this time we had lost all faith and hope with NP long ago. We wouldn't even have bothered to report this incident if it wasn't for the fact we had the CCTV footage. It is hard to put into words the desperation we all felt regarding this incident, both in the Heads conduct and even more importantly, the disgraceful and unbelievable decision by NP to take No Further Action.

We did object to the decision of NP to take no further action but as usual and expected, that just led to more bullshit. NP told us that they would interview Mrs Head to allow her to tell the truth, that was their words to us. So, they knew Mrs Head was lying, but to my knowledge, Mrs Head was not interviewed. More talking a good fight to the victims of crime to do absolutely fuck all. Yet again, the Heads were left laughing their socks off while we were left to suffer.

Mrs Head did what she did because she knew she could. She and any member of her family could do whatever they wanted to our family and NP would do nothing about it, no matter what evidence there was. To my reckoning, there can be no other explanation, it had happened so many times before and had happened again. Mrs Head knew that she could steal and smash our ornament because she knew she and her entire family had some sort of immunity with NP.

But what could it be? Could it be the friends in high places? Could it be that Mr Head was a retired member of the Emergency Services? Could it be that the Heads had previously been the victims of police misconduct themselves and NP were trying to 'make it up' to them? Could it be that because of the misconduct, NP had been instructed not to take any action against the Heads? Who knows, probably one, some or none of the above, but there was definitely something and whatever it was, it was powerful and very influential.

To be clear, many of these officers from NP were committing acts that would ordinarily amount to Gross Misconduct, failing to record or action criminal offences, refusing to show a suspect Key Evidence, disclosing evidence to a suspect, failing to disclose a conflict of interests regarding personal relationships with fellow officers and so on, and so on, and so on!

Why would these officers risk placing their whole career in jeopardy? I will tell you why I believe they would do this, because they were as sure as the Heads that no matter what they did, they too would have No Further Action taken against them. These officers would simply not risk their career for the Heads, what would be in it for them? Whatever was at play here was powerful. Although I may never be successful, I will not stop until I find out what or who it is.

The chain of misconduct by NP has many links, I haven't even mentioned some of the worst officers and members of staff of NP yet, and I cannot wait to introduce some of them to you. An officer I will call PS Pinocchio was a particular favourite of mine.

Like everything else, NP are only as strong as their weakest link, and with all these links to choose from, one of them will be weak and will break. When that link breaks, the whole machine will grind to a halt. Take PC Pinky for example, he might think he was a big man when he is hiding behind his uniform, but he was a coward, picking on victims of crime and young women to fulfil his Narcissistic Personality Disorder. But when push comes to shove, he will break, and he will not give a second thought to throwing his colleagues under the bus if it would help to save his own neck.

I have come across so many people like him in my life, and they all have one thing in common, they underestimate their enemy because they think they are untouchable. That was Pinky's biggest mistake, he underestimated me and my family, he mistook our kindness for softness, and when the time comes, I will be standing tall, and I will see him break – just like our garden ornament, smashed to pieces beyond repair.

"Stand by the riverbank long enough and the body of your enemy will come floating by."

Chapter Twenty-Two
It's A Kind A Magic

Well, well, well, amazingly, the County Court had found our Case File. It somehow managed to reappear in the very place it should have been all along. It must have got a bit lonely having run away and decided it would be better off where it belonged, after all. Due to this piece of magic, we were able to arrange and attend the Case Management Conference at the County Court in mid-March 2017. The date was set for a five-day trial in October that year. This was a longer wait than we had hoped for of course, but at least we had a date.

At this meeting, the Head's solicitor stated that she hoped there would be another round of civil mediation before the trial due to the partial success of the previous one!!! Excuse me, but how could she possibly say that the last round of mediation was in any way successful? The only thing that resulted in the last round of mediation was that the Heads refused to make any concessions, refused to agree to any of our proposals and compromises, and after six hours, they were forced to accept the fence was on our land. They then signed an agreement that they would remove the entire fence from our land, which they have not done. Also, when they employed Trigger to move the fence, they alleged that I verbally abused him.

On top of that, the Heads have now moved out of their property, so there is absolutely no chance of this work ever being done by the Heads, which in turn leaves us to sort their mess with the new owners of next door. If the Head's solicitor considered that to be a success, then she was as deluded as her clients.

The Head's solicitor went on to make what by now had become the familiar string of false allegations against our family, but, as always, she was unable to specify any particular incidents or provide any evidence of the alleged acts of harassment. No change there then.

She also claimed that due to our non-stop harassment of her clients, Mrs Head was hospitalised and the Heads moved out of their house because they could no longer bear living next door to us. For the Heads to claim that our non-stop harassment was the reason they had to move out was as sick as it was unbelievable. And for their solicitor to put these claims forward to the Judge proved to us that the Head's solicitor was as dishonest as her clients. How could their solicitor even claim such a thing?

At one point, my wife became very upset at what was being said against our family. When their solicitor heard my wife sobbing, she turned around and smirked at my wife, clearly delighted that her false claims and all-round unprofessional conduct were causing my wife distress. I haven't forgotten her name, and I will even the score.

When we returned home from the Case Management Conference, we received a visit from the potential new owners of next door. Quite by chance, the potential new owners aunty lived next door to our former next-door neighbours who sold their house to the Heads.

We spoke about the usual things you would expect between potential new neighbours and then the subject of the harassment arose. The potential new owners told us that our former next-door neighbours had told their aunt that we were a good family, and due to their experience with the Heads when they moved house, it would be the Heads that were responsible for any issues. We were very grateful to hear this and thought it best to leave it there. We did not want to tell our potential new neighbours about the extent of the problems we were having as we did not want to make them feel uncomfortable or prejudice them in any way.

So, all in all, a typical day in the life of our family. It started with the Case Management Conference when yet more despicable lies and allegations were made against our family and finished with a visit from our potential new next-door neighbours who said they had been told we were a good family. Talk about a roller coaster ride of emotions.

In early June 2017, we eventually received a copy of the Heads Counterclaim that had now been signed and submitted to court. It was a repeat of the unsigned version we had received previously, so I will not repeat the content here. They were very lengthy documents, and as they had now been filed with the Court, we needed to make a response as the claims against us would be upheld if we did not provide a defence.

I kid you not, as with our witness statements to NP, and the Notice to Admit Facts documents, my wife and I spent hundreds of hours on this Counterclaim, all the time knowing it was a pack of lies, and the Heads knew it was a pack of lies and we would need to spend our time defending it. Ridiculous. Of course, we couldn't just say we didn't do it, or it didn't happen, we had to provide a defence which meant gathering and issuing any evidence to support our defence. And when there are so many allegations to defend, I am sure you can understand the task.

This paragraph is just a small example of the impact the harassment was having on our lives.

We had a bad storm and a large piece of felt blew off the shed roof of the family whose back garden ran adjacent to ours, and landed in our back garden. These neighbours had been listed by the Heads as witnesses in the civil and criminal cases and the husband was the witness the Heads claimed I intimidated in the Summer of 2016. Because of this, we had been advised by our solicitor not to have any contact with these neighbours, so we did not feel able to ask these neighbours ourselves what they wanted us to do with the felt. So, one of our other neighbours offered to call at this neighbour's house and ask them what they wanted us to do with the felt.

This neighbour later informed us that when she explained the circumstances for her visit, the male neighbour told her that he remembered the conversation between us and that he certainly did not feel intimidated by me. This confirmed what I already knew anyway, that the allegation by the Heads that I intimidated their witness was totally false. However, the female neighbour told her that she had only heard good things about the Heads and that nobody had defended our family.

Defended our family from what? We had done nothing to be defended from, so why would anyone need to defend us? For these neighbours to have said that, it was clear to us that yet again, the Heads had been spreading malicious gossip around the neighbourhood. I am sure if we knew half of what the Heads had said about us to our neighbours, we would be shocked, even now. She also said that Trigger had knocked on her door to tell her of his conviction for harassing me and that she felt sorry for him.

Sorry for him! He had been convicted of Harassment including threats of violence and Homophobic Hate crime, and she felt sorry for him! Give me strength.

That is what we were up against. The Heads were harassing our family nonstop, including assaulting me and my wife, and Trigger had been criminally convicted for harassment. Somehow, according to this neighbour, we were still the villains. This was just an example of what gossip and lies can do, it only takes one bad apple, and it quickly spreads to the whole barrel. Particularly when people want to believe the drama, even though they have nothing to confirm or support the gossip, and even though what they know goes against what they have heard or been told, they still believe what they want to believe. Talk about being isolated in our neighbourhood. Incredible.

Anyway, after being told this, I couldn't give a shit what they wanted me to do with the felt, so I threw it over the fence into their garden. I wasn't going to waste the space in my bin for them, fuck um. Another neighbourly relationship of fifteen years up in smoke thanks to the Heads.

On the 27th of March 2017, Trigger was sentenced at the County Magistrates Court, he received a fine of £342 and ordered to pay costs of £434 and, wait for it, compensation to the victim of the grand sum of £50. Woohoo, get the fucking flags out, a whole £50 to do with whatever I wanted. Maybe I will put it towards one of the therapy sessions I will need, thanks to the horrific vision of my grandson being killed, or put it towards the hundreds of pounds in income I lost because I couldn't work due to the state of my mental health and being on Diazepam.

Being awarded nothing at all would have been less demeaning, at least then I could have consoled myself with the thought that the Judge had forgotten about compensating the victim. But to have considered it and determined that the impact of what Trigger had done was worth £50, was an insult. Does anyone in the criminal justice system ever give a second thought to the victims?

In my experience, the answer to that question is an emphatic NO. The justice system seems to bend over backwards to help the offenders,

'Oh poor man, no wonder he robbed that pensioner of her life savings, his Mum wouldn't let him have warm milk at bedtime when he was a child, let's send him on a course of fishing lessons to aid his rehabilitation and mental wellbeing.'

'Oi, what about the victim?'

'Oh, give her fifty quid and tell her to fuck off.'

It is an absolute joke and an embarrassment.

On top of that and as mentioned earlier, Trigger was not issued with a Restraining Order as the Magistrates deemed it to be disproportionate to the crime. That was an even bigger joke, and the consequences of that decision would prove to have a huge impact on our family, and me in particular. All will be explained very soon!

You are going to be absolutely gobsmacked at this bit. This is how incomprehensible things had become. It may seem like a small point to you, but when this happened it just took what little wind there was left in our sails, clean away. No sooner had the new neighbours moved in next door, and we were hoping for quieter times, our solicitor informed us that he had received a letter from the Head's solicitor requesting that we pay the Heads moving costs of £15,000!

Yes, you read right. The Heads were requesting we pay their moving costs of £15,000. The letter stated that the reason for this was that it was our non-stop harassment of the Heads that had forced them to move from their beloved home. Also, following the settlement of the £15,000, all four of the Heads would then be considering a claim for Personal Injury due to the stress of our conduct had caused them and being forced out of their home.

What the hell do I say to you about that? I could babble on about how could this be happening? What could the Heads and their solicitor be thinking? But I hope you can get the picture. All I can say is that it wasn't like being kicked when we were down, it was more like a ten-tonne weight being dropped on our head from a great height.

Even in a civil case, if one side accuses another of doing something so serious as to force someone out of their home, they have to provide the evidence to support the claim. Of course, there was no evidence, and their solicitor knew that the sending of the letter was threatening, intimidating, unprofessional, and inappropriate. What did the Heads and their solicitor expect us to do, just hand over £15,000 because they said they wanted it.

In another unprofessional act, the letter also requested that we inform the Heads how we were funding our civil case against them. What! What business was it of theirs how we were funding our case? One thing was for sure, our civil case wasn't being bankrolled by the Parish Council!

Now, it wasn't just the Heads, NP, Trigger, the Parish Council and most of our neighbours that were harassing us, it was the Head's solicitor as well. Again, as with NP and the Parish Council, why would the Head's solicitor act so unprofessional? Was it the friends in high places again, or was this solicitor just another Cowboy, well, Cowgirl to be gender specific.

Needless to say, we didn't pay the Heads £15,000, over my dead body. However, there would be consequences, as there always were with the Heads. They were like petulant little kids, if they didn't get exactly what they wanted, they would scream and scream and scream until they did. Well, if they didn't get what they wanted, they would harass, harass, harass, and then tell NP we had done to them what they had done to us and then threaten to commit suicide while NP turned us over.

Seriously, even after the conduct of the Heads at mediation, they contacted PC Clueless and told her that they were yet again contemplating suicide due to our actions. I am not kidding you; they did this and I have the evidence in writing to prove it. They really were sick people.

Anyway, the consequences of not paying the £15,000 were that Mr and Mrs Head turned up at our daughter's place of work. Because of the previous incidents, notably when Sponger harassed our daughter at her place of work and then made a complaint to our daughter's employer, all the Heads had been advised by NP not to attend our daughter's place of work.

As they were no longer living next door nor able to visit as there were new occupiers, they had to find another way to make contact with our family, and they knew where our daughter worked. So she was, if not their only option, she was their obvious and easiest option. The Heads did the same as

Sponger, they wandered around the Pet Shop Department for several minutes staring at our daughter before leaving without buying anything.

Don't ask me why we bothered, but we reported this incident to NP and although the Heads visit was recorded on the Garden Centre and Pet Shop CCTV system. NP informed us that,

'The Heads said they thought that our daughter no longer worked at the Garden Centre so it would be okay to visit.'

Of course, that was yet more lies. What would give them that idea and as expected, the CCTV footage counted for nothing and it was a good enough excuse for NP to take No Further Action, in fact, we were told by NP that as the Heads were no longer our next door neighbours and were not harassing us, there was now no reason why they shouldn't visit the Garden Centre and the Pet Shop if they chose to do so.

Brilliant, so, not only did the Heads attend our daughter's place of work after NP had told them not to do so. NP had now decided that, as the Heads were no longer living next door, they couldn't possibly still be harassing us, so they could visit our daughter's place of work whenever they wanted. NP strikes again.

That was too much for our daughter. She couldn't bear the thought of going to work every day, wondering whether the Heads or their relatives or friends would turn up at the Garden Centre, as they surely would from now on, having not only been allowed to get away with the visits by Sponger and the Hopterty's in October 2015. Now this visit by the Heads and now basically given license by NP to visit whenever they wanted.

Enough was enough for our daughter and she quit her job. Nice one Heads and NP, your collaboration in the destruction of our family has achieved yet another milestone for you all. You have a jolly good time together celebrating this victory. Never before had you quite managed to force a member of our family to become unemployed. Now you have, enjoy!

C U Next Tuesdays.

Chapter Twenty-Three
For Better or Worse

I think this will be a good point to update you on the impact this was having on our health. I will keep it brief as I know this may not be what you want to read about. If you believe just a fraction of what you have read so far, I am sure you can imagine the impact anyway, but I will clarify a few things. You may have already noticed that the past few paragraphs have been lacking in the usual humorous take I try to have on things. Simply because I cannot think of anything slightly humorous about where we were at this time. Survival was the only aim.

Due to the impact of the harassment by the Heads and Trigger, and particularly the conduct of NP, I was placed on a second course of Diazepam. When that course came to an end, I was placed on a continuous course of Antidepressants to accompany the Beta

Blockers I had been prescribed since my suspected Heart Attacks. I was also prescribed Statins for High Cholesterol. I was not and never had been on any of this medication before the harassment started.

I had also been having problems with my right eye. Over the past few months, the white of my eye had become partially red on six of seven occasions. I eventually went to see my GP about this, and she made an emergency referral to the Eye Department of the Local Hospital. My GP also advised me to take time off work as my vital statistics indicated I was struggling due to stress. Easier said than done when I had been very inconsistent in being able to work since November 2014. I was self-employed, and the civil case was eating money like there was no tomorrow. If I didn't work, I did not get paid, rock and a hard place springs to mind.

I attended my appointment at the Eye Department, where, surprise, surprise, I was diagnosed with a stress-related condition called Anterior Uveitis. This is when the white of the eye becomes inflamed from the inside, causing the eye to haemorrhage, which causes the redness. It is a serious condition which can lead to sight problems including blindness. I was prescribed Steroid eye drops which dilate the pupil, so I could not drive, so I could not work anyway, again. I was also advised that if my eye turned red again, I was to go straight to the Eye Department without delay, where I will be treated as an emergency, as the longer it is left, the greater the danger of it affecting my sight. I would continue to have major problems with my right eye for several years.

The ophthalmologist also thought that the Uveitis might be a symptom of Arthritis and referred me to the Rheumatology Department. I had several tests and eventually it was diagnosed that my immune system had gone haywire and was attacking itself. This was causing painful and swollen joints, which was not the best thing when you are a Sports Coach.

In June of 2018, I was also diagnosed with Ehlers Danlos Syndrome, this is an inherent condition which I now know I inherited from my mum. She obviously had it much worse than me and was more than likely responsible for her kidney failure. Unfortunately, my daughter inherited it from me and is also more severe than I am. She often tells me that the only thing I have ever given her is Ehlers Danlos Syndrome. That's me, share and share alike.

I won't go into the details of the condition, but it has many different forms which can affect many different parts of the body. This diagnosis explained many things that had happened in my life up to this point, especially regarding my health. I was advised that although I had this condition since birth, it had laid pretty much dormant until I reached the age of fifty-four and was more than likely triggered into action by the stress of the harassment. There's a thing!

My wife was also struggling, of course. She, like me, often needed to take time off work because she couldn't cope with the stress of the harassment. It is not my place to talk about her or anyone else's medical problems though.

As for our daughter, I will have to write a separate book on her health issues. Bless her! Our son, he is deep, he wouldn't tell you what was wrong if his life depended on it. Whatever you asked him, are you okay, did you enjoy that, did you like your tea, whatever the question, the answer was always the same, alright. And that was it, alright.

As for our mental health, as part of our civil claim against the Heads, my wife, our daughter, and I needed to have a report compiled by a Forensic Psychiatrist to assess the impact of the harassment on our mental health. The reports were very detailed and a difficult read to be fair. To read what an expert in the field concluded about the impact on our mental health was very distressing, but I have to say, he was spot on. The reports on each of us were more than fifty pages in length. So, to cut a long story short, I will just include his fundamental findings.

Firstly, I was diagnosed with Post Traumatic Stress Disorder. This was due to the assault by Mr Head and the many threats of violence that have been made against me. I hadn't considered this until now, but when I read the report, it made so much sense. It explained the severe reaction I had to the harassment by Trigger when he threatened to have me beaten up and stood outside our front door holding a claw hammer. It explained the nightmares, the vision and why I was hypervigilant whenever I was out of the house, particularly in the neighbourhood. I would try to memorise what people looked like and what they were wearing and I would try to memorise part of every car registration plate that passed me, and also why I felt only four feet small.

My wife was diagnosed with an adjustment disorder. The psychiatrists considered that my wife had lost control of their life, and again, he was spot on. What happened in our lives was not dependent on us, it depended on what the harassers and NP decided would happen.

Our daughter was diagnosed with a deterioration in her already existing mental health condition. This was a real shame, our daughter had really struggled with her mental health at times and had put so much effort into regaining a standard of life that was mostly okay and occasionally rewarding, like her job at the Garden Centre. She was only able to do that because we knew the son of the owner who understood her condition and was understanding when it impacted on her work.

Of course, our daughter had to give that job up due to the harassment by the Heads and their relatives at her place of work, you remember, the harassment that NP said did not happen. Our daughter would not have given that job up unless she was desperate to escape the clutches of the Heads.

It was considered that the impact on the mental health of our son did not warrant an assessment. The psychiatrist would only have concluded our son was, alright!

The psychiatrist also concluded that our recovery from these conditions was dependent on the successful conclusion of the investigation by NP into the harassment. That's us fucked for life then!

Around this time, it was a couple of months further on in fact, but I will include it in this Chapter as it is a health issue I suppose. I had the third of the horrific nightmares that had and would continue to blight my life for years. This one involved my wife's sister and PC's Pinky and Perky.

There had been a lot of stuff going on around this time regarding the civil case and the trial was looming, that was what must have triggered this particular nightmare. Like the others, they are not as regular as they were around this time. But writing this book brings them to the fore again of course, but that is a necessary evil I have to deal with.

The nightmare was as follows. We were in the Courtroom at the County Court for the Civil trial, I was in the witness box giving evidence. The Head's barrister said to me, *'Did you assault Mrs Head?'*

I said,

'No'

When I said that, my wife's sister burst into the Courtroom and shouted,

'Yes, he did, I saw him do it.'

The Judge then shouted,

'Take him down.'

Then, out of nowhere, PC's Pinky and Perky rushed into the courtroom. They grabbed me by my arms and marched me out of the court and into a cell below. They then kicked the shit out of me until I was motionless on the floor. I was lying on my side and Pinky and Perky took it in turns to jump on my head, not just stamping, but full on jumping as high as they could and coming down double footed as hard as they could.

They were laughing and joking with each other as they did it. As they continued, my head became flatter and flatter, eventually, my brain started to appear out of my mouth, each time they jumped on my head, my brain became longer and longer out of my mouth. By the time they stopped, I was dead, my head was wafer thin and my brain was a foot long out of my mouth. There was no blood, just brain. That was where it ended, it was horrific. What more can I say other than thank you to Heads, Trigger and NP for making me live through this. I hope you are proud of yourselves. If any of you ever read this, I hope you are somewhere where you deserve to be, prison, or hell maybe, I won't hold my breath though.

I also had another nightmare where all the harassers, including the Heads, the Hopertys and Trigger, trapped me outside the front of our house, they were all carrying machetes and they hacked me to bits. Thankfully, that was a one-off.

Chapter Twenty-Four
Civil Case or No Civil Case, that is the Question

Just two months after finally being issued with the Counterclaim by the Heads, and after spending hundreds of hours defending the outrageous claims made in it, our solicitor informed us that the Heads had discontinued their Counterclaim. To be fair, this was no surprise to us. We knew from the very beginning that the Heads would not be able to back up their claims with evidence as these events did not happen.

In fact, I was a little disappointed that they discontinued their Counterclaim as I was looking forward to their lies being exposed in Court. When you consider the fuss and length of time the Heads took to issue their Counterclaim in the first place and the obvious stress this caused our family, we found it to be an absolute disgrace to all concerned, including the Court, that they had now withdrawn it.

Our solicitor believed that the Court would take a dim view of the fact that the Heads discontinued their Counterclaim so soon after filing it. What difference would that make though, our solicitor would still be able to charge us for his time in dealing with it and we had already spent all that time defending ourselves from the total bullshit contained in it. I know we would be entitled to all our legal costs in dealing with the Counterclaim, but we were not compensated for the time we spent on it and how it impacted our lives. C U Next Tuesdays.

I have mentioned that we were not entirely happy with our solicitor's actions regarding costs. It was their responsibility to protect their clients from the actions of the other side, causing unnecessary and spiralling costs. Our solicitor gave us an estimate at the start of the case that the likely cost would be between £60,000 and £70,000. Astronomical, I am sure you will agree. Well, we were already well past that point, and we hadn't even got to the trial yet, far from it.

On top of that, we received a call from our solicitor urgently requesting the sum of £1090 for the Court Fee for the Listings Questionnaire! We thought this to be unprofessional at best, I couldn't see it to be best practice for a solicitor to contact a client urgently requesting what was not a small sum of money. Obviously, many people, including ourselves, would not have this amount of money lying about, especially as our solicitor had already taken every penny we had and more, much more. However, we begged, stole or borrowed to pay him, what choice did we have? There were several occasions throughout the case when our solicitor phoned us urgently requesting we forward him £100 here and a £100 there. Is that normal practice? If it is, it needs to stop.

We also had a chat about the case in general. Our solicitor advised us that the likely cost of just the trial itself would be around £30,000. That would take the total cost of the case to in the region of £140,000, that was at least double the original estimate. That cannot be right, our solicitor was very experienced in this field and should not have been so far out in his estimate. I feel it's fair to say, we were not given the appropriate level of protection from our solicitor regarding costs. He would and did dispute that of course.

What can you do though, you are up a creek without a paddle? You cannot go back and start again, you cannot stay where you are, you must keep moving forward, at all costs, and the solicitor knew that. They have you over a barrel.

Our solicitor also informed us that the Heads had dispensed with the services of their latest solicitor and were now representing themselves. This came as no great surprise to us. We knew it wouldn't be long before even their cowgirl solicitor had enough of their shenanigans. If their solicitor wasn't prepared to do what the Heads wanted, it must have been bad. I could see nothing but trouble ahead.

It wasn't long before the fun and games started. The next we heard from our solicitor was that he had received no further correspondence from the Heads since they had ditched their solicitor and had not replied to our solicitor's letter regarding an exchange of evidence that was due to take place the next day under the instruction of the court. The exchange of evidence needs to be co-ordinated by both sides so as not to allow one side to adapt their statements and evidence to suit. My hunch was that the Heads would not respond to our solicitor at all as they knew that they had no credible evidence to exchange, and they were going to lose the case.

A week later and still no contact from the Heads to our solicitor. Yet another deadline set by the Court that the Heads failed to comply with, just like the delay in issuing their Counterclaim. This meant that the Heads were yet again in contempt of court, but nothing was done about it, nothing was ever done about the conduct of the Heads, if it was, we wouldn't' be where we were. Simple as.

Eventually, at the very end of August 2017, we managed to exchange evidence with the Heads. Amongst other things, this evidence included Police Statements completed by several of the Heads witnesses to the alleged harassment regarding the criminal investigation being carried out by NP, an investigation that was still live! These statements were also completely unredacted.

To clarify, when an authority such as the police disclose information via a Subject Access Request or to comply with the Data Protection and Freedom of Information Acts. Any disclosure cannot contain any information that might identify a third party, such as names and addresses of suspects, witnesses or victims for example, for obvious reasons. If a suspect or convicted offender were to make a subject access request and that request disclosed details of the alleged victim or witnesses, it would place the victim and witnesses in danger of intimidation or revenge by the suspect. Any third-party data must be blacked out or removed from the disclosure. This is called Redaction.

To be clear, these statements could only have been provided to the Heads by NP. They contained the names and addresses of our family members as well as other personal details such as our height, hair colour, etc., that would identify us to anyone who read the statements.

Clearly, NP should not have disclosed these statements to the Heads during a live police investigation in which these statements were related. The Heads were suspects in the live investigation, there was no way on this earth that NP should have disclosed these statements to them or anyone in any format. But to disclose them to the Heads during a live police investigation and completely unredacted was a serious breach of the Data Protection and Freedom of Information Acts and an absolute outrage.

312

NP will have to answer some questions about how this happened at some point in the future. To be honest, I have a very strong hunch how it happened, but it will be interesting to hear what bullshit NP will come up with to defend this clear act of gross misconduct, negligence and criminality.

To be clear, these were not statements provided to NP by the Heads, these were statements provided to NP by Heads alleged witnesses to the alleged harassment by our family against the Heads. It was clear, NP had disclosed evidence to the Heads that they should not have done and which the Heads were not entitled to. That was bad enough, but to have disclosed these statements to the Heads during a live police investigation and in a completely unredacted format, cannot have been a mistake or accident. This must have been a deliberate act by an officer or member of staff of NP.

An even more pressing point these statements showed at this time was that these statements were only from witnesses who allege they witnessed our family harassing the Heads, but did not refer to any evidence of the alleged acts of harassment contained in the statements, why? Because they were of course total bullshit. This alerted us to the fact that PC Clueless had contacted and taken statements from all the Heads witnesses listed in their criminal allegation of harassment against us, but PC Clueless had made no attempt to even contact any of our witnesses, let alone taken statements from them. This caused us great concern.

To recap. From being told by Arsewipe at our meeting with him and PS Quack in November 2015,

'If you want to make an allegation of Harassment against the Heads, you may find yourselves being investigated for the same offence as these things have a habit of backfiring'

To the failure by Arsewipe and Quack at this same meeting to inform us of the personal relationship between Quack and Pinky.

To the tasking of PC Clueless by Arsewipe to conduct an *'impartial evidence gathering exercise'*, that had only gathered statements from the Heads witnesses.

To PC Clueless parking her police car on the Heads drive.

To PC Clueless carrying the Heads shopping in for them, laughing and joking with them while she did it.

To refusing to provide me with the evidence to support my statement regarding the harassment by the Heads, the CCTV footage APC1.

To knowingly and deliberately lie to our family regarding a clear act of Harassment by Mrs Head, the 'Hand of God'.

To providing the Heads with unredacted statements of witnesses to the harassment during a live police investigation.

It is clear to me. Inspector Arsewipe had never tasked PC Clueless to conduct an 'impartial evidence gathering exercise' into the allegations of harassment by both sides. But instead, he tasked PC Clueless to conduct a Witch Hunt against our family.

It must be clear to anyone, Arsewipe, Quack, Clueless and NP, had knowingly and deliberately failed in their duty to investigate with openness, transparency, honesty and with the slightest level of equality and impartiality, that was at best, at worst, it was an absolute stitch up. Arsewipe, Clueless and Quack were determined to punish and discriminate against our family because I had made a complaint against one of their own, PC Pinky, who was also in a personal relationship with PS Quack.

From this and what was to follow, it was clear that the Heads were never the subjects of an investigation by NP, it was only our family that were being investigated.

We contacted NP to express our concern that Clueless had taken statements from the Heads witnesses in the criminal investigation, but none of our witnesses had even been contacted by Clueless, let alone statements taken from them. And yet again, NP were clearly treating our family with inequality and discrimination. We also asked for an update regarding the investigation. We received a call from PC Willis who informed us he did not know what was going on. That makes two of us then!

He also told us that his understanding was that the original Detective Inspector who had been tasked with reviewing the evidence, had now been taken off the case and NP were looking for someone else to conduct the review. The next day, we received further contact from NP informing us the investigation into the harassment had been passed to another Detective Inspector.

A couple of days after that, we received a visit from PC Willis who wanted to confirm that the matter was now being dealt with by a Detective Inspector, whom I will call DI Custard, and he was a member of the Criminal Justice Unit. PC Willis also told us that in his conversations with DI Custard he was told that he would be enlisting the use of a crime analyst to help him with his review. Bollocks.

PC Willis also informed us that in the conversation with Custard, he said to him,

'I will only be able to conduct the review in my down time as more serious matters would take preference and therefore the review would take weeks if not months to complete,

We fully understand NP had more pressing matters to deal with than Harassment, but clearly, the level of the harassment and the length of time it had been going on, was a serious matter. I know he must have a lot on his plate, I mean, a police officer working in the Criminal Justice Unit must be flat out, but he didn't have to be so flippant about our situation. This just showed the attitude of the police towards harassment. Maybe he should have come to live with us for a while, and he might not be so dismissive of our plight. Sometimes, if you haven't got anything nice to say, don't say anything at all.

More to the point, to discover the case had already been passed to a Detective Inspector to review the evidence when Clueless had only taken statements from the Heads witnesses, was of course, extremely worrying and disturbing.

How could NP be conducting an open, honest, transparent, and fair investigation with any sort of impartiality and equality when the reviewing officer only had the statements from the Heads witnesses and not ours, it was impossible. To me, this proved it was a stitch-up from the start, it had to be, there was no doubt in my mind. Even though we raised our concerns to NP that statements had not been taken from our witnesses, the review went ahead without those statements ever being taken.

In a rare compliment about an officer of NP, I would like to say that PC Willis was a good cop, not on our side, just good, fair, and as honest as he could be, or allowed to be. I believe he knew what NP was doing to our family, and he didn't approve and would have no part in it. Ironically, PC Willis was soon to be, and much to his surprise, moved to another station and had no further involvement in the case. Ironically!

How Close Were We

Anyway, back to the Disclosure of Evidence by the Heads in the civil case. Along with these police statements by the Heads witnesses, the evidence also contained a police log of the 999-call made to NP by Mr Head following his assault against me in July 2014.

In this call, Mr Head said to Force Control,

'I am going to put my fist through the door of my neighbour's and get the male.'

Three points. Firstly, when you consider Mr Head had already assaulted me that evening, and now he had called NP via 999 and told NP that he was going to assault me again. Surely, at the very least, NP should have taken some measures to prevent Mr Head from carrying out this threat of further assaults, but no, the attending officers,

'Had a word with Mr Head and managed to calm him down.'

And then left him next door and our family unprotected from whatever Mr Head decided he wanted to do when they had gone. The officers didn't even have the decency to inform us of what Mr Head had said in his call to NP, so we would at least have been aware and taken our own precautions. I know Mr Head did not commit any further assaults that evening, so you may think, no harm done, but that was down to sheer luck, not judgement or correct policing. How close were we to being attacked again that night!

Secondly, in the entire Log of this incident, there was no mention whatsoever of the allegation the Heads would later make in both the criminal and civil case that I assaulted Mrs Head.

Thirdly, why would the Heads disclose this evidence? It was clearly incriminating and would do their case no favours. How could the Heads continue to defend their actions regarding this matter, when they had now provided us with the evidence to prove their defence to be false? Durr.

There was so much more contained in this disclosure that you may find interesting. In particular, a statement allegedly written by Mrs Head that made absolutely no sense whatsoever. It was as if it had been written by a young child, not an elderly lady (I say lady in the loosest sense of the word).

It wasn't just what was contained in the disclosure that was the problem, it was what wasn't contained in the disclosure that was equally upsetting and extremely frustrating. This evidence had been requested by ourselves and ordered by the Judge to be contained in the disclosure, it was, yes, you've guessed it, the elusive CCTV footage APC1. The Heads were now again in contempt of Court for failing to disclose this evidence ordered by the Judge.

Our solicitor contacted the Heads on multiple occasions between now and the trial, requesting the disclosure of the CCTV footage APC1, but it was never disclosed, and nothing was ever done about it. Even though there was a court order for them to disclose it. The whole thing was a total farce.

Chapter Twenty-Five
Eat, Sleep, Harass, Repeat

It was mid-May 2017, less than two months since Trigger had been sentenced for his conviction of Harassment against me. I pulled up at the junction at the top of our road opposite the house of Trigger, he was on his drive and when he saw me at the junction he shouted,

'Fuck off.'

At me and shooed me away with his hands. I was just waiting at the junction for traffic to pass, what the fuck did he think I was doing, parking my van there on purpose just to stare at him all day. Twat.

I thought, oh no, not again. Even he wouldn't be so stupid to continue to harass me, would he? No, it would just have been a one off, a reaction to seeing me for the first time since the sentencing. But no, he really was that stupid. Even though Trigger had been convicted of harassment against me, he still hadn't learned his lesson, what must have been going through his head. What did he think would happen to him if he harassed me again? I know he was a thick a shit to have allowed himself to be incited by the Heads to the point that he now had a criminal conviction. But to be that stupid to do it all again was beyond my comprehension.

The next occasion was at the beginning of June. I was cutting the hedge at the front of our house when I heard a male voice shouting. I looked in the direction of the voice and there was Trigger standing on his drive shouting abuse at me, things like,

'You're a fucking coward and a big girl's blouse, yea, run along and call the police.'

So, I did exactly that, as I had done with the other incident a few weeks ago.

This was how ridiculous the situation with Trigger had become and how deluded he was. It was early July, and by this time, Trigger was permanently camped on his drive stalking our house, waiting for either myself or my wife to leave so he could harass us.

He had even taken to sitting in a deck chair on his porch all day every day, dawn till dusk.

Seriously, I am not joking, he was actually doing this.

Every time I left the house in daylight, which was most of the time in July, Trigger would be there, and he would start singing, shouting, and swearing at me. Half of me was saying to myself, don't go out, wait until it's dark and the other half was saying, no fuck him, don't let him intimidate you into not leaving your own house, you have lived your life like this for far too long, don't let him beat you. Life should not be like this.

Some of these incidents were so bizarre. One day, I noticed Trigger was not on his drive, so I took the opportunity to walk to the local shop to buy the newspaper. We were collecting the tokens for the Sun Holidays, so I needed to get the paper. Unfortunately, Trigger must have seen me leave the house because when I returned from the shop, he was on his drive. When I neared the corner of our road, he started to sing to me. I could not make out what he was singing but he was looking straight at me grinning like a Cheshire cat.

A couple of days later, the same thing happened. I was once again returning from the local shop and as I neared the corner, Trigger appeared on his drive and started to sing to me again. This time it was louder and clearer, and I could hear what he was singing. It was not a song I recognised, it went,

"I'm gonna write a letter to the Council but I'm not gonna put my name on it." Not an Ed Sheeran classic that I can recall!

Trigger repeated this line several times until I eventually said to Trigger,

"What are you on about?"

Trigger replied,

"I'm just singing."

I did not respond to Trigger who then said,

"Are you threatening me?"

Trigger then repeated his song and beckoned me over to him before saying,

"Come here, you're not close enough."

I again did not respond, I just stood there in disbelief. Trigger then said,

"Go on, go and call the Police."

So, I did exactly that.

I was subjected to further acts of harassment by Trigger on the 12th, 13th and 15th July, sometimes several times in the same day. This was the usual mix of insults and strange comments. The same shit as when he had harassed me previously in October and November 2016.

The harassment by Trigger reached a whole new level in mid-July. I left the house for work, as I got to the junction at the top of our road, opposite the house of Trigger, even though it was a Saturday morning, Trigger was on his drive as always. Trigger aggressively waved his arms at me and told me to fuck off. I pulled off from the junction and, though I wasn't aware of it at the time, Trigger jumped into his van, slammed the door, and drove after me along the road. He was so angry he even managed to make his old builder's van wheel spin along the road.

My wife and daughter watched Trigger do this as we always kept an eye on each other when one of us left the house. That was how scared and concerned for our safety we were due to the multiple acts and threats of violence, that was how we had lived our lives for the past three years.

My wife and daughter were so concerned for my safety if Trigger caught up with me that they both got in our car and drove to where they knew I was working. While they were driving, our daughter phoned me several times but as I was driving, I did not answer. When I got to my work, I called our daughter back and she told me Trigger had chased after me and he was very angry. Luckily, I was about to do some one-to-one coaching and was at a local playing field with lots of people around. So, I assumed when Trigger saw where I was, he must have thought twice about harassing me in front of all these witnesses, including the person who I was about to coach, who was a former police officer, funnily enough. This person was a good person though, which was why he was a former police officer. He resigned from the Force because he could not stand the *'politics'* as he called it.

Something must have been fuelling the fire of hate Trigger clearly had for me. Whatever it was, it must have been powerful, so powerful that he simply could not control himself when he saw me. He must have been aware of the consequences for him if he was convicted of harassment again.

When I returned home from work, it was lunch time, we needed some fresh bread but neither I nor my wife would let the other go to the shop on their own, so we decided to go together, and it was a good job we did. As we neared the corner, there was the fuel for the fire of Trigger. He was on his drive talking to Mrs Head, as we got to the corner, we saw Mr Head sitting in his car. There was no way on this earth anyone would be so stupid to do what Trigger was doing without being incited. We did nothing to him; we did nothing to anyone in fact. I cannot think of any reason why Trigger would have started his harassment against our family, let alone continue with it when he was already convicted once. If he was being incited by the Heads and he was too stupid to realise what he was being told by them was a pack of lies and the trouble it would get him into, then he is even more stupid than I thought. Either that or they were paying him to do it! Due to these incidents, I made a statement to NP, and I was later informed that Trigger was due to be interviewed under caution by NP, but he had failed to attend his appointment. To cut a long story short, following the failure by Trigger to attend his interview, he made several attempts to contact the officer assigned to deal with the continued harassment who I would call PC Chatshit. When Chatshit failed to respond to the attempts by Trigger to contact him, he then contacted NP and made an allegation against me, for what I have no idea, and an appointment was made for Trigger to meet with an officer of NP regarding this allegation. But when NP realised that Trigger was in fact the suspect for his harassment of me, and that he failed to attend his interview, the appointment was cancelled. I would love to know what allegation Trigger made against me.

NP contacted Trigger to give him another opportunity to attend for interview. Initially, Trigger refused this offer but then changed his mind and he attended the interview at the end of August 2017, some six weeks after the last incident was reported to NP. As a result of this interview, Trigger was again charged with Harassment. He subsequently attended his Plea Hearing in early October where he again pleaded Not Guilty, and a trial date was set for the 30th of January 2018 at a Magistrates Court in a nearby town.

Family Ties

Some of you may not think too much about this next bit, but for those of you who believe what I have written so far, you may want to make sure you are sitting down. If you are reading this book, you are probably sitting down anyway, most people are sitting down when they read a book, unless you are on the tube, for example, or have a bad case of Haemorrhoids maybe.

Talking of Haemorrhoids, due to My Ehlers Danlos Syndrome (EDS), I have had major problems with my bowel for all my adult life, including having Haemorrhoids, and having them surgically removed as well as needing major surgery in January 2020. This surgery was due to a Fistula, which is an abnormal connection between two bodily organs, in my case, between my bowel and my bladder. That may not seem too bad compared to some other illnesses, and I agree, it is not, it even has its funny side. Because of this connection between my bowel and bladder, I started to pass wind out of my willy, you can imagine my shock when this first happened, I was actually farting out of my dick. I even entered Britain's Got Talent where I played the National Anthem on my penis. I never got past the auditions for some reason, but me and Amanda Holden have never looked back.

Seriously though, I felt very poorly for a long time and by the time my surgery came round, I was on a continuous course of antibiotics due to the constant Urine Infections the fistula caused. The fun definitely stopped when I started to pass poop out of my willy, that was not nice. Luckily, I escaped the need for a Stoma, that is a little treat in store for the future I suppose.

Although I had problems with my bowel all my adult life, I managed to get to the age of fifty-six without needing this surgery. There was no doubt in my mind, the stress of the harassment and misconduct of NP substantially contributed to my increasingly severe mental and physical health problems.

If the harassers and NP really knew the full impact of their actions at the time, would they still have done what they did?

Of course they would, that was the whole point. They gained pleasure from what they did, they didn't just do it for a laugh or because they think might be fun, they did it to fuck up our family. They are sick bastards.

Anyway, back to the point. On the 01st of November, just a few weeks after Trigger had pleaded Not Guilty and was on Bail awaiting trial, again. Our son received a series of messages via Facebook from a woman we did not know. These messages claimed a member of our family had slashed her car tyre and she was coming around our house that evening *'to get the money'* for the cost of a new tyre and she would call the police if we did not pay her!

No connection there you might think, nothing untoward, just something that happens to everyone all the time. We all get messages making allegations of Criminal Damage against us and demanding money with threats to call the police if we don't pay, don't we? No, it must just be us then!

The first question you might ask is, if this person did have her car tyre slashed and she knew it was a member of our family who did it, why didn't she call the police in the first place.

I will tell you why, through a little detective work by our daughter on social media, we very quickly discovered that this woman was in fact the granddaughter of Trigger! The same Trigger who was on Bail awaiting trial for his harassment against me for the second time.

This woman was so brazen or stupid, like her granddad, that she made no attempt to hide her identity in these messages. They were sent via her Facebook page which included her name and even her photograph. She must have known we would very quickly find out who she was and her connection to Trigger, maybe that was the whole point. We saved and printed a copy of these messages as evidence.

As well as these messages being an offence in their own right. They are also a clear and blatant attempt to intimidate and threaten our family because we were victims and witnesses to the harassment by her grandfather. Even though Trigger was awaiting trial for the second time. Having been convicted once less than a year ago, he was still prepared to continue

to harass our family, to the point of enlisting his own granddaughter to do so.

To be clear. Trigger was awaiting trial for the second time for his harassment against me.

And Trigger enlisted his own granddaughter to commit further harassment and intimidation. It was astonishing.

But that astonishment was nothing compared to the complete bollocks we were told by NP regarding those messages. I swear, you will not believe what we were told by NP about this.

We reported this incident to NP as clearly these messages amounted to serious criminal offences. It cannot be a coincidence that out of all the families in the world, the family that this woman falsely accused of slashing her car tyre, was the one family her grandfather was awaiting trial for his harassment of, having already been convicted once.

We were informed by NP that PC Chatshit had been assigned to the investigation. I called him that because that was what he did, Chat Shit. Almost three weeks later having received no contact from Chatshit and despite making several requests for an update, I contacted Force Control of NP to ask if they could help. Force Control informed me, *'There is nothing on the system regarding the 1st of November 2017.'*

Oh my God. No wonder we had not received any contact from Chatshit. NP completely failed to record the incident onto their Logs, so there was no record of this serious incident even being reported. It was as astonishing as it was unbelievable!

Without hearing anything else in the meantime, a week later, we received a telephone call from PC Chatshit informing us that NP would be taking NO FURTHER ACTION against Trigger or his granddaughter. The next day, I emailed Chatshit to tell him we were not happy about the decision and asked him to explain why this had been taken.

That evening we received an unexpected visit from Chatshit, he was accompanied by another officer. Chatshit informed us,

'The messages received by your son do not amount to any offences and there was nothing to link Trigger to this incident, so the police will not be speaking to either Trigger or his granddaughter.'

You see why I have named him Chatshit!

Just in case Chatshit had missed the point, I told him that the woman who sent the messages to our son was the granddaughter of Trigger and Trigger was awaiting trial for his harassment of me for the second time having previously been convicted of the same offence. However, Chatshit had not missed the point and replied, '

This does not constitute a link between the two.'

FUCK OFF, YOU C U NEXT TUESDAY.

How stupid did he think we are? That's a stupid thing to say, Chatshit knew we were not that stupid, no one is that stupid, except, the Heads, and Trigger, and his granddaughter, and what seemed to be every single member of Numpty Police, he just didn't care what he told us or how stupid or not we were, he didn't have to. He knew he could tell us whatever he wanted, what could we do about it?

It wasn't the taking us for fools that hurt, it was the humiliation that he could say something he knew was so blatantly wrong and that he and NP did not consider our family to be worthy of their protection from criminality and to live our life in peace. How do people like him sleep at night? Oh yes, I know how, because they are total arseholes. To be clear, the granddaughter of Trigger sent multiple messages to our son via Facebook, accusing a member of our family of causing Criminal Damage to her car and that she was coming around our house that night to get the money for a new tyre and if we do not pay her she will call the police. We provided NP with a printed copy of these messages.

Trigger was on Bail awaiting trial for the second time having already been convicted for his Harassment including Threats of Violence and Homophobic Hate Crime against our family, less than a year ago.

And NP concluded this incident does not amount to any offences and there is NO LINK between Trigger and the sender of the messages, even though the sender of the messages is the granddaughter of Trigger. Therefore, NP will be taking No Further Action! INCREDIBLE BEYOND BELIEF.

I then said to Chatshit that if NP were not going to do anything about it, I would like to make a statement regarding this incident and for this statement to be provided to the CPS and used as evidence of the continued harassment by Trigger while he was on bail awaiting trial for the second time.

Chatshit refused my request and said to me,

'If I go to the CPS with this, they will laugh at me.'

I know I am babbling a bit, but I feel it is a very important point, I hope you agree.

In my opinion, given the situation, the granddaughter of Trigger would not do something so stupid and incriminating against her and her own grandfather if she thought for a second, NP were ever going to take any action against her or Trigger.

Trigger would not do something so stupid as to enlist his own granddaughter to send those messages to our son while he is awaiting trial for the second time for his harassment against me, if he thought for a second NP were ever going to take any action against him or his granddaughter.

Trigger and his granddaughter must have known before the messages being sent to our son that NP were never going to take any action against them, there can be no doubt about that.

If NP were to take what no one can honestly deny would be the appropriate course of action regarding this blatant and serious criminal conduct, the consequences for Trigger and his granddaughter would be so severe, to the point of Trigger losing his liberty, that neither of them would have taken such a stupid risk. They must have known it would not be a risk.

It is absolutely crystal clear, NP, and PC Chatshit condoned, encouraged, facilitated, were complicit and actively joined in with the harassment of our family by Trigger and his granddaughter. Exactly the same as they had done on multiple occasions with the harassment by the Heads.

Yet again, I have the same burning question. WHY?

Trial Times Two

30th January 2017. It was the day of the second trial of Trigger, it was one of the most bizarre experiences of my life. Before I could even finish reading my oath in the witness box, Trigger started to harass me by shouting from the Dock,

"I hope you're going to swear on your grandson's life to tell the truth, Mr Bean."

Yep, no problem, that's all I have to do, tell the truth and you will be fucked. In fact, I didn't even have to do that as the conduct of Trigger fucked himself up. Twat.

This harassment continued for the whole time I was giving evidence. Trigger was warned on several occasions by the Magistrate to keep quiet or he would be held in Contempt of Court, but it made no difference. Trigger kept up his harassment and the Magistrate did nothing else but warn him about his conduct time after time. Trigger even said to the Magistrates,

"What's the point of all this, I know I am guilty, you know I am guilty, you have been told to find me guilty, the police are corrupt (agreed) *and this court reminds me of 1950's Russia."*

Not the best way to win over and influence the Magistrates I thought, particularly as he pleaded Not Guilty! Twat.

The conduct of Trigger was so bad that following the completion of my evidence, the CPS barrister submitted his case to the court to save my wife and daughter from the harassment of Trigger while they were giving evidence. The CPS barrister advised us it would be better if we left the court building due to the irrational and unpredictable behaviour of Trigger and he would call us later that day with the result of the trial.

We received the call from the CPS barrister that afternoon, what he told us was even more bizarre and shocking than being in the witness box. He informed us that the Magistrates had found Trigger Guilty of Harassment, but Trigger refused to accept the verdict of the Court, refused to accept any sanction from the Court, refused to cooperate with the probation officer, and refused to take part in any Community Service Resolution. As such, the Court had no choice but to serve Trigger with a two-and-a-half-year prison sentence, suspended for eighteen months.

That may give you some idea of the level of the harassment and conduct of Trigger during the trial, and he had no one else to blame but himself. He was now a twiceconvicted criminal serving a two-and-a-half-year suspended prison sentence, and for what? For allowing himself to be manipulated and incited by the Heads to do their dirty work? Because he wanted the Heads to think he was a big man? Because he thought he was a big man himself and got a buzz from picking on victims of crime? Fucking hell, he would make a great police officer.

And that was without being allowed to submit a statement to the CPS regarding the contact from his granddaughter, what would have been the outcome then. The refusal by PC Chatshit to take any action against Trigger and his granddaughter and to refuse my request to submit a statement to the CPS regarding this contact, really did Trigger a huge favour, to the point of keeping his freedom probably.

The very next day following the trial, Trigger was on his drive for most of the day, loading his van, cleaning his van, sitting in his van, unloading his van, cleaning his van again, loading his van again. He was clearly waiting for me to leave the house.

My wife came home from work in our car as usual, when she approached the corner, Trigger was in his van. When he saw my wife, he revved the engine loudly and let the clutch out, so the van would jolt forward towards our car as if he was going to ram her. He would then let the van roll back onto his drive, rev the engine and then let the clutch out again.

What an idiot, just the day before, the man was found guilty of harassment for the second time and was now on a suspended prison sentence, but he still would not stop his harassment. What did he think was going to happen if he carried on, and for what, because he had a bond with the Heads? Incredible.

It also occurred to me at this time that as part of the civil disclosure from the Heads, we received copies of the police statements made to NP by their witnesses in both the criminal and civil cases. Included in these police statements was one from Trigger, this statement was dated April 2016. That meant Trigger was a witness for the Heads in the criminal investigation being carried out by NP at the same time he committed and was convicted for his Harassment against me in Autumn of 2016 and in the summer of 2017.

In other words, Trigger was convicted of the very offence he claims to have witnessed our family committing against the Heads. Pot, kettle, black maybe! It was also reminiscent of the time when Inspector Tool threatened us with Perverting the Course of Justice when he and PC Pinky were committing that very offence against us.

So, the harassment by Trigger was much more than just that. It was without doubt a further attempt to yet again Pervert the Course of Justice by intimidating a witness. As Trigger was working for and accompanied by the Heads on several of the occasions when he committed these acts, the law is clear, the Heads were considered to be as guilty as Trigger of both the offences of Harassment and Perverting the Course of Justice. I won't bore you with the ins and outs of the law regarding this point, but it is very clear.

How ironic is it though? Although Trigger deserved everything he got and more, and has only himself to blame for being a convicted criminal. Compared to the Heads, what Trigger did was a drop in the ocean, but other than the Conditional Caution given to Mr Head for Common Assault, the Heads have not received the slightest sanction for the many and much more serious criminal offences than Trigger ever did.

Including the numerous acts that were so reckless and dangerous that they could have caused any member of our family, the public, their property and pets, serious harm or even worse. The screws through the fence, the base of a broken bottle on the verge, the scattering of broken glass also on the verge, to name but three. The power of the dark side at work again?

Chapter Twenty-Six
Low Life

Eyes Down

Just a week after Trigger had been convicted of harassment for the second time, our daughter's friend was visiting. Well, I say visiting, what I mean was she was basically living here. But we didn't mind as she was fun to have around and a rare friendly face in our troubled times. Anyway, she left to go home at about 10.00 pm as usual, she generally parked her car on the verge in front of our house and she had done so on this occasion. Just a few seconds later our daughter received a phone call from her friend to say there was something on both her and our cars.

We went outside to find that there was a substance all down one side of both cars. The substance was clearly corrosive as the paint had started to bubble and peel from the cars. From my experience as a carpenter, it appeared the substance was a mixture of paint stripper and PVA Glue. Whoever had done this, as we assume it didn't happen by accident, knew what they were doing, the glue makes the substance stick to the car so the paint stripper can do more damage. But who would do such a thing, apart from the Heads, the Hopertys, Trigger, his granddaughter, and half the neighbourhood who seemed to hate our family with a passion? But who would have paint stripper and PVA Glue hanging about? Someone like a builder maybe, someone like Trigger perhaps, he was a builder.

I tried to wash the substance off, but the damage had been done. The substance peeled the paint down to the bare metal on both cars. The damage to our daughter's friend's car was worse than ours, what had she ever done to deserve this? She wasn't a member of our family; she was just a friend visiting our home and she was targeted by some low-life coward who hadn't got the balls to face his victims. The damage to her car alone was estimated at £900. Thankfully, she was a very kind and supportive person and knew what we were going through and we were able to sort this with her. Thanks

Eric, not just for this but for all the support and understanding you gave our family at our most desperate of times.

We returned indoors and started to look through our CCTV footage, which showed at 18.48, a person turned the corner into our road on the opposite side. The person crossed the road to be on the same side as our house, as the person walked past our friend's car, they poured the substance from the bottle they were holding in their left hand, down the side and over the bonnet of her car. The person then stopped at the end of our drive and threw more of the substance over the back and side of our car, which was on our drive. The person then turned around and walked back to the top of the road and turned the corner in the direction of the local Pub.

Bingo. This person was wearing a dark coat with a distinctive reflective strip on the collar and an even more distinctive reflective badge on the left sleeve, which was the logo for the designer label Heller Hansen. The person was also wearing a dark hoodie with the hood pulled up, dark jogging bottoms, and trainers with reflective silver stripes, three stripes in fact, like the Adidas stripes. The coat was an absolute giveaway, how many Heller Hansen coats could there be in our area?

It was clear from our CCTV footage this was a deliberate, targeted and premeditated attack on our and our friend's property. The person knew exactly what they were doing and as the substance was a mixture of paint stripper and glue, it must have been prepared in advance.

We were extremely relieved that our CCTV captured this incident, and the footage could easily identify the person due to the coat, we thought it to be gold dust. This incident signified a serious escalation in the harassment and followed on from the incident at the beginning of November 2016 when our son received messages from the granddaughter of Trigger. This incident or something very similar was inevitable due to the failure of NP to take the appropriate action regarding that incident. If NP had taken reasonable and proportionate action regarding that incident, I am convinced this incident would not have happened.

It was no coincidence that this incident happened just a week after Trigger had been convicted for the second time and there was no doubt in my mind, this incident will either involve or be connected to Trigger and was in revenge for his second conviction.

This incident had a very dramatic impact on our family. We were already struggling to cope with the continued harassment. Only a week ago, we were in Court giving evidence against Trigger who further harassed me when I was in the witness box, and now this. This incident wasn't just words, lies, threats, or false allegations though, it was a targeted attack on ours and our friend's property.

Because of this incident, we did not feel safe either inside or outside our home. It was clear, the harassers would go to any lengths to continue their persecution of our family, and the harassers are getting more and more brazen, and the actions more severe, and therefore, more dangerous for our family. If the attack on our property didn't satisfy the harassers, and NP failed yet again to take the appropriate action, would it be Paint Stripper thrown in our face next time? You might think I am being silly, but it happens, it happens all too often, and all too often because of police failure. Clearly, nothing was off limits, and we wondered what could possibly happen next?

Just to remind you, this is a true story by the way.

But NP couldn't possibly fail our family again, could they? Na, this had got to do it. Now that the harassment had escalated to such a level where paint stripper was being poured over our cars. NP would eventually have to put two and two together and the penny would surely drop. We would report the incident and provide NP with our CCTV footage; they would then make enquiries, and the culprit would be identified. Game over, surely!

We called the police to report the incident, and an appointment was made for us to visit the local Police Station at 4.30 pm the next day. We talked the officer through the recent history and the current situation and provided him with a copy of our CCTV footage of the person pouring the substance over the cars. We also told the officer the person in the footage walked off in the direction of the local Pub and they might have further CCTV which might help.

The officer said he would place an image of the suspect on the police website and in the local evening paper, conduct door-to-door inquiries, and contact the local Pub regarding the possibility of obtaining any CCTV of the suspect. He said that he would update us with the progress before his shift pattern changed in a couple of days.

Great, finally NP had decided enough was enough and they needed to do something and do it quickly before the harassment became tragic. I bet some of you actually believed that, oh no, NP took their disdain for our family to a whole new level regarding this incident.

In a favourable coincidence for a change, our daughter was friends with the daughter of the Landlord of the local Pub, so she contacted her and told her what had happened to our cars. Her friend said that she and my wife could go around to the Pub and look at their CCTV.

Bingo. The CCTV footage from the Pub showed the same person wearing the same clothing, including the same coat with the Heller Hansen logo on the left sleeve and in the exact time frame, walking along the road, passing the Pub in the direction of the local shop. As the person walked past a bush in the Pub grounds, they dumped a bottle they were holding in their left hand in a bush. The wife and daughter went outside of the Pub with her friend to see if the bottle was still in the bush.

Bingo. There it was, it was still there. There was no doubt it was the same bottle that was used to pour the substance over our cars as there was still some of the substance inside the bottle. The wife and daughter didn't know what to do for the best, should they leave the bottle there and report it to NP, or should they retrieve the bottle, so we had it as evidence. As we were dealing with NP, they very sensibly decided to retrieve the bottle themselves, so our daughter's friend went back into the Pub to get a plastic bag to put the bottle in. The wife and daughter came straight home with the bottle and called NP to inform them they had retrieved the bottle used in the Criminal Damage to our cars. NP said they would collect the bottle and send it away for forensic testing. Guess what, they actually did this, no seriously, they actually collected the bottle and sent it away for analysis, allegedly!

We then realised, if this person continued in the direction they were going when they passed the Pub, they would come to the local shop, which was only about 30 metres along the road, and which also had CCTV.

We visited the shop and explained what had happened to our cars and asked if we could look at their CCTV of the time of the incident to see if there was any footage of this person.

Bingo. To our amazement, the footage showed the same person, wearing the same coat, joggers, and trainers, walking past the front of the shop and putting something in a rubbish bin. The same person then returned to the shop and went in, yes, straight in the front door of the shop in full view of the CCTV camera.

Bingo. The person had pulled the hood down of the hoodie and had undone their coat. The hoodie he was wearing had distinctive writing on it, it was one of those pieces of clothing that celebrated your year of birth, this one was the Class of 62. This meant that the suspect was most likely born in 1962 (I worked that one out myself). This CCTV also showed crystal-clear footage of the person's face, which was quite distinctive. He wandered around the shop for a couple of minutes before buying some chocolate and even laughing and joking with the manager for a while before leaving.

We could not believe our eyes, this man had just committed a blatant act of Criminal Damage to our cars and then dumped the bottle in a bush on the grounds of the local Pub, and then walked to the local shop to buy chocolate, as casual as you like, without a care in the world. It beggars' belief, and we had all this on CCTV, not just our CCTV, but the CCTV from the local Pub and local shop. Not just Bingo, but the Jackpot on the Lottery as well.

We asked the manager if we could record the footage on our daughter's phone and he very kindly obliged. We again informed NP that we had this additional footage. To be clear, we had the CCTV footage of this person pouring the substance over our cars, the CCTV footage of the person walking past the local Pub and dumping the bottle in the bush, and the CCTV footage from the local shop showing the crystal-clear image of the person's face. In all versions of the footage, the person was wearing the same clothing, including the distinctive coat, and all versions of the CCTV were in the exact time frame to confirm this person's movements. We also had the bottle that was used to hold the substance, and we had the most likely year of birth of the person who did this. Pretty conclusive, you would think. Our survey said, Aa Aa.

Protect and Serve!

At this point, I would like to introduce you to yet another officer of NP who I will call PS Pinocchio. Honestly, if you think NP had been dishonest and untruthful to our family up to this point, you haven't read anything yet.

I kid you not, if this officer's nose grew just a fraction of a millimetre for each time he lied to our family, he wouldn't need to use the remote control to turn the Telly off. He once went for a picnic at a local Country Park and when he laid down for a snooze, someone complained to the Local Council because they thought someone was erecting a wind turbine. When he needed to do a COVID Test, he would have to use a sheep for a nose swab. If there was an officer of NP that I would rather see held accountable for his actions than PC Pinky, it would be this one, no, PS Quack, no, Inspector Arsewipe, no, Inspector Tool, no, PC Clueless, no, oh, I don't know, shoot them all.

He was what I would describe as the new breed of Police Officer. I would imagine he had been to university to study some random course like *'how to be a proper C U Next Tuesday*, got his degree, and went straight into the Police Force as a Sergeant. Where officers like PC Pinky who hadn't been to university and did not have a degree in *'how to be a proper C U Next Tuesday'*, had to start at the bottom of the ladder as a Constable and work their way up the ladder by screwing over innocent people until he was promoted to a *'proper C U Next Tuesday'*. Bit strong? Maybe!

Anyway, back to the serious stuff. We were contacted by PS Pinocchio regarding the Criminal Damage to our cars. He informed us the incident had been passed to the Community Policing Team, of which he was the Sergeant. He said he had been made aware of the footage from the local shop and would arrange for it to be collected. That was all the contact we had from Pinocchio for weeks. Despite our repeated requests to him for an update, we received no response.

We then received an email from another officer from NP, whom I will call PC Goffer. He informed us that PS Pinocchio had tasked him with investigating the damage to our cars and he was contacting us with an update. He said they had placed an image of the man captured on the CCTV cameras at the local shop on the NP Facebook page and they would see what comes of that. Positive, we thought.

We subsequently received a call from PC Goffer who informed us he had received a call from a man asking why a photo of him was on the NP Facebook page. Goffer informed us that the man who contacted him lived very close to us, but he would not tell us who he was or exactly where he lived.

Brilliant, so now we know the man identified in the CCTV footage from the local shop and the only suspect for the Criminal Damage to our cars was a close neighbour, but NP would not tell us who that neighbour was. We knew it wasn't any of the neighbours that harassed us up to this point as we did not recognise the man in the CCTV footage from the shop. So, it must be another neighbour who had joined in with the harassment.

The fact that this person was a neighbour and prepared to do something so sick as to pour a corrosive fluid over our cars, clearly placed our family at risk of further attacks. If he was prepared to do that, what else might he do? He was clearly a low-life. But NP thought it to be sensible policing not to inform us of who this man was so that we could take necessary steps to try and ensure our safety when in and about our neighbourhood.

I was aware the police may not be able to completely identify this man as he had not been charged with an offence at this stage. But the number one priority of the Community Policing Team was to protect the Community from crime. NP had a Duty of Care to our family as the victims of crime and to enable us to feel and be safe both inside and outside our home. They clearly neglected that Duty of Care in favour of protecting the identity of the suspect.

NP knew that by telling us this man was a neighbour but not telling us who he was or where he lived, would cause our family more distress than if they hadn't told us anything. This was a needless, pointless and deliberate act by PC Goffer to cause our family further suffering. In due course, this failure would have further implications for our family and me, in particular.

Having this information also heightened our fears when we were out of our house. I was already struggling with being in the neighbourhood alone and now this. Every time any of our family members was out in the neighbourhood, whenever we passed or saw anyone, we would look to see if they were wearing the Heller Hansen coat. We knew it was a neighbour, but which one, thanks to PC Goffer, only he and the suspect knew.

A couple of weeks passed without any further contact from NP and without us knowing which neighbour was the only suspect of damaging our cars. Can you imagine what it was like for our family to know that we could walk past this neighbour at any time, or he could be following us. We wouldn't have a clue if that was going to happen or more to the point, what he was going to do.

Yes, we knew what the person in the CCTV footage from the local shop looked like, but he could easily be in disguise as he was when he poured the fluid over our cars. Or he could approach us from behind, it was unbelievably stressful. It wasn't as if this was the only thing on our plate at the time. There were so many other matters to deal with, not just the matters like the harassment, the civil trial, and police failure, but also the usual family stuff, such as finances, children, and work. It was like we were living like Zombies, constantly in a daze, and we were really struggling to cope. If I hadn't lived it, I would never have understood how harassment can destroy a family both individually and collectively, and in so many ways. It truly is a devastating and cowardly crime.

A short while later, maybe a couple of weeks or so, I was returning home from work in my van. As I neared the corner of our road, I noticed a man on the drive of the house next door to Trigger. I instantly recognised this man to be the same man as in the CCTV footage captured at the local shop of the person who poured the fluid over our cars, and he was on the drive of the house next door to Trigger. No wonder NP wouldn't tell us who he was or where he lived.

To be clear, the man who was identified in the CCTV footage as the man who poured the corrosive fluid over our cars, was the next-door neighbour of Trigger who had been convicted of harassment against me, twice, and was on a suspended prison sentence for those convictions. And NP considered it to be sensible and appropriate policing not to inform our family of this. C U Next Tuesdays.

The penny dropped, Trigger must have either incited or paid this man to pour the fluid over our cars because he had been found Guilty of Harassment for the second time just one week earlier. Trigger was found guilty for the second time just a week before, and he was still harassing our family. Although I cannot be sure of that, why else would the next-door neighbour of Trigger pour a corrosive fluid over our cars? Just like the Heads had done with Trigger, as Trigger wasn't able to continue his harassment himself, he incited or paid someone else to do it. What a deranged bastard.

Bingo. I came into the house and told our daughter what I saw. Our daughter, like most of her generation, was very proficient on social media. So, she quickly did some research and soon discovered who the man I had seen on the drive next door to Trigger was. I will call him Cupid Stunt. Social media confirmed the age of Cupid Stunt would mean he was born in 1962. This of course matched the "*Class of 62*" hoodie of the man in the CCTV footage from the local shop.

I contacted PC Goffer to inform him I had seen the man in the CCTV footage from the local shop on the drive of the house next door to Trigger. Goffer said he could not comment at this stage! I asked Goffer why that was, but he would not tell me, he just repeated the line '*I cannot comment,*' I then asked him,

"*Is the man you suspect of causing Criminal Damage to our cars called Cupid Stunt?*" Goffer again said he could not comment. What a C U Next Tuesday.

It was beyond ridiculous that PC Goffer knew this man lived so close to us and even more ridiculous, that he lived next door to Trigger who had been convicted of

Harassment including threats of violence and Hate Crime, twice, the last of which was a just one week before the Criminal Damage to our cars. Also, that Trigger was a friend of the Heads who assaulted me and my wife as well as committing several other serious acts of Harassment causing Fear of Violence, and who were under investigation by NP for the harassment of our family, that Goffer did not and would not make us aware of this. What about our safety, what about just a little consideration for our family, what about just a little consideration for the victims, what about the fundamental role of the police to Protect and Serve the Public. That wouldn't even enter the heads of NP, they simply do not care.

The next thing we heard from PC Goffer is that the Forensic Examination on the bottle containing the fluid that was poured over our cars had not produced any evidence, but he would be interviewing the suspect anyway. I doubt if the bottle was ever sent to Forensics.

Matters got even worse, as only they could. We received an email from PC Goffer who told us the man who contacted him asking why an image of him was on the NP Facebook page, who was the man I had seen on the drive next door to Trigger, had now been interviewed and he completely denied it was him in our CCTV footage. Oh, that classic tactic again, just say it wasn't you and everything would be okay, clever! He wasn't going to get away with that, the evidence was too strong, wasn't it?

Considering the fact that this man was the only suspect for the criminal damage to our cars, the fact he lived so close to us and he was the next-door neighbour of Trigger, and the fact the CCTV footage from the local shop clearly identified this man wearing the same clothing as in our CCTV footage including the Heller Hansen coat, and that this incident marked yet another clear escalation in the level of the harassment – surely, NP would not just accept that because this man denied it was him in one version of the CCTV footage. They would say,

'So, we have the CCTV footage of the person pouring the fluid over the cars wearing the distinctive coat. We have the CCTV footage from the Pub showing the same person wearing the same distinctive coat, dumping the bottle containing the fluid in the bush. We also have the CCTV footage from the local shop showing the same man wearing the same distinctive coat and clearly identifying him. All the CCTV footage is in the exact time frame to confirm the person in all the CCTV footage is the same, but he said it wasn't him, so what can we do?

No, not this time, NP would not do this to our family. I know they are incompetent, incapable, inept, inefficient, and above all dishonest, but they are not downright evil, are they? No, this time would be different, it had to be, right?

Well, here is your answer, wrong. Yes, they would do this, and yes, they did do this, and yes, they are just downright evil.

We received an email from PC Goffer which stated, you've guessed it,

'NP will be taking NO FURTHER ACTION regarding the Criminal Damage to your cars due to a LACK OF EVIDENCE.'

We just could not believe it. To say NP would be taking no further action was bad enough, but to say the reason was because of a lack of evidence was so soul destroying. You could not get stronger, more complete evidence of this crime and the person who did it.

If this incident happened to any other family and the police had the same level of evidence against the only suspect, then the matter would have proceeded to Court and I am 100% confident, there was not a Judge, Jury or Magistrate in the land that would have found anything other than it was Cupid Stunt who committed this offence. No doubt.

I emailed Goffer to inform him of our utter disgust that yet again Numpty Police have failed in their Duty of Care to our family in knowingly and deliberately allowing yet another blatant criminal act against our family to go unpunished, giving the harassers further encouragement to continue their campaign of hate. Why I wasted my time telling Goffer something he already knew anyway, I don't know.

We then received an email from PS Pinocchio. He told us the lack of evidence was due to the lack of continuity in the various clips of CCTV footage. Lack of continuity, what the fuck, there was perfect continuity. I accept that there were three clips of CCTV footage and therefore the footage may not have been completely continuous, but the clothing and time frame of the three clips left no doubt it was the same person in all the clips, no doubt whatsoever.

In any case, when is CCTV footage ever completely continuous? Just as an example, you only have to watch the News or a crime programme such as Crimewatch and when showing the CCTV footage the police are using as evidence they will say, first you see the suspect following the woman at 10.00 pm on Baker Street, then you see the suspect still following the woman at 10.15 on Abbey Road, and then at 10.30 you see the suspect running in the opposite direction along Abbey Road shortly after the incident had taken place. Clearly, that would be enough for the police to progress their investigation or it wouldn't be on Crimewatch.

Not in our case, however, the three clips of CCTV from three different locations showing the person wearing the same distinctive clothing in the exact time frame, which was over only two and a half minutes, was not enough. Not enough to charge the suspect, not enough to refer the case to the CPS for guidance, and not enough for NP to do anything other than let this man get away scott-free with causing criminal damage to our and our friend's cars.

I contacted Pinocchio and told him there was complete continuity of the movements of the person in all of the clips of CCTV footage and the person was wearing the same clothing in all versions and they are in the exact time frame, so there could be no doubt that the person in all versions of the footage is the same.

Time to sit down again. In fact, lie down as I reckon you would even fall off your chair when you read this. PS Pinocchio replied,

"Ah, but the suspect in your footage and the footage from the pub may not have been the same person in the footage from the local shop as from when you lose sight of the suspect at the pub, to when he reappears in CCTV footage from the shop, he may have met with someone and swapped clothes."

I am not kidding you. A Sergeant in the Police Force actually wrote that in an email to the victims of crime. To be clear, there was a ten-second gap from when you lose sight of the person in the footage from the pub to when they reappear in the footage from the shop. PS Pinocchio was trying to tell me that in those ten seconds, the suspect managed to meet with an accomplice, strip off in the middle of the street with no one seeing him and his accomplice almost naked, and change clothes, not just the coat but hoodie, Joggers, even trainers. And then the accomplice walked the 30 metres to the local shop to buy chocolate, all in ten seconds. Absolute bullshit.

You see now why I call him PC Pinocchio. But this wasn't a make-believe character in a Walt Disney film, it was a real-life police officer, incredible. The level of utter disdain this officer would display to our family on several occasions which I will detail later, was an absolute disgrace.

Of course, this wasn't the first or last time NP would break their backs to protect the offenders, but because of the severity of the incident and the evidence NP had of the offence, it was one of, if not their most blatant, deliberate, and shocking failures.

PS Pinocchio was not only a proper C U Next Tuesday, but he was also the epitome of the modern-day police officer. He was young, far too young to be a Sergeant in the Police Force if you ask me, he had no life experience to call on. Everything he did was what he had been taught, or read in a book, although I would love to meet the author of the book this twat read!

When the police come to a decision to take No Further Action against a suspect for an alleged offence, the victim can exercise their right to a Victim's Right for Review. In that case, another officer from the same force will review the case to determine if the original decision was correct.

So, a police officer will review the decision of his fellow police officer and determine that his fellow police officer was correct in their original determination. In other words, it is a complete farce used by the police to place yet another barrier in the way of the victim getting justice or even equality.

The same as when you must make a complaint about the police, to the police. Come on, one officer is not going to throw his fellow officer under the bus, are they?

When the Victims Right for Review is upheld in favour of the police, as it is on almost every occasion, it then makes it doubly hard for the victim to progress the matter any further as the police will say. *'Well, Officer Dumb agrees with the determination of Officer Dumber, so two officers have the same opinion, so both cannot be wrong.'* The thin blue line and all that.

Anyway, if I haven't given too much away. I exercised my right for a Victim's Right for Review regarding the decision by NP to take No Further Action against Cupid Stunt for the Criminal Damage to our cars. I will return to this in a bit.

I suppose all we had to do now was to wait for Cupid Stunt to decide when he felt he would like to have another go at our family, and if he followed the same pattern as the others.

I am sure we will not have to wait very long before that happens. Then I would say that as I know what happens in just a few months!

Chapter Twenty-Seven
Trying Times

The civil trial against the Heads scheduled for October 2017 was delayed due to the Heads ditching their latest solicitor and deciding to represent themselves. Although I think it was a matter of having no choice to represent themselves as no reputable firm of solicitors would embarrass themselves in a Court of Law. It would appear the same firm of solicitors used by the Parish Council of which Mr Head was the Vice Chair, was their last hope and even they could not cope with the Heads lies. The delay in the trial was to allow the Heads time to prepare, and a new date was set for the 12th of March 2018.

As the trial date loomed, the Heads defence started to unravel. I knew it would, but even I was surprised at the level and speed of the unravelling. The Heads must have been thinking,

'Fuck, what have we done and what are we going to do now?'

As the Heads discontinued their Counterclaim, they would not be able to make any allegations against our family during the trial. It would just be a matter of them attempting to defend our claim. This did make the lead up to the trial a little less stressful than it might have been, not that we had anything to hide or fear, but just knowing that the Heads would not be able to make their disgusting allegations against us in a court of law was comforting in a way.

I say less stressful; it was still unbelievably stressful. If we won, we would be vindicated and some of the financial burden of the case would be alleviated, but if we lost, we would not only be liable for our astronomical costs, but those of the Heads also. Loss would mean financial ruin; we would have to sell our home and live in a tent in the woods. Although that seemed very appealing at the time, knowing our luck, we would set up camp next to a family of deranged badgers who would harass our family day and night.

That was one of the many risks of civil litigation, as our barrister told us, nothing is certain in law. The result was in the hands of one Judge and if they saw it differently to you, you are fucked. I don't have an alternative, but the risk of financial ruin should not be at the cost of justice. I guess, many civil cases are played like a hand of Poker, one side keeps raising the financial stakes until the other side has no choice but to fold. Democracy, do me a favour.

The first indication of the Heads expected unravelling was when our solicitor informed us that the Heads wanted to withdraw three of their witnesses from the trial. Those witnesses were Mr and Mrs Hoperty and, wait for it, Mrs Head herself. Seriously, the Heads wanted to withdraw one of the defendants from the trial, and the other two witnesses were their relatives!

Mr and Mrs Hoperty were, of course, the brother and sister-in-law of Mrs Head. Why would the Heads relatives withdraw? Lies, that was why. The Heads, as well as us, knew that what the Heads had claimed in their Counterclaim and was allegedly witnessed by the Hopertys, did not happen. I wouldn't have been at all surprised if the Hopertys were completely unaware that they had even been listed as witnesses by the Heads.

Even more bizarre, the Heads wanted to withdraw Mrs Head! Why would they want to do that? How are they able to do that? Mrs Head is not just a witness but a defendant. In most circumstances, if a defendant does not attend court to defend themselves, then the case against them is upheld. If Mrs Head did not attend the trial, it would severely impact the Heads defence.

My view was that all the Heads knew Mrs Head would be a liability in court. She is a compulsive and pathological liar and would not last five minutes under crossexamination before being exposed. She also has a non-existent fuse and would blow at the first tiny hurdle. The Heads all knew they could not let her attend court as a defendant, witness or even as support.

Our solicitor and Barrister had discussed the request by the Heads to withdraw these witnesses and it was decided that this would be to the detriment of our case and had therefore, requested the court to summon these people to attend court and give evidence.

However, the Court refused our request to summon these witnesses to the Court. Our barrister said that he had never known a Judge to refuse a request by a Claimant to summon a defendant or witness to court. Was it the dark side at play again?

Well, well, well, on the Thursday before the trial was to begin on the Monday, we were informed by our solicitor that three more of the Heads witnesses would not be attending court. These were the neighbour whom the Heads claimed I intimidated in July 2016, and his wife. The other witness the Heads wanted to withdraw was none other than Trigger himself. Smart move in a way, having a witness who had been convicted of Harassment against the Claimants, twice, was hardly a feather in their cap. Let's be honest, if Trigger was the best witness the Heads could manage, and even he was withdrawn, they must have known they were fucked.

What a disappointment that was though. Can you imagine the fun our barrister would have had cross examining Trigger?

'So, Mr Trigger, can you tell me how you know the first claimant?'

'Yea, I have been convicted of harassing him twice and I am on a two-and-a-half-year suspended prison sentence for those convictions.'

'And can you tell me why you harassed the first claimant?'

'Yea, the Heads told me to.'

It would have been brilliant and to be fair, I was really looking forward to that bit. What pissed me off the most was that I had been selling tickets for the Public Gallery for that day and now I would have to issue a full refund, it was a sell out as well. Damn you Trigger.

If it wasn't bad enough that Trigger would not be a witness in court, the Heads even had the gall to tell our solicitor the reason Trigger would not be attending court was because I had harassed him, and he was a broken man due to his convictions. Ahh, bless him, if you can't do the time, don't do the crime, old man.

This left the Heads with, uum, wait a minute, let me just tot up how many witnesses the Heads had left, there was, ah no, they had withdrawn, there was, oh no, they were not coming. That leaves, oh yes, ONE. One witness who was an alcoholic. What a defence the Heads had, they must have been shitting themselves. Well and truly up the creek without a paddle, even their own relatives had deserted them. Roll on Monday.

12th March 2018

We attended the County Court for the start of the civil trial against the Heads. I could write a book just on the events of the trial itself, but I think you would rather watch the Dulux Chanel showing an hour-long episode on Magnolia Matt Emulsion drying, so I will just stick to the main events.

Day One

All four members of our family were there of course, and we were represented by our barrister who was supported by our solicitor. We also had a few friends and relatives in the public gallery who came to show their support. For every day of the trial, we always had someone in the Public Gallery supporting us, true friends, neighbours and relatives. Then there was the Heads, Mr Head, Little Head, and Sponger, and that was it, no Mrs Head. It was quite ironic that out of all the other neighbours who joined in with the harassment of our family, not one of them turned up in court to support the Heads. In fact, the Heads had no one for the entire trial, no friends, no neighbours and not even a relative came to support them. The only person to turn up for the Heads for the whole trial was their one and only witness, the alcoholic, who turned up for the morning she was scheduled to give evidence. At times like these you find out who your true friends are, if you have any! Clearly, the Heads had been arseholes all their lives and not just for the time they had lived next door to us.

And there was the Judge, who I will call, the Judge (appropriate name I thought).

Not surprisingly, the very first words uttered by Mr Head were a lie. The Judge asked Mr Head who was with him, and he replied,

"My two sons."

Of course, they were not his two sons, they were his son and his son's husband. They were a married gay couple, and Mr Head clearly had a problem with that. He was obviously embarrassed and ashamed of his son's sexuality to the point of trying to conceal it from the Judge. Mr Head was the stereotypical, old-fashioned, male chauvinist bigot.

To the credit of Little Head, he stood up and told the Judge that Sponger was in fact his husband. It was just a pity Little Head didn't have the same strength to stand up to his parents and tell them to stop their harassment of our family, it would have saved both families an awful lot of misery.

The Judge asked Mr Head if Mrs Head was attending. Mr Head informed the Judge that Mrs Head would not be attending the trial as she couldn't be away from a toilet because she couldn't control her bowel when she was stressed. Fair enough, although she seemed to cope okay with the '*stress*' of harassing our family!

The Judge advised Mr Head it would harm their case if Mrs Head did not attend to give evidence and asked Mr Head if he wanted to delay the trial until such a time when Mrs Head could attend. Our hearts sank, we thought, oh no, not a further delay, please no. Mr Head said he wanted to carry on with the trial as there would never be a time when Mrs Head would be able to attend.

Phew, thank fuck for that. To be honest, I thought that was the whole idea why Mrs Head was not attending court, for the Judge to delay the trial. If that was not the Heads plan, then they must have something else up their sleeve. There was no doubt in my mind that Mrs Head could have attended court if she and the rest of them wanted. The fact that she didn't was for a reason, with the Heads, everything was for a reason.

The Heads did not have any legal representation in court. Mr Head informed the Judge that he was going to represent all four of the Head family. However, the Judge informed Mr Head that as Little Head and Sponger were attending court as defendants, they would have to represent themselves. I could sense that sent them into a right kerfuffle. The reason for that would become clear later in the trial.

The Judge was very hostile to our barrister from the start, and this continued throughout the whole trial. The Judge did not even let our barrister finish his opening submissions without arguing with him. The Judge repeatedly said throughout the trial,

"This is a very simple case."

We would later realise why the Judge had this attitude. As stated earlier, most Judges do not like civil cases as they feel the matter should have been sorted before it gets to court. He was clearly, and made no secret of the fact, that he was very annoyed that the trial had been scheduled for five days and that our barrister had listed all the major acts of harassment committed by the Heads against our family in our Particulars of Claim.

In any event, it might have appeared a very simple case to him, but it is anything but simple to us. It was the destruction of our family over what was at that time, five years. We all found this repeated comment by the Judge to be unnecessary and offensive, as with NP, it showed a complete lack of understanding for the impact of harassment and crime in general, on the victims.

After all the preliminaries, I was first to give evidence. It was clear to see and hear the frustration in the voice and actions of the Judge. He would not let me answer the questions in the way I wanted, he had clearly not read my witness statement and did not appear interested in what I was saying. In fact, he spent more time staring at the ceiling than paying attention to what was happening in his Court. I did not like his attitude, and I was not alone in that.

When I was being cross-examined by Mr Head, it was an absolute joke. He was so far out of his depth and made himself look like the complete idiot that he was. As expected, Mr Head lied constantly, even when he was proven by the evidence in front of him to be lying, he just continued to lie. One of the strangest moments in the questioning by Mr Head was when he repeated the claim made to our solicitor before the trial that I had harassed Trigger and that he was a broken man due to my harassment of him. Work that one out?

Mr Head was clutching at straws as there was nothing else he could do.

My wife was next to give evidence. Mr Head was his usual horrible self by trying to intimidate and upset her by repeatedly asking her about the assault on her by Mr Head. To be fair, the Judge did tell Mr Head to stop his line of questioning as it was unnecessarily intimidating and distressing to the witness.

Our son was the last to give evidence on day one, he was not in the witness stand for very long at all. Mr Head did not ask many questions and following his questioning we adjourned for the day, but not before the Judge gave our barrister a lecture about how he should present his case and what he expected from our barrister the next day.

Day Two

Day two was all about the Judge, he made sure of that. He continued to criticise our barrister at every opportunity, mainly about the number of incidents listed in our Particulars of Claim. What our barrister was supposed to do about that, I don't know. We hadn't asked the Heads to commit all these acts of harassment against us.

At the end of day one, the Judge asked, no, told, our barrister that before the start of day two, he must whittle down the number of incidents to just the most serious. Our barrister told the Judge he had already done so, which would have become clear if the Judge had allowed him to make his opening submissions.

However, our barrister began day two by informing the Judge he had done what was asked of him the day before and highlighted the most serious incidents which totalled seventeen of the forty-seven incidents listed in our Particulars of Claim.

This still was not good enough for the Judge however, although by this point, we were all aware nothing would ever be good enough for him.

The Judge loved the sound of his own voice, he made it clear to everyone in the court that he was in charge, he was the Alpha Male, the Billy Big Bollocks. I have never met a man with such a degree of self-importance, although several members of Numpty Police would push him close.

After the trial ended, I looked up the Judge on social media. His status and posts were all about how important and successful he thought he was, how much he was worth, what he did for charity, what car he drove, all that self-obsessed, ego-boosting, obnoxious look at me, look at me bollocks.

As far as the actual trial was concerned, on day two, our daughter was the first to give evidence. She was very strong and stood up to Mr Head during his questioning. In fact, she wasn't just strong, she destroyed Mr Head, he didn't know whether he was coming or going.

Mr Head clearly thought our daughter would be the weak link in our case and tried the same tactic as he had with my wife on day one by trying to intimidate our daughter. She was having none of it though, and at one point, she completely embarrassed Mr Head. Even Little Head and Sponger exhaled sharply as if to say,

'For fuck sake dad, shut up,'

I have to say and to his credit, the Judge was kind to our daughter, not just while she was being cross-examined but throughout the whole trial. For all his apparent faults, the Judge felt very strongly about the abuse of women and took a dim view of the horrible and distressing questioning of my wife and daughter by Mr Head. I thank him for that, he was still a dick, but I thank him all the same.

Our witnesses then started to give evidence. This did not take as long as expected, as Mr Head did not contest the content of most of their statements, so they did not need to give evidence in person. However, this was why the trial had been booked for five days. As in the Case Conference a few weeks before the trial, Mr Head had disputed the content of all our witnesses' statements and said he wanted to cross-examine them all, but when it came to the trial, Mr Head changed his mind.

The Judge never mentioned that though, he never mentioned the fact that the trial was booked for five days because Mr Head insisted on questioning our witnesses. But when it came to the trial, Mr Head changed his mind, funny that. I do understand that the Judge had to consider the fact that Mr Head was representing himself and needed to give him some leeway, but at the end of the day, it was the Heads choice to represent themselves. So, that should not impact our case.

Day Three

It was the turn of the Heads to give evidence. They all lied from start to finish and were proven time and time again to be dishonest.

Mr Head again stated I assaulted his wife, even though he was not supposed to make any allegations against our family. He also admitted to assaulting my wife and that he had lied to NP when being interviewed under caution regarding this assault. Little Head continued his allegation that our daughter had tailgated him. And Sponger completely lost his temper with our barrister and said that my wife had called Mr Head a *'Fucking C U Next Tuesday.'*

But thirty seconds later, he admitted that she didn't call him that at all. What a mess they were making of it. Not surprising when everything in their armoury was based on lies. The truth will out in the end.

They were all a joke, crying and sniffling like little children, trying to convince the Judge they were the victims of our harassment. They also claimed they all suffered from mental health conditions, which meant they could not remember certain things that happened.

Get this, at one-point, Little Head and Sponger admitted they had not even written their statements, and that Mr Head had written them. The reason they both gave for this was that they would find it too stressful to write them themselves, and due to their mental health conditions, the stress would cause them to self-harm. Sick bastards. They both admitted they hadn't even read their statements, let alone written them.

This was why Mr Head wanted to represent Little Head and Sponger, because he had written their statements for them and Little Head and Sponger hadn't got a clue what was contained in them.

Mr Head also claimed they had to discontinue their Counterclaim as they had no money. Total bollocks. They had no choice but to discontinue their Counterclaim because they had no evidence to support the disgusting lies contained in it. If they were confident their Counterclaim was truthful and would be successful, they wouldn't need to worry about money as the Judge would order us to pay their costs.

The last remaining witness for the Heads also gave her evidence. She claimed to have witnessed an act of harassment by my wife against Mr Head. But when she described what she claimed to have witnessed, she described an act of harassment by Mr Head against my wife. So, the only remaining witness for the Heads, witnessed an act of harassment by Mr Head against my wife, trifik. I am not usually one to give advice, particularly when I have not been asked to do so, but one piece of advice I would give is to never rely on an alcoholic as a witness in a trial.

Of course, our barrister had the opportunity to cross-examine the Heads, apart from Mrs Head as she wasn't there. However, the Judge seemed determined not to let our barrister cross-examine Mr Head. He really went in on our barrister on this, at one point, when our barrister was asking Mr Head about the erecting of the fence on our land in the summer of 2014, the Judge told our barrister that he wanted the trial conducted his way. Our barrister informed the Judge that he was conducting the trial correctly and he was cross-examining Mr Head as he was supposed to do.

The Judge was extremely rude to our barrister to the point he was completely bemused, as were the rest of us. At the end of day three, our barrister told us he had never heard such a thing as a Judge not wanting a barrister to cross-examine a defendant and that he had never been spoken to like that in a court before, not even by a witness let alone a Judge. It was a disgrace to be fair.

It was clear to me then, and even more so after the trial, the Judge did not want our barrister to cross-examine Mr Head regarding the erecting of the fence on our land in the summer of 2014. During the civil case, the Heads always maintained the fence was on their land to enable them to defend the fact that when I removed the fence in September

2014, they were within their rights to make the allegation of criminal damage against me.

As the Judge failed to prevent Mr Head from being cross-examined. When being questioned about the fence, Mr Head panicked and admitted at the time he erected the fence in the summer of 2014, he knew he was erecting the fence on our land by saying, *"I am a layman, not a carpenter so the easiest way to erect the fence was to attach it to the gate post, which I knew was on the Bean's land, I did not think they would mind."*

Did not think we would mind! By the summer of 2014, Mr Head assaulted both me and my wife. Of course we would mind if he erected the fence on our land.

He went on to say,

It was the police who told me to say about the hammer being used."

Of course, this was a clear admission under oath in a court of law, that Mr Head had knowingly lied in his statement to NP regarding his allegation of Criminal Damage, and NP had told him to lie about me using a hammer to damage the fence. Because of his lies and the failure by PC's Pinky and Perky to conduct a reasonable, proportionate, and impartial investigation into the allegation, what happened to me because of that allegation, the suspected Heart Attacks, the hospital admission, the six weeks of work, the appearance in Court, the nightmares, the prosecution and the undoubted life-long impact on my mental and physical health, should not have happened.

And that was why the Judge was so determined to prevent our barrister from crossexamining Mr Head on this point, because the Judge did not want Mr Head to slip up and expose the deliberate failings of NP. The dark side had even got to the Judge in our civil case. Or am I being paranoid?

On a more positive note, at the end of day three, our barrister cautiously advised us that we had won our case. He said this because of his experience in court, the way the Judge had spoken to Mr Head, it was clear he was trying to tell Mr Head that they were going to be found liable for the harassment of our family including the Personal Injury part of our claim.

Day Four

The day focused on both sides closing submissions. Mr Head did not have much to say, what little he had brought to the party had been obliterated and exposed as complete and utter garbage. He still tried to play them as the victims though. Once again, the Judge was very combative with our barrister, he would not let our barrister present his final submissions in the way he wanted, which was the way it should be done. Like with the cross-examination of Mr Head, the Judge was blocking our barrister from doing his job exactly the way it should be done, very strange. By lunchtime, both sides had finished their final submissions, and the Judge adjourned early for the day to consider his findings.

Day Five

Findings

On the positive side, Mr Head, Mrs Head and Little Head were all found liable for the harassment of all four members of our family. On the negative side, for some reason, none of us could understand, Sponger was found not to be liable for the harassment of any member of our family. What the fuck was going on there?

Our barrister was completely baffled as to how the Judge could find three members of the Head family liable for harassment, but not the fourth. The Judge had said many times during the trial,

"An act of harassment by one member of the family is an act of harassment by all members of the family as they live in the same house and are a closely-knit family unit. It would not be possible for any one of them not to know what is happening."

But then he found Sponger was not liable. Talk about a contradiction.

The Judge also made a point of emphasising that it was not an act of harassment or any other offence for Mr Head to make an allegation of Criminal Damage to the police against me for removing the fence in September 2014 as at the time of the allegation Mr Head genuinely believed the fence was on his land.

Absolute bollocks. Mr Head admitted while giving evidence under oath that at the time he erected the fence he knew it was on our land. Despite that admission under oath, the Judge still made a specific Judgement that Mr Head was within his rights to make the allegation. Total bollocks.

Again, and I stress, I am convinced this is why the Judge did not want our barrister to cross-examine Mr Head about the fence. The Judge was clearly aware of the allegation by Mr Head and the malicious prosecution by

NP and he did not want Mr Head to disclose anything that would incriminate the police. You failed, not that it would make any difference anyway.

This, of course, was a very important point for me. This false allegation and malicious prosecution had a dramatic impact on my life. I had spent 50 years on this planet trying to do my best and being a good person. No one can ever take away the fact that now, I have been offered a Conditional Caution by the police, charged with an offence, summoned to appear in Court, stood in the Dock to make my plea, and prosecuted by the CPS. It is something that will always impact my life negatively.

I will have to right that wrong if I am ever to come to terms with this.

We adjourned for lunch while the Judge prepared his Order, and he would give Judgement when we returned.

Suicide is Painless

Time to make sure you are sitting down again. In fact, if you intend to keep reading for a while, it might be best if you lay down again, maybe as close to the floor as possible.

Our family, friends, barrister, and solicitor, retired to the café at the Court building for lunch, not that any of our family could eat anything. We were all sitting round a table when Mr Head walked in and tapped our barrister on the shoulder. Mr Head then said to our barrister,

"The wife has taken some tablets in an attempt to commit suicide, so I have got to go home straight away."

Oh my God, not again!

Mr Head then left the cafe.

However, a few minutes later, one of our friends went outside of the court building to have a cigarette before we returned to the courtroom. While she was standing outside the court building, who should she see walking down the street smiling and joking with each other, none other than Mr Head and Sponger? Not the sort of behaviour you would expect from a man who had just been told that his wife had attempted to commit suicide.

Something was telling me, and I don't know what it was, maybe it was because of the previous occasions when the Heads contacted NP and told them they were going to commit suicide because we harassed them. Maybe it was because of their vile abuse of mental health conditions as an excuse for their behaviour, maybe it was because our friend had seen Mr Head and Sponger outside the Court Building just a few minutes after Mr Head told our barrister that his wife had attempted suicide. I couldn't quite put my finger on it, but something was telling me this was not a genuine suicide attempt. There are no flies on me you know!

When we reconvened, our barrister asked the Judge if he was aware of what had happened over lunch. The Judge said he was aware and adjourned the case until Monday morning for him to give his Judgement.

Our barrister asked the Judge if he was aware of the gravity of what had happened and suggested that Monday morning might be a bit soon. The Judge then adjourned the Judgement until the following Friday at 11 am.

The Judge did not seem shocked or even bothered that Mrs Head had allegedly tried to commit suicide, he thought the same as the rest of us. This was how deranged the Heads were, they would and have on several occasions threatened to commit suicide unless they got what they wanted, which in this case was an adjournment of the Judgement.

Let's be honest, the Heads are both Pensioners, in just the short time we have known them, they have allegedly attempted suicide on numerous occasions. But they were still here, alive and kicking. So, either they were not very good at attempting suicide, or they did not attempt suicide at all!

Later that day, our barrister contacted Little Head to ask how Mrs Head was. Our barrister was not as familiar with this tactic of the Heads and was therefore more concerned and sympathetic than maybe our family was. Little Head said he was at home with Mrs Head, and they were waiting for an ambulance. Lying little bastard, we have a friend who was a paramedic, and he confirmed there was not an ambulance dispatched to the Heads address that day. Sick, evil bastards.

It might appear a bit sad, but later that day we contacted the local hospital and asked how Mrs Head was doing following her attempted suicide. Guess what, we were told there was no record of a Mrs Head attending or being admitted to the hospital. Oh my God, how strange. Could it be that Mrs Head feigned her suicide attempt, again? DA, DA, DA.

I bet you thought I was joking or exaggerating when I said earlier that the Heads regularly used suicide and mental health as their get-out-of-jail-free card.

We returned to the Court the following Friday for the Judgement. The Judge started by very insincerely asking Mr Head how Mrs Head was following her near-death experience. Mr Head told the Judge that Mrs Head was in A&E for 8 hours the previous Friday following her attempted suicide, liar. The Judge asked Mr Head if he could provide any evidence to the Court to support that, but guess what, he couldn't. Well, well, well, would you believe it!

The Judgement

To cut a long story short, I was awarded damages of 25k, my wife was awarded 20k, our daughter 10k, and our son 3k, which was 58k in total. Our barrister was disappointed but not surprised with the awards. In his experience, the awards were on the low side of the bracket for Personal Injury for myself, wife and daughter and the award for our son of 3k likened our son's damages to that of someone who may have suffered mild whiplash due to a minor car accident, rather than someone who had suffered five years of harassment.

Anyway, we still had the matter of costs to deal with and from the way the Judge constantly criticised our barrister from day one of the trial, we were not optimistic of being awarded a high percentage of our costs. The loser of the case is normally ordered to pay around 90% of the winner's costs. However, the Judge ordered the Heads to pay just 65% of our costs.

Coincidentally, I am sure, I will not go into the figures at this stage as they will be covered in more important points regarding these awards later, but basically, 65% of our costs would mean that the shortfall between the cost of bringing the case against the Heads and the amount of costs we were awarded, would be almost exactly, yes you've guessed it 58k.

So, the award of damages and costs would equate to the same amount as the cost of bringing the claim against the Heads, which of course, meant that we would have absolutely nothing to show for the five years of absolute hell on earth that cost our family so much more than just money. When you consider things like the interest we have paid on our loans, and the lost income due to time off work, etc, we would be thousands and thousands of pounds out of pocket. It really was an absolute insult.

The Judge ordered that the award should be paid in instalments with the first instalment of 80k to be paid on the 18th of April 2018.

To be clear. It was never about the money. Taking civil action was the only avenue left open to us if we ever wanted the harassment to stop, legal avenue anyway. It was a last resort when everything else, including the many attempts at mediation and relying on NP to treat us with equality and respect, had failed.

But it has to be said, there is no other way to compensate victims of crime. Unless or until someone events a time machine that can take people back to a time before whatever crime was committed against them had happened, the only form of recompense is financial.

Following the Judgement, we adjourned to discuss the award. Our barrister was of the view that we should appeal on the grounds that the award of damages was too low for the severity of the harassment and the award of 65% of our costs was very low considering the conduct of the Heads during the entire case. Also, and more importantly, the fact that two of the judgments were completely and obviously wrong and would considerably affect the amount of damages awarded. These two judgments were Sponger not being found liable, which did not make any sense to any of us, and the finding regarding the allegation of Criminal Damage made by Mr Head for the removal of the fence. We agreed that when we returned following the adjournment, our barrister would ask the Judge for Leave to Appeal but he expected the Judge would refuse his request.

When we returned, that was exactly what happened, the Judge refused our Leave to Appeal. This didn't mean it was the end of the road as far as an appeal was concerned, but it would make an appeal more difficult and expensive. No wonder our solicitor was smiling!

Our barrister then suggested that we should make the Heads an offer whereby if they agreed to pay the sum of £150,000 as full and final settlement, which was 9k more than the award of damages and costs combined. We would agree not to appeal the Judgement or take any further civil action.

Before we left the Court Building, our barrister put this offer to Mr Head who said he would think about it and agreed to meet with our barrister the following week regarding a decision. Mr Head later contacted our barrister to reject the offer and cancelled their meeting. We would soon find out why the Heads did this, they had a plan, they always had a plan!

By the end of the trial, Mr Head was all by himself. His wife had not attended court at all, they had no support from friends, relatives, or neighbours throughout the entire trial, his son did not attend on the final day and even Sponger disappeared at lunchtime. Mr Head was all alone. I can vividly remember watching him walking down the corridor toward the exit at the end of the day all by himself. It was a sorrowful sight, and I remember thinking to myself. **Serves yourself right, you horrible little cunt.** Sorry, but that one is staying in.

Interlude

Remember PC David Carrick, the Met Police Officer who was one of the worst serial rapists in British History. On the news today, it was confirmed that four officers from the Professional Standards Department of the Metropolitan Police Force have been suspended while under investigation for failing to take appropriate action regarding reports to the Met about the conduct of PC David Carrick.

Just another example of how the police fail victims of crime to protect their own, not just from standard crimes like Harassment, Burglary, and Theft but also from heinous crimes such as rape and domestic abuse. Also, just another example of how things have not changed, despite the promises we have heard time after time for decades,

'We have learned from our mistakes and have taken measures to ensure this can never happen again.'

But sadly, it does keep happening again, and again, and again.

ChapterTwenty-Eight
You Cannot Be Serious

Murder in Slow Motion

Going back to just before the start of the civil trial. It was the Friday evening before the trial began on the Monday morning. We received a visit from PC Goffer to take statements from me and our daughter's friend regarding the Criminal Damage to our cars at the beginning of February.

After he took our statements, he said that he had been tasked by the Detective

Inspector who had investigated the allegations of harassment by ourselves and the Heads, to write a letter to inform us of his determination of that investigation, but as he had a copy of the letter with him, he felt he could not leave without reading it to us. I bet he couldn't!

Just to remind you. We knew the so-called *'impartial evidence gathering exercise'* conducted by PC Clueless had included taking statements from the Heads alleged witnesses as the Heads had disclosed these statements to us as part of the civil case. We also knew the *'impartial evidence gathering exercise'* conducted by PC Clueless had **not** taken statements from any of our witnesses.

We had pointed this fact out to NP on more than one occasion before this point in time, so you can imagine our shock to be told by Goffer, totally out of the blue that the investigation had been concluded and a determination had been reached by the Detective Inspector. This instantly made me think the news was going to be bad, the look on the face of PC Goffer confirmed that, pure disdain. Just how bad even I could not have imagined.

My wife, daughter, our daughter's friend, and I were all in our front room with Goffer. When he told us of the letter, the atmosphere in the room completely changed, to say you could cut the atmosphere with a knife does not do it justice. This was the conclusion of an investigation by NP that had taken TWO AND A HALF YEARS to complete and the determination of which was so important to our family for so many reasons.

Goffer started to read the letter, and after the initial introduction, Goffer read,

'DI Custard has completed the final review and has deemed that there was sufficient evidence to charge all parties from both sides with Harassment'

We were all absolutely stunned. I just sat on the floor in the middle of the room, I could not speak, talk, hear, or think, I couldn't even move. I just sat there in the middle of the room staring into space. My wife was just the same, it was like we were instantly frozen solid. Our daughter became very distressed and needed to leave the room, and her friend went to look after her.

We could not believe our ears, it was right up there with the worst news we had ever heard or could ever hear, I know that may be hard to believe but I swear it's true. After all we had endured, all the harassment, intimidation, provocation, discrimination, inequality, and misconduct by NP, and not once did any member of our family initiate or react to any of the multitude of serious criminal offences committed against our family. Mr Head had even assaulted my wife, and we still did the right thing in reporting it to NP and trusted them to deal with it appropriately. We remained the good, honest, lawabiding family that we have always been, and still are.

I cannot put into words the emotion we all felt regarding this. I have been through quite a lot in my life, but I can honestly say, I have never felt the way this instantly made me feel. If I had to pick a word to describe the feeling, the only word I can think of is empty, but that does not do it justice, nowhere near. It was as if everything instantly left my body, my ability to speak, hear, think, and even move. I was an empty shell.

Despite Goffer seeing the impact his words had on our family, he continued to read the rest of the letter but, probably thankfully, I did not hear a word he said after that. I just sat on the floor for I don't know how long. I cannot even remember seeing Goffer out, I assume he just left of his own accord when his job was done. Probably with a big smile on his face, no, it would be wrong of me to say that, he would definitely have had a big smile on his face, he had written the letter himself after all!

The same as when NP could not have investigated the allegations of the Public Order offences made by ourselves against Mrs Head, how could NP have investigated the allegation of harassment made by ourselves against the Heads when they had failed to gather the evidence from our witnesses?

All this just two days before the start of the civil trial. It had taken DI Custard two and a half years to conduct his totally fucked up investigation and reach a determination that was so wrong. How could he have conducted a fair and equal investigation when he only had the statements from the Head's witnesses, it is impossible. After waiting for two and a half years, NP decided to drop this bombshell on us just two days before the start of the civil trial. I am sure you can imagine that the stress was incredible and unbearable. How we did not suffer even more serious health implications than we did, I will never know.

I know it might sound silly, but it genuinely felt as though NP were trying to kill us. They were deliberately piling so much pressure on our shoulders hoping we would suffer a breakdown, stroke, or heart attack. The same as the conduct of PC Pinky regarding the Conditional Caution offered to me for removing the fence.

This wasn't NP playing games, just making us a little stressed or worried. This was NP deliberately trying to cause our family serious harm. It was like murder in slow motion, and they were loving it and probably closer than even they thought to achieving their goal. Everyone has their limits, and their breaking point and I think it is fair to say, that we had passed most people's breaking point a long time ago.

I can only speak for myself, but I hope these past few chapters may help you understand that although I did survive, I am not intact, I am not the same person I was before the harassment started. The past few years have taken so much from me, things that cannot be replaced, repaired, or returned to how they were. Not just my mental and physical health, but things like pride, self-worth, and trust. There is no doubt in my mind, the events since 2014 may not have ended my life, but they have definitely shortened it.

An example of how I have changed, and I am sure most of you will understand this. I have been a member of a badminton club for the past few years on and off, I had a break for a while due to health issues, not surprisingly. However, I went to the club's Christmas get-together, and one of the members told me that they had a few new members and one of them was a Police Officer. That was it for me, there was no way I could return to the club and enjoy playing badminton with a police officer. Obviously, it is impossible to totally escape contact from the police and I would not care if I was in the company of a police officer at a wedding or funeral for example, but to have to interact with one is a step too far at this time. It's a real shame, she may be the nicest person in the world, I doubt it, but you never know, but I just cannot do it.

At this time, we had even more important matters to deal with. Even more important than being considered by NP as having harassed our next-door neighbours, such as the civil trial. We received the letter that Goffer had read to us on the Friday evening through the post on the Monday or Tuesday of the following week, during the civil trial. As we needed to focus all our efforts on the trial, we decided it would be best not to open it until the trial ended as we were sure the rest of the letter would be as distressing as what we had heard on Friday.

Even after the way we had been treated by NP up to this point, it did not enter our heads that DI Custard could possibly conclude we were as much to blame for what happened as the Heads and all the other harassers. We could not understand how DI Custard could find we were to blame at all.

We had done nothing wrong to anyone. To be clear, as confirmed by Inspector Arsewipe and PS Quack in our meeting with them in November 2105, this investigation was to include all reported incidents to NP including those by the Heads, their friends, relatives, and neighbours.

Following the completion of the civil trial, we opened the letter. Trust me, even a week later, it wasn't much easier seeing it in black and white, especially with the emblem of NP at the top of the page.

On reading it through however, it was clear that after being under investigation for the past two and a half years by NP, DI Custard knowingly and deliberately lied in his determination. He, and I, knew there could not be any evidence of our alleged offending as we did not offend at all. We had done nothing wrong so there could not be anything to say that we had, nothing that was legitimate at least.

As well as the part that stated there was enough evidence to charge all parties from both sides with harassment. The letter also stated,

"DI Custard noted in his review, however, that the offence of Harassment is a 'summary only' crime and as such is bound by prosecution time limits. The date for the case to be presented to the Crown Prosecution Service has passed meaning this matter cannot be pursued any further".

"DI Custard, in reviewing the material, considered other criminal offences which would not be bound by time scales and therefore allow for a criminal prosecution. No evidence of more serious offending could be found which led DI Custard to taking the only option available to him. No further action is to be taken against any person from either family for the offense of harassment."

That is absolute bollocks. I'm afraid I will have to go into a bit of detail regarding the Prevention of Harassment Act again to explain why the above is wrong. I hope it doesn't bore you too much.

The Protection from Harassment Act, which came into force in 1997, was amended in 2012, to include the Section 4 offences of Harassment causing Fear of Violence and Stalking Causing Fear of Violence. The standard offence of Harassment is indeed a Section 2 offence and is *'summary only'* and is bound by prosecution time limits for the case to be presented to the Crown Prosecution Service (CPS). DI Custard is correct about that.

Harassment Causing Fear of Violence however, is a Section 4 offence and therefore not *'summary only'* and is not bound by the same prosecution time limits for the case to be presented to the CPS. So, DI Custard is wrong to say the offence of Harassment is solely a Section 2 *'summary only'* offence.

DI Custard claimed he could not find any evidence of more serious offending other than Section 2 *'summary only'* harassment offences. However, if our statements and evidence had been considered in his investigation, he would have seen the many acts of Harassment Causing Fear of Violence that had been committed against our family by the

Heads and their associates, including but may not limited to, the assault on my wife on the 05th June 2014, the assault on myself on the 24th July

2014, the threat to attack our daughter also on the 24th July 2014, the screws through the fence in August 2014, the Malicious Communications via Social Media on the 11th September 2014, the placing of the broken bottle on the verge in January 2016, and as the investigation was to include all incidents that had been reported to NP, the investigation should also have included the many acts of Harassment Causing Fear of Violence committed by Trigger in the Autumn of 2016 and the summer of 2017, the threatening messages sent by the granddaughter of Trigger in the Autumn of 2017 and the Criminal Damage to our cars in February 2018.

All these offences are either acts of Harassment Causing Fear of Violence or evidence of more serious offending, all of which were reported to NP and all of which were fully and irrefutably evidenced. Trigger had even been convicted of Harassment including threats of violence and Homophobic Hate Crime, TWICE!

However, DI Custard still claimed there was no evidence of any offences other than

Section 2 harassment. DI Custard was a senior investigating officer with Numpty Police. If, after taking two and a half years to investigate this case, DI Custard could find **No Evidence** of a Section 4 offence of Harassment causing Fear of Violence, and **No Evidence** of more serious offending, either he was knowingly and deliberately lying or he did not have the required level of intelligence to enable him to conduct his duties to an appropriate standard to allow the general public to have confidence in the police. Either way you choose to look at it, it is clear, DI Custard should not be a Detective Inspector in the Police Force. He was either completely bent or completely stupid, neither of those are complimentary I know, but they are true, in my opinion.

There is no way on this earth that PC Clueless conducted an *'impartial evidence gathering exercise'* for this investigation when she had only taken statements from the Heads witnesses. Therefore, there is no way on this earth DI Custard could have conducted a fair and impartial investigation when he only had the statements from the Heads witnesses. There is no way on this earth DI Custard could claim there was no evidence of any acts of Harassment Causing Fear of Violence or other more serious offending. There is no way on this earth DI Custard could honestly claim that after conducting an investigation into Harassment that lasted for two and a half years, he was not aware that Harassment Causing Fear of Violence was a section 4 offence.

Surely, there is no way on this earth any reasonable person could believe anything other than this investigation was a complete and utter sham from the very start of the socalled *'impartial evidence gathering exercise'*, right through to the determination. It is clear to me, the sole purpose of the investigation which must have cost tens of thousands of pounds, was to protect the offenders, incriminate the victims and protect the various officers of NP from their misconduct and criminality. Yet again, NP condoned, encouraged, facilitated, was complicit too, and actively joined in, with the continued harassment of our family to a shocking level.

After all our family had endured from the Heads, Hopertys, Trigger, his granddaughter, Cupid Stunt, and the many members of NP who joined in with the harassment in many ways and on many different occasions. For DI Custard to conclude that it was our family who harassed the Heads, was absolutely devastating and beyond our comprehension.

All the effort we had put into doing the right thing, clinging on to the hope that this investigation would see the truth and stop the harassment. To then be blamed by a senior officer of NP, not only for the harassment we endured but also for being the harassers ourselves, was a complete waste of time.

We might as well have taken a different path. I will be honest with you, I do not think there are many families out there who would have possessed the tolerance and strength that we have. Most families would have cracked and taken matters into their own hands with potentially tragic consequences for either themselves or others. To be fair, I do not think there are many men out there who would have tolerated their wife or partner being assaulted by their next-door neighbour, before taking matters into their own hands, let alone all the other stuff. Believe me, I wanted to confront Mr Head for what he did, but I didn't, was that the right thing to do? I genuinely do not know.

In terms of stopping the harassment, no, it was the wrong thing to do as the failure by NP to deal with the assault appropriately, gave the Heads the green light to continue their harassment. Was it the right thing morally and ethically? Yes, it was, it allowed me and my family to be able to hold our heads high and be forever proud of ourselves and each other for having the strength to do the right thing and not to lower ourselves to the level of the Heads, their associates and NP. Once you do that, you are as bad as them, in the eyes of the law anyway, that's British Law, by the way, not the law unto NP.

After being under investigation by NP for TWO AND A HALF YEARS, the net result of that investigation and determination by a Detective Inspector with NP was a one-page letter that was the most compelling evidence of inequality, discrimination, incompetence and above all, blatant dishonesty and misconduct by an officer of NP, it is possible to imagine.

It now became even more obvious what was meant by Inspector Arsewipe at our meeting with him and PS Quack, when he said,

"If you want to make an allegation of Harassment against the Heads you may find yourselves being investigated for the same offence as these things have a habit of backfiring."

Inspector Arsewipe must have tasked PC Clueless to only take statements from the heads witnesses and not ours to facilitate the premeditated determination by DI Custard.

It is clear. NP never had any intention of conducting an impartial evidencegathering exercise, investigation and determination into the harassment, and it is clearly evident that NP were not and would not ever take the desperate plight of our family seriously. Even worse than that, NP were hell-bent on trying to prove it was our family that are the guilty ones. WORDS FAIL ME, AGAIN.

I cannot emphasise strongly enough the impact this determination by DI Custard had on all members of our family. It was beyond devastating.

Eat, Sleep, False Allegation, Repeat

Due to the content of the letter, I contacted PC Goffer to ask if we could arrange a meeting with DI Custard to discuss the matter with him. To my great surprise, DI Custard agreed to meet with us at our home address.

We met with DI Custard towards the end of April 2018. It would be fair to say the meeting did not get off to the best of starts. DI Custard was early, so it was just me and our daughter as the wife was still at work. Time to lie down again I'm afraid. Are you ready?

The first thing DI Custard said to me was,

"I have to inform you that an allegation of a Public Order Offence has been made against you by a Mr and Mrs Hoperty and as you are a KNOWN OFFENDER you will be required to provide an interview under caution."

WTF, to be clear, the police cannot require you to provide an interview under caution, it is voluntary, and there is a clue in the name. If you refuse to provide a voluntary interview under caution, you can face arrest.

Just to remind you, Mr and Mrs Hoperty are the brother and sister-in-law of Mrs Head. The same Mrs Head who had been found liable for the harassment of all four members of our family just a few weeks prior!

That feeling of emptiness came over me again. Here we were, meeting with DI Custard to discuss his fucked-up investigation, and the first thing he did was to tell me that yet another false allegation by the harassers had been made against me. But even worse, DI Custard referred to me as a known offender, I really took exception to being called that. Again, as with several previous meetings with officers of NP, Custard tried to intimidate me and put me on the back foot from the start.

I said to Custard,

"I am not a KNOWN OFFENDER."

He replied,

"Oh, don't worry about it, it's just a term we use."

Bollocks. The police do not refer to members of the public or victims of crime as KNOWN OFFENDERS unless they are known offenders. If they did, they would be sued left right and centre and rightly so. Being regarded by the police and recorded on the local police system as a Known Offender, has a massive impact on that person's life. It leads to prejudice, discrimination, being treated differently and to being considered as an offender for every allegation that is made against you, as I was finding out right now.

As Custard regarded me as a Known Offender, there was no question in his mind that I committed the offence, and I would be interviewed under caution. Not because NP had any evidence of the allegation, because there was no evidence, because the allegation was false, but because I was regarded as a Known Offender.

After what happened to me the last time I was interviewed under caution by Pinky and Perky for another false allegation of Criminal Damage made by Mr Head, the thought of this happening again was very hard to hear, especially as this allegation was made by his brother and sister-in-law!

It was no coincidence that the Hopertys made this allegation just a few weeks after we won our court case against their relatives the Heads. This was a clear act of retribution by the Heads and Hopertys and confirmed what we had known for a long time. The Heads and their associates were never going to stop their harassment of our family, even after the Heads were found liable and Trigger was convicted, twice. While they can harass, they will harass.

It was also no coincidence that Custard started the meeting by telling me of this allegation. It was clearly done to try to undermine our belief that Custard must have known his determination was a total travesty. What had this allegation got to do with Custard or the purpose of the meeting? Why would a Detective Inspector be informing me about this false allegation? Why would he tell me I was a Known Offender? Why would he tell me I would be required to provide an interview under caution, even though the allegation had not been investigated at that time? It had nothing to do with him and it had no relevance to our meeting.

This was the same tactic used by Inspector Arsewipe at the start of our meeting with him and PS Quack when he started the meeting by saying,

"If you want to make an allegation of harassment, you may find yourself being investigated for the same offence as these things have a habit of backfiring."

It is a popular tactic with the police, to intimidate, undermine and threaten you and to put you on the back foot. It is part of their training and is the same method used when interviewing suspects, unless you are one of the Heads, of course, and then you won't be interviewed or investigated at all!

The wife returned home at this point, and I told her of the allegation. Custard then said to my wife,

"The allegation is that your husband used foul and abusive language towards the Hopertys on the 19th of April 2018 and your husband will be required to provide the police with an interview under caution as he is a KNOWN OFFENDER."

I again told Custard that I was not a KNOWN OFFENDER.

Custard did not reply.

To be referred to as a "KNOWN OFFENDER" again by Custard after I had told him I was not a known offender was extremely insulting and offensive.

Again, after all we had endured as the victims of harassment, it was NP who considered me to be a known offender, not the Heads or the Hopertys, but me. There was no reason why NP should refer to me as that, I have never been arrested, cautioned or convicted of any offence, ever. So, there should not be anything on either the Local Police System (LPS) or the Police National Computer (PNC), that would indicate that I am.

I would later find out that wasn't the case, and Custard knew that because following his *'investigation and determination'*, it was he who added all four members of our family onto the Local Police System of NP for the offence of harassment. Bastard, cowardly bastard.

And he didn't even have the balls or respect to tell us he did this either before, during or after our meeting. That's why I have named him Custard, because he is a cowardly custard and a C U Next Tuesday to boot.

I would also later discover that PC Pinky also recorded me onto the LPC of NP for Criminal Damage. Even more shocking, was that NP submitted false information to the

Association of Criminal Records Office (ACRO) to facilitate the addition of my name to the Police National Computer. To facilitate this addition, the form submitted by NP to ACRO, stated, *'Arresting Officer: PC Pinky.'*

This was completely untrue. I was not arrested for this offence by PC Pinky. In fact, I have never been arrested for any offence, by anyone, ever. More on this later.

I could not believe that once again a false allegation was made against a member of this family by the Heads or their relatives and yet again a member of this family was being told they would be interviewed under caution by NP, even before any investigation. Clearly, this is wrong.

For all you law-abiding citizens out there who have never been interviewed under caution by the police as a suspect, I am sure you can understand, it is not a pleasurable experience, particularly when the police conduct the interview in the way they did with myself, son and daughter, and even more particularly when you are not only innocent, but when you are the victim of the harassment of the people who made the false allegation against you.

This will be the FOURTH time a member of our family had been interviewed under caution by NP, all because of false allegations to NP by the harassers and all with no evidence to support them.

The start of this meeting with DI Custard clearly confirmed the level of discrimination displayed by NP towards our family knew no bounds. It did not seem to matter what level of misconduct and indeed criminality NP used to discriminate against us. If it served their purpose, they would use it.

Failed

Anyway, back to the purpose of the meeting. I am sure DI Custard thought his 'tactic' to undermine me would work and we would be putty in his hands, and a few years ago, he would have been correct, but not now. Like so many others before him, he underestimated the strength of our family, it was one of those occasions where I knew I was 100% right. There was not a single shred of doubt in my mind that DI Custard was wrong in his determination and when I am like that, nothing and no one will stop me from seeing it through, win or lose.

Despite that, the rest of the meeting was still very difficult. Custard had the usual arrogance we had become accustomed to by a member of NP. However, I was about to humble him. I asked Custard what evidence he had of our offending, Custard stuck to the content of his letter by stating,

"I have conducted a thorough investigation and concluded there is enough evidence to charge all parties from both sides with harassment." I said,

"That's not what I asked, I asked you what evidence do you have of our offending. Whatever evidence you have will be false as we have not harassed the Heads, and whatever allegations they have made against us in their statements will also be false, and we have the right to know what those allegations are, and what evidence you have to support them in order to defend ourselves. You have just referred to me as a Known Offender so you must have compelling evidence to support that statement considering you have not provided me with my legal right to defend myself. So, can you show me the evidence of our offending please?"

Custard said,

"It does not matter what the evidence is as we have passed the time limit to lay the case to the CPS, so we cannot take it any further."

"Yes, it does matter, we have spent the last two and a half years under investigation by the police for allegations we know will be false. So, not only does it matter, but it is also vital, and we have the right to know what the specific allegations are."

"The Heads statements are their evidence."

"The Heads statements are not evidence; they are just allegations. You cannot write a letter to us saying you have enough evidence to charge all members of this family with the criminal offence of harassment when you do not have the evidence to support your determination. Do you not understand the impact that will have on this family?"

"I have to say the Heads statements were very vague compared to yours and the Heads had not submitted any evidence to support their statements. Having read their statements I just accepted the content to be true which I can now see was wrong."

Fucking hell! A police officer admitting they were wrong, miracles never cease. I then asked Custard about his comment in the letter written by PC Goffer which stated,

"DI Custard noted in his review however, that the offence of Harassment is a 'summary only' crime and as such is bound by prosecution time limits. The date for the case to be presented to the Crown Prosecution Service has passed meaning this matter cannot be pursued any further.

DI Custard, in reviewing the material, considered other criminal offences which would not be bound by time scales and therefore, allow for a criminal prosecution. No evidence of more serious offending could be found which led DI Custard to making the only option available to him. No further action is to be taken against any person from either family for the offence of harassment."

I informed Custard that not all harassment was a Section 2 *'summary only'* offence and that an act of Harassment Causing Fear of Violence, was in fact a Section 4 offence and not *'summary only'* and is not subject to the same time frame to present the case to the CPS. And that is clearly stated in the CPS Guidelines for prosecutors.

Custard told me that was not the case and that I was wrong in my interpretation of the law on Harassment. I told Custard I was not wrong and asked him to look up the CPS

Guidelines for Prosecutors regarding the Prevention of Harassment Act on his laptop. There was no way I was going to let this man out of my house until either he or I was proved wrong. Police officer or not, he was in my house, and I would not let him bully or intimidate me.

Custard got his laptop out and after a couple of minutes, he said,

"You're right, I have looked on the CPS website and it clearly states Harassment causing Fear of Violence is a Section 4 offence."

OMG, a police officer admitting he was wrong again, twice in a matter of minutes. I was on a roll.

DI Custard then said,

"It is clear Numpty Police has FAILED your family; I will order a review of my investigation immediately to include Section 4 offences and I will inform you of my investigative strategy as soon as possible."

Wow, a third time in one visit, that's got to be a record!

Custard then left our house with his tail between his legs. Not only had his plan to intimidate me at the start of the meeting failed, but he also had to eat a great big slice of Humble Pie. Although it was satisfying, I knew we were dealing with NP and Custard would not be happy with being shot down like that by a civilian. If I knew anything about NP, I knew there would be a price to pay, but so what, what else could they do to us?

At this meeting, DI Custard was banking on the fact that we would not have any knowledge of the Prevention of Harassment Act 1997 as amended in 2012 to include the Section 4 Offence of Harassment Causing Fear of Violence, or the CPS guidelines for prosecutors, or the information contained on the Government Legislation website.

It is a very sorry situation when an ordinary member of the public with no qualifications or experience of the criminal justice system, knows more about the law, the CPS guidelines for prosecutors, Government legislation, and correct investigative procedure, than a Detective Inspector.

Of course, I do not know more or better than Custard. He clearly knew the law regarding Harassment, he just chose to be dishonest about it.

This was a clear and deliberate attempt by Custard to mislead our family regarding the law on Harassment to protect the offenders from prosecution and amounts to a clear and blatant act of Gross Misconduct. It is also, in my opinion, a clear and blatant attempt to Pervert the Course of Justice and yet again, another clear example of yet another officer of NP to condone, encourage, facilitate, be complicit to, and actively joining in with the Harassment of our family.

It all started to make sense. This is why NP were so reluctant and even refused on several occasions to record or progress many of the incidents we reported to NP since our meeting with Arsewipe and Quack in November 2015, because if they did NP could not use the six-month time limit since the last reported incident to submit the case to the CPS as an excuse for not progressing the case. That is also why DI Custard refused to acknowledge that there was any evidence of the section 4 offence of Harassment Causing Fear of Violence or any evidence of more serious offending because the six-month time limit would then not apply. The last thing in the world NP wanted was for this case to get into the hands of the CPS as it would also expose their misconduct. What complete and utter bastards.

This meeting also highlighted to me how I had changed as a person, not through choice but through necessity. I have mentioned before that when

I do something I have to be 100% sure it is the right thing to do. When I removed the fence from our own land,

I knew 100% it was the right thing to do, it wasn't a belief or an opinion, it was a fact of British Law that I was entitled to remove someone else's property from our own land.

Being 100% sure was usually enough for me, I wouldn't have to prove my point to anyone. The difference on this occasion was that I had to prove my point. Before the harassment, even if I was 100% sure, I would not have been able to stand up to a Detective Inspector with the Police Force in the way that I did at this meeting. Even if I found the strength to stand up to a police officer, I would have been a nervous wreck, but at this meeting, there wasn't a nerve in my body. We knew we were 100% right and, in the end, it wasn't that difficult.

I think the police rely on ordinary citizens being afraid or intimidated by the police, I think they thrive on the fear factor they can have over people, and they will not be challenged. I am sure Custard thought that about our family before this meeting and I am sure he couldn't give a toss after the meeting. He couldn't give a shit that he was exposed as a failure. Too thick-skinned and protected.

Later that day, we received an email from DI Custard which stated,

"*It was good to meet with you today and gain an understanding of the impact these events have had upon you. Before I go any further I would wholeheartedly like to apologise for providing you with a decision which failed to take into account Section 4 Harassment (with violence). An oversight on my part and my failing alone. I am sorry for the stress and upset the letter will have caused. Having spent a few hours with you I can appreciate the impact of my decision.*

I will order a review of my investigation immediately to include Section 4 offences and I will inform you of my investigative strategy as soon as possible." Total bollocks. He could not give a shit.

Whilst at that time. we were grateful for the acknowledgement of NP's failure. It is not often a police officer will admit their failings and even less often for them to put it in writing. We hoped more than anything, this would be the beginning of the end of the discrimination and misconduct by NP against our family. The only way is up from here, surely! It is a fact, we can't get any lower, can we?

With that said, it did not change our situation. I was still facing being interviewed under caution for the false allegation by the Hopertys. This is something I was dreading more than you can imagine. It may sound soft, but I was traumatised by the events following the previous time I was interviewed under caution, and being in that situation again, brought all those feelings back. Life was so difficult, not just for me but for all of us.

Although Custard openly and fully admitted he failed our family in his investigation and that failure had a huge impact on us all. That admittance could not take away the fact that it happened when it should not have happened and that his failure was deliberate. We were all still regarded as being offenders for the very offence we were the victims of.

Although at this stage, we were still not aware we had been added to the Local Police System of NP by Custard for the offence of harassment.

As it turned out, the apology and content of the email received from DI Custard were as false as his investigation and determination. He was not apologetic or sorry for the stress and upset his failure had caused, anything but. He was pissed off with us for not bowing our heads to him and accepting what he considered to be our punishment for making a complaint against a fellow officer. The content of his email was a complete and utter lie.

Chapter Twenty-Nine
Trauma Times Two

Eat, Sleep, Voluntary Interview, Repeat

A few weeks later, I received a call from an officer from NP who I will call PC Cheek. He informed me he had been allocated the allegation of a Public Order offence made against me by Mr and Mrs Hoperty and he would call me again when he had investigated the allegation and because I was a *'KNOWN OFFENDER'*, a decision had been made regarding providing a taped interview. I told PC Cheek I was not a Known Offender.

A week or so later, I received another call from PC Cheek who informed me he had finished his investigation into the allegation of a Public Order Offence by Mr and Mrs

Hoperty, and requested I attend an interview under caution at the Crooked Cop Justice Centre or face arrest. Seriously, that's what he said, if I refused to attend for interview under caution I would be arrested because the Hopertys had made an allegation to NP that I used foul and abusive language. What a fucking joke.

No, not the fact that I would be arrested if I refused, but the fact NP called it the Crooked Cop Justice Centre. I have no objection to them calling it the Crooked Cop Centre, but the Crookd Cop Justice Centre, surely that is an offence under the Trade Descriptions Act!

I attended the Crooked Cop Injustice Centre for the interview as arranged. I had asked our barrister from our civil case if he would accompany me to the interview and he kindly agreed. After the formality of being cautioned, which was anything but a formality for an ordinary member of the public, that is something the police do not understand. Because it is an everyday part of their job, they think nothing of it, but for ordinary people, being interviewed or cautioned by the police in any circumstance, is a big thing. PC

Cheek informed me that the allegation was that on the 18 April 2018, I called Mr Hoperty a *'Fucking Scumbag'*.

Really, I was being interviewed under caution by NP because someone said I called them a fucking scumbag!

Cheek asked me some questions regarding the allegation but did not show me any evidence. Sound familiar! At the end of the interview, Cheek informed me that he would speak with his Sergeant and be in touch in due course to inform me of what method of disposal would be taken. As stated, during the entire interview, PC Cheek did not show me any evidence of the allegation, why? Because the allegation was false, I had not called Mr Hoperty a fucking scumbag. Trust me, if I was to call Mr Hoperty anything, it would be far worse than a fucking scumbag and I would probably have my hands around his throat as I was saying it.

So, to be clear, because the Hopertys had alleged that I had called Mr Hoperty a *'Fucking Scumbag'* and despite an investigation by PC Cheek which obviously found no evidence to support the allegation, I was still required to provide an interview under caution or face arrest.

NP would not have treated anyone else in the same way they treated me regarding this alleged offence. I was clearly being discriminated against and treated differently to any other member of the public because I was considered by NP to be a Known Offender.

And also, I had made a complaint against an officer of NP, and this was not the first time.

The first thing my barrister said to me following the interview was,

"Why are you being interviewed by the police under caution because someone said you called them a Fucking Scumbag, that must happen a thousand times a day."

It was unfair and unjust that I was asked by NP to provide an interview under caution or face arrest for this petty and in any event false allegation. What an absolute waste of police time and resources. Someone must have been pulling the strings of NP, but who could it be?

To be clear, there is no suspense here, if you are reading this book just to find out who was pulling those strings, stop now, because I still don't know and I guess I never will.

When you consider what the Heads and their associates, including the Hopertys, had done to this family for the past five years for which NP had not only failed to interview under caution but point blank refused to take statements, gather evidence or even record the incident, let alone investigate, for me to be interviewed by NP for this ridiculous reason is pathetic.

None of the Heads were ever prosecuted, none of the Heads ever had to stand in the dock of a criminal court and be spoken to like a criminal by a magistrate, none of them had to deal with the trauma, but I had to deal with all of that, and now this. It is an absolute travesty.

For NP to go to the effort and expense to investigate and then interview me under caution for such a ridiculous and false allegation just demonstrates the lengths NP will go to try and pin something on this family. This was yet another clear example of the inequality and discrimination by NP and now, yet again, a member of this family was being put through the trauma of being interviewed under caution by NP for yet another false allegation. When will it ever end? How will it ever end?

I later received a call from PC Cheek to inform me NP will be taking No Further Action regarding the allegation of a Public Order offence made by the Hopertys. Not because they didn't want to, but because they couldn't, they had no evidence to support the allegation. In fact, NP never had any intention of taking any further action, they knew they would not be able to do that from the very start. It is clear, that NP only progressed this matter to the point of interviewing me under caution to inflict as much pain, stress and misery on this family as they possibly could. C U Next Tuesdays.

In all seriousness though, I was very relieved to hear this, I knew I was innocent, and the allegation was false, but I still could not help but think NP would say I did commit a Public Order Offence or some other weird and wonderful crime dating back to the Magna Carta,

'Thou shalt not call thy next-door neighbour's relative a fucking scumbag.'

The whole cycle of Cautions, Summons, Prosecutions and Court appearances would start again. To be honest, after what happened to me the last time, I do not think I could have coped with that. I think that would have pushed me over the edge. In fact, I am sure it would.

Even though NP took no further action, the impact this had on me was immense. I was already trying to drag some more water out of a well that was bone dry just to get through each day. Sometimes, even now, we wonder how we managed to survive. Everyone has a breaking point and thankfully most people do not get close to it. For most people, that breaking point is far beyond what they may think it is. But for everyone, when the tank is truly empty, the engine stops working, end of.

My extreme reaction to this was due to the impact the previous occasion had on me.

The thought of history repeating itself was very scary. I am no expert in Post Traumatic Stress Disorder, and we all differ anyway, but I think this is one of the main symptoms of PTSD. There is a clue in the name, Post Traumatic, the person has suffered trauma because of a previous incident such as a car crash, explosion, fire, assault or prosecution, for example. So, when that trauma is repeated or something similar, it brings all the stress of the previous trauma to the fore again.

Like if a soldier has suffered PTSD from being close to a bomb, for example, every time they hear a loud bang, they have what others may seem to be an extreme reaction to it. It wasn't just reliving the trauma of the past; it was thinking it was going to happen again that was even more scary. Even more scary was the fact that it was out of my hands, it was up to NP whether the investigation progressed, and I had no control over what was and would happen.

For example, if someone had been in a car crash which had caused them to have PTSD, they could choose whether or not they wanted to drive down the road where the crash happened again, they may be okay with it or they may want to avoid it, either way, the choice is theirs, they are in control and they will do what is best for them. I could not do that, I did not have that choice, and NP did. I don't know if that is a very good description or not, most of you probably know better than me anyway. Sorry if the above offends anyone who may feel differently.

So, even though NP took no further action, the damage was done and the aim of the Heads, Hopertys, and NP was achieved. They had collaborated to cause yet more pain, misery and suffering on our family.

Interlude

I kid you not. It is the 18th of April 2024. On the news this morning, it was reported that nine officers from Numpty Police have been suspended for a range of criminal offences including Rape and Serious Sexual assault. Even more shocking, on watching the evening news hoping for an in-depth update to this major news story which most people would consider to be a very important local issue. Not a mention, not a single word on the matter whatsoever.

The news did find time to report on an injured seal, but not a mention of the nine police officers who had been suspended for allegations of serious criminal activity. That is what we are up against, I understand at that stage they may only be under investigation, and I would not expect these officers to be identified, but to not mention it at all must mean that the news programme had been told not to, or they were too afraid to. If nine members of any other organisation, such as the Church or a Local Council, had been suspended for the same, would it be mentioned on the evening news?

One thing is for sure, our family are not alone in being victims of NP. This confirms what I have thought for a long time and have made no secret of the fact, Numpty Police are incompetent, incapable, inept, inefficient and above all, dishonest. They are rotten to the core, out of control and unfit for purpose.

This will not change unless they are made to change. Bringing in new laws, codes of practice or tougher disciplinary procedures and punishments will not make a blind bit of difference, NP will just ignore them. In any event, those laws and Codes of Practice are in place now, they are just not abided by or even recognised and not enforced. Just like the Heads, if they can harass, they will harass, if NP can abuse their position and powers, they will abuse their position and powers. Nothing will change until they are made to change. Sad, but the evidence suggests it to be true.

Chapter Thirty
Sting in The Tail

It was the 18th of April 2018; the day the Judge ordered the Heads to pay the first instalment of the Damages and Costs. I tell you; we desperately needed this money; we were up to our eyeballs in debt and still owed our Solicitor over £30,000 for the cost of the trial. My wife was working full-time just to make the repayments on our loans. The stress of our financial situation was enough on its own without all the other stuff. Sometimes it's the little things that have the greatest impact, things like trying to stretch the fuel out in the car until the end of the month so we could fill the car up using the credit card, so we didn't have to pay it off until the end of the next month. Doing the shopping and having to buy all the offers and reduced stock. I'll tell you one thing, if we ever get back on our feet financially, the first thing I will do is go to the supermarket and put whatever I want in the trolley without even looking at the price. A bit maverick I know but fuck it.

Seriously though, this day couldn't't come soon enough.

We received the call from our solicitor to tell us that the money had been transferred to their account by the Heads, and he would then transfer it to our account when it had cleared. Woohoo!

Get real. Do you think that really happened? Not a chance. We did get the call from our solicitor alright, but it wasn't to tell us the Heads had transferred the money. Instead, he informed us that Mr Head, Mrs Head and Little Head had all declared themselves voluntarily bankrupt and we would not be receiving any money for the foreseeable future.

How many of you saw that one coming? I bet some of you are holding your heads in your hands and thinking,

'Oh my God, you have got to be kidding me.'

Kidding I am not. We were absolutely devastated; would our nightmare ever end?

Not if the Heads and NP had anything to do with it, especially now this has happened.

Our solicitor advised us that we would need to employ an Insolvency Practitioner to deal with the Heads bankruptcy and recommended a company based in a nearby town, I will call them BRB, which is short for Bloody Robbing Bastards.

Can I just say, if you are ever in a similar situation to ours and you are advised by your solicitor to employ an Insolvency Practitioner, if you have any choice, DON'T. Particularly, if you are advised by your solicitor to employ a certain firm of Insolvency Practitioners who are based in the same town and whose Chief Executives probably play golf together of a Sunday morning.

What could I possibly be insinuating? Could it be that the Insolvency Practitioner and our solicitors planned to work together to make as much money for each other as they could, *'You scratch my back and I'll scratch yours'* sort of thing? No, surely not, there cannot be this sort of arrangement between two professional and reputable companies as an Insolvency Practitioner and a firm of solicitors, could there?

Yes, of course there is, they're all at it all the time. Do not be fooled for a second in thinking they are or will act in your best interests, they will act in their best interests. They do not give a flying fig about their clients, no matter what their situation or what they have been through.

The saddest thing is that when you do need a solicitor or Insolvency Practitioner, you are often at your most vulnerable, you have no choice but to use their services, often you are legally required to. They know this, they know they have you by the short and curlies, but do they care, not on your nelly my son, not on your nelly. You are one thing and one thing only to them, a cash cow, a means to acquiring wealth, your wealth. End of.

If by some miracle you ever do see a solicitor riding a bike, they will probably be riding alongside an Insolvency Practitioner, helping each other carry their ill-gotten gains to the bank.

If ever you want to take up a career that requires a zero level of morality, consider becoming an Insolvency Practitioner, if you fail, you can always try the Police Force. I wouldn't go as far as saying any or all Insolvency Practitioners break the law, far from it, it is the law that is fucked up and Insolvency Practitioners take advantage of these flaws to line their pockets with gold, our gold, your gold, anyone's gold.

Here's me whinging and whining about someone else now. What a moaning little git I am!

There were two main people we dealt with from BRB, there was the office manager, who I will call the Artful Dodger or Dodger for short (from the film Oliver Twist), he looked like a weasel and definitely suffered from short man syndrome, and the Trustee for the Heads Estate (a posh title for dirty rotten scoundrel), who I will call Fagin (also from the film Oliver Twist), to be honest, she even looked like the character in the film. The resemblance didn't stop there though, she was very stern, and I wondered if she had ever smiled. Silly me, of course she had, every time she robbed a client. She reminded me of someone who would empty her money box at the end of every day to count her pennies just in case one had gone missing or by some miracle they had given birth to a gold sovereign. You've got to pick a pocket or two!

The first contact we had with BRB was a call from Dodger. He informed us of the details of the bankruptcy, he also said he had conducted a search on the Heads current property and the search had revealed Mr and Mrs Head had added Little Head and Sponger as part owners of their current property just before declaring themselves bankrupt. This is what is called an Attempt to Disperse Assets, which is illegal if it is done during or just before declaring bankruptcy. But it's the Heads so a little bit of crime doesn't matter. I haven't said that for a while have I?

It became clear, that this is what the Heads were up to during the delay in the Judgement. This is why they falsely claimed Mrs Head had attempted suicide, to delay the Judgement to get the advice to attempt to disperse their assets and then declare voluntary bankruptcy. Is that not just sick?

It would prove to be the case that the Heads had in fact sought the advice of an Insolvency Practitioner who did advise the Heads to do this. This firm was a right shower of shit. Of course, it is illegal for an Insolvency Practitioner to advise their clients to do something illegal. But it's the Heads Insolvency Practitioner, so a little bit of crime doesn't matter.

This shower of shit didn't care about the Heads as their advice would lead to the Heads losing everything, including their home. Having said that, knowing the Heads as I do, I think they would rather lose everything they had ever worked for than have to pay us a penny of the award of the court, that was how deluded they were. Their Insolvency Practitioners must have loved it when they walked in the door of their offices, all their Christmases and birthdays rolled into one.

To be clear. This was right at the beginning of the bankruptcy and BRB had already discovered that the Heads had not complied with the laws of Bankruptcy. This gave BRB the opportunity to take action to prevent this and further criminality or non-compliance by the Heads from happening. It is also an offence to fail to cooperate with an Insolvency Practitioner, but it's the Head's, so a little bit of crime doesn't matter.

But if BRB did what I believe they should have done, then they wouldn't have been able to make tens and tens and tens of thousands of pounds from the bankruptcy, would they?

Maybe they did take the appropriate action in reporting the conduct of the Heads and their Insolvency Practitioner to the Insolvency Service and it was them who failed to take the appropriate action against the Heads. Whoever it was, one or maybe both failed to do anything about the Heads continued offending and yet again, it would be our family who would pay a huge price for that failure. Just as we had done with the failure of NP to protect us from the Harassment.

I truly believe there is not a justice system in this or maybe any country. There is a legal system, and if you can afford it, you can get what you want, justice does not enter the equation. If the legal system decides it wants to turn you over, they will and there is nothing the ordinary person can do about it. Justice is for the rich, or those with friends in high places!

At that time, we were as naive as most of you regarding the laws of bankruptcy, I would imagine. There is no need to know anything about it unless you are involved in it, and we hadn't been involved in it until now. Even if a layman like me tries to understand the laws of bankruptcy and insolvency, it is so complicated and like a lot of other laws, can be manipulated and interpreted to suit whatever you need, or can afford. In this sort of situation, you rely on professionals like solicitors, Insolvency Practitioners and lawyers, and whilst I have not got a bad word to say about our barrister who I do and always will regard as a friend, the rest of these people did take advantage of our naivety at our time of greatest need, desperation and vulnerability.

The overriding feeling I have regarding the way we were treated by those who were best placed to help and indeed were legally obligated to always act in our best interests, is that they do not care about their clients. Their attitude is that their clients are bottom of the pile, and they can have what's left when we have had our fill.

The word vulture comes to mind. They circle above their wounded prey waiting for them to become too weak and vulnerable to defend themselves. Then they swoop and start to peck the flesh from their prey's bones until there is nothing left. They don't even wait for their prey to die before they start to devour it. They gorge themselves until they cannot eat any more and then just fly away in search of their next victim.

That is just my honest view based on my experience. I am sure many people will have a completely opposite opinion. I can imagine if you are fortunate enough to have professionals who do put their clients first, it can make a world of difference to your situation. Unfortunately, I can only imagine, because apart from our barrister, we were not that fortunate.

Dodger also told us his investigations had discovered the Heads have another son. This other son would go on to have a big part to play in the Heads bankruptcy, and as you can imagine, it was not to be a positive one. If it were possible, this other son, who I will call Stupid Head, was as bad as his mum, dad and brother. A total arsehole.

Chapter Thirty-One
Fight, Flight, Or Freeze

Following the decision by NP to take No Further Action against me for the allegation of the Public Order Offence made by the Hopertys, our barrister advised us that in his experience and given the conduct of the Heads and NP, the Hopertys would continue to harass our family and make further false allegations to NP as they now knew, if they didn't before, that was all they had to do to inflict suffering on our family.

All they had to do was tell NP that we did something, and NP would treat us like we were not just *'Known Offenders'* but Public Enemy's number one and put us through absolute hell. He advised that we write to Mr Hoperty offering him the opportunity to mediate a solution to the issues between us and if he did not respond within seven days, we will consider taking legal action against him to stop his unlawful behaviour. We therefore, wrote to Mr Hoperty explaining our position and waited for his response.

I also kept an eye on the Minutes of the Parish Council of which Mr Head was still Vice Chair. These minutes confirmed that although Mr Head was a bankrupt he was having an active part in the running of the Parish Council, he was also the Parish Council representative on several of their subgroups. The minutes also confirmed that as the Parish Council Representative for one of these groups he would be meeting with an Inspector from NP to discuss the issuing of High Visibility Vest to the members of the Parish Council for use in an emergency. A right little Dads Army the Parish Council were turning into.

The minutes also confirmed that PC Goffer was attending the monthly meetings of the Parish Council at the same time as he was involved in the review of the failed investigation by DI Custard. I know it may sound a bit petty under the circumstances, but I do not think it to be sensible or best practice for Goffer to be attending meetings of the Parish Council when the Vice Chair is a suspect in that investigation. That is clearly creating a Conflict of Interests and would lead the public to believe all parties were not being treated with equality and impartiality.

By the way, the Inspector that Mr Head was meeting with to discuss the issuing of High Visibility Vest, was the Inspector of the Community Policing Team, PC Goffer's Inspector!

Oh, and one other point, the minutes also confirmed that not only was Mr Head playing an active role in the running of the Parish Council while being bankrupt, which I couldn't give a shit about, they also confirmed Mr Head was having an active role in the finances of the Parish Council, countersigning cheques and the like, that I know to be wrong and I do give shit about.

To be clear, at this point in time, the Parish Council had a precept, or in other words, a balance in excess of £150,000 in their bank account, and Mr Head had access to this account and was signing cheques for the Parish Council business. Whether any fraud was taking place or not, I couldn't possibly say! I mean, it is not as if anything untoward had happened in the past like the Parish Council solicitors also representing the Heads in their civil case!

However, this situation would clearly give the public, and particularly the residents of the Parish, the impression not everything was above board. My opinion is, why would the Parish Council do something that is wrong and illegal, if there was no reason for them doing so, why risk getting in trouble for nothing? Someone must be getting something out of it, in any event, why would a Parish Council need to have £150,000 in its account? Rightly or wrongly, we had been advised by BRB that it was against the law for Mr Head to undertake a role in Public Office (Vice Chair of the Parish Council) while being bankrupt. But even I know it is against the law for a bankrupt to be involved in any way, shape or form with the financial running of any public service. But it's the Heads, so a little bit of crime doesn't matter.

I did consider attending one of the monthly Parish Council meetings, but I decided it would be more trouble than it was worth as Mr Head would surely make an allegation to NP that I was harassing him. It would have been very interesting to see the faces of Mr Head and the representative of NP when I walked in. That's if they weren't too busy kissing and cuddling each other in the corner to even notice I was there.

I did email PS Pinocchio regarding my concerns that Mr Head was regularly meeting with officers of NP who were investigating him for his suspected involvement in the harassment of his next-door neighbours and this would give public the impression that not all sides in the investigation were being treated with equality and impartiality.

PS Pinocchio replied telling me that NP are not going to stop sending officers to the monthly meetings of the Parish Council just because I don't like it. Charming. What about the fact it is against correct policing policy, investigative procedure and the law. Surely, that is more important than me not liking it. Obviously not!

It was about this time, that I had been researching the offence of harassment more thoroughly and I had found some very interesting information about what I have mentioned earlier regarding Group, Community or Organised Harassment. What I had read summed up our situation to a tee, we were the victims of Organised Harassment which is defined in the Protection from Harassment Act (PHA) as,

'When an individual or group of individuals embark on a course of conduct that would amount to the Harassment of another group or individuals of a group, a family, gay club, or members of a mosque for example, which would cause the member or members of the group alarm, anxiety or distress.'

I therefore emailed DI Custard to inform him we were the victims of Organised Harassment as defined in the PHA and requested this offence to be included in the Review he had ordered due to his failed two-and-a-half-year investigation.

Therefore, it cannot be disputed by NP that I had not informed them or reported the fact that our family were the victims of this offence and that what was happening to our family was exactly as it was described in the PHA. The definition in the CPS Guidelines for Prosecutors even referenced 'a family' as one of the groups to be the target of Organised Harassment. I even copied and pasted the definition of Organised Harassment from the Crown Prosecution Service Guide for Prosecutors webpage into the email to Custard.

But NP already knew we were the victims of Organised Harassment, as they were involved in it. When the police decide to harass someone, it might be a criminal or someone who has made a complaint against a police officer, for example, they completely take over the life of their target or targets, in this case, our family, and to be fair, I was a particular target.

I don't want to give too much away here as it may spoil your read later, but I will try to explain what happens with this kind of organised harassment and you may get the gist. I know some of you will be a little sceptical of my views regarding NP being involved in the harassment. If I were you, I would be sceptical too, things like this don't really happen, things like this only happen in Eastenders, not real life, right! Wrong!

All police forces have what they call 'Local Information'. This is where the police can record onto the Local Police System anything they want about an individual or group. It can be anything from information regarding a crime, being a suspect, witness or victim of an offence, what an officer deems to be someone's *mental health issues* or a person's propensity for making complaints for example, anything.

When you are recorded onto one Government system, i.e., the police, a flag is put against your name. When you are flagged on one Government system, you are likely to be flagged on all Government systems such as the NHS, Borough and County Councils, and even things like Libraries and Museums. This causes all these authorities to consider you to be what the flag states you to be.

A good thing you may think, forewarned is forearmed so to speak. I agree, but only when the information entered onto the local system is correct. Being recorded or *'flagged'* onto the local police system for a legitimate reason can have a massive impact on the individual's life, but when the information is incorrect, misleading, false, or blatantly untrue, the impact is magnified and leads to either primary or inadvertent discrimination and prejudice.

It also makes it almost impossible for the victims to get help, because everyone who can help has the preconceived opinion that you are the person that the *'local information'* states that you are. This leads to the individual or group being isolated, unable to get any help, and left at the mercy of the harassers. Even if you move to another part of the country, you cannot escape because the authorities in that part of the country have the same information. I have already mentioned that following the failed investigation by DI Custard, he stated,

'There is enough evidence to charge all parties from both sides with the offence of harassment.'

What I did not know at that time was that DI Custard had also added all four members of our family onto the local police system of NP for the offense of harassment, the very offence that we were the victims of. So, all four members of our family were flagged on the *local system* as offenders, and probably troublemakers and complainers, but of course, DI Custard didn't have the balls to tell us he had done this.

To be clear, you do not have to have been cautioned, convicted, or arrested for an offence for you to be recorded onto the local police system as an offender, and the police do not have to tell you what they have recorded about you. How is that right, just or fair?

That leaves the system open to abuse by any corrupt officer who wants to screw you over. You can make a Subject Access Request for the information the police hold on you, but even then, they can refuse to disclose the information, but why would anyone make a Subject Access Request for information they do not even know exists? The police can add whatever they want about you onto the local police system, and you would be none the wiser.

Even now, ten years down the line, to our knowledge, that information about our family is still on the local police system of NP. So, whoever accesses that information for whatever reason, will be under the impression our family are offenders when we are not. I often wonder how many people are walking around this country believing they are clean when in fact the local police force has recorded them as dirty, I bet the number would shock even me. I have read of several cases of Organised Harassment which have resulted in absolutely tragic endings, and I can fully understand why. Now, our family is living it.

The fact that Mr Head was Vice Chair of the Parish Council had really been grating on my mind over the past few months. Compared to the main issues facing our family, this was a relatively minor matter you might think. It wasn't just the fact that Mr Head was the Vice Chair of our Parish Council, or that he had assaulted my wife, and me, or that he had been found liable for the harassment of all four members of our family, or that he was a bankrupt.

I think some of you will get this and some may think I have gone too far. As part of our Council Tax, every household in the Parish contributes to the Parish Council, this contribution is compulsory.

Under the circumstances, I did not think it to be morally or ethically correct for our family to contribute to a Parish Council whose Vice Chair had assaulted my wife and me and been found liable for the harassment of our family.

I therefore emailed the chairman of the Parish Council to request a refund of the contributions we had made to the Parish Council through our Council Tax for the time Mr Head had been a member of the Parish Council. A reasonable and fair request, I thought, I hope you agree.

Over the following few weeks, I exchanged several emails with the Clerk to the Parish Council regarding the refund. This exchange resulted in an email from the Chair of the Parish Council, who is in fact a Knight of the Realm, you remember.

Surprise, surprise, the letter stated my request had been refused as Mr Head had not breached the Code of Conduct for Parish Councillors. It gets worse, the letter went on to say,

"Please be advised not to withhold any future payments of Council Tax to avoid any debt recovery process being initiated."

Oh my God, the Chair of the Parish Council has not only refused my request for a refund, a request which I am sure any reasonable person would feel to be legitimate, but he has also threatened me with debt recovery proceedings if I withhold payment of our Council Tax.

I know you might think I am overreacting to this and indeed you may feel it to be sensible advice, but, I have never stated to the Parish Council that if I do not receive a refund from them, I will stop paying my Council Tax. Furthermore, the Chair of the Parish Council does not have the right to threaten and intimidate members of the parish with debt collection proceedings. It is not within the remit of either the Chair or the Parish Council as a whole, to send a letter of this nature to a member of the Parish. On top of that, it is a clear attempt to heap shit upon shit.

Due to the content of my letter requesting a refund, the Parish Council was fully aware that Mr Head assaulted my wife and me, and he, his wife, and son have all been found liable in the civil court for the harassment of all four members of our family, who were the next-door neighbours of Mr Head.

It is therefore clear, the Parish Council as a whole but in particular, the Chair has abused their position in public office to threaten, intimidate and join in with the harassment of our family because Mr Head is the Vice Chair. They have clearly taken sides when they should at the very least have remained impartial and not allowed their relationship with Mr Head to influence their decision making.

The grounds given by the Parish Council for the refusal was that during the time Mr Head had been a member of the Parish Council, our family was just as entitled to the services of the Parish Council as any other member of the Parish.

The only problem with that was the Parish Council did absolutely fuck all for the members of the Parish. That was why they had a surplus of over £150,000 in their bank account, even after they had paid the Heads solicitors (sorry, shouldn't have said that). Even during the COVID-19 pandemic, with that huge surplus, the Parish Council did nothing to help the people of the Parish. To think, with all the hardship so many people faced in the COVID-19 pandemic and now in the cost of living crisis, we still had no choice but to contribute to a Parish Council that had over £150,000 of our money in its coffers, but they just kept on taking it and giving nothing back.

I wonder if they ever heard of Misconduct or Misfeasance in Public Office, both of which are serious criminal offences. If they haven't heard of them yet, maybe they will soon. Mr Chair, you may be a Knight of the Realm, but you are not above the law. Having said that as you are a Sir, you probably are above the law.

Now, I hope this doesn't inspire any of the residents of the Parish where I live to write or make peaceful protest against the Parish Council who meet at 7 pm every second Thursday of the month at the local Community Centre by the way.

It is enough for me to know the Parish Council has absolutely no morals or ethics and will allow anyone to serve on their committee and become Vice Chair, even criminals and bankrupts, and will continue to take your money no matter what your circumstances while not giving a tiny fraction of it back to the residents of the Parish, even to a family whose lives have been destroyed by their Vice Chair. Shame on you, Parish Council, shame on you.

I will leave it there for now as I have bigger wars to win but rest assured, I will get my money back. Pathetic jumped-up shower of self-important shit, don't forget to wear your High Vis Vest at your monthly meetings will you?

Fuck sake, though, if things weren't bad enough, now even the Parish Council is having a go.

Chapter Thirty-Two
Cupid Stunt Plus One

It was early July 2018. I was returning home from posting some letters in the post box on the main road near our house, Cupid Stunt (the only suspect for causing the criminal damage to our cars), came charging out of his drive and crossed the road to be on the same side as me. He walked straight towards me until he was directly in front of me and stopped me from walking. He was very angry and repeatedly shouted at me,

"Why are you staring at my family?"

I remained perfectly calm as I have always been able to do in this sort of situation. To be fair, I think the fact that I keep my cool in situations like this, wound some people up, but that is not my intention or my fault. If they didn't act like idiots and take me for a soft touch, there wouldn't be a problem. I said to him,

"Stop shouting at me, I wasn't staring at your family, what are you on about?"

Cupid Stunt shouted some more and then started to cross back over the road towards his house. I continued to walk home quite bemused. As I got nearer to the corner, Cupid Stunt crossed back over the road towards me, he put his head right in my face, so I moved back, and he moved forward, so he was right in my face again. It was very unpleasant, he was even uglier than in the CCTV footage from the local shop, and his breath stank.

He was even angrier by now and repeatedly shouted,

"Make something happen, make something happen."

What a dick, a man of his age and he wanted a fight in the middle of the street. One thing I have learned in my time when faced with a situation like this is don't give them what they want. Cupid wanted me to throw the first punch, so he could then claim I started the fight. I said to him,

"That's not going to happen."

Cupid then turned away and started to walk across the road again. As he was about halfway across the road, he turned around, pointed at me and shouted,

"I will fucking kill you."

Well, he clearly wasn't going to kill me as he had just had his chance and did fuck all except shout and wave his arms. Prick.

At this point, I noticed Trigger was on his drive. When Cupid crossed the road, he and Trigger had a lovely little chat about what just happened before they walked down their drives together like a couple of naughty little children.

When I got home, I looked at our CCTV which I had angled to cover the drive of Trigger. NP advised me not to do this, but I thought fuck um, you won't help our family, so we will have to help ourselves and get all the evidence we can to stop the harassment and hold you to account for your failings. I have no regrets about doing this and one day it will prove invaluable I am sure. The camera doesn't lie, allegedly, except when it captures the Heads harassing our family, or Mrs Head stealing and smashing our garden ornament, or Mrs Head *'weeding'* our back garden, or when I remove a fence from my own land or Cupid Stunt pouring a corrosive fluid over our cars. Sorry, am I babbling again?

Anyway, the footage showed, surprise, surprise, Trigger was on his drive the whole time. Did he plan or incite Cupid to confront me? Did he pay him? Why would Cupid do this? He must have known he would be walking a tightrope having been the only suspect for the Criminal Damage to our cars. Unless he knew nothing would happen to him this time as well as the last. Fucking hell, how many more times is this going to happen.

I feel this was Cupid's reaction to being told by NP that no further action was to be taken against him for the Criminal Damage to our cars. He never thought we would get the CCTV footage from the pub or the local shop and clearly didn't care if we did. He never thought we would be able to identify him as the person who poured the fluid over our cars and despite NP having all of this compelling evidence of the movements and identity of

Cupid, but still allowed him to get away with such a cowardly crime scottfree, he, like the Heads, now knew he could do whatever he wanted to our family without consequence.

Let's face it, NP was never going to do anything about the Criminal Damage to our cars. Who pours a corrosive fluid over two cars, then casually disposes of the bottle containing the fluid in a bush at the local pub, and then, even more casually, walks into the local shop revealing their identity and buys chocolate? No one who thinks they might be held accountable for their crimes, that's who. Maybe Cupid wanted us to know it was him and that he would get away with it.

Anyway, I reported the incident to NP via 101. They advised me to stay indoors and to call back on 999 if anything else happened. What do you think people, do you think anything else happened?

Spot on, of course it did.

About two hours later, a car pulled up outside our house blocking our drive. A woman got out of the car, walked down our drive, and knocked on our front door. Well, I say a woman, she was more like an Oompa Loompa from Willy Wonka's Chocolate Factory, quite short, chubby, and bright orange, God knows how much fake tan she had on, either that or she had just been Tangoed. Anyway, I do not have to think too hard for a name for her, Oompa Loompa will do just fine.

By coincidence, our daughter had ordered a takeaway for her and her partner who was here, again! And she thought the knock on the door was the food being delivered. Luckily, because of what had happened just a few hours before, and because of what had happened for the previous four years, we never answered the door to anyone we did not recognise. That is a habit we still have to this day, and it is not a bad thing, you never know who it might be on the other side of the door! They could be holding a claw hammer or something!

Our daughter went to the front door and asked,

"Who is it?"

Expecting the reply, *'McDelivery'*, or whatever it was they had ordered. Instead, the reply was,

"*Get your dad.*"

Our daughter asked the person,

"Who are you?"

The woman replied,

"*Just get your dad.*"

As we were accustomed to events like this, believe me when I say I have only mentioned half of the events that happened up to this point, our daughter, like the rest of us, is very quick thinking in situations like this and started to record the exchange through the letterbox on her mobile phone. It was clear that this incident was related to the events earlier in the day with Cupid, so our daughter said to Oompa,

"I will call the police."

Oompa replied,

"*Call the police, your dad's in the wrong, tell the police your dad has been staring at my children. Tell me, why has your dad been staring at my children, they feel unsafe in their grandad's home, you must be so proud to have a dad like that, is he a paedophile, I'm thinking he is a paedophile right now.*"

This confirmed that it was connected to earlier in the day. Oompa Loompa was the daughter of Cupid Stunt.

By this time our daughter had called NP on our landline and was speaking to Force Control informing them of what was happening. Our daughter gave the officer a description of Oompa and was given the usual advice,

'*Stay indoors, lock all windows and doors, and call us back if anything else happens.*' DURR, it was already happening!

What does it have to take before NP spring into action and does something! This was one of the very few times I would criticise Force Control. Most of the many times, we needed to call them, they were very polite, understanding and helpful. It was only when matters passed from their hands that the problems started.

Anyway, Oompa stayed outside our front door for about 20 minutes and refused the many requests by our daughter to leave our property. She repeatedly called me a paedophile along with many other insults. When she eventually left our drive, she walked over to her dad's house and had a conversation with him and Trigger who were both on their driveways, funnily enough.

Although Oompa left our property after about 20 minutes, she did not move her car from blocking our drive for a further 20 minutes or so. When she finished her conversation with Cupid and Trigger, she walked back and forth up and down the street stalking our house, waiting for one of us to come outside, I suppose.

Eventually, after about 40 minutes, she moved her car from in front of our drive and parked outside Cupid's house.

During this entire incident, I was in the house the whole time. And even though this woman who I had never seen before was on our drive repeatedly calling me a paedophile, I did not react, I did the right thing and followed the advice of the police to avoid confrontation and danger,

'Stay indoors, lock all doors and windows, and call us back if anything else happens.'

For what good that advice had done us in the past. And for what good that advice would do us on this occasion also. Why we still listened to the advice of NP and why I thought it would be different this time I do not know, IDIOT. Oh yes, I know why, because we are good people, simple.

Once again, our CCTV had recorded the whole incident, and the footage recorded on our daughter's phone had audio as well as visual. In any event, Force Control heard Oompa calling me a paedophile while our daughter was on the phone with them. So, there were three pieces of evidence of the same incident, surely that would be enough for NP to do something about it!

Clearly, someone must have told Oompa that I had been staring at her children, and that person could only have been her dad, Cupid. So, Cupid deliberately lied to his own daughter to incite her to harass our family. Even for a low life like Cupid who pours corrosive fluid over cars, that is low, very low.

Hello, hello, hello, what do have we here then? Two officers from NP eventually turned up at our house about 11 pm that night, some 5 hours later. It was the usual routine of *'good cop, bad cop'*. Although that can't be right as there are no good cops! Silly me.

The *'bad cop'* was a PC Mound, his attitude was complete shit. I cannot recall the name of the *'good cop'* as it was next to pointless him being there. PC Mound said that it had been reported as a *'Threat to Kill'* but he said it could not be considered as a threat to kill as the suspect did not have a weapon.

Excuse me. How the fuck could PC Mound have known whether Cupid had a weapon or not? I did not know whether Cupid had a weapon or not and I was there! Anyway, it is total bollocks, you do not need to have a weapon to kill someone. Some of you may remember the very high-profile police campaign which had the slogan,

'One punch can kill.'

Obviously, PC Mound doesn't remember! Maybe he was too busy lying to victims of crime!

In any event saying to someone, *'I will fucking kill you'*, sounds like a threat to kill if you ask me.

Getting technical (and probably boring) again. It clearly states in the CPS guidelines a threat to kill is if the victim believes the threat to be real and feels in danger of harm.

As Cupid had poured the corrosive fluid over our cars in February 2018 and was the next-door neighbour and sidekick of Trigger who had been

400

convicted of harassment against me, twice, I considered the threat to be very real. I believe that to be reasonable.

My daughter and I tried to put our point across politely and respectfully. Suddenly, PC Mound shouted,

"You're not listening to me."

My daughter became upset at this point, so I said to Mound,

"No, you're not listening to us and if you are not prepared to listen there is no point in you being here so you might as well leave."

Again, before the harassment, I would never have been able to speak to a police officer like that. PC Mound seemed to realise we were not going to roll over and have our belly tickled as he expected.

PC Mound reluctantly took a statement from me and we provided him with a copy of our CCTV footage of both incidents that happened that day involving Cupid Stunt and Oompa Loompa.

We were not able to transfer the footage from our daughter's phone to a memory stick by this time, so the other officer recorded the footage from our daughter's phone on his bodycam. He said he would go into the hallway to do this to avoid any background noise.

I did not think anything of this at the time as it made sense, but now, I am not so sure, I wonder if he recorded the footage at all. Read on.

The officers left saying that they would go back to the station to write it up and Cupid would be arrested that night.

Chapter Thirty-Three
Victims Right for Review

Car Crash

Four days on from the recent incident regarding Cupid Stunt and Oompa Loompa, I contacted PC Mound for an update. As it was clear Cupid and Oompa posed a significant threat to our family, I thought it would be best to keep up to speed with any developments such as the arrest of Cupid or his daughter. PC Mound informed me that he had not had time to do anything about it and the incident had now been passed to another department. Standard.

So, four days after Cupid threatened to kill me, and his daughter stood on our drive and repeatedly called me a paedophile, and despite Cupid being the only suspect for the criminal damage to our cars, and despite PC Mound saying Cupid would be arrested on the night of the incident, and despite all of the other incidents that happened to our family, and despite the clear escalation of the harassment, NP did absolutely fuck all about it.

To be fair, I do understand the police have many and much more serious incidents to deal with daily, but part of the reason for that is that the police do not deal with things promptly, which allows the situation to escalate. Recent history is littered with examples of this particularly concerning certain crimes. How many times do we need to hear that yet another woman has been murdered by her ex-partner who stalked her for months if not years and the woman reported this behaviour to the police on numerous occasions, but the police failed to act on these reports or even blamed the victim. How many times do we need to hear the police saying after the murder,

'We made mistakes, but we will learn from those mistakes to make sure this can never happen again.'

We will continue to hear this forever because the police do not learn because they don't want to learn. If they did want to learn, they would have done so by now, surely.

This has been happening for decade after decade, that is enough time to learn some basic skills in dealing with and tackling this sort of offense, isn't it?

Although these cases grab the headlines, and rightly so, they are not the only offences the police have the same attitude towards. It is the same for all forms of Domestic Abuse, Stalking, and Harassment. The attitude of the police towards the victim is,

'Well, you must have done something to deserve it.'

It is not just me saying that, ask the survivors of domestic abuse, stalking, and harassment and almost all will say this is the case. The police did not believe them and made them feel like they were the offenders. That is certainly the case with our family, NP repeatedly did not believe us, they also blamed and incriminated us at every opportunity, often without us even knowing. When it comes to crimes like this, the police have the time but cannot be bothered.

'Oh, it's just a bit of a falling out between ex-partners, or a bit of a neighbour dispute, it will peter out if we leave it alone. Okay, onwards and upwards, let's pop to McDonald's for an apple pie and coffee.'

Anyway, my call must have touched a nerve as the next evening Cupid was arrested. However, before the officers could even get out of their car, guess who appeared on his drive, none other than Trigger himself, it was as if he knew the police were coming. As the officers walked down the drive of Cupid, Trigger spoke with the officers. What he said to them I have no idea, but I can guess it wasn't favourable to me.

Later that evening, I received a call from a PC Locks who informed me Cupid had been arrested, interviewed, and released pending further investigation and that we should take extra care when leaving our house or in the neighbourhood.

Wow, credit to her for informing us of the danger, but that did leave me to wonder what Cupid must have said to NP in his interview that would have caused NP to warn us. The fact is, we could not take any more care than we were already other than never leaving the house. We were already living like prisoners, we did not go out alone, even to the local shop and I had given up walking as I used to do almost every day.

It wasn't just because of the fear of what might happen or because walking around the neighbourhood was no longer enjoyable, it was just as much because I simply did not have the energy. I know that may be hard to understand, but the Harassment was the hardest thing I have ever had to deal with in my life, and like most people of my age, I have been through some very difficult times. Trying to deal with what had just happened and not knowing what and when the next incident was going to happen was so exhausting and stressful. Drip, drip, drip.

The best way I can describe the impact of harassment on the victim(s) is the following. When someone suffers a severe trauma such as a serious car crash for example. When the crash happens, that is it, it happened at a certain time on a certain day and it is over. From that day on, the person starts to process the incident and starts to recover from the physical and mental trauma and can start to get closure. It may take weeks, months, or years and in some cases, they will never fully recover and will suffer the consequences of whatever the incident was for the rest of their lives.

With harassment, it is never over, you do not get the opportunity to process what happened before the next incident happens so, therefore, you cannot start to recover. The longer the harassment goes on, the greater the impact it has because of the cumulative effect it has. You become a little weaker, a little more exhausted, a little more isolated, a little more scared and vulnerable. It is like having a car crash over and over again. Drip, drip, drip.

It wasn't just the harassment; we could deal with a bit of name-calling or swearing and shouting and all that sort of petty stuff. It was the fact these people, and by this time, it was many people, many of which were our neighbours or police officers, were hellbent on really hurting our family in any way they could. They literally hated our family with a passion that drove them to commit serious offences against us to the point of being arrested, prosecuted, and convicted, and many officers of NP committed serious crimes and acts of Gross Misconduct.

Why? We had never done anything to them. Apart from the Heads, we had been neighbours with these people for well over a decade and never had any problems with them. What could be fueling their hatred to such an extreme level? Although they were all adults and capable of making up their minds so there is no excuse, and they cannot blame anyone else for their behaviour. Someone must be fuelling their hatred with lies about our family. There is only one logical conclusion, the Heads were not only using social media to spread false and malicious gossip, but they were also spreading these lies around the neighbourhood and even further to anyone who would listen, including of course, Numpty Police.

PC Locks went on to say that she had been made aware of further CCTV footage that is in the possession of a neighbour of Cupid, and they would need to acquire this footage as part of the investigation. She also informed me the woman who attended our property had been identified and Trigger would need to be spoken to as part of the investigation.

Great, more CCTV footage that NP would claim showed Cupid being the victim of my criminality and which NP would refuse to let me see, I just know it. And why would Trigger need to be spoken to, I suppose he would claim to have witnessed the whole thing, and it was me who threatened Cupid. I cannot wait to see how NP are going to twist this one. For now though, at least it seemed NP was taking the matter seriously, you would not believe the difference that made to our family, just to know or believe something was being done.

I know Trigger is a horrible person, but he is also a joke. Even though he must be in his 70s, he still thinks he is a big man, a hard man. Whenever our paths had crossed in the recent past, he would always flex his muscles as if he were some kind of bodybuilder or something. To be fair, he did seem to have a good physique for an old fella, but his best days were long gone. I know he had been seriously ill in the past and had a knee replacement. So, even if he was once a bit of a boy, a fighting man, he should really accept he is now an old man and stop playing games that he is no longer able. If he plays with fire at his age, he can expect to get burnt.

More Bull

Back to the main topic. Is that the harassment by the Heads and their cronies or the fucked-up police force? Mmm, let's go fifty-fifty on that one.

As part of the Review ordered by DI Custard into his failed two-and-a-half-year investigation into the allegations of harassment made by ourselves and the Heads. We met with an Inspector Stuart at our home address to discuss the scope of that Review. All four members of our family were present along with our civil barrister who had again very kindly agreed to attend, he really was a diamond.

Stuart started by informing us the scope of the review would include all allegations and reports that have been made to NP from the very start to the present day, including those allegations by ourselves against other parties, not just the Heads. He said he was aware that NP failed to take statements from our witnesses for the original investigation and he tasked PC Goffer with gaining these statements and gathering any further evidence. PS Pinocchio would be overseeing this process, and this would be completed within six weeks.

He also said NP would be working with the Crown Prosecution Service for advice to see if they can use evidence from the civil case in the criminal investigation and if there are grounds for early intervention by the CPS.

Quite randomly, Stuart then said,

'There is nothing on the police system to say you are troublemakers or time wasters.'

What! If there was nothing on the police system to say our family were troublemakers or time wasters, then why would he say this? We hadn't asked him about it, it wasn't the topic of conversation or the purpose of the meeting. We felt this was a very unusual thing to randomly say and as it came from a member of NP, this led me to believe that there was in fact something on the police system to say we are troublemakers or time wasters. In fact, I think it was Stuart's way of letting us know that we were flagged as troublemakers and time wasters. Bit cynical maybe!

The meeting lasted a good hour and a half and there were a lot of matters that were discussed. The whole meeting was recorded on the Body Cam of Inspector Stuart, of which I have a copy, and once again, following the meeting, we all felt a little more positive about the situation. Finally, the truth would come out and our nightmare would start to come to an end. We knew there wasn't a magic wand, and it would take time, but at least we were now being listened to, and justice would be done.

One thing I will give NP credit for is that in face-to-face meetings, they do talk a good fight. They reassure you that they would do this and that to sort the matter, they make you feel as though you have been listened to. It is just a shame that in the past, that talk turned out to be a complete pack of lies. Would it be the same this time, surely not! This was an Inspector in the Police Force, he wouldn't be a bare-faced liar to an entire family, would he? Particularly as the meeting had been recorded on his own Body Cam!

I received a call from PC Locks of NP with an update to her investigation regarding the Threat to Kill by Cupid Stunt and the attendance to our property by his daughter Oompa Loompa just a few hours later. She informed me that she had not progressed the investigation, and it consisted of two elements that needed to be completed before Cupid could be re-interviewed. Firstly, door-to-door inquiries had been completed (so they had progressed the investigation), and secondly, the other CCTV footage still needed to be obtained as evidence but she was still waiting to hear from the officers who arrested Cupid which neighbour it was who told them they had CCTV footage of the incident.

Obviously, both points cannot be true, if NP had done door-to-door inquiries then they would have spoken to the neighbour who said they had the CCTV footage! In any event, if these door-to-door inquiries had taken place then NP did not knock on the door of any of the neighbours that were still talking to us, and the officers that conducted the door-to-door inquiries must have been invisible as they were nowhere to be seen on our CCTV, amazingly!

I will guarantee the neighbour who said they had CCTV footage of the incident was Trigger. I bet that was what he told the officers when they arrested Cupid. I will also bet it is complete bollocks. I bet a pound a pinch of shit that Trigger nor anyone other than ourselves would have any footage or evidence of the incident. I would also bet my bottom-dollar NP did not conduct any door-to-door inquiries. I hope you're lying down for this next bit, again!

I received another call from PC Locks to inform me,

'NP are struggling to identify any offences committed by Cupid Stunt and the matter has been passed to the neighbourhood policing team to arrange mediation between Cupid and yourself.'

If that wasn't bad enough Locks then said,

'The actions of Oompa Loompa did not amount to any offences, and they will be taking NO FURTHER ACTION against her.'

What the Fuck!

Locks went on to say that when Oompa viewed the CCTV footage of her dad threatening me, she accepted I had not been staring at her children, and she reacted the way she did due to

'Ongoing stalking issues.'

So, unless Oompa was alleging it was me who was stalking her, I couldn't see what the hell that had got to do with this incident. If Oompa was not claiming I was stalking her, then what NP was telling me was that because Oompa was being stalked by someone else, that gave her and her dad the right to commit multiple offences against me including a threat to kill and calling me a paedophile!

What about the harassment this family endured for the past five years? We were all going through absolute hell on earth with all manner of people committing an endless list of offences against us including assaults, threats, criminal damage, theft, false allegations, malicious communications, and harassment and NP had done nothing to protect us. In fact, it is the exact opposite. NP actually joined in with the harassment and the above was just another example of that. More to the point, when I did one thing to protect ourselves and our property by removing the fence from our own land, which I was perfectly entitled to do, I was prosecuted, but Locks was telling me that because Oompa claimed she was the victim of Stalking, it was okay for her to join in with the harassment of our family.

To put this into context, if that was possible. If I had retaliated to the threat to kill by Cupid Stunt. Would NP have concluded it was okay because we were suffering 'ongoing harassment issues? No. I don't think they would.

The absolute and total disdain displayed by PC Locks towards our family was shocking and a complete disgrace, just when we thought NP was starting to take the matter seriously.

It only just dawned on me how outrageous it was that NP considered it okay for someone, anyone, to commit criminal offences because they claimed to be victims of criminal offences themselves. Two wrongs don't make a right. Not only that, but it was also okay for Oompa to commit offences against other victims of crime.

If Oompa was being stalked, then I really do feel for her. Well, I would have done so if she hadn't done what she did. If she was being stalked, then she of all people would know the impact this sort of crime has on the victim, yet she still committed the offence anyway. If she thought she could stand on my drive and call me a paedophile in front of my neighbours, she had another thing coming. I won't go looking for her because she is a woman, and I won't go looking for her dad either, they are not worth it, but one day they might just realise what sort of people they are. What goes around comes around.

Don't get on your high horse about me speaking like that about a woman. Before the harassment, I would never have dreamed of speaking like that about a woman and I would never physically harm a woman in any way. But now, if you cross me, you are fair game, whoever you are. I fully agree that women should have equal rights, but they cannot then hide behind the fact that men should treat them differently than if a man had done the same. Equal rights, equal fights.

My reason for this is simple, Mrs Head is the most evil, not just woman, but person I have ever met in my entire life, she was the instigator and motivator for the harassment. It was she who would whip Mr Head into a frenzy to commit assaults, it was her who would spread malicious lies on social media and around the neighbourhood, it was her who lied to NP about their and our her families conduct and it was her who was somehow able to make all of these people, including NP, believe what she was telling them was the truth and that it was her family who were the victims of our harassment. She was pure evil.

So now, I look at women differently, they can hurt you as much as any man, so I have to treat them as equals. However, one thing remains the same as it always has, you leave me alone and I will leave you alone.

PC Locks also informed me Trigger had not and would not be spoken to in relation to this incident as due to the history between myself and Trigger he would not be considered an independent witness.

I asked Locks about the other version of CCTV footage that needed to be obtained. She told me there had been some confusion about this and there wasn't any other footage. Absolute bollocks, there was no confusion, there never was any other footage. More lies, disrespect, and disdain.

The conduct of Cupid and Oompa could not have been a clearer example of Harassment Causing Fear of Violence and many more offences besides, and the evidence could not be stronger. Yet here we are again with those words ringing in our ears, NO FURTHER ACTION. So now, we had two more people who were fully aware they could do whatever they wanted to our family, and NP would take No Further Action.

Great work NP, I hope you are very proud of yourselves for hammering home yet another nail in the coffin of our family. Anyway, I seem to be getting quite good at guessing what NP would do next. It was not that difficult I suppose, basically just think of the most outrageous thing they could possibly do, and it wouldn't be too far off the mark.

The call from PC Locks had an even bigger impact on our family than the incidents themselves, which had been the case many times before. Thanks to the latest deliberate fuck up by NP we now had a man who lived no more than 50 metres away who had poured a corrosive fluid over our cars and now threatened to kill and who also lived next door to a man who had been convicted of harassment against me twice, he had also incited his daughter to harass me and call me a paedophile, and NP told him and his daughter that what they did was all okay.

Of course, NP would have known the impact this would have on our family, that was why they did it, but why were they doing it? Was it because they simply didn't like us or didn't care? Was it because Mr Head was a retired member of the emergency services, and the registration plate of his car was N999 Head? Or was it because I had made a complaint against a police officer, hmm, I wonder. I know I have mentioned this several times in this book already, but it really baffles and frustrates me. I wish I knew the answer, but then, maybe I should be careful what I wish for!

Later that day, I emailed PC Locks and requested she put the content of our telephone conversation in an email I did not get a reply! Oh, and guess what, I never did hear from the Community Policing Team regarding arranging mediation between Cupid and myself. More bullshit. I fucking hate NP.

We had known for a long time that NP were never going to protect us from the harassment. Let's face it, NP were among the harassers, but the level of utter disdain they had for our family was, and still to this day, shocks me. This incident and conduct by NP made it clear, that NP was as determined as the Heads and their friends, relatives, and neighbours to destroy our family. Not just to hurt us or punish us for making a complaint or whatever reason it was for their conduct, but to destroy us. Did I mention I fucking hate NP, oh yes, just a few moments ago as it happens, silly me!

This hit our family hard. It reinforced our already deeply held belief of being abandoned by the only people who can protect us from crime. We were very concerned for our safety and wondered what could possibly happen next.

Over the next few days, I emailed Locks and her senior officer to request a copy of the Crime Report to assist me in submitting another Victims Right for Review, even though I knew it would be a complete waste of time but in this type of situation, you have to follow procedure, or at least we do, the offenders and police can do what they like.

If you try to take it to level two let's, say without going through level one, they can and will refuse to deal with your concern and tell you that you haven't followed the correct procedure. They hope that the complainant will get fed up with being made to jump through hoops and give up, which in most cases is what must happen. The complainant is already struggling to deal with the offence that was committed against them, then they have to deal with the fuck up by the police, then they have to make a complaint against the police, which is not an easy thing to do, then they are treated like they are an even bigger piece of shit where the police close ranks and discriminate against them even more.

The Police complaints procedure and the Victims Right for Review are a complete waste of time for the complainant and a complete waste of precious police resources. We constantly hear about how the police are underfunded, bollocks, they are not underfunded. The Government knows the police are adequately funded to be able to do what they should do; it's in their interests to have a well-funded police force. The Government also knows that the police waste so much of their resources on firstly, fuck ups, corruption, and misconduct, and secondly, the police waste even more resources on their Professional Standards Departments whose sole purpose is to protect and defend their bent officers from their fuck ups, corruption, and misconduct. Talk about throwing good money after bad, but why should the police care about that, it's not their money after all, it's yours and mine!

Needless to say, I did not receive a response from either officer to any of my emails. One other trick the police have up their sleeve to make it harder for anyone to even communicate with the officers involved in a case, particularly when they know they are being bent, is to set their computer to reject emails from your address. On more than one occasion I have sent emails to officers of NP including the Chief Constable, only to receive a response from my email provider stating,

'We have tried to send your message to the recipient but your message has repeatedly been rejected. It would appear the recipient has set their system to reject your email address.'

The police will also not respond to your emails and when you chase them, they say they have not received your email and could you send it by post. Very professional, I don't think.

I knew from the very start that I would not get a copy of the Crime Report. If they provided me with a copy of the report it would be like shooting themselves in the foot. For NP to arrive at No Further Action for these offences, the Crime Report would either have to be a complete lie, in which case I would be able to prove it was, or the Crime Report would prove the decision to take No Further Action was wrong. Either way, NP was never going to provide me with a copy. Personally, I don't think there was a Crime Report at all. I guess that NP never produced a Crime Report to allow them to not even record the crimes.

But I would not be deterred. Without being provided with the evidence and information I was entitled to be able to resent the best case possible to support my application, I exercised my Victims Right for Review regard-

412

ing these determinations anyway. So that was now two Victims Right for Review cases I had submitted, this one regarding the conduct of Cupid Stunt and his daughter and the one regarding the Criminal Damage to our cars on the 9th of February, also by Cupid Stunt. Let the games begin.

I was really struggling to cope with the impact of recent events. It was not just the actions of Cupid Stunt and Oompa, which would be difficult for anyone to cope with. It was the decision by NP that as far as they were concerned, the actions of Cupid and his daughter did not amount to any offences and no further action would be taken. I just cannot get my head around that. What does someone have to do to our family for NP to take action against them? As it is at this time, NP has made it clear to all the harassers that they can do what they want, which makes it a very scary situation to be in. There are no lengths the Heads will not go to harass our family or incite others to do their dirty work for them and there was no way they would stop of their own accord. If they could harass, they would harass.

All these people think they can bully me and my family, and the police have given them the green light to do so. Although it is completely out of my comfort zone and character, I must do something to let these people know I will not be bullied, intimidated, threatened, or harassed by them and I am not scared of them. I must stand up to the bullies if I ever expect them to stop. I am not sure what I can do but whatever it is, it will be legal. I am not an offender and one thing I am determined to do is not let the harassers and NP turn me into one. If that happens, I am as bad as them.

I spoke to our civil barrister about this, and he advised me that I should write to Trigger and Cupid and inform them that if there are any further incidents involving them or their friends and relatives then I will take civil action against them. It sounds a bit weak I know and I was sure it wouldn't make a blind bit of difference but my barrister again advised that if the matter was to progress to court or any sort of civil action you have to be able to show the court that you have tried to either mediate or warn the other party of the consequences of their continued behaviour.

Any judge will look very unfavourably on anyone who has not tried their best to resolve an issue before it wastes their precious time on the golf course. It is all about following the correct procedure again. What did we have to lose?

Interlude

Jumping to real-time for a moment, it is the 16th of August 2024. How ironic is life sometimes, I have just written about how evil Mrs Head was, and low and behold we were informed by a neighbour that Mrs Head had died. It would appear she died of cancer, well, she was a cancer so why shouldn't she die from it? I knew she had previously had cancer before she moved next door, it was one of the very first things she told me, to be fair, both my dad and sister died of lung cancer and I was with them both when they drew their final breath and it was not nice, so I knew the impact it had and the suffering the person went through and I would not wish it on my worst enemy. But Mrs Head was not my worst enemy, she was far more than that, so good riddance to her, and may she rot in hell. And whoever is already in hell, look out, you have a bad one coming your way, even by your standards. I think the clearest indication of the person she was and the family the Heads are was that they were not even going to have a funeral for her. Who cares.

DING DONG, THE WITCH IS DEAD.

Chapter Thirty-Four
The Enemy Within

Around this time, we attended a meeting with Dodger and Fagin from BRB at their offices. They firstly informed us of their estimated costs of dealing with all three bankruptcies, these costs totalled around £50,000. They explained that we were the only unsecured creditors of the Heads estate. That means we were third in line to receive a dividend from the Heads estate after the debts to the Heads secured creditors had been settled and BRB had taken their costs. Why we were considered unsecured creditors after the court had awarded us damages and costs, I have no idea, I would have thought it to be the other way around or at least equal, but there you go, the victims of crime were at the bottom of the pile yet again.

They said they had met with Mr Head and his other son who did not live with them, Stupid Head, and at this meeting both the Heads were very hostile and aggressive and told Dodger and Fagin they intended to be as awkward as possible throughout the Insolvency process and they intended to whittle away all of the money, so there was nothing left for the Beans. I could have told you that one, but thanks anyway. They went on to say, that all three of the Heads, Mr, Mrs, and Little Head, were claiming they had mental health illnesses, but they had not provided BRB with any evidence of this. Because it's more bullshit, of course.

What we were told next was not surprising, but we didn't realise the huge impact this would have on our family. Although, BRB knew the impact it would have as it was all part of their plan to fleece as much money from the Heads estate as they possibly could, not just for themselves but for their partner in crime, metaphorically speaking of course, that being their solicitors who I will call Sikes (After the character Bill Sikes also out of Oliver Twist).

So, we had Dodger, Fagin and Sikes all working together, not for us as they should have been, but for themselves. A formidable trio, particularly when they were up against complete novices in the field of bankruptcy. I did try to read up on the bankruptcy legislation but with everything else that was going on there was only so much I could do, but there would be a twist in the tale, if you pardon the pun, Oliver, Oliver Twist, get it! Comic genius.

Dodger informed us the Heads had made allegations of harassment against BRB and the Trustee for the Estate, Fagin, had come in for some particularly nasty allegations that had caused her so much distress that she needed to take time off work. Dodger also told us that some of the emails they received from the Heads were vile and claimed the harassment by BRB and Fagin in particular, was so bad that Little Head had self-harmed and threatened suicide and needed to go on holiday with his husband for two weeks to recover.

Oh my God, welcome to our world for the past five years. When the Heads backs were against the wall, claim self-harm and suicide. This does prove that to claim selfharm and suicide was the Heads go-to plan when things got tough, not just to NP and the civil court but to everyone and anyone. This must have been a tactic they had used before. Now, if I was as big an arsehole as the Heads, that's a video I would love to watch, Little Head self-harming and attempting suicide.

Anyway, this holiday wasn't just a weekend in a caravan in Skeggy, it was two weeks in southern Spain! Quite by chance, I am sure, it just happened to be that the hotel they were staying in was owned by the husband of their Insolvency Practitioner, what a coincidence. Not bad for a bankrupt who claimed not to have any assets or a penny to his name, is it?

Fuck me though, BRB are telling us that because the Heads made allegations of harassment against them, it is the end of the world and Fagin was struggling to cope and was off work.

Whilst I do understand it is not nice being accused of something you haven't done; you would have thought it would have given BRB an insight into our life for the past five years. If we were as weak as them, we would have been dead long ago, seriously, but not a bit of it, they couldn't give shit about what we were going through, it was all about them and how distressed they were. Although at that time, we thought they were our Allie, as that was what they had told us and an Insolvency Practitioner is always supposed to work in the best interests of the creditors, just like a solicitor is always supposed to work in the best interests of their clients. I should have known better!

They were in fact working against us from the start and their sole aim was to benefit themselves. They had no time for empathy, sympathy, understanding or compassion. They were the enemy within. Heartless.

In my opinion, looking back, Dodger was telling us this because BRB had an ulterior motive regarding the harassment they claimed to have been subjected to by the Heads.

Dodger then informed us that due to the allegations of harassment by the Heads, they were not able to contact any of the Heads directly and all communications will have to be conducted through a third party and they have instructed their solicitors, Sikes, to act on their behalf who have quoted £60,000 for their work!

Yes, you read right, Sikes had quoted BRB £60,000 for representing them in the Bankruptcy of the Heads. Ulterior motive uncovered, I think!

Of course, this 60k is on top of the 50k BRB estimated for their work, all of which will be taken from the Heads estate before we even get a look in. Dodger then said,

'But don't worry, you will still get your money.'

Lying little bastard. He and Fagin knew full well we would not get our money, not all of it anyway. Even though both Dodger and Fagin knew more than most of what our family had been through, they could still look us in the eye and lie, cheat and deceive us, scum of the earth. Dodger would go on to be especially twisted. I hope at some point in the future our paths cross, I will probably find him hiding under the same rock as Pinky, Pinocchio and the like. Or maybe one day, I will stumble across a dead sewer rat and on that sewer rat there will be some parasites called Pinky, Pinocchio, Dodger and Fagin.

In the human race, as with everything else, there are levels. On the top of the pile are your doctors, nurses, surgeons, firefighters, and people who risk their lives to save others. Then you have the volunteers, carers, fundraisers, people who selflessly give up their own time to help others. Then you have the ordinary person, teachers, bricklayers, factory workers, good, honest, law-abiding citizens. Then you have the petty criminals, shoplifters, robbers, trespassers. Then you have the serious criminals, armed robbers, fraudsters, stalkers and harassers. Then you have the depraved, rapists, domestic abusers, paedophiles. I'm babbling again, sorry, I will get to the point. Then you have rats, then you have sewer rats, then you have parasites that live on sewer rats, the Head family, bent coppers, Insolvency Practitioners, solicitors and the like. Some, not all, I'm sure.

Anyway, back to the point. I am going to get a bit technical again about the law, sorry if it gets a bit tedious for a while. It is regarding the offence of Fraud, basically, there are three main provisions to the Fraud Act 2006, Fraud by false representation, Fraud by failing to disclose information and Fraud by abuse of position. This is how it is written on the Government Legislation Website.

Fraud by false representation.

A person is in breach of this section if he —

a.   dishonestly makes a false representation, and

b.   intends, by making the representation —

i.   to make a gain for himself or another, or

ii.   to cause loss to another or to expose another to a risk of loss.

A representation is false if —

a.   it is untrue or misleading, and

b.   the person making it knows that it is, or might be, untrue or misleading.

Fraud by failing to disclose information.

A person is in breach of this section if he —

a.   dishonestly fails to disclose to another person information which he is under a legal duty to disclose, and

b.   intends by failing to disclose the information —

i.   to make a gain for himself or another, or   ii.   to cause loss to another or to expose another to a risk of loss.

Fraud by abuse of position.

A person is in breach of this section if he —

a.   occupies a position in which he is expected to safeguard, or not to act against, the financial interests of another person,

b.   dishonestly abuses that position, and

c.   intends, by means of the abuse of that position —

i. to make a gain for himself or another, or

ii.   to cause loss to another or to expose another to a risk of loss.

Well, excuse me, according to the Fraud Act 2006, the bankruptcy had only just started and both the Head family and BRB had already contravened all three of these provisions and on many occasions. I will highlight just one example regarding what happened so far which hopefully makes my point.

BRB claim the Heads made allegations of harassment against them, so BRB have now employed their solicitors to act on their behalf. So, either the allegations against BRB by the Heads are false and, therefore, it is Fraud by False Representation by the Heads. But it's the Heads, so a little bit of crime doesn't matter.

Or the allegations of harassment made against BRB by the Heads are true. If that is the case, then for BRB to employ their solicitors to represent them and to pay them out of the Heads estate is Fraud by Abuse of Position.

To be clear, whether the allegations of harassment are true or false, it is not our liability or the liability of the creditors of the estate of the Heads to fund the legal cost of BRB due to allegations of harassment being made against them by the debtors.

It is clearly Fraud by Abuse of Position to make a gain for themselves or another (Sikes) and to cause loss to another or to expose another to a risk of loss (our family). I could give you many more examples of acts of Fraud by all parties during the bankruptcy but like I said, I think most of you would find it a little tedious. In any event, it only needs one act of Fraud for it to be considered as Fraud, unlike harassment, there does not need to be a Course of Conduct. If I knew then what I know now!

Also, and I may not be quite right about this. It is my understanding that the Insolvency Act allows an Insolvency Practitioner to employ a solicitor for advice during a bankruptcy, but that solicitor can only give advice, they must not administer or be involved in the administration of the Estate of the Bankrupts in any way.

Clearly and by their own admission, BRB employed the services of Sikes to represent them in the administration of the Heads estate, that to my understanding is not allowed.

If BRB do not have the skill set or knowledge to deal with the estate of the Heads due to the allegations of harassment made against them, it is not the liability of the estate of the Heads to fund the advice or training of their staff to be able to deal with something they should already be qualified to do.

As with solicitors, an Insolvency Practitioner is duty bound to work in the best interests of their clients and if they do not feel they have the knowledge, skill or professionalism to deal with a bankrupt's estate they are again duty bound to inform the creditors of this and decline to deal with the bankruptcy. If they do not have the ability to deal with the Heads then they shouldn't be in business as this is what they are supposed to do on a daily basis.

It was all just a rip off for BRB and Sikes to take as much money as they possibly could out of the Heads estate, and boy, did they do that. If you think the figures I have mentioned so far are eye watering, wait until you hear the final amounts. I swear, even if you are lying down, you will fall over.

We don't even know if the Heads did make allegations of harassment against BRB. We did ask BRB to provide us with evidence of these allegations, but they refused to disclose any information that would confirm or deny this. Another act of Fraud, that tells me, and I hope you, all we need to know.

Jack and Fagin gave it the Billy Big Bollocks at this meeting by saying they and Sikes are not going to mess about with the Heads anymore and they had given the Heads ample opportunity to sort the bankruptcy amicably, but the Heads will not cooperate. They said the car of Mr Head was going to be seized next week and that is just the start. What a load of absolute bollocks.

Just like NP, BRB talked a good fight when face to face but in reality, they never had any intention of doing what they said they would. Mr Heads car was never seized and the Heads continued to disrupt the bankruptcy process for years and years. All the time BRB and Sikes were making an absolute fortune out of the Heads estate. Why would they want the Heads disruption and noncompliance to stop? It was lining their pockets with gold, our gold. I could include all of what happened in the bankruptcy, but I think it would be a bit mundane for some if not most of you. I will, however, from time to time, include the most important and relevant bits, just to keep you all in the loop and have enough information to make your own minds up about whether they are the enemy within as I think they are.

Due Legal Process

Staying with the bankruptcy for a bit of news. Just a few weeks after we attended the meeting with BRB. We received a letter from Stupid Head. The letter was the usual pack of lies you would expect from a member of the Head family.

He claimed he was acting as Power of Attorney for his parents as they were no longer able to conduct their own affairs (even though Mr Head was still Vice Chair of the Parish Council). More subtly, he basically repeated what Dodger and Fagin told us that the Heads had threatened them with at their meeting. He stated in the letter that if we agreed to bypass the bankruptcy process, we would then be in possession of substantial funds in a matter of months, but if we did not agree we could wait up to five years, and by that time, there would be nothing left. He also stated in the letter that he had made an offer of £150,000 to BRB as settlement of the bankruptcy but BRB refused his offer.

In basic form, the letter was telling us that if we did not abort the due legal process which his parents and brother had voluntarily entered into, then we would not get any money for at least five years, if at all. Unfortunately, for the Heads and perhaps ourselves, and even though we were the victims in all of this, it was not up to us to abort due legal process. It is not as easy or straightforward for us to do what Stupid Head was suggesting, and probably illegal.

You may recall in December 2014; our family was informed by Inspector Tool that *'any attempt to interfere with due legal process could be construed as an attempt to Pervert the Course of Justice which is a Criminal Offence'*. So, the same rules should apply to Stupid Head, shouldn't they?

Stupid Head had no right to send us this letter or to communicate with our family in any way, shape, or form regarding the bankruptcy of his parents and brother, or regarding any other matter. The Heads, like ourselves, had been informed by NP not to have any unnecessary contact with each other as this could be seen as harassment. This letter from Stupid Head was unnecessary, threatening, intimidating, unsolicited and unwanted contact from yet another member of the Head family and a clear act of harassment and by the rules set by NP themselves, an attempt to Pervert the Course of Justice. But it's the Heads, so a little bit of crime doesn't matter.

For what it was worth, I contacted both BRB and NP to inform them of the letter and provided both with a copy. I informed PS Pinocchio that we regard the letter to be a further act of harassment by another member of the Head family and would like him to include it in his Review.

BRB informed me they were shocked that Stupid Head contacted us at all but also at the content of the letter.

Dodger and Fagin both informed me that as far as they were concerned, Stupid Head was not representing his parents at all and no evidence had been submitted to BRB that he was their Power of Attorney or that Mr and Mrs Head could no longer deal with their affairs and they did not receive an offer of £150,000 from Stupid Head or anyone else! More bullshit, but from who, was it Stupid Head who was lying or was it BRB?

At that time, I would have said Stupid Head, for sure, he was a Head after all. But now, I am not so sure. I know Stupid was not and never had Power of Attorney for his parents. That was easy to determine by contacting the Office of the Attorney General and requesting the information. So Stupid was definitely lying about that point, but had he made an offer of £150,000 to BRB to resolve the bankruptcy? I suspect so, but BRB rejected the offer so they could continue with the bankruptcy process and make the fortune they wanted for themselves and their solicitors.

The fact Stupid Head did not have Power of Attorney for his parents not only proves he was lying but also that he should not have contacted us. He had no right or reason, legal reason anyway. Quite ironically, Stupid Head is, or was the Head Teacher at the Bean Academy, such a shame it must remind him every day he drives through the school gates that he lost his entire inheritance due to the conduct of his mum, dad, and brother. Such a shame.

The letter was also another clear example of Fraud by False Representation. Stupid Head knew he did not have Power of Attorney for his parents and in claiming he did, he was attempting to make a gain for himself or another, or cause loss to another or expose another to the risk of loss.

In any event, even if we had agreed to abort the bankruptcy, Stupid Head had no intention of settling his parents' bankruptcy. If we agreed to do what he suggested he would have led us up the garden path for as long as he could until we had no right to the money or there was nothing left, he was a Head after all. If Stupid Head had any intention of settling the Heads debts, he would have done so before they declared bankruptcy, not after.

Unfortunately for him, we were not as stupid or corrupt as he would have liked.

Twat.

I also received an email from PS Pinocchio who informed me,

'*The letter from Stupid Head did not amount to an act of harassment or any other offences and was in fact conciliatory and No Further Action will be taken and it will not be included in the Review.*'

So, according to NP, the letter was not an act of harassment, perverting the course of justice or fraud, or anything else, hmm, beg to differ. Anyway, it was the Heads, so a little bit of crime doesn't matter. It doesn't matter which member of the Head family it was, they could all do what they wanted. Standard.

That was of course, expected, NP was never going to change course now, but for Pinocchio to say the letter was, in fact, conciliatory, was just unnecessary and insulting and showed yet again, a total lack of understanding, and care for the impact of harassment on a victim.

Chapter Thirty-Five
Next Level Shit

As advised by Inspector Stewart in our meeting with him a few weeks before, about seven weeks actually. The time limit of six weeks given by him for NP to have taken statements from our witnesses for the Review being conducted by NP into the failed investigation by DI Custard, had elapsed and we were aware that our witnesses had still not been contacted by NP. So, I emailed PC Pinocchio for an update and to ask why this had not been done. Low and behold, I did not get a reply. I wonder why that was!

I did however, receive an email from Inspector Stewart requesting a copy of the Transcript of the civil trial against the Heads. Although we thought this to be a bit odd as we were repeatedly told the police cannot get involved in civil matters, as we had nothing to hide and in fact, due to the admissions made by the Heads in the civil trial, such as Mr Head admitting under oath that he assaulted my wife in June 2014 and erected the fence on our land in August 2014, and therefore, his allegation of Criminal Damage and his statement were false, we thought it would be beneficial to ourselves for NP to have a copy.

This is how ridiculous the legal system is in this country. Although the civil trial alone cost us in the region of £30,000, yes, £30,000 for a five-day trial. We still had to pay several thousand pounds more for a copy of the transcript for the case which had already cost us £30,000. I swear, you get ripped off left, right, and centre in our legal system. No wonder justice is only for the rich, but we paid the 'ransom', gained a copy, and provided it to NP as requested.

Imminent Threat to Life.

What you are about to read is God's honest truth and I have all the evidence to prove it. This really happened and NP really did do what I will write. It is, without doubt, the most disgusting and outrageous failure by NP that I have no hesitation in saying literally resulted in an imminent threat to

425

our lives while in our own home. If you are not convinced already that NP deliberately failed our family, then if this next incident does not change your mind, then I am afraid nothing will.

Not totally unexpectedly, Trigger moved house. I knew for a while that he sold his house, so it was not totally unexpected to see the removal van outside. I was, of course, really happy about this.

The Heads were gone from next door and now another of the harassers, a man who had been convicted of harassment on two separate occasions and was clearly as deluded as the Heads, was also going. We had outlasted another arsehole. However, as I knew it would be, that joy would be short-lived. Trigger did not leave without a passing shot.

This is a little complicated to explain but I hope I can write it in a way that can be understood. On the very same day as Trigger moved away, our son received a text from a friend and former work colleague of his who I will call Bob. This text forwarded messages Bob received from a friend of his who our son did not know, I will call him Rabbit. The text sent by Rabbit to Bob said that Bob should steer clear of our son as he had been,

'Playing with children and the whole town are looking for him and they want to know his address, but they know where his dad lives, and it looks like these people are going to set fire to their house.'

This marked another clear escalation in the harassment. I do not think it to be an exaggeration to say the receipt of these messages meant we felt at serious risk of harm or even death both inside and outside of our property. Nothing stokes up hatred in people more than paedophilia and now, as far as we and any reasonable person were concerned, we had a gang thinking our son was a paedophile and who were intent on finding him, but until they do find him, they would come for his parents by setting fire to our house.

We reported the incident to NP via 999, and as you would expect when reporting such a serious incident which could be considered an imminent threat to someone's life, the police turned up straight away!

Well, some five hours later, actually. I know you might think that five hours to respond to a report that someone's house may be set on fire is not that long and I do understand the police have to prioritise between an imminent threat to someone's life and the BOGOF offer on doughnuts at Greggs.

But even then, when the two officers had eaten their doughnuts and arrived at our house, they had the usual attitude of why had we bothered them with this petty matter. They talked a good fight saying we are going to do this and that, but as usual, they did nothing but heap further pain and misery on our family. Not to mention living with the fear that these threats to our welfare and our property may be carried out at any time. We provided the officers with a copy of the messages which included the name and number of Bob and Rabbit.

It was also becoming a theme with the harassers to accuse our family of paedophilia. Firstly, we had Oompa Loompa standing on our drive calling me a paedophile, and now these messages were sent to our son claiming he was also a paedophile. I suppose the harassers do this because there is nothing worse for anyone to be accused of than paedophilia. They know it will cause more fear, alarm, and distress than anything else to their target and because NP had let Oompa get away with it scott-free the first time, the harassers knew they could do it again.

In a case of group harassment, it only needs one member of the group to know how to harass and that person can control the harassment without actually committing the acts themselves. They just tell the others what to do and when to do it, but the law is clear, if they aid, abet, procure, or incite others to commit acts of harassment, even if those acts are not carried out, they are still guilty of harassment as if they had committed the acts of harassment themselves.

In my opinion, it cannot be a coincidence that this happened on the day Trigger moved house. This was Trigger saying,

'I may have moved away but I will not stop harassing you.'

But who was Rabbit, was it a friend of Trigger, or was Trigger inciting or paying someone? My bet is that as the messages inferred our son was a paedophile and as Oompa Loompa did the same to me, somewhere along the line, either she or her dad, Cupid Stunt, had something to do with it. Just a hunch.

427

I am sure we will not find out who is behind it from NP as NP were probably behind it anyway. It was clear by now and had been to us for a long while, NP were as involved in the harassment of our family as much as anyone else. More on this in a bit.

Get off the Bonnet.

We had been informed by a neighbour that Trigger moved to an address in another town in the County which was about eight miles from where we live. We knew the area as we had a family friend who lived on the same housing estate.

A couple of days later, I had a booking for a demonstration of my work at a Community Centre in the next town from the town where Trigger moved to, just a mile or so further on. Our daughter came with me to this demonstration and as we were passing through the town where Trigger moved to, which was the natural route to drive home, I suddenly had the thought that I could confirm in my own mind that Trigger had gone from our neighbourhood. To see it with my own eyes would give me that certainty, peace of mind, and closure.

I know that might sound strange and some of you will struggle to understand that, but for me, it was the same as when someone who had been through a trauma, an assault, a car crash, or the loss of a loved one, a cyclist being hit by a vehicle, for example. We have all seen the shrines or memorials on the side of the road where a loved one had passed. The bereaved need to visit the scene to pay their respects and start to process the trauma to start to get that closure to start their recovery.

I thought if I saw the van of Trigger parked outside of the address I had been told he had moved to, that would give that certainty that he was definitely gone from our neighbourhood, I would gain that closure that was vital for recovery, I hope that explains my reasoning. Little did I know that this decision would lead to a whole load of trouble, initially with Trigger and then with NP.

I turned into the road I was told Trigger had moved to and after about 30 metres, I saw his van parked on the side of the road. Job done, there was the van of Trigger parked outside of the house we were told he moved to, mission accomplished, happy days, let's go home.

I drove past the van and expected to come to the junction at the end of the road. When I got to the end of the road, it was a dead end. Although I knew where the road was due to our family friend living in the area, I had never had cause to drive down it, so I was unaware it was a Cul-De-Sac. So, I turned around and started to drive back along the road. I could see a figure of a man standing in the middle of the road opposite the van of Trigger. I thought,

'Oh no, it couldn't be, could it?'

As I got a little closer, my heart sank, it was Trigger. Although I had not seen him when I drove past his van, to be honest, I wasn't looking, he must have seen me. As I neared Trigger, he did not move so I slowed down to a crawl. I said to our daughter,

'What's he doing?'

Trigger did not move so when I was about a metre from him, I had the choice to either stop or hit him. Guess what I did, I stopped of course. I shouted through the windscreen several times asking him to move, but he would not. After about a minute or so I started to reverse my van back along the road away from Trigger, as I reversed, Trigger followed me along the road. He was clearly very angry as usual, and flexing his muscles, as usual, prick.

Trigger was about 20 metres in front of my van, he was still in the middle of the road and walking towards me. I stopped reversing, put the van into first gear, and slowly moved forward, I mounted the pavement to give Trigger a wide berth. As I mounted the pavement Trigger was on the passenger side of my van, as I drew level with him, rather than letting me pass, he leapt onto the bonnet of my van, it was like being in an episode of the Dukes of Hazzard.

This of course forced me to either stop again or carry on driving and risk causing him injury.

So, guess what I did, I stopped, of course. I shouted through the windscreen to

Trigger,

'Get off the bonnet.'

Trigger would not get off the bonnet and instead, he rang NP on 999 and told them that I ran him over causing a serious injury to his leg. He told NP that the injury was so bad that he could not stand up and therefore could not get off the bonnet of my van.

This was absolute bollocks and could not be further from the truth. I had two opportunities to cause Trigger serious harm and considering what he did to me, I think most people would have taken those opportunities, but I did the right thing as always. I did not run him over when he was standing in the middle of the road, preventing me from continuing my journey, and I stopped when I could easily have kept driving when he leapt on the bonnet of my van, again, preventing me from carrying on with my journey. My actions prevented Trigger from serious injury, not caused a serious injury.

After about ten minutes of Trigger lying right across the bonnet of my van and as I was getting increasingly concerned for my safety and that of my daughter due to the irrational behaviour and nature of Trigger, I called 999 myself. I knew from previous experience that Trigger was incapable of controlling himself and the situation would only escalate the longer it went on. I know this will sound stupid after all that had gone on, but I wanted the police to turn up as soon as possible.

I know some of you will be saying,

'Well, it's your fault for going there.'

Of course, I do understand that. I wish I hadn't, but it wasn't a crime, and it was never my intention to confront or even see Trigger, I never wanted to see him again. I just needed to confirm for myself he was definitely gone from my neighbourhood.

I informed Force Control what was happening, and they told me the police were on their way. About five minutes later another car arrived, when Trigger saw this car arriving, he waved to the driver to park in front of my van. The car did this at speed and stopped just short of the front bumper. I did not recognise the driver, but I assumed it was either his son or another relative as he was much younger than Trigger.

Whoever he was, by the way he drove his car towards the front of my van, his intentions were clearly to intimidate me and my daughter. After what we have been through for the past five years, you will have to do better than that my son.

The driver of the car got out, glared, and shook his head at me as if it was my fault Trigger was lying across the bonnet of my van. Thinking about it, he must have been a relative as he clearly shared the same amount of brain cells as Trigger. That being none!

A few minutes later, the police arrived. When the driver of the other car saw the police, he got in his car and reversed it away from the front of my van. Brave!

Trigger was still on the bonnet of my van, and he stayed there while the officers passed my van, parked their car along the road, and walked back to where we were. As the officers got to my van, Trigger slid off the bonnet. He then had a conversation with the officers before walking across the road towards his house showing no sign of the alleged serious leg injury I had caused him when I had run him over! What amazing powers of recovery this man had. Sorry, in this day and age I should be more politically correct, I said man, I should have said shit stain.

One of the officers walked with Trigger into his house while the other officer asked me for my version of events. I told him what happened and informed the officer that Trigger had two criminal convictions for harassment against me and was on a suspended prison sentence due to those convictions, the officer then went into the house of Trigger. About ten minutes later, he came back and spoke to me. He said they were going to sit on the fence with this one and would be taking No Further Action.

So, you have a man who has been convicted of harassment against me twice and is on a suspended prison sentence for those convictions and has clearly just committed further acts of harassment and criminality against me and my daughter, and NP sits on the fence. Great policing!

I informed the officers again that Trigger was on a suspended prison sentence. I know I drove past the van of Trigger, but that did not give him the right to do what he did. If it was an offence for me to drive past the van of Trigger to help my physical and mental well-being after the harm Trigger had caused me, then I was as guilty as hell, lock me up and throw away the key, boy, how NP would love to do that.

Whatever your view, it may well be that if I had not driven past the van of Trigger, there would not have been an issue, but that was all I did. But if Trigger had not prevented me from continuing my journey, twice, intimidating myself and my daughter, leaping onto the bonnet of my van, forcing contact with me, and lying to the police, all of which are offences, there would also not have been an issue. Of course, you can make up your own mind.

To be fair, I understood the rationale of the officers as they had no previous involvement in the harassment, and it would have been hard for them to consider the history when they were not aware of it. Although, that is what local police intelligence is for. To be honest, by that stage, my only concern was to get my daughter away from there and get us both home.

What I did not mention to the officers was that the whole incident had been recorded on my Car Cam and my daughter had also recorded several parts of the incident on her phone. Not that it would make any difference. I could have recorded Trigger decapitating my daughter with an axe and they wouldn't do anything about it, except buy more BOGOF doughnuts to celebrate.

When I got home, I told my wife what happened, and the events started to sink in. As the day went on, I started to feel more and more disturbed and after trying to get some sleep for several hours, at about 2 am I decided to call NP on 101 to report the actions of Trigger as an act of Harassment. Force Control were their usual helpful and polite selves (seriously, that's not sarcasm) and a scheduled appointment was made for me to meet with an officer at the local Police Station.

Bastards

Due to the events of the previous day and the fact I had not been able to sleep, I did not feel up to going to work. So, I busied myself by writing down the events of the previous day in as much detail as possible as we were advised by NP to do at the very start of their involvement. I thought this would also help with easing my mind and it would save time at the scheduled appointment.

Unfortunately, NP had other ideas for our family that day. The incident with Trigger shook me more than I thought. Once I wrote down the incident, it would have been nice to have a bit of downtime to try to relax and even get some sleep, maybe.

Not a bit of it. Although my wife and daughter tried to protect me from this because they could see I was struggling, we received separate emails from both PS Pinocchio and PC Goffer regarding the text messages sent to our son which stated he was a paedophile and there was a gang looking for him and they are threatening to set fire to our house. The initial emails from both officers were exactly the same, so either these two officers were not communicating with each other, or they sent them separately to deliberately cause as much distress as possible. Whatever the reason, that was exactly the impact these messages had.

Both emails stated,

'These messages do not pose any risk to yourselves or your property and do not amount to any offences therefore, NP will be taking No Further Action.'

What the fuck. How can any reasonably minded person determine these messages do not pose a risk to ourselves and our property and do not amount to any offences. Surely, not a single reader of this book, all two of them, would come to that conclusion, let alone two police officers whose primary aim is to detect and prevent crime and to protect the public.

There is no way these officers believed what they were telling us. What they did believe they were telling us in no uncertain terms, was that our family was not worthy of their time or protection, and if these people were to attack our son or set fire to our house, it would be no great loss. These emails made us all feel less than worthless, our lives did not matter. C U Next Tuesdays.

During the day, several emails were exchanged between my wife and daughter to Pinocchio and Goffer. Eventually Pinocchio said that the rationale for their decision was because the messages were *'Hearsay'*.

They were not hearsay. We had the messages and had provided them to NP, they were the exact opposite of hearsay. I mean, these threats were not whispered in the ear of our son by a stranger in a pub or as he passed him in the street, that's '*hearsay*'.

They were sent to our son by his friend and were there in black and white, fully evidenced and with the name and number of the sender, Rabbit, included in the messages. So, NP not only had the evidence, they had the identity of the sender of the messages, but still, they would not do anything. That was not just poor policing, that was a deliberate failure that placed our family in danger.

Over the next few days, more emails were exchanged between us and Pinocchio. We asked Pinocchio if he could contact Rabbit on the number in the messages to ask him if he knew who said this about our son. Pinocchio said he would not be phoning Rabbit as it would be considered Computer Misuse as no crime had been committed. Work that one out if you can! We were not going to give up on this because of how threatened we felt. Not just when we were outside of our house, but now inside as well. Would we be awoken in the middle of the night by someone pouring petrol through the letterbox and setting light to it? Would we wake up at all if this happened? Even if we did wake up, would we be able to escape? Would this gang find our son and attack him leaving him in a coma or even kill him? Who knows what could have happened? One thing is for sure, NP did not care one way or the other. How can these two police officers have such a disregard for human life? If they were in our position, would they expect to be treated how we were being treated by them? Would you expect to be treated the same as we were by them? Probably not! Sick beyond belief. Bastards.

Of course, they would not know the threats were not real unless they were involved in sending the messages!

Even sitting in our front room, we did not feel safe. We half expected someone to throw a petrol bomb through our front window, these were very difficult and scary times. Eventually, Pinocchio got fed up with our emails and we received the pathetic cowardly response,

'I have given you my determination and rationale and I will not be replying to your emails regarding this matter any further. If you remain dissatisfied with the performance of the police there is a complaints procedure to follow."

Thanks for that. Been there done that and got the scars to prove it. C U Next Tuesday.

You would not believe the amount of times NP said this to us,

'If you're not happy, make a complaint.'

The reason they say it is because they know they are protected from the complaint by the PSD. NP, and maybe every other police force, would rather use up precious resources by spending countless hours dealing with a complaint, than a few hours doing what they should in conducting simple, basic investigations into clear criminal offences which may lead to solving the crimes that have been committed and equally important, preventing serious crime that could even result in loss of life.

It is the priority of the police to protect the public and to detect and prevent crime, but Pinocchio blatantly chose not to do that, no wonder we are in a mess. Anyway, thanks for the advice Pinocchio, I may just make a complaint at some point in the future, when I am strong enough to do so. Rest assured, if I do make a complaint against you or NP, I will win, I have all the evidence of your failure and that cannot be ignored by everyone forever. I will find someone who you cannot treat like a piece of shit. Maybe that someone will read this book and find me, who knows!

A couple of days later, it was a Saturday morning, and what happened was an experience I will never forget. It was one of those things that on the face of it you might think is relatively minor compared to some of the stuff that has happened but it is a moment in my life that made me realise that no matter what you are going through in life and you think it cannot possibly get any worse, it can always get worse.

We received an unexpected visit from PS Pinocchio. He said he wanted to clarify the situation regarding the messages sent from Rabbit via Bob to our son. Pinocchio insisted the messages did not pose a risk to ourselves or our property but he would notify the Crime Prevention Unit as a matter of procedure to see if they want to take any steps or have any advice to help us feel safe in our home.

Well fuck me, the messages sent by Rabbit either pose a risk or they don't. If they don't then fuck off. If they do, then do something about it. Why

435

contact the Crime Prevention Team if a crime has not and is not going to be committed?

Why I will never forget this visit is because when Pinocchio sat in the chair in our front room, just a few feet away from me and my wife. He looked me straight in the eye and said,

'These messages do not pose a risk to yourselves or your property.'

It wasn't just what he said, we had heard shit like that countless times before, it was the look on his face when he said it. It was an expression of emptiness, void of any emotion, compassion, or care. The sort of look I would imagine someone having just at the moment they plunged a knife into your chest. A mixture of pure pleasure and pure evil.

Now, I could have imagined it, but it seemed clear to me Pinocchio knew exactly what he was doing. He was pissed off with us because we had *'pestered'* him about the messages and he wanted to put us in our place. To make it clear to us he was the boss and he was in control of our lives. He made it absolutely crystal clear that we knew he couldn't give a shit if our son was attacked by a mob or that our house was set on fire. That was why he visited without warning, so there was no record of what he said, no paper chain, and no evidence.

As far as he and NP were concerned, we were worthless. Why else would he visit, we hadn't asked him to, he hadn't offered or said that he would be visiting and he didn't offer us anything new, he just wanted to re-peat what he had already said, but to our face.

He did what he did to hurt our family even more than we had been hurt already. It was the look on his face. Police officers are trained in how to use and detect body language and facial expressions to not only detect if peo-ple are lying but also to intimidate people and make them feel uncomfortable. He knew exactly what he was doing.

I have made my views clear regarding PC Perky having Narcissistic Personality Disorder. Well, if I am wrong about him, I am not wrong about Pinocchio. In my opinion, Pinocchio could write a book on NPD. In fact, I wouldn't be surprised if Pinocchio taught Pinky everything he knows about being a proper C U Next Tuesday.

So, whether you agree with the previous paragraph or not. There can be no doubt, here we were, yet again the victims of blatant criminality on many levels, and NP has yet again failed our family. We were left more vulnerable, harassed, abandoned, disillusioned, and really scared for our lives than ever before. You may think that is an exaggeration, but it happens all too often, people commit arson, ex-partners, people with a grudge, stalkers and harassers, set fire to their target's property and whole families die because of it. That is the reality of our lives. Would our family be headline news for tragic reasons and would NP be telling the public, yet again,

'We made mistakes and failed the Bean family but we will learn from those mistakes and make changes so a tragedy like this can never happen again.'

Thankfully, our son wasn't attacked, and our house wasn't set on fire, which was a plus. Having said that, if our house had been set on fire and we had all perished, at least we would not be living the life we were at this time, it really was a life not worth living. The number of times I put my head on my pillow at the end of another shit day and said to myself,

'I hope I don't wake up.'

Many times, I didn't wake up, because I never managed to fall asleep. Lying there thinking that your house could be set on fire at any moment is not the best way to relax, unwind, and eventually drift off into a blissful night's sleep and wake up fully refreshed to face another day in paradise. But get up I did and the fight went on and on and on.

I found this time in my life to be right up there with the time I was being prosecuted for Criminal Damage. The stress was unbelievable.

To prove a point. A week or so after the visit by Pinocchio, we were visited by two officers from the Crime Prevention Unit of NP. One was a Crime Prevention Officer, and the other was a Fire Safety Officer from the Fire and Rescue Service. We spoke for a while about the reason for their visit and they had a copy of the messages that were sent to our son.

Both officers expressed their shock at the attitude and rationale of Pinocchio and Goffer. They questioned why Pinocchio did not refer the matter to their department sooner as they only received the referral and a copy of the messages that morning and due to the content of the messages they prioritised their visit. I would not be surprised if Pinocchio deliberately delayed the referral to allow the mob time carry out their threats or at the very least, to make our family stew for as long as possible.

The officers provided us with an internal lock for our letterbox to prevent petrol from being poured through it during the night and said they would make inquiries regarding the supply and fitting of a ballistic membrane for our windows, but they were not hopeful due to budget restrictions.

We were also advised on how to protect ourselves and our property. This advice included not sitting near our front downstairs windows in case our property was attacked.

Clearly, this approach and attitude by these two officers regarding the messages and the risk posed to ourselves and our property was more realistic and sensible and the complete opposite to that of Pinocchio, but I think anyone would tell you that.

Pinocchio's attitude was not just wrong but very dangerous, to us anyway. Not to him, of course, it wasn't his son being hunted by a mob thinking he was a paedophile, or his property or life being threatened, so why should he care?

To be fair to PC Goffer on this point. Goffer was just Pinocchio's puppet and Pinocchio pulled his strings. Wait a minute, isn't that the wrong way around, isn't Pinocchio supposed to have the strings? NP fuck everything up, even a Walt Disney classic.

Not another C U Next Tuesday!

Just a couple of days after this visit from Pinocchio, I attended the scheduled appointment at the local Police Station regarding the incident with Trigger where he laid on the bonnet of my van for about twenty minutes.

As you can hopefully comprehend, it was relentless at this time. It had been relentless for years to be fair.

The officer I met with who I will call PC Anus, was the usual rude, ignorant, arrogant arsehole we had become familiar with over the years.

Nothing special, just an all-round twat. Here I go again, whinging and whining about yet another officer of NP. Read on my friends.

Anyway, without even letting me speak, Anus started to lay into me, verbally I mean, although I could understand if you thought otherwise. He said,

"I have read your file regarding the Heads and Trigger so why are you still dragging it on?

Why don't you just let it go?"

Another attempt to put me on the back foot at the start of the appointment. I had taken a copy of the details of the incident with Trigger that I wrote the day after. I informed Anus of this and offered him a copy explaining that it might help save time when making a statement. He said,

"I am not going to take a statement from you because it was your fault for going there and even if I did the CPS would not be interested as any defence lawyer would have a field day."

I then informed him of the Car Cam and mobile phone footage I had of the incident.

Anus replied,

"It doesn't matter what evidence you have as I am not going to do anything about it."

Anus then finished the appointment by saying,

"I am not going to waste my time in taking a statement from you but I will record a crime of harassment and have a word with my Sergeant but as far as I am concerned, the police will be taking No Further Action."

Anus then stood up and started to walk towards the door. I said to him I was not happy with that and Anus replied with the classic,

"If you're not happy, make a complaint."

He then left the room, leaving me sitting there on my own, so, I got up and left, I couldn't do anything else. To be honest, I was still struggling with the impact of the visit by Pinocchio a couple of days before, so my head was spinning. I walked to my van and just sat there for ages; it wouldn't have been safe for me to drive home as my head was in such a mess. After a while, I decided to go for a walk to a nearby park to get some fresh air and clear my head. I then returned to my van and drove home.

So, yet another officer of NP refused to take a statement, gather evidence, and investigate, an allegation, which is their duty. This time, however, the allegation was against a known and convicted offender. Anus did not treat me with impartiality and equality at this appointment. He had preconceived opinions regarding the history between myself, the Heads, and Trigger and had formed the view that I was the one at fault for the harassment. I was left feeling shell-shocked at the attitude and conduct of PC Anus.

As we had never met each other before this appointment. It must have been the case that Anus formed his opinion of me from the information held on the Local Police System of NP.

He said at the start of the appointment if you can call it that,

'I have read your file regarding the Heads and Trigger so why are you still dragging it on? Why don't you just let it go?'

Clearly, to start the meeting with that comment indicated that what he read in the police file suggested our family were the offenders and the Heads and Trigger were the victims. Even though we won our civil case against the Heads and Trigger had been convicted of harassment against me, twice, somehow, our family was still in the wrong. This further fuelled my belief that the information held on the local police system of NP regarding our family was not just false, incriminating, and discriminatory, but I am sure, totally outrageous.

So, that was it for this one. . However, there was a lot more to come regarding this incident and the conduct of the officer involved. I knew from the appointment with PC Anus that he considered me to be in the wrong for driving past the house of Trigger, which I can understand to a degree, but the lengths to which Anus went to incriminate me and our whole family, not just for this incident, but for the entire harassment, was shocking. This was something I did not become aware of until sometime later.

I have stated earlier that NP were like Vultures, but they are also like a pack of Hyenas. They wander about the wilderness looking for their victim, usually selecting the most vulnerable target. Once they have selected their victim, they isolate them from the rest of the herd or group, then they start chasing their victim until the victim cannot run anymore, then they surround and start biting their victim, going for their most vulnerable and painful parts, usually the bollocks if they have any, then they keep biting their victim until their victim eventually succumbs to their relentless snapping and cannot fight anymore and lies down and accepts their fate, then they start to eat their victim alive, then, when they have had their fill of fresh flesh, they jog on, laughing like a pack of Hyenas. Oh, they are Hyenas, silly me. Great analogy though.

Chapter Thirty-Six
Dilemma

I have a dilemma. I have so much more I want to tell you, but I have been faffing about whether I should do it all in one or split it into two separate books. My feeling is that as this book is over 400 pages long already and I am only halfway through, it may be a bit of an information overload to put it all into one, particularly as the second half has more to do with my fight for justice than the harassment itself and will be a difficult read at times. So, I have decided to split it into two, I think, yes, yes, definitely two, no more faffing, no, decision made, perhaps. Seriously, that means this book is nearly at an end, thank God, I hear you cry.

If you are still reading, then well done, and thank you, if you have given up by now, then fuck off.

To be honest with you, I need a break. Although writing this book is part of my therapy and recovery, it has been at times, emotional and distressing but it had to be done. Short-term pain for long-term gain, I hope.

Call it Quits

There is at least as much again that I could have included in this book but most of the more serious and interesting acts of harassment that were committed against our family by the many members of the public have been covered. I am sure there will be a great fallout for me due to the content of the book and maybe some of the characters will come looking for me.

What I will say to any of the harassers who may want to come after me, please don't. I and my family just want to live our lives in peace, we have suffered enough and if you recognise yourself in this book, maybe take a second to think about what is written and ask yourself that same question, haven't we suffered enough?

I do not want to fight you, any of you. At the end of the day, you will know what is written is the truth, so maybe we can call it quits. You had a go at our family, and I have had a go back, scores even, let's leave it there shall we?

Unforgiven

If I do survive and I am not in prison or holding up a bridge somewhere and if this book is well received, the second book will focus on the fight back against NP. I have taken the advice of Pinocchio and made several complaints against various officers of NP and NP as a whole. This book ends in 2018, and it is now 2025, a lot has happened in the past seven years and is still happening as I write.

So, to NP, I cannot be as forgiving towards you as I can to the harassers. Why? That one word, **JUSTICE.**

When justice was denied to our family it hurt more than anything else, more than any of the acts of harassment, more than all of the acts of harassment put together. That hurt will always be there no matter what, so I have to do all I can to lessen that hurt, to make it bearable, bearable enough to feel that vindication and closure that is essential for our family to live the rest of our lives as the people that we want to be and the people we were before the harassment.

You should have protected our family from the harassment, instead, you joined in with it. If you had done your job none of this would have happened and I would not have been able to write this book. So, you can blame me for exposing your failings if you like, but in reality, you have no one to blame but yourselves. So, if you do come after me in any form, I have no choice but to fight you, and although you hold all the aces, it will be a no retreat, no surrender, no holds barred, fight to the finish, last man standing war. Hopefully, that will not be the case, hopefully, there is one decent officer amongst you who will read this and think, fuck sake, did we really do that, not just to an innocent family but a family that were the victims of multiple serious criminal offences. I will not hold my breath on that one though.

I did mention earlier that I might finish with a line or two regarding the content of this book has had on our health. I have decided not to do that here for several reasons.

Firstly, I hope the impact will be obvious to you. After reading this book, I do not think there is anything I could write here that would change your opinion now anyway. Secondly, even though it is now April 2025, it is still not over. Far from it. Thirdly, if I were to detail the impact on our health, I am sure certain members of the public and NP would gain great pleasure from learning their actions caused so much distress. I do not want to give them that pleasure.

It is *our health* of course, although this book is focused on my version of events and how I feel about them and the people involved, those events have affected all four members of our family. I would not want any reader to think this book is just a selfcentred, self-indulgent, me, me, attention-seeking exercise. As stated at the start of this book, I do not feel I have the right to speak for anyone else. I hope you can understand that.

Anyway, back to me! I am slowly working my way down the long winding road of recovery. How far I get down that road before the wheels might come off again is not up to me, it is up to the result of my complaints against Numpty Police and whether or not they will ever accept, admit, or be held accountable for their failings. Like I have always done, I will do my best and do whatever it takes to enable me to grow again and who knows, one day I might not feel Four Feet Small anymore.

So, for now at least. That's all folks!

www.ingramcontent.com/pod-product-compliance
Lightning Source LLC
Chambersburg PA
CBHW052014030426
42335CB00026B/3140